Vietnam Battle Chronology

Vietnam Battle Chronology

U.S. Army and Marine Corps
Combat Operations, 1965–1973

by
David Burns Sigler

McFarland & Company, Inc., Publishers
Jefferson, North Carolina, and London

British Library Cataloguing-in-Publication data are available

Library of Congress Cataloguing-in-Publication Data

Sigler, David Burns, 1956–
    Vietnam battle chronology : U.S. Army and Marine Corps combat
operations, 1965–1973 / by David Burns Sigler.
        p.   cm.
    Includes bibliographical references and index.
    ISBN 0-89950-683-6 (lib. bdg. : 50# alk. paper) ∞
    1. Vietnamese Conflict, 1961–1975 — Campaigns — Chronology.
2. United States.   Army. — History — Vietnamese Conflict, 1961–1975 —
Chronology.   3. United States.   Marine Corps — History — Vietnamese
Conflict, 1961–1975 — Chronology.   I. Title.
DS557.7.S57   1992
959.704′34′0202 — dc20   91-50941
                                                                        CIP

McFarland & Company, Inc., Publishers
  Box 611, Jefferson, North Carolina 28640

for R., Riss and Mom
. . . the women in my life

Contents

Introduction

Khe Sanh, Dak To, Hamburger Hill... Like most Americans in the late sixties, I had heard of those places. I knew they were the sites of some of the major battles of the Vietnam War. Exotic names half remembered from the occasionally read newspaper story and the evening news: As was true for many of my generation, that was about the extent of my knowledge.

I grew up with Vietnam on television. Vague images of death and destruction came on at dinnertime. Though I largely ignored it, I wondered if one day I too would have to participate in a war that was unpopular and not well defined.

It wasn't until ten years after the war ended that I truly became interested in the causes and effects of Vietnam. In one of my college classes, Al Santoli's *Everything We Had* was recommended. Reading the brief personal accounts of those soldiers' Vietnam experiences gave me, for the first time, an idea of what it must have been like to be in Vietnam.

I began to collect and read all the personal narratives and oral histories about the Vietnam War I could find, among them Mark Baker's *Nam,* Phil Caputo's *A Rumor of War* and Michael Herr's *Dispatches.* These books were all great, full of the power and raw emotion of the war. However, as interesting as they were, they could be very frustrating to read. My frustration stemmed from the books' inherent lack of adequate details and my own ignorance of the war.

To me it seemed that the details those books lacked were critical to an overall understanding. I needed to be able to place all of their events into context. I wanted to be able to see the total scope of the war and yet not lose sight of how these individual stories fit into that larger picture.

I turned to some of the many general histories of the war and began reading and taking careful, chronologically arranged notes. This too proved frustrating because of the length and complexity of the war. I was determined to put together a picture of the war that I could understand. I felt that this "picture" I was assembling would help me to better understand the personal stories of the men and women with which I began my study of Vietnam. In essence, I was trying to create for myself the reference work I wish had been available when I started trying to understand the war.

For the sake of brevity and clarity I chose Army and Marine combat operations for the years 1965–1973 as the framework of my project. There were many reasons for this. First, members of the Army and Marines saw the vast majority of combat during the war and their participation was almost entirely limited to that specific eight-year period.

Second, the operations themselves represented a finite time frame. Each had a date of beginning and ending and thus lent itself to being arranged in chronological order. I feel this helps place the events into perspective and makes the larger picture of the war easier to see.

Also, most of the oral histories and personal narratives of the war concern combat action, which is what most interested me. I was seeking to provide the minute, complex details that would fill in the What, When and Where to those first-person accounts of battle.

So I continued my research along those lines with little or no thought of publication. I was working strictly for myself: it wasn't until much later that I considered that other people might be interested in a book of this nature. I had run some ads in a variety of military journals, magazines and newspapers asking for input from combat veterans and it was some of their responses that suggested that a book of this type was more vital or important than I had ever considered.

My confidence and efforts were bolstered by Bill Noyes (B–2/22 Infantry, 25th Infantry Division, Sept. 68–Sept. 69), who wrote: "I think you've sensed a very important difference between Vietnam and other recent historical events. Previously, it was the emotional, the personal, the minutiae of life that faded fastest from the record. The firm structure of facts, overviews, etc., tended to dominate our historical memory and the understanding of the events. Vietnam seems to be headed in the other direction. Very little of the facts and figures seems to catch the public's attention . . . How can a people hope to deal realistically with their history if they are inadequately aware of important historical facts? I think your book should serve a timely and important purpose in aiding people's perspective on the Vietnam War. The information may be available, but your concise volume should make it less likely that it will be overlooked or ignored."

Bill's letter, and others like it, gave me the incentive to continue with my work and ultimately to finish the book. More important, these letters also showed me that a work of this nature can make a significant contribution to an understanding of the war. I began writing for myself and ended up writing for others.

I worked for the generation before me, in the hope that they can now make more sense of a troubled time. Included in this generation are the men and women themselves who served in Vietnam. In my correspondence with the veterans who answered my ad, I was constantly amazed at how little they were told of how their efforts contributed to the overall war effort. Often they were unaware of the names of the operations they participated in or what the goals and objectives of that campaign were. I wrote for them, to help them make their contribution "real," to help those that want to put the pieces of the puzzle together, to help those that want to remember and perhaps understand.

I wrote for my generation. I wrote to help overcome the ignorance and the apathy that surround the war and cloud perceptions of the men and women that fought in it. The Vietnam War and its impact on the people of the United States and on the men and women who fought it are too important to be forgotten. Without effort and knowledge there can be no understanding.

Finally, I wrote for the generations to come. Those who are now children, and their children, must not grow up ignorant of the events and implications of Vietnam. For them, Vietnam could easily become nothing more than a documentary video and a grudgingly read homework assignment. It is hoped that this book will contribute to the kind of detailed, factual base that these children can use to learn about Vietnam and its problems, and thus avoid making the same mistakes themselves.

So what began as a series of notes to help a single reader make some sense of the Vietnam War has evolved into *Vietnam Battle Chronology: U.S. Army and Marine Corps Combat Operations, 1965–1973*, a sequential and chronological history of Army and Marine combat operations presented in an encyclopedic format. It is the goal of this book to replace the reader's vague images and memories with concrete facts.

It is my hope also that readers can use this book to derive more satisfaction from reading the ever-growing body of Vietnam War literature.

Dave Sigler
Orangevale, California
January 1992

A Note on the Arrangement

Vietnam Battle Chronology is primarily intended as a reference work for use in conjunction with other Vietnam War literature. This book strives to provide the details that the general histories and personal accounts of the war often lack. My goal is to show the reader how specific combat operations and incidents fit into the larger picture of the war.

The format of the book was designed to make its information readily available to the reader and resembles an encylopedia. The following explains the organization of the entries:

Dates: The date or dates that an operation or combat-related incident took place.

Name: The name given to a particular operation.

Location: The general area where an operation took place. This element of the entry begins with the Military Region (I–IV Corps) and province and then progresses to more specific locations.

Type/Objectives: The type of operation (Search and Destroy for example) and its specific goals or targets.

Units: This element identifies the U.S., allied and enemy units present for a given operation or incident.

Events: This element of the entry lists and describes specific, individual events that occurred within the area of operations and the operational time frame.

Casualties: This element contains the number of known (confirmed) killed, wounded, captured and missing troops from the United States, its allies and the North Vietnamese regular army (NVA) and Viet Cong (VC). *Note:* In many cases the number of dead and wounded was not available in the source used because the unit reported their casualties on a monthly or quarterly basis rather than by the individual operation.

In the interest of brevity, many abbreviations are used throughout the operational listings. They are as follows:

Abn: Airborne
ARVN: Army of the Republic of Vietnam (South Vietnam)
Bde: Brigade (3000 troops: 3–4 battalions)   .
BLT: Battalion Landing Team
Bn: Battalion (750–920 troops: 3–5 companies)
Co: Company (150–250 troops: 3–4 platoons)
Div: Division (12,000–18,000 troops: 3 brigades)
Inf: Infantry
(M):   Mechanized
NVA: North Vietnamese Army
Plt: Platoon (40 troops: 3–4 squads)
Rgt: Regiment (3000 troops: 2–4 battalions)
ROK: Republic of Korea
SLF: Special Landing Force
Sqdn: Squadron (Cavalry equivalent to a battalion)
Trp: Troop — usually a single soldier, in this case the cavalry
            equivalent to a company
USA: United States Army
USMC: United States Marine Corps
VC: Viet Cong
VNAF: Vietnamese Armed Forces (South Vietnamese)
VNMC: Vietnamese Marine Corps (South Vietnamese)

Unit Identification Listings

Army operations are listed with the division first, followed by the brigade number and then the specific subunits. Each subunit will then be listed by its smallest increment first. For example, a unit entry that appears as USA: 101st Abn Div–1st Bde (A–2/501st Abn) would be read as United States Army: 101st Airborne Division–1st Brigade (A Company–2nd Battalion/501st Airborne Regiment). Companies and cavalry troops are always identified by letters and battalions are identified by numerals.

Marine Corps unit designations will begin at the regimental level. This is done in the interest of clarity because units were detached and reattached often between the 3d and 1st Marine divisions and keeping up can be very confusing. For the sake of accuracy, it can be noted that the 3d Marine Division was active in the Northern I Corps area, principally in Quang Tri and Thua Thien provinces, and consisted of the 3d, 4th and 9th Marines.

The 1st Marine Division was more associated with the Central and Southern I Corps area: Quang Nam, Quang Tin and Quang Ngai provinces, and was made up of the 1st, 5th and 7th Marines. The 26th and 27th Marines of the 5th Marine Division were also attached to the 1st Marine Division.

The Marine Corps unit names will be the same as those for the Army;

for example: 2/2d Marines would be read as the 2d Battalion/2d Marine Regiment.

The reader will immediately recognize the omission of Aviation, Artillery, Engineer, Signal, Medical and Support units. This was done strictly for the sake of brevity and clarity within the entries and should in no way be considered a slight on those units or their important contributions to the war. For a complete listing of all Army divisional assets please see Shelby Stanton's landmark work, *Vietnam Order of Battle* (Galahad Books, 1986).

At this point I would like to advise the reader that what follows in the heart of the book is as thorough and accurate a record of Army and Marine combat operations for the years 1965–1973 as I could assemble. I make no pretense that this work contains the *complete* documentation of all combat activity during the Vietnam War. Using existing publications and hundreds of government documents, I was able to identify more than 600 combat operations; hundreds more were, however, actually conducted.

My research was limited by several factors. The major hindrance was that I live on the West Coast and all archival material for the Army and Marines is located in the East. The Army documents are catalogued and readily available from the National Technical Information Service in Virginia. Using the phone and my credit card, I was able to obtain copies of practically every legible and declassified Army document the NTIS has to offer; only lack of adequate funds and the absence of a readable copy precluded my obtaining every single document.

Unfortunately the Marine Corps' documentation is much harder to come by. The Marines' records are not catalogued and I simply could not afford to pay the fees for their researchers to find the records I needed; nor could I afford to go to Washington, D.C., and dig through the archives myself. Thus I was forced to rely primarily on the Marines' own historical monographs. This did not present a major problem due to the thoroughness and quality of the works.

1965

As of 1 January 1965, there are approximately 23,000 U.S. personnel in South Vietnam. Thus far, 140 Americans have been killed, 1138 wounded and 11 declared as missing. ARVN strength: 265,000 regular Army and 290,000 militia. The strength of the NVA/VC is estimated at more than 34,000.

7 February: *Location:* II Corps; Pleiku Province; Camp Holloway. *Action:* VC forces attack the U.S. advisory compound and ARVN II Corps Headquarters. *Units:* USA—Special Forces and 52d Aviation Battalion. *Casualties:* U.S.—8 KIA, 128 WIA (five helicopters destroyed and 123 other aircraft damaged). *Result:* President Johnson orders immediate retaliatory air strikes against targets in North Vietnam.

10 February: *Location:* I Corps; Binh Dinh Province; Qui Nhon. *Action:* VC sappers detonate suitcases containing 100 pounds of TNT at the Viet Cuong Hotel. The hotel is being used as housing for U.S. enlisted personnel. *Casualties:* U.S.—23 KIA, 21 WIA. *Result:* President Johnson orders further retaliatory bombings of North Vietnam.

March–May: The 3d Marines of the 3d Marine Division arrives in South Vietnam. They are stationed in Da-Nang (I Corps; Quang Nam Province).

March–June: The 9th Marines of the 3rd Marine Division arrives in South Vietnam. They are stationed at DaNang (I Corps; Quang Nam Province).

2 March: *Rolling Thunder,* the sustained bombing of North Vietnam begins. The objective of *Rolling Thunder* is to crush the enemy's ability to wage war against the south.

8 March: The first U.S. combat troops arrive in South Vietnam. Battalion Landing Team 3/9th Marines (BLT 3/9) of the 3d Marine Division comes ashore at 9:02 a.m. on Red Beach 2. Two hours later, Battalion Landing Team 1/3 Marines (BLT 1/3) of the 3d Marine Division lands at DaNang Air Base.

19–21 March: The first U.S. Army troops arrive in South Vietnam. The 716th Military Police Battalion lands at Tan Son Nhut Airport, Saigon.

April–May: The 4th Marines of the 3d Marine Division arrives in South Vietnam. They are stationed at Hue (I Corps; Thua Thien Province).

22 April: *Location:* I Corps; Quang

Nam Province; Binh Thai. *Action:* First firefight between the Viet Cong and the Marines. The battle takes place nine miles southwest of DaNang. *Units:* USMC — D–3d Recon Battalion; VNAF —1 platoon (38 troops); NVA/VC —1 company of Viet Cong reported. *Casualties:* U.S. —1 WIA; NVA/VC —1 KIA.

26 April: Secretary of Defense Robert McNamara reports that *Rolling Thunder* has "slowed down the movement of men and materiel . . . however, infiltration of both men and arms into South Vietnam has increased."

May: The Monsoon (rainy) season ends in the northern provinces and begins in the south.

5 May: The 173d Airborne Brigade (The Sky Soldiers) arrives in South Vietnam. The 173d is stationed at Bien Hoa (III Corps; Bien Hoa Province). The 173d is made up of the 1st, 2d and 3d battalions of the 503d Airborne Regiment. They are joined by the 4/503d on 25 June 1966.

6 May: The 3d Marine Division officially arrives in South Vietnam. The 3d is stationed at DaNang (I Corps; Quang Nam Province). The 3d Marine Division is made up of the 3d, 4th and 9th Marines.

7 May: The 3d Marine Expeditionary Force becomes the 3d Marine Amphibious Force (III MAF).

11 May: *Location:* III Corps; Phuoc Long Province; Song Be. *Action:* Viet Cong attack an MACV/Special Forces compound at Song Be, approximately 75 miles northwest of Saigon. *Units:* USA — Special Forces Detachment B–34; VNAF — 34th and 35th ARVN Ranger battalions, Regional/Popular Force troops; NVA/VC — 761st and 763d VC Main Force regiments (attacking force estimated at 2500 VC). *Casualties:* U.S. —5 KIA, 16 WIA.

13–18 May: The United States stops all air strikes over North Vietnam. The cessation of the bombing is meant to induce the North Vietnamese to begin peace talks. The American gesture is ignored.

16 May: A bomb is accidentally detonated at Bien Hoa Air Base. Twenty-seven people are killed and 95 others wounded. Forty aircraft are destroyed.

19 May: *Rolling Thunder* bombing raids over North Vietnam resume.

25 May: The 1st battalion of the Royal Australian Regiment arrives in South Vietnam. The battalion is attached to the 173d Airborne and is stationed at Bien Hoa (III Corps; Bien Hoa Province).

31 May: The 1st and 2d battalions of the 503d Airborne Regiment (The Rock Regiment) arrive in South Vietnam. The battalions join their parent unit, the 173d Airborne Brigade, at Bien Hoa (III Corps; Bien Hoa Province).

•*There are now 50,000 U.S. troops in South Vietnam.*

10–20 June: *Location:* III Corps; Phuoc Long Province: War Zone D. *Action:* Three Viet Cong regiments attack U.S. Special Forces camp at Dong Xoai, approximately 60 miles northwest of Saigon. *Units:* USA — Special Forces A–342 Detachment; VNAF — 1/7th ARVN Rgt, 1/48th ARVN Rgt, ARVN 7th Abn Bn, 52d ARVN Ranger Group, Regional Force troopers. *Casualties:* Allied — 416 KIA, 233 reported as missing.

21 June: *Location:* I Corps; Quang Nam Province; DaNang. *Action:* Viet Cong ambush of two squads of Marines. *Unit:* USMC — 2/3d Marines. *Casualties:* U.S. —1 KIA, 3 WIA; VC —4 KIA, 2 POWs.

27 June: *Locations:* III Corps; Binh Duong Province; War Zone D; "Iron Triangle." *Actions:* Army units attack "Iron Triangle" area just northwest of Saigon. *Units:* USA—173d Abn Bde + (E/17th Cavalry, D/16th Armor); VNAF—ARVN 2d Abn Bde, 4th ARVN Rgt; Aust—1/Royal Australian Regiment. *Casualties:* Casualties not reported in source document.

6–10 July: *Locations:* III Corps; War Zone D; Dong Nai River. *Type:* Search and Clear operation. *Units:* USA—173d Airborne Brigade; VNAF—48th ARVN Regiment; Aust—1/Royal Australian Regiment; NVA/VC—D-800 Viet Cong Battalion. *Comment:* Allied units discover and destroy an enemy staging area capable of supporting 800–1200 men.

11 July: The 2/16th Infantry, 1/18th Infantry and the 2/18th Infantry battalions arrive in South Vietnam. These units are part of the 1st Infantry Division. Initially, the 2/16th and 2/18th are stationed at Qui Nhon (II Corps; Binh Dinh Province) and Nha Trang (II Corps; Khanh Hoa Province). The 2/18th is first stationed at Cam Ranh Bay (II Corps; Khanh Hoa Province).

12 July: *Locations:* I Corps; Quang Nam Province; Duong Son; Phong Le Bridge. *Type/Objective:* Cordon and Search of the Duong Son (1) hamlet. *Note:* In Vietnam, a group of neighboring villages often have the same name. Numbers follow the name to identify it and avoid confusion or error. *Units:* USMC—2/9th Marines, B-1/9th Marines and D-3d Recon Battalion. *Casualties:* U.S.—3 KIA, 12 WIA; NVA/VC—6 KIA.

28 July: President Johnson announces that U.S. force levels in South Vietnam will be immediately expanded to 125,000 troops. However, in an effort to quiet negative public reaction to the buildup, Johnson says there will be no mobilization of the National Guard or Reserves. This effort at public relations hinders the war effort by depriving the front-line troops of needed replacements, especially officers and non-coms.

29 July: The first troops of the 1st Brigade/101st Airborne Division (The Screaming Eagles) arrive in South Vietnam. The 1/327th and 2/327th Airborne (The Bastogne Bulldogs) are stationed at Bien Hoa (III Corps; Bien Hoa Province) and Vung Tau (III Corps; Phuoc Tuy Province). The 2/502d Airborne are initially stationed at Qui Nhon (II Corps; Binh Dinh Province).

August–September: The 7th Marines of the 1st Marine Division arrives in South Vietnam. They are stationed at Chu Lai (I Corps; Quang Tin Province).

August 1965–January 1966: The 1st Marines of the 1st Marine Division arrives in South Vietnam. They are stationed at Chu Lai (I Corps; Quang Tin Province).

2–3 August: *Operation Blastout I. Locations:* I Corps; Quang Nam Province; Yen River; DaNang. *Type:* Search and Clear. *Units:* USMC—1/3d Marines, 1/9th Marines; VNAF—4th ARVN Regiment. *Event:* **3 August**—While conducting a sweep of Cam Ne village, in conjunction with the 3d Marines' *Blastout I,* D-1/9th Marines receives heavy small arms fire. Orders are given to raze the village. Fifty-one huts are destroyed as Morley Safer and a CBS camera crew are filming. *Casualties:* U.S.—4 WIA (NVA/VC losses not in source).

6–7 August: *Operation Thunderbolt. Locations:* I Corps; Quang Ngai Province; Song Tra Bong River. *Type:* Search and Destroy. *Units:* USMC—4th Marines; VNAF—51st ARVN Regiment; NVA/VC—1st Viet Cong Regiment. *Casualties:* U.S.—2 WIA. The

Marines suffer 43 heat-related casualties in two days of 105-degree heat.

12 August: *Operation Midnight. Location:* I Corps; Quang Nam Province; "Elephant Valley." *Type:* Search and Destroy 10 miles northwest of DaNang. *Units:* USMC—F,H–2/3d Marines. *Casualties:* NVA/VC—2 KIA (U.S. losses not in source).

18–24 August: *Operation Starlite. Locations:* I Corps; Quang Ngai Province; Van Tuong Peninsula; Phuoc Thuan Peninsula; Nho Na Bay; An Cuong (1); An Thoi; Nom Yen; Hill 43; LZs Red, White and Blue. *Type/Objectives:* Search and Destroy 15 miles south of Chu Lai. The mission is to exploit sightings of enemy troops in the area and prevent an attack on the Chu Lai enclave. *Units:* USMC–3/3d Marines, 2/4th Marines, 3/7th Marines; NVA/VC–1st VC Rgt (60th and 80th VC bns) (estimated strength of 1500–2000 men). *Events:* **18 August**—H–2/4th Marines lands at LZ Blue only to find almost the entire 60th VC Battalion waiting for them. **18 August**—A rescue force, I–2/4th Marines, is ambushed near An Cuong (2). Five Marines are KIA, 17 WIA. **18 August**—BLT L–3/7th Marines is ambushed by elements of the 60th VC Battalion while crossing a rice paddy just east of An Cuong (2). Four Marines are KIA, 17 WIA.

22 August–2 October: *Operation Highland. Locations:* II Corps; Binh Dinh Province; An Khe. *Type/Objective:* Clearing operation to secure An Khe base area for the incoming 1st Cavalry Division. *Units:* USA–101st Abn Div, 1st Bde (Task Force Collins: 1/327th Abn, 2/327th Abn and 2/502d Abn). *Event:* **25 August**—The first 1000 troopers of the 1st Cavalry Division arrive at An Khe and begin work on constructing Camp Radcliffe. *Casualties:* U.S.–21 KIA; NVA/VC–692 KIA.

5–7 September: *Operation Stomp.*

Locations: II Corps; Binh Dinh Province; Ky Son Mountain; LZs Palomino and Shetland. *Type:* Search and Destroy 10 miles north of Qui Nhon. *Units:* USMC–BLT 2/7th Marines (Cos F and H). *Casualties:* U.S.—none reported; NVA/VC—26 KIA, 3 POWs.

7–10 September: *Operation Piranha. Locations:* I Corps; Quang Ngai Province; An Ky Peninsula; Batangan Peninsula; Khe, Chau Me Dong and Cho Moi Rivers; LZs Bitch, Oak and Pine. *Type/ Objective:* Search and Destroy. *Piranha* is an aggressive follow-up to *Starlite* aimed at the remnants of the 1st VC Regiment. Its secondary purpose is to shut down reported places of entry for a Viet Cong network of seaborne infiltration. *Units:* USMC–3/3d Marines, 1/7th Marines, 3/7th Marines; VNAF–2/4th ARVN Rgt, 3d VNMC Battalion; NVA/VC–1st Viet Cong Regiment. *Casualties:* U.S.–2 KIA, 14 WIA; VNAF–5 KIA, 33 WIA; NVA/VC–183 KIA, 360 POWs.

8 September–27 October: *Operation Golden Fleece. Location:* I Corps; Quang Nam Province; DaNang. *Type/ Objective:* Security operation to protect local rice harvest. *Units:* USMC–1/9th Marines, 2/9th Marines, 3/9th Marines. *Results:* An estimated 250 tons of rice are kept from the enemy.

11 September: The 1st Cavalry Division (Airmobile) (The First Team), arrives in South Vietnam. The 1st is stationed at An Khe (II Corps; Binh Dinh Province).

14–28 September: *Locations:* III Corps; Binh Duong Province; Ben Cat; Cau Thi Tinh. *Type/Objective:* Search and Destroy seeking a reported regimental-sized enemy force. *Unit:* USA–173d Airborne Brigade (1/503d Abn). *Casualties:* Not reported in source document.

15 September: The first combat

troops of the 1st Cavalry Division arrive in South Vietnam: 1/5th and 2/5th Cavalry (The Black Knights); 1/7th and 2/7th Cavalry (Garry Owen); 1/12th and 2/12th Cavalry and the 1/9th Cavalry. The new battalions are initially stationed at An Khe (II Corps; Binh Dinh Province).

18–21 September: *Operation Gibraltar. Locations:* II Corps; Binh Dinh Province; Song Con River; An Khe; An Ninh. *Type/Objective:* Search and Destroy. *Gibraltar* is a companion mission to *Highland;* a sweep north of An Khe to secure 1st Cavalry's base camp. *Units:* USA—101st Airborne Division: 1st Bde (2/502d Abn); NVA/VC—2d VC Regiment. *Comments:* This operation is the first major contact for the 101st Airborne and the first defeat of a Main Force Viet Cong unit by the U.S. Army. *Casualties:* U.S.—13 KIA, 44 WIA; NVA/VC—226 KIA, 9 POWs.

25 September: *Operation Dagger Thrust I. Locations:* II Corps; Phu Yen Province; Vung Mu. *Type/Objective:* Amphibious raids into suspected enemy concentration 20 miles south of Qui Nhon. *Unit:* USMC—SLF 2/1st Marines. *Results:* No enemy contact.

29 September: The Republic of Korea (ROK) Capital Division arrives in South Vietnam. The Division is stationed at Qui Nhon (II Corps; Binh Dinh Province).

October: American forces begin *Operation Shining Brass.* Coordinated by MACV/SOG (Special Operations Group), *Shining Brass* is a clandestine intelligence operation. Specially trained teams are inserted into Laos to watch and disrupt traffic along the Ho Chi Minh Trail. These high-risk missions are launched from Kham Duc Special Forces Camp (I Corps; Quang Tin Province).

2 October: The 1st Infantry Division (The Big Red One), officially arrives in South Vietnam with the 2/28th Infantry. They are initially stationed at Bien Hoa (III Corps; Bien Hoa Province).

3–14 October: *Operation Shiny Bayonet. Locations:* II Corps; Binh Dinh Province; Soui Ca Valley; La Tinh Valley; Deo Mang Pass; An Khe; Binh Khe. *Type:* Search and Destroy. *Units:* USA—1st Cavalry Division: 3d Bde (1/7th Cav, 2/7th Cav, 2/12th Cav). *Casualties:* Not reported in source document.

5 October: The 1/16th Infantry (M) and 1/28th Infantry of the 1st Infantry Division arrive in South Vietnam. The new units are initially stationed at Bien Hoa (III Corps; Bien Hoa Province).

6 October–19 November: *Operations Happy Valley I–II. Locations:* II Corps; Binh Dinh Province; Vinh Thanh Valley; Vinh Phu. *Type:* Search and Destroy; Search and Clear. *Units:* USA—1st Cavalry Division: 2d Bde (1/5th Cav, 2/5th Cav, 2/12th Cav), 3d Bde (1/7th Cav, 2/12th Cav). *Casualties:* Not reported in source document.

8–14 October: *Locations:* III Corps; Binh Duong Province; "Iron Triangle," Ben Cat. *Type/Objective:* Search and Destroy mission to clear and open Highway 13 for the 1st Infantry Division's use. *Units:* USA—173d Airborne Brigade (1/503d Abn, 2/503d Abn); Aust—1/Royal Australian Regiment. *Event:* 10 October—B-2/503d Abn is ambushed in the "Iron Triangle" area by a company of Viet Cong. Eight Americans are KIA, 25 WIA. *Casualties:* Total casualty figures not reported for individual operation in the source documents.

14–19 October: *Operation Lonesome End. Locations:* II Corps; Binh Dinh Province; Mang Yang Pass; Highway 19. *Type/Objective:* Security operation to clear Highway 19, allowing resupply convoys to reach west to Pleiku. *Units:* USA—1st Cavalry Division: 1st Bde (1/8th Cav, 2/8th Cav). *Casualties:* Not reported for individual operation. Source documents listed casualties on a monthly or quarterly basis.

17 October: The 1/2d Infantry, 2/2d Infantry (M) and the 1/26th Infantry units of the 1st Infantry Division arrive in South Vietnam. They are initially stationed at Bien Hoa (III Corps; Bien Hoa Province).

18–20 October: *Operation Triple Play. Locations:* I Corps; Quang Tin Province; Chu Lai. *Type:* Search and Destroy—12 miles north of Chu Lai. *Unit:* USMC—3/3d Marines. *Casualties:* U.S.—2 WIA; NVA/VC—16 KIA, 6 POWs.

18–24 October: *Operation Trailblazer. Locations:* I Corps; Quang Nam Province; "Happy Valley"; DaNang. *Type/Objective:* Reconnaissance of enemy concentrations in the hills west of DaNang. *Unit:* USMC: 3d Recon Battalion. *Casualties:* NVA/VC—2 KIA (U.S. losses not included in source).

19–25 October: *Location:* II Corps; Pleiku Province; Plei Me. *Action:* An estimated force of 6000 NVA/VC soldiers attack the Special Forces Camp at Plei Me. *Units:* USA—Special Forces Operations Detachment A-217, 1st Cavalry Division: 1st Bde (2/8th Cav, 2/12th Cav, 1/9th Cav); VNAF—1 squad of South Vietnamese Special Forces (LLDB) and more than 400 Civilian Irregular Defense Group soldiers (CIDG) Reinforcements consist of 3d Armored Cavalry, 1/42d ARVN Rgt, 21st and 22d Ranger battalions; NVA/VC—32d, 33d and 66th NVA regiments. *Casualties:* U.S.—9 KIA/WIA; NVA/VC—850 KIA.

19 October: The Republic of Korea's 2d Marine Brigade (the Blue Dragons), arrives in South Vietnam. The Brigade is stationed at Dong Ba Thin (II Corps; Khanh Hoa Province).

20 October–5 November: *Operation Good Friend. Locations:* II Corps; Binh Dinh Province; An Khe; Binh Khe. *Type/Objective:* Security operation to cover the arrival and establishment of the ROK's Capital Division Cavalry Regiment at Binh Khe. *Units:* USA—1st Cavalry Division: 1st Bde (1/8th Cav, 2/8th Cav), 2d Bde (1/5th Cav, 2/5th Cav, 2/12th Cav). *Casualties:* Not reported in source document.

22–25 October: *Operation Red Snapper. Locations:* I Corps; Thua Thien Province; Phu Gia Peninsula; Dam Lap An Bay. *Type/Objective:* Search and Clear 20 miles north of DaNang. Security of Highway 1 between DaNang and Phu Bai. *Units:* USMC—F,G-2/3d Marines and one company from the 3/4th Marines; VNAF—2 ARVN Infantry battalions; 1 ARVN Ranger battalion and 4 companies of Regional/Popular Forces (RF/PF). *Casualties:* NVA/VC—7 KIA, 1 POW (U.S. losses not reported in source material).

23 October–26 November: *Operation Long Reach. Locations:* II Corps; Pleiku Province; Ia Drang Valley; Chu Pong Massif; Cateckia Tea Plantation; Plei Me. *Type/Objective:* Search and Destroy operation initiated in response to NVA attack on Plei Me Special Forces Camp. **Long Reach** is actually a series of three operations: *All the Way, Silver Bayonet I* and *Silver Bayonet II.* These battles come to be collectively known as the Pleiku Campaign. *Units:* USA—1st Cavalry Division: 1st Bde (1/8th Cav, 2/8th Cav, 1/12th Cav); 2d Bde (1/5th Cav, 2/5th Cav, 2/12th Cav); 3d Bde (1/7th Cav, 2/7th Cav); the 1/9th Cavalry participates with all brigades. NVA/VC—32d, 33d and 66th NVA regiments. *Casualties:* Totals for **Long Reach** (Pleiku Campaign). U.S.—300 KIA, 524 WIA, 4 MIA; NVA/VC—1447 KIA, 177 POWs.

23 October–9 November: *Operation All the Way. Locations:* II Corps; Pleiku Province; Ia Drang Valley; Chu Pong Massif; Plei Me; Duc Co; "Charger City"; *Cavalair,* LZ Wing. *Type/Objective:* Search and Destroy. *Units:* USA— 1st Cavalry Division: 1st Bde (1/8th Cav, 2/8th Cav, 1/12th Cav), 2d Bde (2/12th Cav); VNAF—3d Armored Cavalry Sqdn, 1/42d ARVN Rgt, 21st and 22d ARVN Ranger battalions; NVA/VC— 32d, 33d and 66th NVA regiments. *Events:* **26 October**—32d VC Regiment attacks ARVN relief column near Plei Me. Twenty-seven ARVN soldiers are KIA, 80 others are WIA. The defenders kill 148 VC and capture five POWs. **1 November**—A "Blue Team" rifle platoon from the 1/9th Cavalry engages elements of the 33d VC Regiment and captures an enemy field hospital west of Plei Me. As the battle intensifies, the 1/9th Cavalry is reinforced by troops from the 1/12th and 2/12th Cavalry. Results of the day's fight: U.S.—11 KIA, 47 WIA; NVA/VC—99 KIA, 44 POWs. **3 November**—Troopers from B–1/9th Cavalry ambush a company-sized force from the 8/66th NVA Regiment near the Chu Pong Massif. Taking a page out of the enemy's playbook, American forces kill 73 and take one prisoner. There are no U.S. soldiers killed. **4 November**—Firefights between 1st Cavalry Division battalions (1/8th, 2/8th Cavalry, 1/12th and 2/12th Cavalry) and NVA forces rage throughout the area of operations. Ten U.S. soldiers are KIA, 34 WIA. NVA losses for the day are 39 killed and 21 captured. **6 November**— "The Battle of LZ Wing" begins as a routine patrol for B–2/8th Cavalry and ends up as one of the bloodiest battles of the campaign. B–2/8th Cavalry, later reinforced by C–2/8th Cavalry, battles the well-entrenched 6/33d NVA Regiment. Twenty-six Americans are KIA, 53 are WIA. Seventy-seven NVA soldiers are confirmed KIA and one is captured. *Casualties:* Totals for *All the Way:* U.S.—57 KIA, 192 WIA; NVA/ VC—216 KIA (confirmed), 138 POWs.

26–27 October: *Operation Drum Head. Location:* I Corps; Quang Tin Province. *Type:* Search and Destroy in area southwest of Chu ·Lai. *Unit:* USMC—3/7th Marines. *Casualties:* U.S.—1 KIA, 2 WIA; NVA/VC—1 KIA, 26 POWs.

27–29 October: *Locations:* I Corps; Quang Nam Province; DaNang; Marble Mountain. *Action:* Viet Cong sappers attack Marble Mountain Air Facility. *Units:* USMC. *Results:* Twenty-four aircraft are destroyed and 23 others damaged. *Event:* A 12-man squad of Marines from I–3/9th Marines ambushes a group of VC five miles south of DaNang at An Tu (1). Fifteen VC are KIA. *Casualties:* U.S.—3 KIA, 91 WIA; NVA/ VC—41 KIA.

29–30 October: *Operation Lien Ket–10. Locations:* I Corps; Quang Tin Province; Do Xa Region; Chu Lai. *Type/Objective:* Search and Clear of Viet Cong base area 12 miles west of Chu Lai. *Units:* USMC—2/4th Marines; VNAF—2d ARVN Division (3/6th ARVN Regiment). *Casualties:* None— No enemy contact.

30 October: *Locations:* I Corps; Quang Nam Province; Tuy Loan River; Hill 22. *Action:* Viet Cong forces attack Marine outpost on Hill 22, eight miles south of DaNang Air Base. *Unit:* USMC—A–1/1st Marines. *Casualties:* U.S.—16 KIA, 41 WIA; NVA/VC—47 KIA.

November: The monsoon (rainy) season begins in the northern provinces and ends in the south.

November: *Operation Roadrunner. Locations:* III Corps; Binh Duong Province; Ap Bau Bang; Lai Khe. *Type/Objective:* Security mission to sweep Highway 13 from Lai Khe to Bau Long Pond. *Units:* USA—1st Infantry Division: 3d Bde (2/2d Inf [M], A–1/4th Cav). *Event:* **11–12 November**—"The Battle of Ap

Bau Bang." A night defensive position of A–2/2d Infantry (M) and 1/4th Cavalry is attacked by a Viet Cong force of unknown size. Nine Americans are KIA and 39 WIA. Viet Cong losses are confirmed at 175 KIA. *Casualties:* Not reported for individual operation in source document.

3–5 November: *Operation Black Ferret. Locations:* I Corps; Quang Ngai Province; Song Tra Bong River; Binh Son; LZs Albatross and Condor. *Type:* Search and Destroy 10 miles south of Chu Lai. *Units:* USMC – 1/7th Marines, 2/7th Marines, 1st Recon Bn; VNAF – 2d ARVN Division: (1/4th and 2/4th ARVN rgts). *Event:* **4 November** – A Marine patrol trips a booby trap, wounding six Marines and killing well known combat photographer Dickey Chappelle. *Casualties:* U.S. – 1 KIA, 13 WIA; NVA/VC – 2 KIA, 6 POWs.

10–12 November: *Operation Blue Marlin I. Locations:* I Corps; Quang Tin Province; Tam Ky River; Tam Ky. *Type/ Objective:* Search and Clear of area between Highway 1 and the coast from DaNang to Chu Lai. *Units:* USMC – BLT 2/7th Marines; VNAF – 3/VNMC. *Casualties:* Exact figures not reported.

10–20 November: *Operation Silver Bayonet I. Locations:* II Corps; Pleiku Province; Ia Drang Valley; Chu Pong Massif; Chu Don Mountain; Cateckia Tea Plantation; LZs Albany, Falcon, Stadium and X-Ray. *Type/Objective:* Search and Destroy. The mission of **Silver Bayonet I** is the pursuit and destruction of the enemy forces responsible for the attack on Plei Me. The operation is a follow-up to *All the Way* and the second phase of the 1st Cavalry's Pleiku Campaign. *Units:* USA – 1st Cavalry Division: 2d Bde (1/5th Cav, 2/5th Cav, 2/12th Cav – attached to 3d Bde), 3d Bde (1/7th Cav, 2/7th Cav); NVA/VC – 32d, 33d and 66th NVA regiments. *Events:* **12 November** – Viet Cong units attack the brigade base at

LZ Stadium. More than 90 mortar rounds fall within the base perimeter. The assault kills seven Americans and wounds 23. **14–16 November** – "The Battle of LZ X-Ray." In one of the fiercest battles of the entire war, three 1st Cavalry battalions (1/7th Cavalry, 2/7th Cavalry and the 2/5th Cavalry) battle the whole 66th NVA Regiment near the base of Chu Pong Massif. Only murderous artillery fire and tactical air support prevent the NVA from overrunning the American positions. Casualties at X-Ray: U.S. – 79 KIA, 125 WIA; NVA/VC – 834 KIA (at least 500 more estimated KIA). **16 November** – Eighteen B-52s drop 344 tons of bombs in support of ground troops. **17 November** – "Battle of LZ Albany." While on their way to recon the site of LZ Albany the 2/7th Cavalry and A–1/5th Cavalry are ambushed by the 8/66th NVA Regiment five miles northwest of LZ X-Ray. Losses from this short battle are staggering: 151 Americans are KIA or later die of wounds; 121 are WIA and four are MIA. Confirmed body count for the NVA: 403. **18 November** – "Battle of LZ Columbus." Heavy mortar and rocket fire pound the 1/5th Cavalry. Air strikes as close as 100 meters from friendly positions break up the attack. U.S. – 2 KIA, 31 WIA; NVA – 27 KIA (confirmed). *Casualties:* Totals for *Silver Bayonet I.* U.S. – 239 KIA, 307 WIA; NVA – 1224 KIA (confirmed), 19 POWs.

16–18 November: *Operation Blue Marlin II. Locations:* I Corps; Quang Nam Province; Truong Giang and Cua Dai rivers. *Type/Objective:* Search and Clear; follow-up to *Blue Marlin I. Units:* USMC – 3/3d Marines; VNAF – Two battalions of ARVN Rangers. *Casualties:* U.S. – 3 WIA; NVA/VC – 25 KIA, 15 POWs.

20–26 November: *Operation Green House. Locations:* II Corps; Pleiku Province; Ia Drang Valley; Chu Pong Massif; Duc Co. *Type:* Search and

Destroy. *Units:* USA — 1st Cavalry Division: 2d Bde (1/5th Cav, 2/5th Cav, 2/12th Cav); VNAF — ARVN Airborne Brigade. *Casualties:* NVA/VC — 119 KIA (U.S. losses not in source document).

21–26 November: *Operation Silver Bayonet II. Locations:* II Corps; Pleiku Province; Ia Drang Valley; Chu Pong Massif; Duc Co; LZs Crooks, Golf and Stadium. *Type/Objective:* Search and Destroy; pursuit of NVA forces west, toward Cambodia. Follow-up to *All the Way* and *Silver Bayonet I;* Phase 3 of the Pleiku Campaign. *Units:* USA — 1st Cavalry Division: 1st Bde (1/8th Cav, 1/9th Cav), 2d Bde (1/5th Cav, 2/5th Cav, 2/12th Cav); NVA/VC — 33d and 66th NVA regiments. *Casualties:* U.S. — 4 KIA, 25 WIA; NVA/VC — 7 KIA, 20 POWs.

21 November–late December: *Operation New Life-65. Locations:* III Corps; Binh Tuy Province; La Nga River; Sung Nhon; Than Duc; Vo Dat. *Objective:* Counterinsurgency effort aimed at breaking the Viet Cong hold on the area. The operation calls for the taking and securing of the large, populated valley northwest of Vo Dat to protect the people and the rice crop from the enemy. *Units:* USA — 1st Infantry Division: 3d Bde (1/2d Inf, 1/26th Inf), 173d Abn Bde (1/503d Abn, 2/503d Abn, D–16th Armor); Aust — 1/Royal Australian Regiment; NVA/VC — 1st NVA Regiment with three Viet Cong battalions. *Casualties:* Not reported in source material.

22–24 November: *Location:* I Corps; Quang Ngai Province. *Event:* Marines come to the aid of an ARVN Ranger battalion under attack by an estimated Viet Cong regiment 20 miles south of the city of Quang Ngai. *Units:* USMC — 3/7th Marines; VNAF — ARVN Rangers. *Casualties:* U.S. — 2 KIA, 1 WIA; ARVN — 71 KIA, 75 WIA; NVA/VC — 178 KIA (confirmed).

December: *Operation Bloodhound/*

Bushmaster. Locations: III Corps; Binh Duong and Tay Ninh provinces; Michelin Rubber Plantation; Lai Khe. *Type/Objective:* Sweep of area in and around the Michelin Plantation. *Units:* USA — 1st Infantry Division: 3d Bde (2/2d Infantry [M]); VNAF — 7th ARVN Regiment; NVA/VC — 272d VC Regiment. *Event:* **5 December** — "Battle of Ap Nha Mat." American forces from the 2/2d Infantry (M) kill more than 300 Viet Cong soldiers during a day-long firefight. The enemy force is identified as four battalions from the 272d VC Regiment. *Casualties:* Not reported in source documents.

December: *Operation Checkerboard. Locations:* III Corps; Binh Duong Province; Ben Cat; Lai Khe. *Type:* Search and Destroy. *Units:* USA — 1st Infantry Division (elements), 101st Airborne Division: 1st Bde (1/327th Abn, 2/502d Abn), 173d Abn Bde (elements); ARVN and Australian Royal Regiment forces also participate in *Checkerboard. Comment:* Little enemy contact during operation, although a huge storage area and hospital are discovered.

5–6 December: *Operation Dagger Thrust V. Location:* II Corps; Binh Dinh Province; Phu Thu. *Type/Objective:* Amphibious raid into suspected enemy concentration 40 miles north of Qui Nhon. *Unit:* USMC — BLT 2/1st Marines. *Casualties:* U.S. — 3 KIA, 10 WIA; NVA/VC — 26 KIA.

8–20 December: *Operation Harvest Moon/Lien Ket-18. Locations:* I Corps; Quang Nam and Quang Tin provinces; Phuoc Ha Valley; Que Son Valley; Ly Ly River; Cam La; Hiep Duc; Ky Phu; Son Thanh; Thang Binh and Viet An. *Type/Objective:* Search and Destroy. *Harvest Moon/Lien Ket-18* is a combined USMC/ARVN operation meant to prevent the NVA from overrunning the Que Son Valley and taking the ARVN garrisons at Viet An and Que Son. *Units:* USMC — Task Force Delta

(SLF 2/1st Marines, 3/3d Marines, 2/7th Marines, H–2/9th Marines); VNAF— 2d ARVN Division (1/5th ARVN Rgt, 6th ARVN Rgt, 11th Ranger Battalion); NVA/VC—1st Viet Cong Regiment. *Events:* **9 December**—While attempting to reinforce the ambushed 5th ARVN Regiment, the 3/3d Marines battle 200 Viet Cong. American losses are 11 KIA and 17 WIA. The Marines count 75 VC bodies. **10 December**—Marines of F–2/1st Marines and E–2/7th Marines fight a vicious battle five miles northeast of Que Son, near Cam La. Twenty Americans are killed and more than 80 wounded. **18 December**—"Battle of Ky Phu." The 2/7th Marines (with H–2/9th Marines attached) are ambushed by the VC 80th Battalion near Ky Phu, five miles northwest of Tam Ky. In the ambush and ensuing firefight 11 Marines are KIA, 71 WIA. The enemy body count is 104. *Casualties:* Total casualties for *Harvest Moon/Lien Ket–18.* U.S.—51 KIA, 256 WIA, 1 MIA; ARVN—90 KIA, 141 WIA, 91 MIA; NVA/VC—407 KIA, 33 POWs.

9 December: The *New York Times* runs an article that mirrors a Defense Intelligence Agency (DIA) report that admits the *Rolling Thunder* bombing program has not succeeded in destabilizing the North Vietnamese economy and has not reduced the flow of arms or men into South Vietnam. According to the DIA, to believe that the bombings will ever accomplish this is a "colossal misjudgment." Despite the frankness of the DIA report, the bombings continue for three more years.

16 December: General Westmoreland declares that he needs a total of 443,000 troops in South Vietnam by the end of 1966.

17–31 December: *Operations Clean House I–II–III. Locations:* II Corps; Binh Dinh Province; An Khe; Binh Khe. *Type:* Search and Destroy. *Units:* USA—1st Cavalry Division: 2d Bde (1/8th Cav), 3d Bde (1/7th Cav, 2/7th Cav). *Casualties:* U.S.—15 KIA; NVA/VC—137 KIA.

24 December: In another peace overture, President Johnson stops the bombing of North Vietnam once more. The halt lasts 37 days, resuming on 31 January 1966.

31 December: There are now approximately 184,000 American personnel in South Vietnam: an increase of 160,000 for the year. The U.S. combat forces end the year in the following strengths: Army—116,700, Marines— 41,000. The United States Air Force has more than 500 aircraft and 21,000 pilots and crewmen stationed at eight major bases in South Vietnam. American losses for the year: 1369 KIA, 7645 WIA. 171 planes have been lost in the less-than-successful *Rolling Thunder* program. Vietnamese Armed Forces (VNAF) losses for the year: 11,100 KIA, 22,600 WIA. NVA/VC losses for the year: 34,585 KIA, 5746 POWs.

1966

There are now 157,700 soldiers and Marines in South Vietnam. There are also 27,000 U.S. Air Force personnel, bringing the total number of Americans to 184,000. Enemy strength is estimated at 226,000 combat and support troops, 36,000 being NVA regulars. Intelligence sources report 12 battalions of North Vietnamese enter the south each month.

1–8 January: *Operation Marauder.* *Locations:* III Corps; Hau Nghia Province; "Plain of Reeds"; Oriental and Vaico rivers; Bao Tri; LZ Wine. *Type/ Objectives:* Search and Destroy. *Units:* USA—173d Airborne Brigade (1/503d Abn, 2/503d Abn); Aust—1/Royal Australian Regiment; NVA/VC—267th Viet Cong Battalion, 506th Viet Cong Battalion. *Casualties:* Not included in source.

1–19 January: *Operations Matador I–II.* *Locations:* II Corps; Kontum and Pleiku provinces. *Type/Objectives:* Search and Destroy in western Central Highlands along Cambodian border. The mission is to provide security for the incoming 3d brigade/25th Infantry Division. *Units:* USA—1st Cavalry Division: 1st Bde (1/8th Cav, 2/8th Cav, 1/12th Cav), 2d Bde (1/5th Cav, 2/5th Cav, 2/12th Cav). *Casualties:* U.S.—6 KIA, 41 WIA; NVA/VC—4 KIA, 6 POWs.

3–14 January: *Operations Quick Kick I–II–III.* *Locations:* III Corps; Binh Duong Province; Song Be River; Phuoc Vinh. *Type:* Search and Destroy. *Units:* USA—1st Infantry Division: 1st Bde (1/2 Inf, 1/26th Inf, 1/28th Inf). *Casualties:* Not included in source documents for individual operation.

8–14 January: *Operation Crimp/ Buckskin.* *Locations:* III Corps; Binh Duong Province; "Iron Triangle"; HoBo Woods; An Nhon Tay; Bao Trang; Cu Chi; Goc Chang; Nhuan Doc; Phu Loi; Trung Lap; LZs Jack and Whiskey. *Type/Objective:* Search and Destroy 25 miles northwest of Saigon. *Crimp/Buckskin* is a combined military effort to find and eliminate the headquarters of Viet Cong Military Region IV. *Units:* USA—1st Infantry Division: 3d Bde (1/16th Inf, 1/28th Inf, 2/28th Inf), 173d Abn Bde (1/503d Abn, 2/503d Abn) (8000 U.S. troops involved); Aust—1/Royal Australian Regiment; NVA/VC—Viet Cong 7th Cu Chi Battalion, D–308 VC Company. *Casualties:* NVA/VC—107 KIA, 9 POWs (American losses not included in source for the individual operation).

10–17 January: *Operation Mallard.* *Locations:* I Corps; Quang Nam Province; Vu Gia River; An Hoa; Thu Bon. *Type:* Search and Destroy. *Units:* USMC—1/3d Marines, 3d/7th Marines, G–2/9th Marines; NVA/VC— 5th VC Main Force Bn, R–20 Battalion.

17 January: The 1/14th Infantry (Golden Dragons), 1/35th Infantry and 2/35th Infantry (Cacti) of the 3d Brigade of the 25th Infantry Division arrive in South Vietnam. They are initially stationed at Pleiku (II Corps; Pleiku Province) and will eventually become part of the 3d Brigade of the 4th Infantry Division.

17–19 January: The 1/5th Infantry, 1/27th Infantry and the 2/27th Infantry (Wolfhounds) of the 25th Infantry Division arrive in South Vietnam. The battalions are stationed at Cu Chi (III Corps; Hau Nghia Province).

19 January–21 February: *Operation Van Buren. Locations:* II Corps; Phu Yen Province; My Canh, Tuy Hoa. *Type/Objective:* Combined allied security effort to protect the local rice crop. *Units:* USA—101st Abn Div: 1st Bde (1/327th Abn, 2/502d Abn); VNAF—47th ARVN Regiment; ROK—2d Marine Brigade; NVA/VC— 5/95th NVA Regiment. *Casualties:* NVA/VC—679 KIA (U.S. losses not included in source document).

25 January–6 March: *Operation Masher/Whitewing. Locations:* II Corps; Binh Dinh Province; An Lao Valley; Kim Son Valley; An Thai; Bong Son; Cu Nghi. *Type/Objective:* Search and Destroy. The goal of *Masher/Whitewing* is to drive the NVA out of Binh Dinh Province, destroying recruiting and resupply areas. The operation is run in conjunction with the Marines' *Double Eagle I* to the north in Quang Ngai. *Units:* USA—1st Cavalry Division: 1st Bde (1/8th Cav, 2/8th Cav, 1/12th Cav), 2d Bde (1/5th Cav, 2/5th Cav, 2/12th Cav), 3d Bde (1/7th Cav, 2/7th Cav); VNAF—22d ARVN Division; NVA/VC—3d NVA Division (18th, 22d and 98th NVA regiments; 1st, 2d VC regiments). *Events:* **28–31 January**—"Battle of Cu Nghi." The 1/7th Cav, 2/7th Cav and 2/12th Cav wage a bloody three-day fight in a small village eight miles north of Bong Son against the 7th and 9th battalions of the NVA 22d Regiment. The battle kills 121 cavalrymen and wounds 220. Enemy losses are 660 KIA. **16–28 February**—"Battle of the Kim Son Valley." The 1st Cavalry's 1st brigade and the 2d brigade's 1/5th Cav and 2/5th Cav clash with the 18th and 22d NVA Regiments in the Kim Son Valley area 15 miles south of Bong Son. Losses: U.S.—107 KIA, 561 WIA; NVA/VC—710 KIA (estimated). **20 February**—Elements of the VC 407th Battalion attack the 1st Cavalry's base at Camp Radcliff (An Khe). The attack kills seven Americans and wounds 65. Eight enemy bodies are found after the battle and one prisoner is taken. *Casualties:* Total losses for *Masher/Whitewing.* U.S.—228 KIA, 834 WIA; NVA/VC—1342 KIA, 633 POWs. *Comment:* Enemy soldiers are spotted in the *Masher/Whitewing* AO less than one week after the operation terminates.

28 January–19 February: *Operation Double Eagle I. Locations:* I, II Corps; Quang Ngai and Binh Dinh provinces; Tra Cau River; Ba To; Duc Pho; Nui Dau; Nui Xuong Giong; Quang Ngai; Thach Tru; Hill 829; Red Beach; "Johnson City." *Type/Objective:* Search and Destroy—companion operation to 1st Cavalry's *Masher/Whitewing.* The mission of *Double Eagle I* is to clear the Quang Ngai/Binh Dinh border area. The goal of both operations is to trap the enemy between the two attacking U.S. forces. *Units:* USMC—Task Force Delta (3/1st Marines, 2/3d Marines, 2/4th Marines, 2/9th Marines, elements of 7th Marines, 1st Force Recon Company); more than 5000 Marines involved in operation; NVA/VC—325-A NVA Division (18th, 19th NVA regiments; 2d VC Main Force Regiment; 38th Independent Battalion); an estimated enemy force of 6600 men. *Comments:* **Double Eagle I** ranks among the largest Search and Destroy operations of the war. *Casualties:* U.S.—24 KIA, 156 WIA; NVA/VC—312 KIA (estimated), 9 POWs.

31 January: *Rolling Thunder* bombing missions over North Vietnam resume, ending a 37-day halt.

February: *Operation Mallet. Locations:* III Corps; Bien Hoa Province; Long Than District; Nhon Trach. *Type/Objective:* Search and Destroy aimed at wiping out Viet Cong bases threatening Saigon. *Units:* USA—1st Infantry Division: 2d Bde (2/16th Inf, 1/18th Inf, 2/18th Inf). *Casualties:* Not reported in source material for individual operation.

3–9 February: *Operation Quick Kick IV. Location:* III Corps; Binh Duong Province; Phuoc Vinh. *Type:* Search and Destroy six miles southeast of Phuoc Vinh. *Units:* USA—1st Infantry Division: 1st Bde (1/2d Inf, 1/26th Inf, 1/28th Inf). *Casualties:* Not included in source documents for individual operation.

10 February–2 March: *Operation Rolling Stone. Location:* III Corps; Binh Duong Province; Cau Dinh. *Type/Objective:* Search and Destroy/Pacification. Operation is to provide security for road building crews on road between Routes 13 and 16. *Units:* USA—1st Infantry Division: 1st Bde (1/2d Inf, 1/26th Inf, 1/28th Inf); Aust—1/Royal Australian Regiment; NVA/VC—761st and 763d Main Force regiments (VC). *Casualties:* NVA/VC—173 KIA (U.S. losses not included in source documents for individual operation).

20 February–1 March: *Operation*

Double Eagle II. *Locations:* I Corps; Quang Tin and Quang Nam provinces; Que Son Valley; Ky Phu; Tam Ky; Thach Tru. *Type/Objective:* Search and Destroy. Continuation of **Double Eagle I** with a shift 50 miles north to exploit enemy sightings in the Que Son Valley. *Units:* USMC—Task Force Delta (3/1st Marines, 2/3d Marines, 2/7th Marines, 2/9th Marines); NVA/VC—1st Viet Cong Regiment. *Casualties:* U.S.—6 KIA, 136 WIA; NVA/VC—125 KIA, 15 POWs.

21–27 February: *Operation Mastiff. Location:* III Corps; Tay Ninh Province; Boi Loi Woods. *Type:* Search and Destroy five miles south of the Michelin Rubber Plantation. *Units:* USA—1st Infantry Division: 2d Bde (2/16th Inf, 1/18th Inf, 2/18th Inf), 3d Bde (2/2d Inf [M], 1/16th Inf [M]), 2/28th Inf). *Casualties:* Not reported in source for individual operation.

23 February: 1st Marine Division formally arrives in South Vietnam. They are stationed at Chu Lai (I Corps; Quang Tin Province).

24–25 February: *Operation County Fair. Location:* I Corps; Quang Nam Province; Phong Bac. *Type:* Cordon and Search in coordination with VNAF. *Units:* USMC—3/3d Marines. *Comment:* First such cordon and search operation to bear the name "County Fair." County Fair becomes a generic term for Marine/VNAF cordon and search operations.

27 February–3 March: *Operation New York. Locations:* I Corps; Thua Thien Province; Phu Thu Peninsula; Huong and Dai Giang rivers; Pho Lai; Quang Dien. *Type/Objective:* Reaction/reinforcement operation. The Marines answer an ARVN call for help northeast of Phu Bai. *Units:* USMC—Task Unit Hotel (F,G–2/1st Marines, K/3d Marines, F/9th Marines; VNAF—1/3d ARVN Regiment; NVA/VC—803d VC

Bn, 810th VC Main Force Bn, elements from the 6th VC Regiment and the 1st Provincial VC Regiment. *Casualties:* U.S.—17 KIA, 37 WIA; NVA/VC—122 KIA, 7 POWs.

March: *Operation Honolulu. Locations:* III Corps; Hau Nghia Province; Bao Tri; Duc Hoa. *Type:* Search and Destroy. *Units:* USA—25th Infantry Division: 2d Bde (1/5th Inf [M]). *Casualties:* Not reported in source document.

1–5 March: *Operation Hattiesburg. Location:* III Corps; Tay Ninh Province; Bo Lu Secret Zone. *Type:* Search and Destroy near Cambodian border. *Units:* USA—1st Infantry Division: 2d Bde (2/16th Inf, 1/18th Inf, 2/18th Inf). *Casualties:* Not reported for individual operation.

2–3 March: *Operation Troy. Locations:* I Corps; Thua Thien Province; Truoi River; Phu Bai; Phu Loc; Truoi Bridge. *Type/Objective:* Security operation to prevent the Viet Cong from using the Truoi Bridge as a means of escaping the *New York* operational area. *Units:* USMC—E-2/1st Marines, F-2/9th. Marines; NVA/VC—810th Viet Cong Main Force Battalion. *Casualties:* Little contact, no casualties reported in source.

3–6 March: *Operation Cocoa Beach. Locations:* III Corps; Binh Duong Province; Ap Bau Bang; Ben Cat; Lai Khe; Nha Mat; Lo Ke Rubber Plantation. *Type:* Search and Destroy. *Units:* USA—1st Infantry Division: 3d Bde (2/2d Inf [M], 1/16th Inf [M], 2/28th Inf); NVA/VC—272d Viet Cong Regiment, 441st VC Heavy Weapons Battalion. *Event:* **5 March**—"Battle of Lo Ke Plantation." A night defensive position (NDP) of the 2/28th Inf is attacked by elements of the 272d VC Regiment. The 2/28th is reinforced by the 1/16th Inf during the course of the six-hour battle. Ten U.S. soldiers are killed in the firefight and 25 wounded. Enemy

losses were counted at 199 KIA. *Casualties:* U.S.—10 KIA, 25 WIA; NVA/VC—more than 200 KIA (estimated).

4–8 March: *Operation Utah/Lien Ket-26. Locations:* I Corps; Quang Ngai Province; An Tuyet; Binh Son; Chau Nhai; Khanh My; Quang Ngai City; Son Chau; Buddha Hill (Nui Thien An); Hills 50, 85, and 97; Routes 1 and 527. *Type/Objective:* Reaction mission in response to an ARVN force's call for help seven miles northwest of Quang Ngai City. *Units:* USMC—3/1st Marines, 2d/4th Marines, 1/7th Marines, F,G,H-2/7th Marines; VNAF—2d ARVN Division (1st ARVN Abn Bn, 5th ARVN Abn Bn, 37th Ranger Bn) (more than 7000 allied troops involved in *Utah/Lien Ket-26*); NVA/VC—21st NVA Regiment, 36th NVA Regiment (enemy force estimated at more than 2000). *Casualties:* U.S.—98 KIA, 278 WIA; ARVN—30 KIA, 120 WIA; NVA/VC—632 KIA.

7–23 March: *Operation Silver City. Locations:* III Corps; Binh Duong Province; War Zone D; Song Be River. *Type:* Search and Destroy. *Units:* USA—1st Infantry Division: 1st Bde (1/2d Inf, 1/26th Inf, 1/28th Inf), 173d Airborne Brigade (2/503d Abn); VNAF—10th ARVN Division; NVA/VC—271st Viet Cong Regiment. *Event:* **16 March**—An estimated force of 2000 VC attack positions manned by the 2/503d Abn. Devastating artillery fire turns back the assault, killing a reported 303 enemy soldiers. *Casualties:* Not reported in source documents.

7–28 March: *Operation Jim Bowie. Locations:* II Corps; Binh Dinh Province; Kim Son, Soui Ca; Song Ba and Vinh Thanh valleys; Dak Kron Bung River; An Tuc; LZs Columbus, Eddy, Nail and Phenix City. *Type/Objective:* Search and Destroy aimed at destroying the Kon Truck staging area west of the Kim Son Valley. *Jim Bowie* also included a sweep of the upper Song Ba

Valley to the northwest. *Units:* USA— 1st Cavalry Division: 1st Bde (1/8th Cav, 2/8th Cav, B–1/9th Cav, 1/12th Cav), 2d Bde (2/5th Cav, 1/7th Cav, 2/7th Cav, C–1/9th Cav); NVA/VC—Sao Vang Division; VC Military Region Five Headquarters reported in area but no contact made. *Casualties:* U.S.—3 KIA, 377 WIA (majority of wounds attributed to punji stake booby traps); NVA/VC—27 KIA, 17 POWs.

9–12 March: *Location:* I Corps; Thua Thien Province; Ashau Valley. *Action:* NVA attack on Special Forces/CIDG at Ashau. *Units:* USA—Special Forces (17 Americans); VNAF—Elements of a Mobile Strike Force, South Vietnamese Special Forces (LLDB) and civilians amounting to just over 400; NVA/VC— 325 NVA Division (95th NVA Regiment) (enemy strength estimated at 2000). *Casualties:* U.S.—5 KIA, 12 WIA; VNAF—172 KIA, 248 WIA; NVA/VC—800 KIA (estimated).

14–30 March: *Operation Golden Fleece II. Location:* I Corps; Quang Nam Province; Le My. *Type/Objective:* Security operation to protect the rice harvest in the DaNang area. *Unit:* USMC—1/3d Marines. *Casualties:* None reported in source.

19–23 March: *Operation Oregon. Locations:* I Corps; Thua Thien Province; Ap Chinh An; Ap Dai Phu; Ap Phu An; Ap Tay Hoang; Phong Dien; LZs Eagle, Duck and Robin. *Type:* Search and Destroy. *Units:* USMC—Task Group Foxtrot (2d/1st Marines; 1/4th Marines); VNAF—1st ARVN Division (3d ARVN Regiment); NVA/VC—802d Viet Cong Battalion. *Event:* **20 March**—Company B–1/4th Marines (later reinforced by E–2/1st Marines) battles three companies from the 802d VC Battalion at the village of Ap Chinh An. The Marines repeatedly try to take the hamlet but are turned back. Nine Marines are killed in the assault and 41 wounded. The Marines, following an intense artil-

lery barrage, attack the village the next day to find the enemy have left the area. *Casualties:* Totals for **Oregon.** U.S.—11 KIA, 45 WIA; NVA/VC—48 KIA, 8 POWs.

19–24 March: *Operation Texas/Lien Ket-26. Locations:* I Corps; Quang Ngai Province; Vinh Tuy Valley; An Hoa; Binh Son; Phuoc Loc; Phuong Dinh; Quang Ngai City; Thach An Hoi; Xuan Hoa; Hill 141. *Type/Objective:* Reaction force operation to retake the An Hoa outpost 25 miles northwest of Quang Ngai City. *Units:* USMC—3/1st Marines, 2/4th Marines, 3/7th Marines; VNAF—5th Airborne Battalion, elements of the VNMC; NVA/VC—11/21st NVA Rgt, 60 and 90/1st VC Rgt. *Event:* **22–23 March**—"Battle of Phuoc Loc." Companies K, L–3/7th Marines battle two battalions of VC at Phuoc Loc (1), 10 miles northwest of Quang Ngai City. U.S. losses are seven KIA and 56 WIA. Enemy body count is 60. *Casualties:* Total for **Texas/Lien Ket-26.** U.S.—99 KIA, 212 WIA; NVA/VC—280-405 (estimated).

19–28 March: *Operation Kings. Locations:* I Corps; Quang Nam Province; Ky Lam and La Tho rivers; Dien Ban; Dai Loc; Giao Ai; Hoi An; Phong Thu; Phu Tay. *Type:* Search and Destroy/ Pacification. *Units:* USMC—K,L–3/3d Marines, E,F–2/9th Marines; NVA/ VC—R–20 Doc Lap Battalion (VC). *Event:* **25 March**—A defensive position three miles east of Dien Ban, manned by E–2/9th Marines, is attacked. Five Marines are KIA and 19 WIA in the assault. *Casualties:* U.S.—8 KIA, 60 WIA (9th Marines only); NVA/VC—58 KIA (estimated).

25 March–8 April: *Operation Lincoln. Locations:* II Corps; Darlac, Kontum and Pleiku provinces; Chu Pong Mountain; Ia Muer, Ia Tae and Ya Lop rivers; Duc Co; Pleime. "The Turkey Farm"; LZs Albany, Buck, Bear, Emerald, Ruby, X-Ray. *Type:* Search and Destroy/Reconnaissance in Force. *Units:* USA—1st Cavalry Division: 1st Bde (1/8th Cav, 2/8th Cav, 1/9th Cav, 1/12th Cav), 3d Bde (1/7th Cav, 2/7th Cav), 25th Infantry Division: 3d Bde (B-1/69th Armor, C-3/4th Cav); NVA/VC—32d, 33d and 66th NVA regiments. *Casualties:* U.S.—51 KIA, 136 WIA; NVA/VC—522 KIA, 18 POWs.

26 March–6 April: *Operation Jackstay. Locations:* III Corps; Gia Dinh Province; Rung Sat Special Zone; Long Tao River; Binh Hoa; Can Gio; Quang Xuyen. *Type/Objective:* Search and Destroy to prevent cutting of main water route to Saigon. *Units:* USMC—Special Landing Force–BLT 1/5th Marines; VNAF—4,5/VNMC. *Comment: Jackstay* is the first full-scale U.S. operation in the Mekong Delta. *Casualties:* U.S.—5 KIA, 25 WIA, 2 MIA; NVA/VC—63 KIA.

28 March: The 25th Infantry Division (Tropic Lightning) officially arrives in South Vietnam. The division is stationed at Cu Chi (III Corps; Hau Nghia Province).

28–30 March: *Operation Indiana. Locations:* I Corps; Quang Ngai Province; Lam Loc; Phuoc Loc; Vinh Loc. *Type:* Reaction force operation in the *Texas/Utah* area of operations. *Units:* USMC—1/7th Marines, 2/7th Marines; VNAF—3/5th ARVN Regiment; NVA/VC—1st Viet Cong Regiment. *Casualties:* U.S.—11 KIA, 45 WIA; NVA/VC—69 KIA, 1 POW.

30 March–15 April: *Operation Abilene. Locations:* III Corps; Long Khanh and Phuoc Tuy provinces; May Tao Secret Zone; Courtenay Rubber Plantation. *Type:* Search and Destroy. *Units:* USA—1st Infantry Division: 1st Bde (1/16th Inf [M], 2/28th Inf), 2d Bde (2/16th Inf, 1/18th Inf, 2/18th Inf), 3d Bde (2/2 Inf [M]); NVA/VC—5th and 94th Viet Cong regiments, D–800 Viet Cong Main Force Battalion. *Casualties:*

NVA/VC—800 KIA (U.S. losses not reported in source document).

April: *Operation Hot Springs. Location:* I Corps; Quang Ngai Province. *Type/Objective:* Search and Destroy in the *Utah/Texas/Indiana* area of operations. *Units:* USMC—7th Marines (1st Marine Division); NVA/VC—1st Viet Cong Regiment. *Casualties:* NVA/VC—More than 150 reported killed. (American losses not reported in source.)

April–May: The 5th Marines of the 1st Marine Division arrive in South Vietnam. They are stationed at Chu Lai (I Corps; Quang Tin Province).

1 April: The 1st Signal Brigade arrives in South Vietnam. They are stationed at Saigon (III Corps; Gia Dinh Province).

11–17 April: *Operation Mosby I. Location:* II Corps; Kontum and Pleiku provinces. *Type:* Search and Destroy along Cambodian border. *Units:* USA—1st Cavalry Division: 1st Bde (1/8th Cav, 2/8th Cav, 1/12th Cav), 3d Bde (1/7th Cav, 2/7th Cav, 1/9th Cav). *Casualties:* U.S.—2 KIA, 12 WIA; NVA/VC—3 KIA, 5 WIA.

12 April: First use of USAF B–52s stationed on Guam against targets in North Vietnam. Raid centers on the Mu Gia Pass—a main route for men and supplies into Laos. Thirty aircraft participate in the reported $21,000,000 raid. The pass is reported open and functional two days after the strike.

12 April–18 May: *Operations Austin I and VI. Locations:* II Corps; Binh Thuan, Lam Dong, Quang Duc provinces. III Corps; Binh Tuy, Phuoc Long provinces; La Nga River Valley; Song Be River; Bu Gia Map; Bu Prang; Nhon Co; Phan Thiet; Song Mao. *Type:* Search and Destroy along Cambodian border. *Units:* USA—101st Airborne Division: 1st Bde (1/327th Abn, 2/502d

Abn, A–2/17th Cav), 173d Airborne Brigade (2/503d Abn); VNAF–3d, 4th and 9th ARVN regiments, elements from 45th ARVN Regiment; NVA/VC–602d, 603d and 608th VC battalions and 186th VC Main Force Battalion reported in area of operations. *Casualties:* U.S.–11 KIA, 33 WIA; NVA/VC–123 KIA, 6 POWs.

16 April: *Location:* I Corps; Quang Nam Province; Phong Thu. *Action:* Two Viet Cong companies attack a company of Marines about 10 miles south of DaNang. *Units:* USMC–H–2/9th Marines; NVA/VC–R–20 Doc Lap Battalion (VC). *Casualties:* U.S.–7 KIA, 37 WIA; NVA/VC–12 KIA.

17 April–1 May: *Operation Virginia.* *Locations:* I Corps; Quang Tri Province; Route 9; Ca Lu; Khe Sanh. *Type:* Search and Destroy. *Unit:* USMC–1/1st Marines. *Casualties:* Not reported in source.

17 April–?: *Operation Lexington I.* *Location:* III Corps; Bien Hoa Province; Nhon Trach. *Type:* Search and Destroy in old *Mallet* area of operations. *Units:* USA–1st Infantry Division: 2d Bde (2/16th Inf, 1/18th Inf, 2/18th Inf). *Casualties:* NVA/VC–17 KIA (U.S. losses not reported in source document).

21 April–?: *Operation Mosby II.* *Locations:* II Corps; Kontum and Pleiku provinces; LZ Elwood. *Type:* Search and Destroy. *Units:* USA–1st Cavalry Division: 2d Bde (1/5th Cav, 2/5th Cav, 2/12th Cav). *Casualties:* As of 30 April 1966: U.S.–31 WIA; NVA/VC–4 KIA, 41 POWs.

21 April–10 May: *Operation Georgia.* *Locations:* I Corps; Quang Nam Province; Ky Lam and Thu Bon rivers; An Hoa; Dai Loc; Phong Thu; Phu Loc; Phu Long. *Type/Objective:* Security operation in the hamlets surrounding the An Hoa Combat Base. *Units:* USMC–

3/9th Marines; NVA/VC–R–20 Doc Lap Battalion (VC). *Event:* **3 May**–M–3/9th Marines is attacked by two companies of the R–20 Doc Lap Battalion near Phu Long, 15 miles southwest of DaNang. Five Marines are KIA and 54 WIA. Fifteen VC bodies are counted on the battlefield and 100 more are estimated KIA. *Casualties:* Total for **Georgia.** U.S.–9 KIA, 94 WIA; NVA/VC–103 KIA.

24 April–17 May: *Operation Birmingham.* *Locations:* III Corps; Tay Ninh Province; War Zone C; Michelin Plantation; Cai Bac River; Lo Go; Long Nguyen; Tay Ninh City. *Type:* Search and Destroy. *Units:* USA–1st Infantry Division: 1st Bde (1/16th Inf [M], 1/28th Inf, 2/28th Inf), 2d Bde (2/16th Inf, 1/18th Inf, 2/18th Inf), 3d Bde (1/2d Inf, 2/2d Inf [M]); VNAF–25th ARVN Division, ARVN Airborne Division, ARVN Rangers; NVA/VC–271st and 273d Viet Cong regiments reported but not found in the area. *Casualties:* As of 30 April 1966: NVA/VC–82 KIA (U.S. losses not included in source document).

26 April: *Operation County Fair II.* *Locations:* I Corps; Quang Nam Province; Vinh Dien River; Thanh Quit (3). *Type:* Cordon and Search/Pacification. *Units:* USMC–2/9th Marines; VNAF–3/51st ARVN Regiment (two companies). *Casualties:* U.S.–None; VNAF–1 KIA, 14 WIA; NVA/VC–45 KIA, 17 POWs.

27 April–6 May: *Operation Osage.* *Location:* I Corps; Thua Thien Province; Phu Loc. *Type:* Search and Destroy; amphibious assault into Hai Van Pass area north of DaNang. *Unit:* USMC–Special Landing Force–BLT 1/5th Marines. *Casualties:* U.S.–8 KIA, 9 WIA; NVA/VC–8 KIA.

29 April: The 4/9th Infantry (Manchu), 2/14th Infantry (Golden Dragons) and the 4/23d Infantry battalions of the

25th Infantry Division arrive in South Vietnam. The units are initially stationed at Cu Chi (III Corps; Hau Nghia Province).

May: Monsoon (rainy) season begins in the southern provinces and ends in the north.

May: *Ky Lam Campaign. Locations:* I Corps; Quang Nam Province; Ky Lam, Than Quit, Thu Bon and Vu Gia rivers; Dai Loc; Dien Ban; Do Nam; Hoa Tay; Hoi An. *Type/Objective:* Search and Clear of area 15 miles south of DaNang. *Units:* USMC — 2/4th Marines, 1/9th Marines, 2/9th Marines, 3/9th Marines; NVA/VC — R-20 Doc Lap Battalion (VC). *Events:* **12 May** — A 14-man patrol from B-1/9th Marines is attacked by elements of the R-20 Battalion near Do Nam, 14 miles south of DaNang. Twelve Marines die in the fight. Thirty VC are reported KIA. **20 May** — The 1/9th Marines again battle the R-20 Battalion, this time near An Trach, eight miles south of DaNang. American losses are 12 KIA and 31 WIA. The Marines counted 83 VC bodies. *Casualties:* As of 31 May 1966: U.S. — 75 KIA, 328 WIA; NVA/VC — 270 KIA.

2 May: Secretary of Defense Robert McNamara claims in a speech that 4500 North Vietnamese soldiers infiltrate into South Vietnam each month. This figure is three times higher than in 1965. *Author's note:* The infiltration increases despite the bombing efforts.

3–16 May: *Operation Lewis and Clark. Locations:* II Corps; Binh Dinh and Kontum provinces; Plateau Gi; An Khe. *Type/Objective:* Reconnaissance in Force from Plateau Gi to An Khe. *Units:* USA — 1st Cavalry Division: 2d Bde (1/5th Cav, 2/5th Cav, B-1/9th Cav, 2/12th Cav). *Casualties:* U.S. — 7 KIA, 62 WIA; NVA/VC — 6 KIA, 2 POWs.

3–16 May: *Operation Davy Crockett. Locations:* II Corps; Binh Dinh Prov-

ince; An Lao, Kim Son ("Crows Foot"), Soui Ca valleys; Da Ban Hill; Bung Di; Bong Son; Ninh De (2); Thanh Son (2); Tuong Son (2); LZs Bird, Bullet, Pony, Ralph, Spike and Zulu. *Type:* Search and Destroy. *Units:* USA — 1st Cavalry Division: 3d Bde (1/5th Cav, 1/7th Cav, 2/7th Cav, 1/9th Cav); VNAF: 3/3d ARVN Armored Cavalry; NVA/VC: 2d, 7th and 9th VC Main Force regiments; 22d NVA (Quyet Tam) Regiment reported in the area of operations. *Casualties:* U.S. — 27 KIA, 155 WIA, 1 MIA; NVA/VC — 345 KIA, 82 POWs.

4–6 May: *Operation Dexter. Locations:* III Corps; Bien Hoa Province; Di An; Tan Uyen. *Type:* Search and Destroy. *Units:* USA — 173d Airborne Brigade (1/503d Abn, 2/503d Abn, D/16th Armor, E/17th Cavalry); NVA/VC — 3/165th Viet Cong Regiment. *Casualties:* NVA/VC — 1 KIA (American losses not included in source).

5–7 May: *Operation Cherokee. Location:* I Corps; Thua Thien Province; Co Bi Thanh Tan. *Type:* Search and Destroy. *Units:* USMC — 1/1st Marines, 1/4th Marines, 3/4th Marines. *Casualties:* U.S. — 1 KIA, 17 WIA; NVA/VC — 9 KIA.

10–12 May: *Operation Wayne. Locations:* I Corps; Thua Thien Province; Phu Loc District. *Type/Objective:* Reaction Force operation 10 miles south of Phu Bai. The mission is to check and verify intelligence reports of VC infiltration in the area. *Units:* USMC — 1/1st Marines, 3/4th Marines; NVA/VC — 804th Viet Cong Battalion. *Casualties:* U.S. — 11 WIA; NVA/VC — 5 KIA.

10 May–30 July: *Operation Paul Revere I/Thang Phong 14. Locations:* II Corps; Pleiku Province; Ia Drang Valley; Chu Pong Massif; LZ Oasis. *Type/Objective:* Search and Destroy/ Search and Clear. *Paul Revere's* mission is to perform screening along the Cambodian border and bring Pleiku

Province under Allied control. Its secondary mission is to prevent attacks on Special Forces camps at Duc Co and Pleime. *Type:* Search and Destroy. *Units:* USA—1st Cavalry Division: 2d Bde (2/5th Cav, 1/9th Cav, 2/12 Cav), 25th Infantry Division: 3d Bde (2/14th Inf, 1/35th Inf, 2/35th Inf); NVA/VC—1st NVA Division (Yellow Star): 141st NVA Regiment. *Casualties:* U.S.—10 WIA; NVA/VC—1 KIA.

15–16 June: *Locations:* I Corps; Quang Nam Province; Queson Valley Hill 488 (25 miles west of Chu Lai). *Action:* "Battle of Nui Vu (Howard's Hill)." An 18-man Marine recon patrol is attacked by a battalion of NVA regulars. *Units:* USMC—1st Recon Battalion, C–1/5th Marines (reinforcements); NVA/VC—3d NVA Regiment (1 Bn). *Casualties:* U.S.—8 KIA, 14 WIA; NVA/VC—42 KIA.

17–22 June: *Operation Kansas. Locations:* I Corps; Quang Nam and Quang Tin provinces; Queson Valley; Ly Ly River; Hill 488; Nui Loc Son; Nui Vu; Hiep Duc; Tam Ky; Thang Binh. *Type/ Objective:* Search and Destroy 25 miles south of DaNang. *Units:* USMC—3/1st Marines, 1/5th Marines, 2/5th Marines; VNAF—2d ARVN Division, VNMC (2 Bns); NVA/VC—3d NVA Regiment (1 Bn). *Casualties:* U.S.—9 KIA, 20 WIA; NVA/VC—85 KIA.

17–23 June: *Operation Dodge. Location:* I Corps; Thua Thien Province. *Type:* Search and Destroy. *Unit:* USMC —2/4th Marines. *Casualties:* None reported following light fighting.

18 June: General Westmoreland requests an additional 118,500 troops.

18–30 June: *Operation Deckhouse I. Location:* II Corps; Phu Yen Province. *Type/Objective:* Amphibious assault in support of *Nathan Hale.* *Unit:* USMC—BLT 3/5th Marines. *Casualties:* Not reported in source.

19 June–1 July: *Operation Nathan Hale. Locations:* II Corps; Phu Yen Province; Tuy Hoa Valley Hill 258; Dong Tri; Dinh Phong; La Hai; The Hien; Trung Luong; Trung Thanh; Tuy An; LZs Apple, Axe and Eagle. *Type/ Objective:* Search and Destroy with the mission of securing the Tuy Hoa Valley. *Units:* USA—1st Cavalry Division–Task Force Colt: 1st Bde (1/8th Cav, 2/8th Cav, 1/12th Cav), 3d Bde (1/7th Cav, 2/7th Cav), 101st Abn Division: 1st Bde (1/327th Abn, 2/327th Abn); USMC—3/5th Marines; NVA/VC: 7/18B NVA Rgt, 8/18B NVA Rgt, elements of 32d NVA Rgt, 66th NVA Rgt, 95th NVA Rgt, and 85th Main Force (VC) Battalion reported in area of operations. *Events:* **20 June**—"Battle of LZ Axe." After combat assaulting into LZ Axe, C–2/327th Airborne comes under heavy fire. Eleven Americans are KIA and 27 WIA. **20–21 June**—A–1/327th Airborne is ambushed near Trung Long. In the ensuing battle, 14 U.S. soldiers are KIA, 21 WIA. *Casualties:* U.S.—66 KIA, 353 WIA; NVA/VC—459 KIA, 35 POWs.

23 June: *Operation Turner. Location:* I Corps; Thua Thien Province; Ashau Valley. *Objective:* Destruction of ammo and supplies left behind at the Ashau Special Forces Camp. *Unit:* USMC—I–3/4th Marines. *Casualties:* None.

24 June–9 July: *Operation Yorktown. Location:* III Corps; Long Khanh Province. *Type:* Search and Destroy southeast of Xuan Loc. *Units:* USA—173d Airborne Brigade (2/503d Abn); NVA/VC—5th VC Division (308/274th VC Rgt). *Casualties:* Not included in source document.

24 June–15 July: *Operation Beauregard. Locations:* II Corps; Kontum Province; Dak Poko River; Dak Pek; Dak Sut; Dak To; Mang Buk. *Type/Objective:* Screening and interdiction operation along the South Vietnamese/ Cambodian/Laotian border. *Units:* USA—101st Airborne Division: 1st Bde

(1/327th Abn, 2/502d Abn; A–2/17th Cav); NVA/VC–24th NVA Regiment. *Event:* Four Americans are KIA and six WIA by mines when 2/502d Airborne air assaults into LZ Jim (near Dak Sut). *Casualties:* U.S.–6 KIA, 39 WIA; NVA/VC–23 KIA, 17 POWs.

25 June: 4/503d Airborne, of the 173d Airborne Brigade, arrives in South Vietnam. They are stationed at Bien Hoa (III Corps; Bien Hoa Province).

25 June–4 July: *Operation Jay. Locations:* I Corps; Thua Thien Province; O Lau River; Route 597; Ap Chinh An; My Phu; Phong Dien; LZs Raven and Shrike. *Type:* Search and Destroy 20 miles northwest of Hue. *Units:* USMC–2/1st Marines, 2/4th Marines, 3/4th Marines; VNAF–1st ARVN Division (LAM SON–284); NVA/VC–802d, 806th and 812th Main Force battalions (VC). *Event:* 25–28 June–"Battle of Ap Chinh An." Companies E,F,H–2/4th Marines battle a dug-in force six miles northwest of Phong Dien. Marine losses in the fight: 23 KIA and 58 WIA. Eighty-two enemy bodies are counted. *Casualties:* Casualties not reported in source.

2–6 July: *Operation Holt. Location:* I Corps; Thua Thien Province. *Type/Objective:* Search and Destroy. Follow-up to *Jay* in an attempt to finish off the mauled 802d Main Force Battalion. *Units:* USMC–3/4th Marines; NVA/VC–802d Main Force Battalion (VC). *Casualties:* U.S.–1 WIA; NVA/VC–7 KIA.

2–30 July: *Operation Henry Clay. Locations:* II Corps; Darlac, Phu Bon and Phu Yen provinces. *Type/Objective:* Reconnaissance in Force along Highway 14 to the Cambodian border. *Henry Clay* is a continuation of *Nathan Hale. Units:* USA–1st Cavalry Division: 1st Bde (1/8th Cav, 2/8th Cav), 3d Bde (1/7th Cav, 2/7th Cav, C–1/9th Cav), 101st Airborne Division–1st Bde

(2/327th Abn). *Casualties:* U.S.–4 KIA, 23 WIA; NVA/VC–33 KIA, 8 POWs.

4 July–28 October: *Operation Macon.* *Locations:* I Corps; Quang Nam Province; "Arizona Territory," Ba Ren, Ky Lam and Thu Bon rivers; An Hoa; Cu Ban; Giang Hoa; My Loc; Phu Long. *Type/Objective:* Search and Destroy to provide security for An Hoa industrial complex. *Units:* USMC–1/3d Marines, 3/3d Marines, 3/9th Marines; VNAF–51st ARVN Regiment; NVA/VC–R–20 Doc Lap Main Force Battalion (VC). *Events:* 4 July–K–3/9th Marines is ambushed at My Loc, 20 miles south of DaNang. Eight Marines are KIA and 16 WIA. **20 August**–1/9th Marines battles a company of the R–20 Battalion near Giang Hoa and Phu Long (25 miles southeast of DaNang). Five Marines are KIA and 16 WIA. Ten Viet Cong bodies are found on the battlefield. **3 September**–In a two-hour firefight at Cu Ban, I–3/9th Marines again battles the R–20 Battalion. Losses are U.S.–5 KIA, 10 WIA; NVA/VC–32 KIA. *Casualties:* Totals for *Macon:* U.S.–24 KIA, 172 WIA; NVA/VC–380 KIA.

6–14 July: *Operation Washington. Locations:* I Corps; Quang Tin Province; Do Xa Region; Tranh River; Chu Lai; Hau Duc; Tien Phuoc. *Type:* Reconnaissance and Exploitation. *Unit:* USMC–A/1st Recon Battalion. *Casualties:* U.S.–none; NVA/VC–13 KIA, 4 POWs.

7 July–3 August: *Operation Hastings.* *Locations:* I Corps; Quang Tri Province; Dong Ha Mountains; Song Ngan Valley ("Helicopter Valley"); "The Rockpile"; Hills 208 and 364; Cam Lo; Dong Ha; LZs Crow, Dove and Robin. *Type/Objective:* Search and Destroy. The goal of *Hastings* is to drive the NVA back across the DMZ and thus to preempt and disrupt the enemy's plan to mass and attack Quang Tri and Thua Thien. *Units:* USMC–1/1st Marines, 2/1st Marines, 1/3d Marines, 2/4th

Marines, 3/4th Marines, 2/9th Marines (more than 8000 Marines participate); VNAF–1st ARVN Division, VNMC (LAM SON–289) (more than 3000 VNAF troops); NVA/VC–324–B NVA Division (90th, 803d and 5/812th NVA regiments) (between 8000 and 12,000 enemy troops estimated in the area of operations). *Events:* **15 July**–"Battle of Helicopter Valley." The assault into the Song Ngan Valley is a tough one for the Marines. Fifteen-hundred enemy soldiers from the 90th NVA Regiment lie in waiting at two key landing zones: E,G,H–2/4th Marines at LZ Dove and I,K,L–3/4th Marines at LZ Crow. Fire is so intense that two helicopters taking evasive action collide and crash. Firefights rage all day throughout the valley. More than 36 Marines are KIA and at least 27 WIA. **18 July**–More than 1000 NVA regulars attack the Marine rear guard, K–3/4th Marines near LZ Crow. K Company is reinforced by I,L–3/4th Marines, thereby averting a disaster. Nonetheless, 14 Marines are KIA and 49 WIA. The enemy body count is 138, with hundreds more estimated KIA. **22 July**–B–52s bomb the DMZ for the first time, their target being a supply area one mile north of the Ben Hai River. **24–25 July**–I–3/5th Marines is ambushed by the 6/812th NVA Regiment near Hill 362, three miles northwest of the Rockpile. Eighteen Americans are KIA in the ambush, 82 WIA. *Casualties:* Total for *Hastings:* U.S.–126 KIA, 446 WIA; VNAF–21 KIA, 40 WIA; NVA/VC–882 KIA, 17 POWs.

9–17 July: *Operation Aurora I. Location:* III Corps; Long Khanh Province. *Type/Objective:* Search and Destroy in the area northwest of Xuan Loc. The emphasis of *Aurora I* is on road security and disrupting Viet Cong tax collection. *Unit:* USA–173d Airborne Brigade. *Casualties:* Not reported in source document for individual operation.

13 July–3 September: *Operation El*

Paso III. Locations: III Corps; Binh Long Province; An Loc; Loc Thanh; Quan Loi. *Objective:* Reconnaissance in Force along Route 13 to provide security for the Quan Loi–An Loc complex. *Units:* USA–1st Infantry Division; VNAF–5th ARVN Division. *Casualties:* Not reported in source document.

16–18 July: *Operation Deckhouse II. Locations:* I Corps; Quang Tri Province; Cua Viet River; Blue Beach; Dong Ha. *Type/Objective:* Amphibious and helicopter assault to block NVA routes of entry into Quang Tri through the DMZ. *Unit:* USMC–BLT 3/5th Marines. *Casualties:* NVA/VC–24 KIA (U.S. losses not reported in source).

17–21 July: *Operation Cedar Rapids. Locations:* III Corps; Binh Duong Province; Ong Dong Jungle; Route 16; Phuoc Vinh. *Type:* Search and Destroy. *Units:* USA–1st Infantry Division: 1st Bde (1/2 Inf, 2/2d Inf [M], 1/16th Inf [M], 1/26th Inf). *Casualties:* Not included in source document for individual operation.

17 July–3 August: *Operation Aurora II. Locations:* III Corps; Binh Tuy, Lam Dong and Long Khanh provinces. *Type/Objective:* Search and Destroy. The emphasis of the operation is on road security and the disruption of Viet Cong tax collection. *Unit:* USA–173d Airborne Brigade. *Casualties:* Not included in source document for individual operation.

21 July–5 September: *Operation John Paul Jones. Location:* II Corps; Phu Yen Province; Vung Ro. *Objective:* Security of Vung Ro Pass and Bay area. *Units:* USA–4th Infantry Division: 1st Bde (1/22d Inf), 101st Airborne Division: 1st Bde (1/327th Abn, 2/327th Abn, 2/502 Abn); VNAF–47th ARVN Regiment. ROK–2d ROK Marine Brigade. *Casualties:* U.S.–23 KIA, 132 WIA; NVA/VC–209 KIA, 40 POWs.

22 July–6 August: *Operation Koko Head. Locations:* III Corps; Hau Nghia Province; Bao Tri; Duc Hoa; Trang Bang. *Type:* Search and Destroy. *Units:* USA — 25th Infantry Division: 2d Bde (1/5th Inf [M], 1/27th Inf, 2/27th Inf); VNAF — 3/49th ARVN Regiment. *Casualties:* NVA/VC — 42 KIA, 25 POWs (U.S. losses not included in sources).

27 July–1 August: *Operation Springfield I. Locations:* III Corps; Binh Duong Province; Route 13; Ap Bau Bang; Ben Dong; Lai Khe. *Type/Objective:* Search and Destroy to exploit information given by a Hoi Chanh — a Viet Cong that has defected to the Allies. *Units:* USA — 1st Infantry Division: 1st Bde (1/16th Inf [M]), 3d Bde (1/26th Inf). *Casualties:* NVA/VC — 10 KIA (U.S. losses not included in source for individual operation).

1–25 August: *Operation Paul Revere II. Locations:* II Corps; Darlac and Pleiku provinces; Ia Drang Valley; Chu Pong Mountains; Plei Djereng; Pleime. *Objective:* Continuation of the *Paul Revere* series of border screening/surveillance and area control operations. *Units:* USA — 1st Cavalry Division: 2d Bde (1/5th Cav, 2/5th Cav, 2/12th Cav), 3d Bde (1/7th Cav, 2/7th Cav), 25th Infantry Division–Task Force Walker: 3d Bde (1/14th Inf, 1/35th Inf, 2/35th Inf, 1/69th Armor); ROK — 1st ROK Cavalry Regiment; NVA/VC — 1st NVA Division (32d, 33d, 66th, 88th and 95–B regiments). *Event:* **1–10 August**—"Battle of 27–V." The 3/1st ROK Cavalry and B–1/69th Armor team up to repel an attack by the 5/88th NVA Regiment. One hundred eighty-one of the attackers are killed. *Casualties:* Totals for *Paul Revere II:* U.S. — 80 KIA, 272 WIA, 3 MIA; ROK/ARVN — 97 KIA, 431 WIA; NVA/VC — 861 KIA, 119 POWs.

1–31 August: *Operation Oahu. Locations:* III Corps; Tay Ninh Province; Highway 22; Ben Go; Truong Mit.

Type/Objectives: Search and Destroy in support of *Operation Blue Jay. Units:* USA — 25th Infantry Division: 1st Bde (4/9th Inf, 2/14th Inf, 4/23d Inf [M]), 2d Bde (1/5th Inf [M]). *Casualties:* NVA/VC — 20 KIA, 12 POWs (U.S. losses not included in source document for individual operation).

2–5 August: *Operation Cheyenne. Location:* III Corps; Binh Long Province; An Loc. *Type/Objective:* Reconnaissance in Force to open and secure national Route 13. *Units:* USA — 1st Infantry Division: 1st Bde (1/28th Inf), 2d Bde (2/16 Inf, 1/18th Inf, 2/18th Inf), 3d Bde (1/2d Inf, 1/26th Inf); VNAF — 5th ARVN Division. *Casualties:* Not included in source document for the individual operation.

3 August 1966–31 January 1967: *Operation Prairie I. Locations:* I Corps; Quang Tri Province; Cua Viet River Valley; Ben Hai River; "The Razorback"; Hills 400 and 484 (Nui Cay Tre–"Mutter's Ridge"); "The Rockpile"; Cam Lo; Con Thien; Gio Linh. *Type/Objectives:* Search and Destroy. *Prairie I* is a follow-up to *Hastings* whose mission is to determine the build-up of NVA forces in the DMZ area. *Units:* USMC — 1/4th Marines, 2/4th Marines, 3/4th Marines, 2/7th Marines, 1/26th Marines, 3d Recon Battalion (a total of 11 battalions with a combined strength of 11,000 Marines participate in *Prairie I*); VNAF — 1st ARVN Division; NVA/VC — 324–B NVA Division (803d and 812th NVA regiments), elements of the 304th and 341st NVA divisions also reported in area of operations. *Events:* **8–9 August**—While waiting to be lifted out of a landing zone near "The Rockpile," 25 Marines (E–3/4th Marines) are attacked by an NVA company. Artillery and air support prevent the enemy from overrunning the Marines' position until reinforcements arrive. Five Marines are KIA and 27 WIA in the attack. **23–25 August**—"Battle of the Razorback." E–3/4th Marines is ordered to conduct a Reconnaissance in Force operation to find and disable an enemy machine emplacement on "Razorback Ridge." The Marines come under fire while searching the ridge's caves and are reinforced by F,G–3/4th Marines and 2/4th Marines. In two days of intense fighting 21 Americans are KIA and 99 others WIA. Enemy losses are estimated between 120–170. **26 August** — Two companies from the 812th NVA Regiment attack the Marines' artillery base at Cam Lo. U.S. losses: 9 KIA and 20 WIA. **22 September–5 October** — "Battle of Mutter's Ridge." The 3/4th Marines assault Nui Cay Tre ("Mutter's Ridge"), two miles north of the "Rockpile," against elements of the 324–B NVA Division. Over the next 13 days of vicious combat, 20 Marines are KIA and 110 WIA. The enemy body count is 100. *Casualties:* Totals for *Prairie I*. U.S. — 239 KIA, 1214 WIA, 1 MIA; NVA/VC — 1397 KIA, 27 POWs.

5–15 August: *Operation Evansville. Location:* III Corps; Binh Duong Province; Phuoc Vinh. *Type:* Search and Destroy. *Units:* USA — 1st Infantry Division: 1st Bde (1/2d Inf, 1/26th Inf). *Casualties:* NVA/VC — 3 KIA (U.S. losses not included in source document for individual operation).

6–22 August: *Operation Colorado/Lien Ket–52. Locations:* I Corps; Quang Nam and Quang Tin provinces; Que Son Valley; Ly Ly and Nha Ngu rivers; "Pineapple Forest"; Cam Khe; Dai Dong; Hiep Duc; Ky Phu; Thach Thuong; Thang Binh. *Type/Objectives:* Search and Destroy to drive the enemy from the Que Son Valley. *Units:* USMC — 1/5th Marines, 2/5th Marines; 3/5th Marines (3000 Marines); VNAF — 2d ARVN Division (2d and 4th ARVN rgts), 2/ARVN Arm Cav, 3/ARVN Arm Cav; VNMC; NVA/VC — 2d NVA Division (3d and 21st NVA rgts), 1st Viet Cong Regiment. *Event:* **10 August** — "Battle of Cam Khe." 1/5th Marines

battles two battalions from the 3d NVA Regiment at Cam Khe, 20 miles west of Hiep Duc. Fourteen Marines are KIA and 65 WIA. More than 100 NVA are reported KIA. *Casualties:* NVA/VC — 674 KIA (U.S. losses not included in source).

7 August–1 September: *Operation Lahaina. Location:* III Corps; Hau Nghia Province; Bao Tri. *Type:* Search and Destroy. *Unit:* USA — 25th Infantry Division: 2d Bde (2/27th Inf). *Casualties:* NVA/VC — 29 KIA, 40 POWs (U.S. losses not included in source document for individual operation).

8 August–1 September: *Operation Aiea. Locations:* III Corps; Hau Nghia Province; Boi Loi Forest; Ap Trang Dau. *Type/Objective:* Search and Destroy. Joint U.S./ARVN operation to screen VC infiltration routes in the Boi Loi Forest. *Units:* USA — 25th Infantry Division: 2d Bde (1/27th Inf); VNAF — 2/49th ARVN Regiment, Trang Bang RF/PFs. *Casualties:* U.S. — none; NVA/VC — 22 KIA, 18 POWs.

10 August: The 2/8th Infantry (M) of the 4th Infantry Division arrives in South Vietnam. They are stationed at Pleiku (II Corps; Pleiku Province).

13–14 August: *Operation El Dorado. Locations:* III Corps; Binh Duong Province; Ap Bau Tran. *Type:* Search and Destroy. *Units:* USA — 1st Infantry Division: 1st Bde (1/16th Inf [M], 1/28th Inf), 3d Bde (1/26th Inf). *Casualties:* NVA/VC — 14 KIA (U.S. losses not included in source document for individual operation).

16–29 August: *Operation Deckhouse III. Location:* III Corps; Phuoc Tuy Province; Vung Tau. *Type:* Search and Destroy/Amphibious Assault. *Units:* USA — 173d Airborne Brigade; USMC — BLT 1/26th Marines. *Casualties:* U.S. — 4 KIA, 21 WIA; NVA/VC — 2 KIA.

20 August: The 5/7th Cavalry of the 1st Cavalry Division arrives in South Vietnam. They are stationed at An Khe (II Corps; Binh Dinh Province).

23 August–1 September: *Operation Amarillo. Locations:* III Corps; Bien Hoa and Binh Duong provinces; Di An; Phuoc Vinh. *Type/Objective:* Search and Destroy to clear Inter-Provincial Route 16 from Phuoc Vinh to Di An. *Units:* USA—1st Infantry Division: 1st Bde (1/16th Inf [M], 2/28th Inf), 3d Bde (1/2d Inf, 1/26th Inf); VNAF—48th ARVN Regiment; NVA/VC—Phu Loi Battalion (VC); C–62 VC company. *Casualties:* U.S.—43 KIA, 248 WIA; NVA/VC—102 KIA, 6 POWs.

26 August: The 196th Light Infantry Brigade and three of its battalions (2/1st Infantry, 3/21st Infantry [Gimlets] and the 4/31st Infantry [Polar Bears]) arrive in South Vietnam. The brigade and its battalions are stationed at Tay Ninh (III Corps; Tay Ninh Province).

26 August–18 October: *Operation Paul Revere III. Locations:* II Corps; Pleiku Province; Cateckia Plantation; LZ Oasis. *Type/Objective:* Search and Destroy. *Paul Revere III* is a continuation of the *Paul Revere* series of screening and surveillance operations along the Cambodian/South Vietnamese border. *Units:* USA—1st Cavalry Division: 3d Bde (1/7th Cav), 4th Infantry Division: 2d Bde (2/8th Inf [M], 1/12th Inf, 1/22d Inf), 25th Infantry Division: 3d Bde (1/14th Inf, 1/35th Inf, 2/35th Inf, C–3/4th Cavalry). *Casualties:* Not included in source for individual operation.

26 August 1966–20 January 1968: *Operation Byrd. Location:* II Corps; Binh Thuan Province; Phan Thiet. *Type/Objective:* **Byrd** is an economy of force operation designed to help pacify Binh Thuan Province. *Units:* USA—1st Cavalry Division (the 1st Cav assigned several battalions on a rotational basis,

usually two at a time, to serve on **Byrd**. *Casualties:* As of 31 October 1967 (U.S. only): U.S.—23 KIA, 278 WIA; NVA/VC—849 KIA (total).

31 August–12 September: *Operation Kipapa. Location:* III Corps; Binh Duong Province; Filhol Plantation. *Type:* Search and Destroy. *Units:* USA—25th Infantry Division: 1st Bde (4/9th Inf; A,B–4/23d Inf [M]), 2d Bde (1/5th Inf [M]); VNAF—7/5th ARVN Regiment. *Casualties:* NVA/VC—9 KIA, 2 POWs (U.S. losses not included in source document for individual operation).

2 September–8 October: *Operation Sunset Beach. Locations:* III Corps; Hau Nghia Province; Boi Loi Forest; Bao Tri; Cu Chi; Trang Dau. *Type:* Search and Destroy. *Units:* USA—25th Infantry Division: 2d Bde (1/5th Inf [M], 1/27th Inf, 2/27th Inf); VNAF—25th ARVN Division. *Casualties:* NVA/VC—84 KIA, 46 POWs (American losses not included in source document for individual operation).

2–8 September: *Operation Alice. Location:* III Corps; Tay Ninh Province. *Type:* Search and Destroy. *Units:* USA—196th Light Infantry Brigade (3/21st Inf); NVA/VC—C–40 Local Force Company (VC). *Casualties:* Not included in source document for the individual operation.

3 September–8 October: *Operation Decatur. Locations:* III Corps; Binh Long Province; An Loc; Quan Loi. *Objective:* Security of Quan Loi–An Loc area. *Units:* USA—1st Infantry Division: 3d Bde (1/26th Inf, B–1/4th Cav). *Casualties:* U.S.—2 WIA; NVA/VC losses unknown.

4 September–8 October: *Operation Baton Rouge. Location:* III Corps; Gia Dinh Province; Rung Sat Special Zone. *Type/Objective:* Search and Destroy to prevent VC harassment of ship traffic.

Unit: USA—1st Infantry Division: 2d Bde (1/18th Inf). *Casualties:* NVA/VC—59 KIA, 12 POWs (American losses not included in source document for the individual operation).

5 September–25 October: *Operation Seward.* *Locations:* II Corps; Phu Yen Province; Hieu Xuong Valley; Vung Ro Bay; Ninh Hoa; Tu Bong; Tuy An; Tuy Hoa. *Objective:* Protection of the rice harvest in the Tuy Hoa area. *Units:* USA—4th Infantry Division: 1st Bde (1/8th Inf, 3/8th Inf, 3/12th Inf), 2d Bde (1/22 Inf), 101st Airborne Division: 1st Bde (1/327th Abn, 2/327th Abn, 2/502d Abn); VNAF—47th ARVN Regiment; NVA/VC—18th and 95th NVA regiments. *Event:* **17 September**—The Command Post of B–2/327th Abn is attacked by more than 100 VC. Ten Americans are KIA and 12 WIA. *Casualties:* U.S.—26 KIA, 169 WIA; NVA/VC—239 KIA, 42 POWs.

8 September: The 11th Armored Cavalry Regiment (11th ACR) (the Blackhorse Regiment) officially arrives in South Vietnam. The regiment is stationed at Bien Hoa (III Corps; Bien Hoa Province).

8–13 September: *Operation Athol.* *Locations:* III Corps; Binh Duong Province; Michelin Rubber Plantation; Dau Tieng. *Type:* Search and Destroy. *Units:* USA—196th Light Infantry Brigade (4/31st Inf). *Casualties:* Not included in source document.

8–16 September: *Operation Fresno.* *Location:* I Corps; Quang Ngai Province. *Type/Objective:* Search and Destroy. The goal of **Fresno** is to prevent the enemy from disrupting the elections. *Units:* USMC—1/7th Marines; VNAF—2d ARVN Division; NVA/VC—38th and 44th Main Force battalions (VC). *Casualties:* Not included in source.

13 September–1 October: *Operation*

Thayer I. *Locations:* II Corps; Binh Dinh Province; An Lao, Kim Son and Suoi Ca valleys; Cay Giep and Phu Cat mountains; Phu My. *Type/Objective:* Search and Destroy. The mission **Thayer I** is to pacify Binh Dinh and eliminate the enemy's staging areas in the province's many valleys. *Units:* USA—1st Cavalry Division: 1st Bde (1/8th Cav, 2/8th Cav, 1/12th Cav), 2d Bde (1/5th Cav, 1/9th Cav, 2/12th Cav); VNAF—41st ARVN Regiment; NVA/VC—7/18th NVA Rgt, 8/18th NVA Regt, 2d VC Rgt. *Casualties:* NVA/VC—221 KIA, 72 POWs (American losses not included in sources for operation).

14 September–24 November: *Operation Attleboro.* *Locations:* III Corps; Binh Duong and Tay Ninh provinces; War Zone C; Ten Cui Plantation; Dau Tieng. *Type/Objective:* Search and Destroy. The mission of **Attleboro** is to find and eliminate all enemy troops west of the Michelin Plantation. *Units:* USA—1st Infantry Division: 1st Bde (1/16th [M], 1/28th Inf, 2/28th Inf), 2d Bde (2/16th Inf, 1/18th Inf, 2/18th Inf), 3d Bde (1/2d Inf, 2/2d Inf [M], 1/26th Inf); 4th Infantry Division: 3d Bde (2/12th Inf, 1/14th Inf, 2/22d Inf [M], 3/22 Inf); 25th Infantry Division: 2d Bde (1/5th Inf [M], 1/27th Inf, 2/27th Inf); *note:* The 1/27th and 2/27th Inf were attached to the 196th LIB. 11th ACR (1st, 2d and 3d squadrons); 173d Airborne Brigade (1/503d Abn, 2/503d Abn, 3/503d Abn, 4/503d Abn); 196th Light Infantry Brigade (2/1st Inf, 4/31st Inf); **Attleboro** involved more than 20,000 U.S. and ARVN troops. NVA/VC: 9th Viet Cong Division (70th, 271st, 272d and 273d VC regiments), 101st NVA Regiment. *Events:* **3 November**—A patrol from B–2/1st Inf (196th LIB) is hit by a VC command–detonated mine just northwest of Dau Tieng. Three are KIA and 15 WIA. **4 November**—A–2/27th Infantry (25th Inf Div) is ambushed near Dau Tieng. The attack kills 12 and wounds 11. **4–5 November**—"Battle of

LZ Lima Zulu." The 1/27th Infantry is ambushed by the VC near Dau Tieng. During the battle, C-2/27th combat assaults in to reinforce the 1/27th. Eleven U.S. soldiers are KIA and more than 19 WIA. *Comment: Attleboro* was the largest operation in the war up to that time and was the first use of large-scale, multidivisional Search and Destroy tactics. *Casualties:* Totals for *Attleboro.* NVA/VC—2130 KIA (U.S. losses not included in sources).

15–21 September: *Operation Danbury. Locations:* III Corps; Binh Duong Province; Thanh Dien Forest; Dau Tieng. *Type:* Search and Destroy. *Units:* USA—1st Infantry Division: 1st Bde (1/16th Inf [M], 2/28th Inf), 2d Bde (2/16th Inf), 3d Bde (1/2d Inf). *Casualties:* U.S.—4 KIA, 42 WIA; NVA/VC—10 KIA.

15–24 September: *Operation Deckhouse IV. Locations:* I Corps; Quang Tri Province; Cua Viet River; Blue Beach; Con Thien; Dong Ha; Gio Linh. *Type/Objective:* Reconnaissance in Force to determine enemy infiltration into *Prairie* area. *Units:* USMC—SLF–BLT 1/26th Marines, 3d Recon Bn; NVA/VC—324–B NVA Division (90th NVA Rgt) reported in area of operations. *Casualties:* U.S.—36 KIA, 167 WIA; NVA/VC—200 KIA.

15 September 1966–13 February 1967: *Operation Lanikai. Locations:* III Corps; Long An Province; Ben Luc; Rach Kien. *Type:* Search and Destroy. *Units:* USA—25th Infantry Division: 1st Bde (4/9th Inf, 2/14th Inf, 4/23 Inf [M]); VNAF—3/50th ARVN Rgt, 3/10th ARVN Cav. *Casualties:* NVA/VC—89 KIA, 11 POWs (American losses not included in source document for individual operation).

16–27 September: *Operation Golden Fleece 7-1. Locations:* I Corps; Quang Ngai Province; Mo Duc District; Vo Ha (1). *Objective:* Protection of the local

rice harvest. *Units:* USMC—1/7th Marines; VNAF—2d ARVN Division; NVA/VC—38th and 44th Viet Cong battalions. *Result:* 7000 tons of rice harvested and kept from the enemy. *Casualties:* U.S.—1 KIA, 19 WIA; NVA/VC—240 KIA.

20 September–4 October: *Operation Kamuela. Locations:* III Corps; Tay Ninh Province; Boi Loi Forest; Cu Chi; Dau Tieng. *Type/Objective:* Search and Destroy on the eastern edge of the Boi Loi Forest. *Units:* USA—25th Infantry Division: 1st Bde (2/14th Inf), 196th Light Infantry Brigade (2/1st Inf). *Casualties:* NVA/VC—13 KIA, 3 POWs (American losses not included in source document for individual operation).

23 September: MACV publicly discloses that U.S. aircraft are using chemical defoliants in the area immediately south of the DMZ.

25 September: The 4th Infantry Division (the Ivy Division) arrives in South Vietnam. They are stationed at Pleiku (II Corps; Pleiku Province).

25–29 September: *Operation Boyd. Location:* III Corps; Binh Duong Province; Lai Khe. *Type/Objective:* Reconnaissance in Force operation to exploit information gathered from a POW. *Units:* USA—1st Infantry Division: 1st Bde (1/16th [M], 2/28th Inf). *Casualties:* NVA/VC—5 KIA (U.S. losses not reported in source document for the individual operation).

27 September: The Republic of Korea's (ROK) 9th Infantry Division (the White Horse Division) arrives in South Vietnam. They are stationed at Ninh Hoa (II Corps; Khanh Hoa Province).

1–24 October: *Operation Irving. Locations:* II Corps; Binh Dinh Province; Phu Cat Mountains; Hung Lac Peninsula; Nui Mieu; Hoa Hoi; Phu My; LZ

Two Bits. *Type/Objective:* Search and Destroy. *Irving* is a follow-up to *Thayer I* and its goal is to clear enemy troops from the Phu Cat Mountain area, 28 miles northwest of Qui Nhon. *Units:* USA — 1st Cavalry Division: 1st Bde (1/8th Cav, 2/8th Cav, 1/12th Cav), 2d Bde (1/5th Cav), 3d Bde (1/7th Cav, 5/7th Cav); VNAF — 22d ARVN Division; ROK — ROK Capital Division; NVA/VC — 610th NVA Division (7/18th NVA Rgt, 8/18th NVA Rgt). *Event:* 2–3 October — "Battle of Hoa Hoi." The troops of 1/5th Cavalry, 1/12th Cavalry and A–1/9th Cavalry trap the 7th and 8th battalions of the 18th NVA Regiment at Hoa Hoi, eight miles west of Phu My. Six Americans are KIA and 32 WIA. Enemy body count is 233 KIA and 35 POWs. *Casualties:* Totals for *Irving.* U.S. — 19 KIA, 150 WIA; NVA/VC — 681 KIA (estimated), 690 POWs.

2–4 October: *Operation Little Rock.* *Location:* III Corps; Binh Duong Province; Ong Dong Jungle. *Type:* Search and Destroy. *Units:* USA — 1st Infantry Division: 1st Bde (1/28th Inf), 3d Bde (1/2d Inf), Attached (1/4th Cav, 2/34th Armor). *Casualties:* U.S. — 5 KIA, 26 WIA; NVA/VC — None. *Note:* There was little, if any, enemy contact in *Little Rock.* All casualties were the result of mines or short rounds from ARVN artillery.

4 October: The 1/8th Infantry, 3/8th Infantry and the 3/12th Infantry of the 4th Infantry Division arrive in South Vietnam. The units are initially stationed at Tuy Hoa (II Corps; Phu Yen Province).

7–15 October: *Operation Hickory.* *Locations:* III Corps; Bien Hoa Province; Ap Ba Truong; Ben San; Long Dien; Nhon Trach; Phu Hoi; Phuoc Thien; Phuoc Tho. *Type/Objective:* Reconnaissance in Force operation to help provide security for engineer units. *Units:* USA — 11th Armored Cavalry Regiment: 3d Sqdn (I,K,L and M

troops). *Event:* 14 October — Third platoon–K Troop is ambushed by a VC squad near Ben Cam. One American is KIA and nine WIA in the 10-minute firefight. Seven VC are reported KIA. *Casualties:* Total for *Hickory.* U.S. — 2 KIA, 20 WIA; NVA/VC — 13 KIA, 17 POWs.

9 October: The 2/12th Infantry, 2/22d Infantry (M) and the 3/22nd Infantry of 4th Infantry Division arrive in South Vietnam. The battalions are stationed at Bear Cat (II Corps; Bien Hoa Province).

10 October: *Operation Robin.* *Location:* III Corps; Bien Hoa Province. *Objective:* Road security from Vung Tau to Bear Cat. *Unit:* USA — 4th Infantry Division. *Casualties:* Not included in source document for the individual operation.

18 October–30 December: *Operation Paul Revere IV.* *Locations:* II Corps; Darlac and Pleiku provinces. *Type/Objective:* Search and Destroy. *Paul Revere IV* is a continuation of the *Paul Revere* series of screening and surveillance operations along the Cambodian border. *Units:* USA — 1st Cavalry Division: 2d Bde (1/5th Cav, 2/5th Cav, B–1/9th Cav, 2/12th Cav), 4th Infantry Division: 2d Bde (2/8th Inf [M], 1/12th Inf, 1/22d Inf), 25th Infantry Division: 3d Bde (1/14th Inf, 1/35th Inf, 2/35th Inf, C–3/4th Cav); NVA/VC — 1st NVA (Le Loi) Division (24th, 32d, 95–B and 101–C NVA rgts). *Events:* 21 November — Elements from 1/5th Cavalry overrun an NVA position near the Cambodian border, killing 147 members of the 101–C NVA regiment. 29 October — Companies B and C–2/8th Infantry (M) are mortared west of Duc Co. Six are KIA and 34 WIA. *Casualties:* Totals for *Paul Revere IV* are current to 31 October and reflect U.S. losses from the 1st Cavalry and 4th Infantry divisions only. U.S. — 62 KIA, 158 WIA; NVA/VC — 977 KIA, 18 POWs.

20–27 October: *Operation Bethlehem/Allentown. Location:* III Corps; Binh Duong Province; Phu Cuong. *Type:* Search and Destroy. *Units:* USA—1st Infantry Division: 2d Bde (1/ 18th Inf, 2/16th Inf). *Comment: Bethlehem* merged with *Allentown* on 24 October; the resulting combined operation was in turn merged with the ARVN's *Lam Son II* on 27 October 1966. *Casualties:* NVA/VC—57 KIA, 1 POW (American losses not included in source document for the individual operation).

20 October–8 December: *Operation Atlanta. Locations:* III Corps; Bien Hoa, Long Khanh and Phuoc Tuy provinces; Ong Khe Rubber Plantation; Nui Chua Chan; Gia Huynh; Gia Ray; Soui Cat; Xa Bang; Xuan Loc. *Objective: Atlanta's* mission is to clear and secure lines of communication near Saigon and to provide security for the 11th ACR's Blackhorse Base Camp. *Units:* USA—11th Armored Cavalry Regiment (1st, 2d and 3d squadrons); NVA/VC— 265, 308 and 800/274th Main Force Rgt (VC); 275th Main Force Rgt (VC). *Events:* **21 November**—A U.S. convoy, led by C-1/11th ACR traveling on Highway 1 from Bien Hoa to Xuan Loc is ambushed by elements of the 274th Main Force Regiment. Losses: U.S.—7 KIA, 8 WIA; NVA/VC—30 KIA, 10 POWs. **2 December**—"Battle of Soui Cat." The battle begins as an ambush of B-1/11th ACR on Highway 1, northeast of Soui Cat, by the 275th Main Force Regiment. Losses: U.S.—1 KIA, 22 WIA; NVA/VC—99 KIA, 3 POWs. *Casualties:* Totals for *Atlanta.* U.S.—8 KIA, 49 WIA; NVA/VC—136 KIA, 51 POWs.

25 October–28 November: *Operation Bremerton. Locations:* III Corps; Gia Dinh Province; Rung Sat Special Zone; Ap Binh Son; Bo Bong; Phuoc An; LZ Michelle. *Type/Objective:* Search and Destroy. The mission of *Bremerton* is to prevent VC harassment

of shipping on the Soi Rap River and Long Tau Channel. *Units:* USA—4th Infantry Division: 3d Bde (3/22d Inf). *Casualties:* U.S.—6 KIA, 39 WIA; NVA/VC—25 KIA.

25 October 1966–12 February 1967: *Operation Thayer II. Locations:* II Corps; Binh Dinh Province; Kim Son and Soui Ca valleys; "Oregon" and "Santa Fe" trails; LZs Bird and Pony. *Type/Objective:* Search and Destroy. *Thayer II* is a follow-up to Operations *Irving* and *Thayer I,* whose goal is the pacification of Binh Dinh Province. *Units:* USA—1st Cavalry Division: 1st Bde (1/8th Cav, 2/8th Cav, 1/12th Cav), 2d Bde (1/5th Cav, 2/5th Cav, 2/12th Cav), 3d Bde (1/7th Cav, 5/7th Cav), 25th Infantry Division: 3d Bde (1/14th Inf, 1/35th Inf, C-3/4th Cav); NVA/ VC—18th NVA Rgt, 22d NVA Rgt, 93/2d VC Rgt. *Events:* **1 December**— "Battle of Phu Huu (2)." Troopers from C-1/9th Cavalry encounter an estimated 200 soldiers of the 18th NVA Regiment at the hamlet of Phu Huu (2), just west of LZ Bird (eight miles southeast of Bong Son). The 1/9th is reinforced by troops from the 5/7th Cavalry and the 2/12 Cavalry. More than nine cavalrymen are KIA and at least nine others WIA. Sixty-seven enemy bodies are found. **17–19 December**— C-1/8th Cavalry and A-1/9th Cavalry battle an NVA battalion near Route 506, killing a reported 95 of the enemy. **27 December**—"Battle of LZ Bird." More than 700 soldiers of the 22d NVA Regiment attack the 1st Cavalry's base at LZ Bird in the Kim Son Valley, about eight miles south of Bong Son. The base is defended by 1/12th Cavalry, C-6th/ 16th Artillery and B-2/19th Artillery. After hours of fighting, the attack is finally broken by intense tactical air support and the first use of Bee Hive artillery rounds fired point-blank into the massed enemy infantry. Losses for LZ Bird: U.S.—58 KIA, 77 WIA; NVA/ VC—266 KIA. *Casualties:* Totals for *Thayer II* (as of 31 January 1967).

U.S.—184 KIA, 747 WIA, 2 MIA; NVA/VC—1757 KIA (estimated).

26 October 1966–5 April 1967: *Operation Adams.* *Location:* II Corps; Phu Yen Province. *Objective: Adams* is to provide security for engineer crews and the local rice harvest. *Units:* USA—4th Infantry Division: 1st Bde (1/8th Inf, 3/8th Inf, 3/12th Inf, A–1/10th Cav); VNAF—47th ARVN Regiment; NVA/VC—18–B NVA Rgt, 95th NVA Rgt, 30th Main Force Battalion (VC), 95th Local Force Battalion (VC) are reported in area of operations. *Casualties:* Totals for *Adams* are current as of 31 January 1967. U.S.—26 KIA, 190 WIA (NVA/LC losses not included in source document for the individual operation).

27–29 October: *Operation Spanway.* *Location:* III Corps; Hau Nghia Province. *Type:* Search and Clear. *Units:* USA—4th Infantry Division: 3d Bde (2/12th Inf). *Casualties:* None, no enemy contact made.

29 October–18 December: *Operation Pawnee III.* *Locations:* I Corps; Quang Nam and Thua Thien provinces; Phu Loc District; Hai Van Pas; DaNang. *Objective: Pawnee III* is supposed to provide security on Route 1 between DaNang and Phu Bai. *Units:* USMC—2/26th Marines. *Casualties:* Not included in source.

31 October–4 December: *Operation Geronimo.* *Locations:* II Corps; Khanh Hoa and Phu Yen provinces; Hills 350 and 450; Cung Son; Ha Roi; Tuy Hoa. *Type:* Search and Destroy. *Units:* USA—4th Infantry Division: 1st Bde (1/8th Inf), 101st Airborne Division: 1st Bde (1/327th Abn, 2/327th Abn, 2/502d Abn); VNAF—47th ARVN Regiment; NVA/VC—5/95th NVA Regiment. *Event:* **6–11 November**—2/502d Airborne battles the 5/95th NVA Regiment on Hills 350 and 450 near Phong Cao. Losses: U.S.—5 KIA, 15 WIA; NVA/VC—39 KIA, 36 POWs. *Casual-*

ties: Totals for **Geronimo.** U.S.—16 KIA, 75 WIA; NVA/VC—149 KIA, 76 POWs.

November: The monsoon (rainy) season begins in the northern provinces and ends in the south.

2–8 November: *Operation Marshaltown.* *Location:* III Corps; Hau Nghia Province. *Type:* Search and Destroy. *Units:* USA—4th Infantry Division: 3d Bde (2/12th Inf). *Casualties:* Not included in source document for the individual operation.

7–11 November: *Operation Meridian.* *Locations:* III Corps; Tay Ninh Province; War Zone C; Minh Thanh. *Type:* Search and Destroy. *Units:* USA—173d Airborne Brigade (2/503d Abn); VNAF—33d and 35th ARVN Ranger battalions. *Casualties:* Not included in source document for the individual operation.

12 November: The *New York Times* reports that up to 40 percent of all U.S. economic and military aid to the Saigon government fails to reach its destination due to theft, corruption, black marketeering and waste.

16 November 1966–12 January 1967: *Operation Dan Tam–81.* *Locations:* III Corps; Binh Tuy and Long Khanh provinces; La Nga River; Gia Ray Rock Quarry; Ap Hien; Vo Dat; Xa Bang. *Objective:* Security of the local rice harvest. *Units:* USA—11th Armored Cavalry Regiment (1st Sqdn); VNAF—10th ARVN Division (Task Force 52), 18th ARVN Division (1/43d ARVN Rgt, 3/43d ARVN Rgt); NVA/VC—D–500 Dong Nai Battalion (VC) and 274th Viet Cong Regiment reported in area of operations.

25 November–2 December: *Operation Waco.* *Locations:* III Corps; Bien Hoa and Long Khanh provinces; Mao Tao Secret Zone; Dong Nai River; Bien

Hoa; Xuan Loc. *Type:* Search and Destroy. *Units:* USA—173d Airborne Brigade (1/503d Abn); NVA/VC—D-800 Main Force Battalion (VC) reported in area of operations. *Casualties:* Not included in source document for the individual operation.

25 November 1966-8 April 1967: *Operation Fitchburg. Location:* III Corps; Tay Ninh Province; Nui Ba Den Mountain. *Type:* Search and Destroy. *Units:* USA—196th Light Infantry Brigade: (2/1 Inf, 3/21st Inf, 4/31st Inf). *Casualties:* NVA/VC—55 KIA, 3 POWs (American losses not reported in source document).

30 November 1966-14 December 1967: *Operation Fairfax/Rang Dong. Locations:* III Corps; Gia Dinh Province; Rung Sat Special Zone; Binh Chanh; Cat Lai; Hoc Mon; Nha Be; Nhi Binh; Tan Binh; Thu Duc. *Type/Objective:* Search and Destroy/Cordon and Search. *Fairfax/Rang Dong* is an ambitious joint U.S./ARVN operation to clear and pacify the region around Saigon. *Units:* USA—1st Infantry Division, 4th Infantry Division, 25th Infantry Division (one battalion from each of the above participated on a rotational basis), 199th Light Infantry Brigade (2/3d Inf, 3/7th Inf, 4/12th Inf); *note:* 199th LIB took over operation in January 1967. VNAF—5th ARVN Ranger Group (30th, 33d and 38th ARVN Ranger battalions), 2/VNMC; NVA/VC—165th Main Force Regiment (VC), 2d Local Force Battalion (VC). *Events:* **20 October 1967**—3/7th Infantry (199th LIB) launches an airmobile assault into Long An Province in reaction to a VC attack on a U.S. ambush position. Five Americans KIA; one WIA. Ten VC killed and four captured. **7 August 1967**—E-4/12th Infantry (199th LIB) and the 30th ARVN Ranger Battalion engage a force from the 2d Local Force (VC) Battalion. Nineteen helicopters are destroyed or damaged in the fight. **6 December 1967**—The

4/12th Infantry (199th LIB) clashes with a battalion of enemy troops near Phuoc Lac in Long Khanh Province. The 4/12th is reinforced by A–3/7th Infantry (199th LIB) and D/17th Cavalry. Losses for the battle: U.S.—21 KIA, 74 WIA; NVA/VC—67 KIA.

4-5 December: *Operation Alexandria. Locations:* III Corps; Phuoc Tuy and Long Khanh provinces; Ap Hien; Can My (2); Duc Thanh; Xuan Loc. *Type:* Search and Destroy and Cordon and Search. *Units:* USA—11th Armored Cavalry Regiment (3d Sqdn); VNAF—43d ARVN Regiment; NVA/VC—C-20 Local Force Company (VC). *Casualties:* U.S.—2 KIA, 10 WIA; NVA/VC—4 KIA, 600 POWs/suspected VC.

6 December 1966-19 January 1967: *Operation Pickett. Location:* II Corps; Kontum Province. *Type/Objective:* Search and Destroy near the Cambodian border northeast of Kontum City. *Units:* USA—101st Airborne Division: 1st Brigade (1/327th Abn, 2/327th Abn, 2/502d Abn); VNAF—42d ARVN Regiment. *Casualties:* U.S.—20 KIA, 95 WIA; NVA/VC—63 KIA, 18 POWs.

7 December 1966-5 January 1967: *Operation Canary/Duck. Locations:* III Corps; Bien Hoa and Phuoc Tuy provinces; Nui Chua Chan Mountain; Bear Cat; Phu My; Vung Tau; LZ Stump. *Objective:* Road security operation undertaken in two phases: 1. *Canary*—road security for the newly arriving 199th Light Infantry Brigade. 2. *Duck*—security for convoys from the incoming 9th Infantry Division. *Units:* USA—173d Airborne Brigade (1/503d Abn, 2/503d Abn, 4/503d Abn); NVA/VC—5th Viet Cong Division—elements reported in the operational area. *Casualties:* Not included in the source document for the individual operation.

10 December: The 199th Light Infantry Brigade (the Redcatchers) officially arrives in South Vietnam. The brigade

HQ is stationed at Long Binh (III Corps; Bien Hoa Province). With the 199th came two of their organic infantry battalions: 2/3d Infantry (Old Guard) and the 4/12th Infantry—both are stationed at Song Be (III Corps; Phuoc Long Province).

12 December 1966–21 January 1967: *Operation Sierra. Location:* I Corps; Quang Ngai Province, Mo Duc. *Units:* USMC: Task Force X-Ray (5th and 7th Marines). *Casualties:* U.S.—10 KIA, 50 WIA; NVA/VC—111 KIA, 9 POWs.

16 December: The 9th Infantry Division (the Old Reliables) arrives in South Vietnam. They are stationed initially at Bear Cat (III Corps; Bien Hoa Province).

19 December 1966–6 February 1967: *Operation Chinook I. Locations:* I Corps; Quang Tri and Thua Thien provinces; Co Bi-Than Tan Valley; Huong and O Lau rivers; Dong Ha; Phong Dien. *Type/Objective:* Search and Destroy. *Chinook I*'s mission is to block infiltration routes leading down from the mountains toward Hue and to deny the enemy access to the fertile rice growing areas of the coast. *Units:* USMC—2/26th Marines, 3/26th Marines; NVA/VC—6th NVA Division, 802d VC Battalion. *Casualties:* U.S.—4 KIA, 73 WIA; NVA/VC—159 KIA, 5 POWs.

20 December: The 2/60th Infantry, 3/60th Infantry and 5/60th Infantry (M) of the 9th Infantry Division arrive in South Vietnam. The 2/60th is stationed at Tan Tru (III Corps; Long An Province). The 3/60th and 5/60th are stationed at Bear Cat (III Corps; Bien Hoa Province).

28 December: The 3/7th Infantry (Cottonbalers) of the 199th Light Infantry Brigade arrive in South Vietnam. The battalion is stationed at Song Be (III Corps; Phuoc Long Province).

31 December: There are now approximately 385,000 American soldiers and Marines in South Vietnam; an increase of more than 200,000 for the year. This number does not include 35,000 Americans in Thailand or 60,000 U.S. sailors offshore. American combat forces end the year in the following strengths: Army—319,000; Marines—65,700. ARVN combat strength is a combined 750,000 troops. However, a reported 116,858 ARVN soldiers and personnel deserted in 1966—a 20 percent desertion rate. The Republic of Korea (ROK) has 46,000 troops in-country. Most of the tab for their services is being picked up by the United States however. Enemy strength at the end of 1966 is reported to be 287,000 with between 45,000 and 60,000 of those being North Vietnamese regulars that have infiltrated into the south. American losses for the year: 5008 KIA, 30,093 WIA. Total U.S. losses in Vietnam since 1959: 6377 KIA, 37,738 WIA. VNAF losses for the year: 9500 KIA, 10,100 WIA. NVA/VC losses for the year are placed at 61,631 KIA.

1967

There are now 385,000 U.S. troops in South Vietnam. In addition to the ground forces, there are also 60,000 United States Navy personnel operating in the Southeast Asian theater and 35,000 Americans in Thailand. Vietnamese Armed Forces (VNAF) strength is a combined 750,000 troops. The Republic of Korea (ROK) has contributed 46,000 soldiers and Marines. Rounding out the Allied forces are relatively small contingents from Australia, Thailand and the Philippines. Enemy strength is estimated at between 275,000 and 300,000 troops of which at least 45,000 are thought to be North Vietnamese.

1 January: The 3/39th Infantry (AAA–O) of the 9th Infantry Division arrives in South Vietnam. The battalion is stationed at Rach Kien (IV Corps; Long An Province).

1 January–5 April: *Operation Sam Houston. Locations:* II Corps; Kontum and Pleiku provinces; Plei Trap Valley; Nam Sathay and Se San rivers; Duc Co Special Forces Camp. *Type/Objective:* Search and Destroy. *Sam Houston* is another border surveillance and interdiction operation. *Units:* USA—4th Infantry Division: 1st Bde (1/8th Inf), 2d Bde (2/8th Inf [M], 1/12th Inf, 1/22d Inf, 1/10th Cav), 25th Infantry Division: 3d Bde (2/35th Inf); NVA/VC: 1st NVA Division (32d, 33d and 66th NVA regiments), 10th NVA Division (88th, 95–B and 101–C NVA regiments). *Event:* 12 February—C–1/12th Infantry engages the enemy in a bloody firefight. Twelve Americans are KIA and 32 WIA. One

hundred and thirteen NVA reported KIA. *Casualties:* U.S.—169 KIA; NVA/VC—733 KIA.

3 January: The 2/39th Infantry and the 4/39th Infantry (AAA–O) of the 9th Infantry Division arrive in South Vietnam. The battalions are initially stationed at Bear Cat (III Corps; Bien Hoa Province).

5–7 January: *Operation Niagara Falls. Locations:* III Corps; Binh Duong Province; "Iron Triangle"; Cau Dinh Jungle; LZ Lois. *Type/Objective:* Search and Destroy. *Niagara Falls* is meant to be a deceptive feint, to conceal the U.S. forces' plans to launch the upcoming *Cedar Falls. Units:* USA—173d Airborne Brigade (1/503d Abn, B–2/34th Armor, 1/4th Cav); VNAF—35th Ranger Battalion; NVA/VC—Phu Loi Local Force Battalion (VC), 2d and 3d Main Force battalions (VC) reported in area

32

of operations, but no contact made. *Casualties:* Very little enemy contact. Casualties for *Niagara Falls* reported with *Cedar Falls* totals.

6–15 January: *Operation Deckhouse V. Location:* IV Corps; Kien Hoa Province. *Type:* Joint USMC/ARVN operation 62 miles south of Saigon. *Units:* USMC – SLF–BLT 1/9th Marines; VNAF – VNMC–Brigade Force Bravo (3 and 4/VNMC). *Comment: Deckhouse V* is the first use of United States combat troops in the Mekong Delta. *Casualties:* U.S. – 7 KIA, 35 WIA; NVA/ VC – 21 KIA.

8–26 January: *Operation Cedar Falls. Locations:* III Corps; Binh Duong Province; "Iron Triangle"; Cau Dinh Jungle; Ho Bo Woods; Thanh Dien Forest; Saigon and Song Thi Tinh rivers; Ben Cat; Ben Suc; Lai Khe. *Type/Objective:* Search and Destroy. The mission of *Cedar Falls* is to find and eliminate the Viet Cong Military Region Four Headquarters and to clear the "Iron Triangle." *Units:* USA – 1st Infantry Division: 1st Bde (1/2d Inf, 1/26th Inf, 1/28th Inf), 2d Bde (2/16th Inf, 1/18th Inf, 2/18th Inf), 3d Bde (2/2d Inf [M], 1/16th [M], 2/28th Inf), 25th Infantry Division: 1st Bde (4/9th Inf, 2/14th Inf, 4/23d Inf [M]), 2d Bde (1/15th Inf [M], 1/27th Inf, 2/27th Inf), 3d Bde (2/12th Inf, 1/14th Inf, 1/35th Inf, 2/35th Inf). *Note:* The 4th Infantry Division's 2/22d Inf (M) and 3/22d Inf were attached to the 3d Brigade of the 25th Infantry Division. 173d Airborne Brigade (1/503d Abn, 2/503d Abn, 3/503d Abn, 4/503d Abn), 196th Light Infantry Brigade (2/1st Inf, 1/6th Inf, 3/21st Inf, 4/31st Inf, 1/46th Inf), 11th Armored Cavalry Regiment (2d and 3d squadrons) (16,000 U.S. troops committed to *Cedar Falls*); VNAF – 5th ARVN Division (7th ARVN Rgt, 8th ARVN Rgt, 1st Abn Bde) (14,000 VNAF troops committed to *Cedar Falls*); NVA/VC – 9th Viet Cong Division. *Event:* **8 January** – An air assault force of 60 troop-ferrying

helicopters lands the 1st Infantry Division's 1/26th Infantry at the village of Ben Suc. More than 6000 villagers are relocated and Ben Suc is burned and plowed under. *Comment: Cedar Falls* is the first corps-sized operation in the war. It is also the largest offensive action in Vietnam up to that time. *Casualties:* U.S. – 72 KIA, 337 WIA; VNAF – 11 KIA, 8 WIA; NVA/VC – 750 KIA, 280 POWs.

9–19 January: *Operation Silver Lake. Locations:* III Corps; Bien Hoa Province; Hat Dich Secret Zone; Ap Binh Son; Phuoc Chi. *Type/Objective:* Search and Destroy designed to prevent foodstuffs from reaching enemy forces. *Units:* USA – 9th Infantry Division: 3d Bde (3/39th Inf, 2/60th Inf, 5/60th Inf [M]); NVA/VC – 274th Main Force Regiment (VC). *Casualties:* Not included in source document.

20–28 January: *Operation Colby. Location:* III Corps; Phuoc Tuy Province; Phuoc Chi Secret Zone. *Type/Objective:* Search and Destroy. The goal of *Colby* is the encirclement and search of the Phuoc Chi Secret Zone. *Units:* USA – 9th Infantry Division: 1st Bde (2/39th Inf, 4/39th Inf), 3d Bde (5/60th Inf [M], 3/5th Cav). *Casualties:* Not reported in source document.

26 January–23 March: *Operation Farragut. Location:* II Corps; Ninh Thuan Province, Phan Rang. *Type:* Search and Destroy in area south of Phan Rang. *Units:* USA – 101st Airborne Division: 1st Bde (1/327th Abn, 2/327th Abn, 2/502d Abn); VNAF – 4/8th ARVN Cavalry. *Casualties:* U.S. – 13 KIA, 94 WIA; VNAF – 92 KIA, 19 POWs.

26 January–7 April: *Operation Desoto. Locations:* I Corps; Quang Ngai Province; Quan River; Nui Dang Mountain; Duc Pho; Mo Duc; Sa Binh; Tan Tu; Truong Sanh; Vinh Binh. *Type/Objective:* Search and Clear 25 miles southeast of Quang Ngai City. The Marines are to relieve an ARVN outpost to free the South Vietnamese troops to be used elsewhere. *Units:* USMC—3/5th Marines, F–2/7th Marines, 3/7th Marines; VNAF—2d ARVN Division (4/4th ARVN Rgt); NVA/VC—95th Viet Cong Battalion. *Events:* **24 March**—Nui Dang Base Camp is shelled, killing three Marines and wounding 14. **5 April**—A series of mine explosions southeast of the Nui Dang hill mass kills 11 Marines, wounds 15 others and destroys a Huey. *Casualties:* Totals for *DeSoto.* U.S.—76 KIA, 573 WIA; NVA/VC—383 KIA, 9 POWs.

28 January–18 April: *Operation Uniontown. Locations:* III Corps; Bien Hoa Province; Nui Chua Chanh; Long Binh. *Objective:* Security and defense of Bien Hoa Air Base and the Long Binh complex. *Units:* USA—1st Infantry Division: 3d Bde (2/28th Inf), 9th Infantry Division: 1st Bde (2/39th Inf, 4/39th Inf), 3d Bde (2/60th Inf). *Casualties:* Not included in source documents.

28 January–31 May: *Operation Palm Beach. Locations:* IV Corps; Dinh Tuong Province; Dong Tam; My Tho. *Type/Objective:* Search and Destroy to provide security for the development of the base camp at Dong Tam. *Units:* USA—9th Infantry Division: 3d Bde (3/39th Inf, 2/60th Inf, 3/60th Inf, 5/60th Inf [M]). *Event:* **8 March**—Dong Tam shelled. Two Americans KIA, 10 WIA. *Casualties:* NVA/VC—570 KIA (estimated). (U.S. losses not included in source document for the individual operation.)

30 January: The 2/47th Infantry (M), 3/47th Infantry and the 4/47th Infantry of the 9th Infantry Division arrive in South Vietnam. The battalions are initially stationed at Phu My (III Corps; Bien Hoa Province).

31 January–1 February: *Location:* I Corps; Quang Nam Province. *Action:*

Two-day firefight at the village of Thuy Bo, seven miles southwest of DaNang. *Units:* USMC—H–2/1st Marines; NVA/VC—One battalion of VC Main Force troops. *Casualties:* U.S.—6 KIA, 26 WIA; NVA/VC—101 KIA.

31 January–18 March: *Operation Prairie II. Locations:* I Corps; Quang Tri Province; Hill 124; Cam Lo; Con Thien; Gio Linh. *Type/Objective:* Search and Destroy. *Prairie II* is a continuation of the 3d Marine Division's *Prairie* series in the DMZ area. *Units:* USMC—2/3d Marines, 3/3d Marines, 3/4th Marines; 1/9th Marines; 2/9th Marines; NVA/VC—324–B NVA Division (812th NVA Rgt). *Events:* **28 February**—L–3/4th Marines is attacked by NVA forces (812th Rgt) 2.5 miles northwest of Cam Lo, while trying to link up with a Marine recon team. Four Americans are KIA and 34 WIA. **16 March**—E–9th Marines is ambushed by a force of unknown size near Hill 861 (adjacent to the Khe Sanh Combat Base). The ambush kills 19 Marines and wounds 59 more. Only 11 enemy bodies were found following the skirmish. *Casualties:* Totals for *Prairie II.* U.S.—93 KIA, 483 WIA; NVA/VC—694 KIA, 20 POWs.

1–9 February: *Operation Independence. Location:* I Corps; Quang Nam Province. *Type/Objective:* Search and Destroy in area south of Song Cu Gia River. *Unit:* USMC—9th Marines. *Casualties:* U.S.—9 KIA, 35 WIA; NVA/VC—139 KIA, 20 POWs.

1–15 February: *Operations Gatling I–II. Locations:* II Corps; Binh Thuan and Lam Dong provinces; III Corps; Binh Tuy Province. *Objective:* The *Gatling* operation is a raid against a suspected high-level political meeting of the Viet Cong's Headquarters of Military Region IV. *Units:* USA—101st Airborne Division: 1st Bde (1/327th Abn, 2/327th Abn, 2/502d Abn, A–2/17th Cav). *Casualties:* U.S.—5 KIA, 23 WIA; NVA/VC—27 KIA, 6 POWs.

1–16 February: *Operation Big Spring.*
Locations: III Corps; Bien Hoa and
Long Khanh provinces; War Zone D;
Song Dong Nai and Song Be rivers.
Type: Search and Destroy. *Units:*
USA—9th Infantry Division: 1st Bde
(2/39th Inf, 4/39th Inf), 3d Bde (3/39th
Inf), 173d Airborne Brigade (2/503d
Abn); NVA/VC—2/273d VC Regiment,
3/273d VC Regiment reported in area
of operations. *Casualties:* Not included
in source document for the individual
operation.

2–12 February: *Operation Williston.*
Locations: III Corps; Binh Duong and
Binh Long provinces; An Loc; Ben Cat;
Chon Thanh; Quan Loi. *Objective:*
Search and Destroy. The mission of
Williston is to clear and secure Route
13 from Ben Cat north to Chon Thanh
and An Loc. Also to be cleared is Route
246 from An Loc to Minh Thanh. *Units:*
USA—1st Infantry Division: 1st Bde
(1/28th Inf, 1/4th Cav), 2d Bde (2/16th
Inf), 3d Bde (1/2d Inf, 2/2d Inf [M],
1/16th Inf [M], 2/28th Inf), 11th Armored
Cavalry Regiment (1st Sqdn). *Casual-
ties:* U.S.—6 WIA; NVA/VC—losses
unknown.

2–21 February: *Operation Gadsden.*
Locations: III Corps; Tay Ninh Province; War Zone C; Dau Tieng; Soui Da;
Thien Ngon; Trai Bi; FSB Lee. *Type/
Objective:* Search and Destroy aimed at
blocking both the infiltration and exfil-
tration routes toward the Cambodian
border. *Units:* USA—4th Infantry Division: 3d Bde (2/12th Inf, 2/22d [M],
3/22d Inf), 25th Infantry Division: 1st
Bde (4/9th Inf, 4/23 Inf [M]), 2d Bde
(1/5th Inf [M]), 196th Light Infantry Brigade (2/1st Inf, 3/21st Inf, 4/31st Inf);
NVA/VC—271st Viet Cong Regiment
and 70th Security Guard (VC) reported
in area of operations. *Events:* **5 February**—A-4/23d Infantry (M) battles an
enemy force of unknown size five miles
south of Thien Ngon (12 miles north of
Tay Ninh City). Results of the battle:
U.S.—1 KIA, 6 WIA; NVA/VC—11 KIA.

6 February—2/22d Infantry (M) fights
an eight-hour battle with an estimated
platoon of VC concealed in bunkers
and trenches southeast of Thien Ngon.
Four Americans are KIA and 47 WIA
during the firefight. Only two enemy
bodies are found. **10 February**—Again
near Thien Ngon, the 2/22d Infantry
fights a VC force of unknown size. Four
more U.S. soldiers KIA and 13 WIA.
Enemy losses are unknown. *Casualties:*
Totals for *Gadsden.* U.S.—15 KIA, 123
WIA; NVA/VC—36 KIA, 2 POWs.

4–14 February: *Operation Muncie.*
Location: III Corps; Long Khanh Province; Cam My. *Type/Objective:* Search
and Destroy to provide security for
work details. *Unit:* USA—11th Armored
Cavalry Regiment (3d Sqdn). *Casualties:* Not included in source document.

6–24 February: *Operation Greenleaf.* *Locations:* III Corps; Bien Hoa
Province; Ap Binh Son; Nhon Trach.
Type/Objective: Search and Destroy
aimed at preventing Viet Cong movement during the TET Holiday. *Units:*
USA—9th Infantry Division: 1st Bde
(1/39th Inf), 2d Bde (2/47th Inf [M],
3/47th Inf, 3/5th Cav). *Casualties:*
NVA/VC—3 POWs (U.S. losses not included in source document).

8 February–?: *Operation Lam Son–
67.* *Locations:* III Corps; Bien Hoa and
Binh Duong provinces; Ong Dong
Jungle. *Type:* Search and Destroy/
Pacification. *Units:* USA—1st Infantry
Division: 2d Bde (2/16th Inf, 1/18th Inf,
2/18th Inf); VNAF—5th ARVN Divi-
sion, 18th ARVN Division. *Casualties:*
U.S. (as of 31 October 1967)—9 KIA,
116 WIA; NVA/VC—115 KIA, 81 POWs.

10–12 February: *Operation Stone.*
Location: I Corps; Quang Nam Province; Go Noi Island; Thuy Bo. *Type/Ob-
jective:* Search and Destroy 12 miles
south of DaNang. *Units:* USMC—1/1st
Marines; NVA/VC—R-20 Doc Lap Battalion (VC). *Casualties:* U.S.—9 KIA, 77
WIA; NVA/VC—291 KIA, 65 POWs.

11 February 1967–21 January 1968: *Operation Pershing. Locations:* I Corps; Quang Ngai Province; II Corps; Binh Dinh Province; An Lao, Kim Son, Nuoc Dinh, Phu My; Song Re and Soui Ca valleys; Cay Giep Mountains; Duc Pho; Song Son; Ta Ma; Tam Quan; LZs English, Montezuma, Tom and Two Bits. *Type:* Clearing and Pacification. *Units:* USA—1st Cavalry Division: 1st Bde (1/8th Cav, 2/8th Cav, 1/12th Cav, 1/50th Inf [M]), 2d Bde (1/5th Cav, 2/5th Cav, 2/12th Cav), 3d Bde (1/7th Cav, 5/7th Cav), 25th Infantry Division (3 January 1967–12 February 1967): 3d Bde (1/14th Inf, 1/35th Inf, 2/35th Inf); VNAF—22d ARVN Division (40th ARVN Regiment); ROK—Capital Division; NVA/VC—3d NVA Division, 18th NVA Regiment, 22d NVA Regiment, 95th Viet Cong Battalion. *Events:* **28 June**—"Battle of An Quang-Dam Tra O Lake." 1/9th Cavalry and 2/5th Cavalry clash with the 9/18th NVA Regiment near An Quang, 12 miles southeast of Bong Son. Eighty-nine NVA bodies counted. **2 July**—A U.S. force is attacked by two NVA companies near LZ Geronimo, north of Bong Son. American losses are 15 KIA and 39 WIA. **9 August**—"Battle of LZ Pat." The 1/9th Cavalry and A–2/8th Cavalry engage more than 80 enemy soldiers 32 miles southwest of Quang Ngai City (I Corps; Quang Ngai Province). The 1st Cav losses are 11 KIA. **22 August–3 September**—A–2/5th Cavalry traps an estimated 100 enemy troops in the Nui Mieu Cave complex. A continuous pounding and siege of the area kill 33 and permit the capture of 41 others. Only one cavalryman is wounded in the action. **31 October**—NVA troops launch a rocket and small arms–fire attack on C–1/50th Infantry (M) southwest of the Cay Giep Mountains (II Corps; Binh Dinh Province). Losses: U.S.—3 KIA, 10 WIA; NVA/VC—15 KIA. **6–20 December**—"Battle of Tam Quan." In one of the largest battles of *Pershing*, the 1/9th Cavalry, 1/8th Cavalry, 1/12th Cavalry, 1/50th Infantry (M) and the 40th ARVN Regiment assault the heavily defended village of Tam Quan, about 10 miles northeast of Bong Son (II Corps; Binh Dinh Province). The village is defended by the 7th and 8th battalions of the NVA 22d Regiment. Losses for the battle: U.S.—58 KIA, 250 WIA; NVA/VC—647 KIA, 6 POWs. *Casualties:* Totals for *Pershing.* U.S.—852 KIA, 4119 WIA, 22 MIA; NVA/VC—5401 KIA, 2059 POWs.

13 February 1967–11 March 1968: *Operation Enterprise. Locations:* III Corps; Long An Province; Rach Dia and Rach Doi Ma rivers; Doi Ma Creek; Ap Ben Do; Ap Ray; Ben Luc; Binh Phuoc; Rach Kien; Tan An; Tan Tru. *Objective:* Consolidation operation throughout Long An Province (South Vietnam's most populated) aimed at defeating organized enemy forces, eliminating enemy infrastructure and conducting pacification operations. *Units:* USA—9th Infantry Division: 3d Bde (3/39th Inf, 2/60th Inf, 5/60th Inf [M]), 25th Infantry Division: 1st Bde (2/14th Inf), 199th Light Infantry Brigade (2/3d Inf, 3/7th Inf, 4/12th Inf); NVA/VC—506th Viet Cong Battalion. *Events:* **20 March**—Position "Dike" is attacked by a company-sized enemy force. The defenders, two platoons from A–3/39th Infantry, kill 55 of the enemy, suffering 10 KIA and 26 WIA. **16–17 April**—"Battle of Doi Ma Creek." 5/60th Infantry (M), C–3/60th Infantry and C–3/39th Infantry engage an enemy near the hamlets of Ap Ray and Ap Ben Do, killing 73 NVA/VC. Eleven Americans are killed or wounded. *Casualties:* U.S.—74 KIA, 380 WIA (as of 30 April 1967); total NVA/VC losses—2107 reported KIA.

14–21 February: *Operation Tucson Delta. Locations:* III Corps; Binh Duong Province; Long Nguyen Secret Zone; Michelin Rubber Plantation; Ap Bau Bang. *Type/Objective:* Search and Destroy. *Tucson Delta* is to act as deceptive cover for the preparations for

the upcoming *Junction City*. *Units:*
USA—1st Infantry Division: 1st Bde
(1/2d Inf, 1/28th Inf, 1/4th Cav), 2d Bde
(2/18th Inf), 3d Bde (2/2d Inf, 1/16th Inf
[M], 2/28th Inf, 3/5th Cav); NVA/VC—
272d Viet Cong Regiment and elements of the Phu Loi Battalion (VC)
reported in area of operations. *Casualties:* Totals for *Tucson Delta*. U.S.—3
KIA, 59 WIA; NVA/VC—8 KIA.

14 February 1967–21 March 1968:
Operation Kittyhawk. Locations: III
Corps; Long Khanh Province; Gia Ray
Rock Quarry; Blackhorse Base Camp.
Type/Objective: Search and Destroy.
Kittyhawk is a joint U.S./ARVN operation to secure installations and lines of
communications (LOC) within Long
Khanh Province. *Units:* USA—9th Infantry Division: 1st Bde (3/5th Cav),
11th Armored Cavalry Regiment (3d
Sqdn); NVA/VC—274th Viet Cong
Regiment. *Event:* 21 May—First platoon of K-3/11th ACR is ambushed by a
reinforced enemy battalion on Route 1
near Soui Cat. Twelve Americans are
KIA and 13 WIA in the ambush. Enemy
body count is 30. 31 December—Two
companies of VC ambush C-3/5th Cavalry on Highway 2. Losses for the ambush are 10 KIA, 29 WIA and 3 MIA.
Enemy losses are unknown. *Comment:*
Kittyhawk incorporated into *Alcorn
Cove/Toan Thang. Casualties:* Not included in source document.

16–17 February: *Operation Laurel.*
Locations: III Corps; Binh Duong Prov-
ince; Noa Nhut; Tan Phuoc Khanh.
Type/Objective: Cordon and Search.
Besides the cordon, *Laurel* is to be used
to maneuver forces into position for the
upcoming *Lam Son–67* operations.
Units: USA—1st Infantry Division: 2d
Bde (2/16th Inf, 1/18th Inf); VNAF—5th
ARVN Division. *Casualties:* Not in-
cluded in source document.

16 February–3 March: *Operation
Deckhouse VI. Locations:* I Corps;
Quang Ngai Province; Nui Dau; Duc

Pho; LZ Bat. *Type/Objective:* Search
and Destroy to prevent enemy move-
ment in area of operations. *Deckhouse
VI* is also a companion operation to
Desoto. Units: USMC—SLF–BLT 1/4th
Marines, 1/5th Marines; NVA/VC—
38th Viet Cong Battalion. *Casualties:*
U.S.—5 KIA, 55 WIA; NVA/VC—204
KIA.

16 February–20 March: *Operation
River Raider I. Locations:* III Corps;
Gia Dinh Province; Rung Sat Special
Zone; Nha Be. *Type/Objectives:* Search
and Destroy to disrupt Viet Cong base
areas and protect shipping in the Long
Tau Channel. *Units:* USA—9th Infantry
Division: 2d Bde (3/47th Inf), U.S.
Navy: River Assault Division 91. *Com-
ment: River Raider I* is the first joint
Army/Navy operation of the war and is
the predecessor of the upcoming
Mobile Riverine Force operations.
Casualties: U.S.—8 WIA; NVA/VC—12
KIA.

19–20 February: *Operation Suitland.*
Locations: III Corps; Bien Hoa Prov-
ince; Dong Nai Sensitive Zone; Co Mi
Jungle; Tan Hiep. *Type/Objective:*
Search and Destroy—Cordon and
Search operation in support of *Lam
Son–67. Units:* USA—1st Infantry Divi-
sion: 2d Bde (2/16th Inf); VNAF—52d
ARVN Ranger Battalion. *Casualties:*
Not included in source document.

22 February–17 March: *Operation
Junction City I. Locations:* III Corps;
Tay Ninh Province; War Zone C;
Katum; Prek Klok; Quon Loi; Tay Ninh
City. *Type/Objective:* Search and Destroy. The goals of *Junction City I* are
1) Elimination of COSVN, the Central
Office for South Vietnam. The headquarters used by the North Vietnamese communists to control their military and political efforts in the south;
2) Pacification of War Zone C; 3) Drive
the enemy away from the populated
areas and into the open where supe-
rior American firepower can be more

effectively used. *Units:* USA—1st Infantry Division: 1st Bde (1/2d Inf, 1/26th Inf, 1/28th Inf), 2d Bde (2/18th Inf), 3d Bde (2/2d Inf [M], 1/16th [M], 2/28th Inf), 4th Infantry Division (attached to 25th Div), 3d Bde (2/22d [M], 2/12th Inf), 25th Infantry Division: 2d Bde (1/5th Inf [M], 1/27th Inf, 2/27th Inf), 11th Armored Cavalry Regiment, 173d Airborne Brigade (1/503d Abn, 2/503d Abn, 3/503d Abn, 4/503d Abn), 196th Light Infantry Brigade (2/1st Inf, 3/21st Inf, 4/31st Inf); NVA/VC—7th and 101st NVA rgts, 5th Viet Cong Division, 9th Viet Cong Division (271st, 272d and 273d Viet Cong regiments). *Events:* **22 February**—In one of the largest airmobile assaults in history, more than 240 troop-carrying helicopters descend on the battlefield of *Junction City I.* **22 February**—Seven hundred and seventy-eight "Sky Soldiers" of the 2/503d Airborne (173d Abn Bde) parachute into their *Junction City* area of operations near Katum, approximately 25 miles north of Tay Ninh City. **28 February**—"Battle of Prek Klok." 1/16th Infantry (M) and B–2/18th Infantry (1st Inf Div) engage the 2/101st NVA Regiment at Prek Klok, 20 miles north of Tay Ninh City. Losses for the battle: U.S.—25 KIA, 27 WIA; NVA/VC—167 KIA. **10–11 March**—"Battle of Prek Klok II." In renewed fighting near Prek Klok, the 2/2d Infantry (M) of the 1st Infantry Division, fight a battalion from the 272d Viet Cong Regiment. Three Americans are KIA and 41 WIA; 197 VC are killed in the fight. *Casualties:* Totals for *Junction City I–II.* U.S.—282 KIA, 1576 WIA; NVA/VC—2728 KIA.

25 February–3 March: *Operation Pittsburg. Location:* III Corps; Bien Hoa and Long Khanh provinces. *Type/Objective:* Reconnaissance in Force into southern portion of War Zone D. *Units:* USA—9th Infantry Division: 1st Bde (4/39th Inf), 2d Bde (2/47th Inf [M]); NVA/VC—7th Viet Cong Division. *Casualties:* Not included in source document for the individual operation.

7–11 March: *Operation Cumberland. Locations:* III Corps; Bien Hoa Province; Co Mi Jungle; Dong Nai Sensitive Zone; Binh Tri; Di An; Tan Hiep. *Type:* Combined Search and Destroy/Cordon and Search. *Units:* USA—1st Infantry Division: 2d Bde (2/16th Inf, D–1/4th Cav); VNAF—35th ARVN Ranger Battalion. *Casualties:* Not included in source document for the individual operation.

8 March–8 April: *Operation Waialua. Locations:* III Corps; Hau Nghia Province; Tho Mo; Tra Cu; FSBs Scott and Taylor. *Type/Objective:* Search and Destroy. *Waialua* is designed to stop the flow of VC supplies on the Song Vam Co River in western Hau Nghia Province. *Units:* USA—25th Infantry Division: 2d Bde (1/27th Inf, 2/27th Inf); VNAF—34th ARVN Ranger Battalion. *Casualties:* NVA/VC—67 KIA, 14 POWs (U.S. losses not included in source document for the individual operation).

18 March–19 April: *Operation Prairie III. Locations:* I Corps; Quang Tri Province; Ba Long; Cam Lo; Con Thien; Gio Linh; Mai Loc. *Type/Objective:* Search and Destroy. *Prairie III* is a sweep of the area east of Gio Linh and a continuation of the Marines' *Prairie* series of operations. *Units:* USMC—3/3d Marines, BLT 1/4th Marines, 3/4th Marines, 1/9th Marines, 3/9th Marines; NVA/VC—324–B NVA Division, 341st NVA Division, 808th and 814th Viet Cong battalions. *Events:* **21 March**—A Marine ammo convoy is ambushed by an unidentified enemy force less than a mile south of Gio Linh. Eight Americans are WIA. **30 March**—I–3/9th Marines is attacked four miles northwest of Cam Lo. The Marines repulse three savage enemy ground assaults, killing 67 of their attackers. Marine losses: 16 KIA and 36 WIA. *Casualties:* Totals for

Prairie III. U.S.—56 KIA, 530 WIA; NVA/VC—252 KIA, 4 POWs.

18 March–21 April: *Operation Makalapa.* *Locations:* III Corps; Gia Dinh Province; Ap Tay; Duc Hoa; Vinh Loc; "Pineapple." *Type/Objective:* Search and Destroy assigned the mission of interdicting Viet Cong supply routes. *Units:* USA—25th Infantry Division: 1st Bde (4/9th Inf), 2d Bde (1/27th Inf). *Event:* **16 April**—An "Eagle Flight" from the 1/27th Infantry attacks an enemy company three miles south of Duc Hoa, killing 22 VC. *Casualties:* Totals for *Makalapa.* NVA/VC—58 KIA, 6 POWs (U.S. losses not included in source document for the individual operation).

20 March–1 April: *Operation Beacon Hill.* *Locations:* I Corps; Quang Tri Province; Cam Lo; Cua Viet; Gio Linh. *Type/Objective:* Amphibious assault operation four miles southwest of DMZ, near Gio Linh, in support of *Prairie III.* *Units:* USMC—SLF–BLT 1/4th Marines; NVA/VC—Elements of 324–B and 341st NVA divisions reported in area of operations. *Casualties:* U.S.—29 KIA, 230 WIA; NVA/VC—334 KIA.

21 March–14 May: *Operation Junction City II.* *Locations:* III Corps; Tay Ninh Province; War Zone C; Quan Loi; FSBs Charlie, Gold and Thrust; LZs Bravo and George. *Type/Objective:* Search and Destroy. *Junction City II* is the second phase of the massive operation sweeping War Zone C. *Units:* USA—1st Infantry Division: 1st Bde (1/2d Inf, 1/26th Inf, 1/28th Inf), 2d Bde (2/18th Inf, 2/16th Inf), 3d Bde (2/2d Inf [M], 1/16th Inf [M], 2/28th Inf), 4th Infantry Division: 3d Bde (2/12th Inf, 2/22d Inf [M], 3/22d Inf), 9th Infantry Division: 1st Bde (4/39th Inf, 3/5th Cav), 2d Bde (2/47th Inf [M]), 25th Infantry Division: 2d Bde (2/12th Inf, 1/14th Inf, 1/35th Inf, 2/35th Inf), 11th Armored Cavalry Regiment; VNAF—36th ARVN Ranger Battalion; NVA/

VC—101st NVA Rgt, 9th Viet Cong Division (271st, 272d and 273d Viet Cong regiments). *Events:* **19 March**—Ten U.S. soldiers are KIA and 18 WIA when VC forces ambush the 3/22d Infantry at a landing zone near Fire Support Base Gold, approximately 20 miles northeast of Tay Ninh City. **19–20 March**—"Battle of Ap Bau Bang." The 273d VC Regiment assaults A–3/5th Cavalry near Ap Bau Bang and Soui Tre, 35 miles north of Saigon. Three Americans are KIA and 63 WIA. Viet Cong losses are reported at 227 KIA and three captured. **21 March**—"Battle of FSB Gold." A force of more than 2500 Viet Cong of the 272d Main Force Regiment attack the 3/22d Infantry and 2/77th Artillery (4th Infantry Division) defending FSB Gold. The 3/22d is reinforced by the 2/12th Infantry during the bloody battle in which point-blank artillery fire and hand-to-hand combat finally turned back the human wave attack launched by the VC. Losses in the battle: U.S.—30 KIA, 187 WIA; NVA/VC—423 KIA. **31 March–1 April**—"Battle of LZ George." The 1/26th Infantry (1st Infantry Division), commanded by Lt. Col. Alexander Haig, fights a fierce battle with the 271st VC Regiment near Ap Gu, 28 miles northeast of Tay Ninh City. Reinforcements, 1/16th Infantry (M), heavy artillery fire and tactical air support help turn the tide of battle in favor of the Americans. More than 600 enemy KIAs are reported. U.S. losses are 10 KIA and 62 WIA. *Casualties:* Casualties were reported for both *Junction City I–II.* U.S.—282 KIA, 1576 WIA; NVA/VC—2728 KIA.

22–25 March: *Operation Newcastle.* *Location:* I Corps; Quang Nam Province; An Hoa. *Type:* Search and Destroy. *Units:* USMC—2/5th Marines. *Casualties:* U.S.—5 KIA, 55 WIA; NVA/VC—118 KIA.

30 March–29 April: *Operation Summerall.* *Locations:* II Corps; Darlac,

Khanh Hoa and Phu Yen provinces; Buon Ea Yang; Duc My; Haroi; Hon Ba; Khanh Duong. *Type:* Search and Destroy. *Units:* USA—101st Airborne Division: 1st Bde (1/327th Abn, 2/327th Abn, 2/502d Abn, A–2/17th Cav); NVA/VC—Elements of the 18–B NVA Regiment reported in area of operations. *Casualties:* U.S.—7 KIA, 43 WIA; NVA/VC—72 KIA, 11 POWs.

3–15 April: *Operation Portsea. Locations:* III Corps; Phuoc Tuy Province; Binh Gia; Xuyen Moc. *Objective: Portsea* was charged with the security of Route 327 and the disruption of enemy supply lines. *Units:* USA—9th Infantry Division: 1st Bde (2/39th Inf, 3/5th Cav), 2d Bde (2/47th Inf [M]). *Casualties:* NVA/VC—44 KIA (U.S. losses not included in source document for the individual operation).

4–7 April: *Operation Cussetta. Location:* III Corps; Gia Dinh Province; Hoc Mon. *Objective: Cussetta* is a companion operation to *Fairfax/Rang Dong. Units:* USA—199th Light Infantry Brigade (3/7th Inf, 4/12th Inf, D/17th Cav); VNAF—30th and 33d Ranger battalions). *Casualties:* Not included in source document for the individual operation.

5 April–9 May: *Operation Harvest Moon. Location:* III Corps; Phuoc Long Province; Bu Nard. *Objective:* To secure the engineer's construction site at the Special Forces/CIDG camp at Bu Nard. *Unit:* USA—1st Infantry Division: 3d Bde (1/16th Inf [M]). *Casualties:* U.S.—1 KIA, 6 WIA; NVA/VC—3 KIA, 5 POWs.

5 April–12 October: *Operation Francis Marion. Locations:* II Corps; Pleiku Province; Ia Drang Valley; Ia Meur Valley; Chu Yam Mountains; Duc Co. *Type/Objective:* Search and Destroy. *Francis Marion* is a continuation of *Sam Houston* and is supposed to prevent the NVA from infiltrating through the Ia Drang. *Units:* USA—4th Infantry Division: 1st Bde (1/8th Inf, 3/8th Inf, 3/12th Inf), 2d Bde (2/8th Inf [M], 1/12th Inf, 1/22d Inf), 173d Airborne Brigade (elements); NVA/VC—32d, 66th, 88th and 95–B NVA regiments (more than 10,000 enemy troops were estimated in the area). *Events:* 18 May—B–1/8th Infantry is ambushed by the K–4 Battalion of the 32d NVA Regiment. Losses in the ensuing firefight: U.S.—29 KIA, 31 WIA, 1 MIA; NVA—119 KIA. 18–28 May—"Nine Days in May." The "Nine Days in May" were a string of continuous battles between 2000 U.S. troops of the 4th Infantry Division and 1500 men of the 32d and 66th NVA regiments. Losses for the "Nine Days": U.S.—79 KIA; NVA—300+ KIA. *Casualties:* NVA/VC—1203 KIA (U.S. losses not included in source document for the individual operation).

7–22 April: *Operation Lejeune. Locations:* I Corps; Quang Ngai Province; II Corps; Binh Dinh Province; An Khe; Duc Pho; Razorback Beach; LZ Montezuma. *Type/Objective: Lejeune* is a logistical operation to move the 2d Brigade of the 1st Cavalry Division into Quang Ngai Province. The purpose of the operation is to free up the Marines in Quang Ngai and allow them to be redeployed into northern I Corps. *Units:* USA—1st Cavalry Division: 2d Bde (1/5th Cav, 2/5th Cav, 2/12th Cav). *Comment: Lejeune* puts the first U.S. Army troops into I Corps. *Casualties:* NVA/VC—176 KIA, 127 POWs (U.S. losses not included in sources).

12 April: Task Force Oregon is formed in South Vietnam in response to MACV's need for reinforcements in I Corps. The task force is stationed at Chu Lai (Quang Tin Province) and is made up of the following units: 25th Infantry Division: 3d Bde (1/14th Inf, 1/35th Inf, 2/35th Inf), 101st Airborne Division: 1st Bde (1/327th Abn, 2/327th Abn, 2/502d Abn), 196th Light Infantry Brigade (2/1st Inf, 3/21st Inf, 4/31st Inf), 11th Armored Cavalry Regiment (2d Sqdn).

18 April: General Westmoreland tells the Joint Chiefs of Staff he needs 201,250 additional troops in South Vietnam to achieve an "optimum" level.

18–30 April: *Operation Newark. Locations:* III Corps; Bien Hoa and Binh Duong provinces; War Zone D; Song Be and Song Dong Nai rivers. *Type:* Search and Destroy. *Units:* USA—173d Airborne Brigade (1/503d Abn); NVA/VC—141st NVA Rgt and D–800 VC Battalion reported in area of operations. *Casualties:* None reported in source document.

19 April–20 September: *Operation Baker. Locations:* I Corps; Quang Ngai Province; An Ba; Ba To; Dien Truong; Duc Pho; Gia Vuc; Ha Thanh; Minh Long; Mo Duc; Pho Nghia. *Type/Objective:* Search and Destroy. The purpose of *Baker* is to deny the enemy the use of the lowlands near Duc Pho, thus cutting his food supply and recruiting ability. *Units:* USA—Task Force Oregon: 25th Infantry Division: 3d Bde (1/14th Inf, 1/35th Inf, 2/35th Inf, C–3/4th Cav, C–1/10th Cav); NVA/VC—3d NVA Division, 22d NVA Rgt, 60/1st VC Rgt, 97/2d VC Rgt. *Events:* **19–20 May**—"Battle of Vinh Hiem." American units from A,C–2/35th Infantry, B–1/9th Cavalry and C–3/4th Cavalry clash with the NVA north of Duc Pho. Five U.S. soldiers are KIA and 24 WIA. The enemy body count is 89 KIA and 3 captured. **27–30 May**—"Battle of Tan Phong." B–1/9th Cavalry, C–3/4th Cavalry and B–2/35th Infantry are embroiled in a two-day firefight north of Duc Pho with an NVA company-sized force. Losses: U.S.—4 KIA, 27 WIA; NVA—116 KIA, 8 POWs. **15 July**—C–1/35th Infantry battles a well entrenched enemy force of unknown size 15 miles southwest of Duc Pho. The eight-hour fight ends as U.S. troops frontally assault the enemy bunkers. Two Americans are KIA and 16 WIA in the firefight. The NVA body count is 25. *Casualties:* Totals for *Baker*. U.S.—

32 KIA, 70 WIA; NVA/VC—371 KIA, 3+ POWs.

20 April–31 May: *Operation Prairie IV. Locations:* I Corps; Quang Tri Province; "Leatherneck Square"; "Ryan's Road"; Hill 174; Cam Lo; Con Thien; Khe Sanh. *Type/Objective:* Search and Destroy Clearing to ease the pressure on the Khe Sanh Combat Base. *Prairie IV* is the last in the series of *Prairie* operations. *Units:* USMC—3/3d Marines, 1/4th Marines, 1/9th Marines, 3/9th Marines. *Events:* **8 May**—Two NVA battalions launch a bloody attack on Con Thien. The defenders, companies A and D–1/4th Marines, kill 197 of the enemy. U.S. losses are 44 KIA and 110 WIA. **28–31 May**—"Battle of Hill 174." Companies M and L–3/4th Marines make heavy contact with an NVA force in bunkers and trenches five miles southwest of Con Thien. The two-day battle to take the hill costs the lives of 10 Marines; 99 are WIA. Only 20 enemy bodies are found after the fight. *Casualties:* Totals for *Prairie IV*. U.S.—164 KIA, 1240 WIA; NVA/VC—489 KIA, 9 POWs.

21 April–17 May: *Operation Union. Locations:* I Corps; Quang Nam and Quang Tin provinces; Que Son Valley; Nui Nong Ham; Nui Loc Son; Song Chang and Suoi Cho Dun rivers; Binh Son; Phu Thai; Phuoc Thuong; Thang Binh. *Type/Objective:* Search and Destroy. *Union's* mission is to eliminate the last VC stronghold between Chu Lai and DaNang; the Que Son Valley. (*Note:* The Que Son is also known as the Nui Loc Son Basin and the Phuoc Ha Valley.) *Units:* USMC—1/1st Marines, 2/1st Marines, 3d/1st Marines, SLF Alpha–BLT 1/3d Marines, 1/5th Marines, 3/5th Marines; VNAF—1st ARVN Ranger Group; NVA/VC—2d NVA Division (3d NVA Regiment). *Events:* **27 April**—A marine from the 3/5th Marines accidentally trips a string of land mines that kills one American and wounds 43 others. **10 May**—"Battle of Hill 110." In a vicious day-long battle, the marines of 1/5th and 1/3d Marines assault and finally capture the crests of Hill 110 and Nui Nong Ham, 2.5 miles from Que Son. Casualties for the day: U.S.—33 KIA, 135 WIA; NVA/VC—116 KIA. Tragically, five of the dead and 24 of the wounded marines are the result of an accidental bombing by American F–4s. *Casualties:* Totals for *Union.* U.S.—110 KIA, 473 WIA, 2 MIA; NVA/VC—865 KIA.

22 April–12 May: *Operation Beacon Star. Location:* I Corps; Quang Tri and Thua Thien provinces; O'Lau River. *Type/Objective:* Amphibious assault into VC stronghold near Quang Tri and Thua Thien border. *Units:* USMC—SLF Bravo–BLT 2/3d Marines; NVA/VC—6th NVA Rgt, 810th and 814th VC Main Force battalions. *Comment: Beacon Star* is interrupted on 26 April when BLT 2/3d Marines is ordered to Khe Sanh area to reinforce the 3/3d Marines.

22 April–12 May: *Operation Manhattan. Locations:* III Corps; Binh Duong Province; Ho Bo Woods; "Iron Triangle"; Long Nguyen Secret Zone; Michelin Plantation; Thanh Dien Forest; LZ Joe. *Type/Objective:* Search and Destroy. *Manhattan* is a follow-up operation in the Iron Triangle area of operations aimed at eliminating the Binh Duong Province Committee and any elements of the VC Military Region IV left in the vicinity. *Units:* USA—1st Infantry Division: 1st Bde (1/2 Inf), 2d Bde (2/18th Inf), 3d Bde (2/28th Inf), 4th Infantry Division (attached to 25th), 3d Bde (3/22d Inf), 25th Infantry Division: 1st Bde (4/9th Inf, 2/14th Inf), 2d Bde (1/27th Inf), 11th Armored Cavalry Regiment; VNAF—34th Ranger Battalion; NVA/VC—273d Viet Cong Regiment. *Casualties:* U.S.—15 KIA, 133 WIA; NVA/VC—123 KIA, 7 POWs.

22 April–10 July: *Operation Shawnee/ Choctaw. Location:* I Corps; Thua

Thien Province. *Type:* Search and Destroy. *Units:* USMC—BLT 2/3 Marines (*Choctaw*—12–23 June), 4th Marines (*Shawnee*). *Comments: Shawnee* begins as a three-battalion operation and then is cut back to one battalion and redesignated *Choctaw* on 22 May. *Casualties:* U.S.—31 KIA, 292 WIA; NVA/VC—292 KIA, 27 POWs.

24 April–11 May: *The Hill Fights of Khe Sanh. Locations:* I Corps; Quang Tri Province; Hills 558, 861, 881 North and 881 South. *Objective:* Technically a part of *Beacon Star,* this first battle of Khe Sanh is a USMC effort to gain the high ground surrounding the Khe Sanh Combat Base and airstrip. *Units:* USMC—BLT 2/3d Marines (Cos E,F,G,H), 3/3d Marines, 1/9th Marines (Cos B,E,K,M); NVA/VC—325–C NVA Division. *Events:* **24 April**—Second platoon, B–1/9th Marines is attacked five miles northwest of Khe Sanh. Thirteen Marines are KIA, 17 WIA. Two are reported MIA. Only five enemy bodies are found. **25–28 April**—2/3d and 3/3d Marines battle a battalion-sized NVA force on Hill 861, 3.25 miles northwest of the Khe Sanh Combat Base. The Marines finally take the summit on 28 April following a devasting aircraft and artillery pounding: 518,700 lbs of bombs and 2000 artillery shells. **30 April**—H–2/3d Marines runs up against an entrenched unit of NVA near Hill 881 South, 4.35 miles northwest of Khe Sanh Base. Marines losses: 9 KIA, 43 WIA. **30 April**—K–1/9th Marines and M–3/3d Marines unsuccessfully assault Hill 881 South. Forty-three Marines KIA and 109 WIA. Enemy losses are placed at 163 KIA. **1 May**—Marine aircraft and artillery pound Hills 881 North and 881 South, delivering more than 650,000 lbs. of ordnance on the targets. **2 May**—Hill 881 South seized by 3/3d Marines after more than four days of fighting. **3 May**—2/3d Marines turn back a strong enemy counterattack by two NVA companies, just south of Hill 881 North. The Marines kill 137 NVA, but their losses are high: 27 KIA and 84 WIA. **5 May**—2/3d Marines secure the last of the hills; Hill 881 North is in the hands of the Americans. **9 May**—While patrolling 2.5 miles northwest of Hill 881 North, F–2/3d Marines finds more than 200 enemy graves and comes under heavy fire. Twenty-four Marines are KIA and 19 WIA in the firefight. *Comments:* After-action reports state an estimated 50 percent failure rate for the M–16 rifles used by the Marines. The malfunctioning rifles are blamed for many Marine deaths. *Casualties:* Totals for the **Hill Fights of Khe Sanh.** U.S.—155 KIA, 424 WIA; NVA/VC—940+ reported KIA.

26 April–22 May: *Operation Hancock I. Location:* II Corps; Pleiku Province; Ban Blech; Pleime. *Type:* Search and Destroy. *Units:* USA—4th Infantry Division: 1st Bde (3/8th Inf). *Casualties:* Not included in source.

28 April–12 May: *Operation Beaver Cage. Locations:* I Corps; Quang Nam Province; Que Son Valley. *Type/Objective:* Search and Destroy 25 miles south of DaNang. *Units:* USMC—SLF Alpha–BLT 1/3d Marines. *Casualties:* Totals for **Beaver Cage.** U.S.—55 KIA, 151 WIA; NVA/VC—181 KIA, 66 POWs.

May: The monsoon (rainy) season begins in the southern provinces and ends in the north.

May: *Operation Daniel Boone* begins. *Daniel Boone* is the code name for covert intelligence missions into Cambodia to recon the Ho Chi Minh trail and staging areas. The operations are part of MACV's Special Operations Group (SOG) *Shining Brass/Prairie Fire* program. *Prairie Fire* is the code name for Laotian missions.

1–4 May: *Operation Fort Wayne. Locations:* III Corps; Long Khanh Province; Song Dong Nai River. *Type:* Search and Destroy. *Units:* USA—173d Airborne Brigade; NVA/VC—141st NVA Regiment reported in area. *Casualties:* Not included in source document for the individual operation.

5–17 May: *Operation Dayton. Locations:* III Corps; Phuoc Tuy Province; Mao Tao Secret Zone; Chau Chan Mountain; Nui Re Mountain. *Type:* Search and Destroy. *Units:* USA—173d Airborne Brigade (1/503d Abn, 2/503d Abn, D/16th Armor); NVA/VC—274th and 275th Main Force regiments (VC). *Casualties:* Only casualties in source document were those for a 17 May mortar attack. U.S.—1 KIA, 19 WIA.

11 May–2 August: *Operations Malheur I–II. Locations:* I Corps; Quang Ngai Province; Song Ne and Song Tra Cau valleys; Duc Pho; Minh Long; Mo Duc; FSB Champs. *Type/Objective:* Search and Destroy designed to keep Route 1 open to the Binh Dinh Provincial border and to assist in the area's revolutionary development programs. *Units:* USA—Task Force Oregon–25th Infantry Division: 3d Bde (1/14th Inf, 1/35th Inf, 2/35th Inf), 101st Airborne Division: 1st Bde (1/327th Abn, 2/327th Abn, 2/502d Abn), 196th Light Infantry Brigade (2/1st Inf, 3/21st Inf, 4/31st Inf); NVA/VC—2d NVA Division. *Event:* **18 June**—Second platoon of A–3/21st Infantry (196th LIB) ambushes an NVA unit 16 miles south of Chu Lai. Two Americans are WIA, two NVA KIA and two captured. *Casualties:* U.S. casualties are from the 101st Airborne only; other figures not included in source documents. NVA/VC totals are for entire operation. U.S.—45 KIA, 433 WIA; NVA/VC—869 KIA, 80 POWs.

13 May–16 July: *Operation Hickory. Locations:* I Corps; Quang Tri Province; Hills 869, 950 and 881 South; Khe Sanh. *Type/Objective:* Search and Destroy with extensive patrolling to occupy and hold the hard-won hills of

Khe Sanh and prevent enemy infiltration. *Unit:* USMC—1/26th Marines; NVA/VC—325-C NVA Division. *Events:* 6 June—An estimated 50 NVA soldiers attack 18 Marines manning a radio relay station on Hill 950, five miles north of the Khe Sanh Combat Base. Six Marines are KIA and two WIA in the attack. Ten NVA reported KIA. 7 June—B-1/26th Marines clash with two NVA companies one mile northwest of Hill 881 South. Sixty-three enemy troops are KIA in the two-hour firefight. U.S. losses are 18 KIA and 27 WIA. 26 June—NVA forces launch heavy rocket and mortar attacks on five different Marine positions throughout the area of operations. The incoming rounds kill five Marines and wound 125. 27 June—The Khe Sanh Combat Base is mortared and rocketed. Ten Marines are KIA and 139 WIA in the attack. 27 June—"Battle of Hill 869." Companies I and L-1/26th Marines encounter two NVA companies one mile west of Hill 881 South. Losses: U.S.—10 KIA, 28 WIA; NVA/VC—28 KIA. *Casualties:* Totals for *Crockett.* U.S.—52 KIA, 555 WIA; NVA/VC—206 KIA, 2 POWs.

14 May–7 December: *Operation Kole Kole. Locations:* III Corps; Hau Nghia and Tay Ninh provinces; Nui Ba Den; Oriental River; Bao Tri; Loc Giang; Loc Thanh; FSB Buell. *Type/ Objective:* Search and Destroy. *Kole Kole* is also used to provide security for work crews. *Units:* USA—25th Infantry Division: 2d Bde (1/27th Inf, 2/27th Inf, 1/5th Inf [M]); NVA/VC—5th NVA/VC Division, 269th Viet Cong Battalion, 2d Go Mon Battalion (VC). *Events:* 17 August—Elements from the 5th NVA/ VC Division attack FSB Buell and the communications station on Nui Ba Den (Tay Ninh Province). The defenders, 2/27th Infantry, kill a reported 120 of the enemy. U.S. casualties: 6 KIA, 49 WIA. 21 October—Companies A,B-1/ 27th Infantry battle an estimated Viet Cong platoon just south of Tay Ninh City. Enemy body count is 18. *Casual-*

ties: Totals for *Kole Kole.* U.S.—144 KIA, 876 WIA; NVA/VC—797 KIA, 150 POWs.

17–25 May: *Operation Dallas. Locations:* III Corps; Bien Hoa and Binh Duong provinces; War Zone D; Ong Dong Jungle; Vinh Loi Woods; Song Be River; Di An; Phuoc Vinh; Tan Uyen. *Type/Objective:* Search and Destroy operation in reaction to 12 May rocket and mortar attacks on Bien Hoa, Phuoc Vinh and Tan Uyen. *Units:* USA—1st Infantry Division: 2d Bde (2/18th Inf, B-2/34th Armor), 3d Bde (2/2d Inf [M]), 11th Armored Cavalry Regiment (1st Sqdn); NVA/VC—7th NVA Division (101st NVA Regiment), 273d Viet Cong Regiment. *Casualties:* U.S.—4 KIA, 81 WIA; NVA/VC—17 KIA.

18–25 May: *Operation Cincinnati. Locations:* III Corps; Bien Hoa and Long Khanh provinces; Cay Gao; Long Binh. *Type/Objective:* Search and Destroy aimed at securing the Bien Hoa–Long Binh area from ground, mortar and rocket attacks. *Units:* USA—173d Airborne Brigade; NVA/VC—273d Viet Cong Regiment, D-800 Main Force Battalion (VC) reported in area. *Casualties:* Not included in source document for the individual operation.

18–26 May: *Operation Beau Charger. Locations:* I Corps; Quang Tri Province; Ben Hai River; LZs Goose and Owl. *Objective: Beau Charger* is a companion operation to the Marines' *Hickory* and *Belt Tight,* which are being conducted in support of *Prairie IV. Units:* USMC—SLF Alpha–BLT 1/3d Marines. *Casualties:* Included in *Hickory* casualty figures (see next entry).

18–28 May: *Operation Hickory. Locations:* I Corps; Quang Tri Province; Ben Hai and Mieu Giang rivers; Cam Lo; Con Thien. *Objective: Hickory* is the western prong of a multiforce offensive aimed at clearing the area southeast of the DMZ in preparation for the construction of the Strong Point Obstacle System—"The McNamara Line." *Units:* USMC—1/4th Marines, 3/4th Marines, 1/9th Marines, 2/9th Marines, 3/9th Marines, 2/26th Marines; NVA/VC—31st, 32d and 812th NVA regiments. *Events:* 17–18 May—Rocket and artillery attacks throughout the area of operations kill 12 Marines and wound 103. **18 May**—Marines from the 2/9th and 2/26th Marines battle two NVA battalions northwest of Con Thien. Losses: U.S.—5 KIA, 142 WIA; NVA/VC—31 KIA. 19 May—H–2/9th Marines suffers seven KIA and 12 WIA in a brief firefight. 20–21 May—Companies K,L and M–3/9th Marines fight a fierce two-day battle with an NVA company-sized force. Casualties in the fight: U.S.—26 KIA, 59 WIA; NVA/VC—36 KIA. 25 May—H–2/26th Marines and K–3/4th Marines engage an enemy force of unknown size on Hill 117, three miles west of Con Thien. The Marines lose 14 KIA and 92 WIA, but kill 41 NVA. *Comment:* **Hickory** is the first major Marine incursion into the DMZ. The operation involved the relocation of more than 10,000 civilians from the DMZ and buffer zone to the Cam Lo refugee area. *Casualties:* Casualty figures listed are the combined totals for *Hickory/Belt Tight* and *Beau Charger:* U.S.—142 KIA, 896 WIA; NVA/VC—789 KIA, 37 POWs.

18 May–7 December: *Operation Barking Sands. Locations:* III Corps; Binh Duong and Hau Nghia provinces; "Iron Triangle"; Saigon River; Filhol Plantation; Cu Chi; Phu Hoa; Trang Bang. *Type: Barking Sands* is a pacification effort incorporating Search and Destroy, Cordon and Search, ambushes and jungle clearing efforts. *Units:* USA—25th Infantry Division: 1st Bde (4/9th Inf, 2/14th Inf, 4/23d Inf [M]). *Event:* 30 August—4/9th Infantry conducts an airmobile assault into the "Iron Triangle" area just northwest of Cu Chi against an entrenched VC bat-

talion. Eleven U.S. soldiers KIA and 43 WIA. Four enemy bodies are found. *Casualties:* Total for **Barking Sands.** NVA/VC—320 KIA, 38 POWs (U.S. losses not included in source document for the individual operation).

18 May–7 December: *Operation Diamond Head. Locations:* III Corps; Binh Duong and Tay Ninh provinces; "The Trapezoid"; Boi Loi Woods; Ben Cui Plantation; Dau Tieng; Lau Thien; Soui Da. *Type/Objective:* Search and Destroy. *Units:* USA—4th Infantry Division: 3d Bde (under control of 25th Infantry Division: 2/22d Inf [M]; 3/22 Inf), 25th Infantry Division: 3d Bde (2/12th Inf). *Event:* 24–25 November—2/22d Inf (M) battles a Viet Cong company near the "Mushroom Bend" in the Saigon River, killing 20 of the enemy. *Casualties:* NVA/VC—237 KIA, 37 POWs (U.S. losses not included in source document for the individual operation).

20–23 May: *Operation Belt Tight. Locations:* I Corps; Quang Tri Province; Ben Hai River; Gio Linh; LZs Mockingbird and Parrot. *Type/Objective:* Search and Destroy in the northeast portion of the **Hickory** area of operations. **Belt Tight** is a companion operation to **Hickory** and **Beau Charger.** *Units:* USMC—SLF Bravo–BLT 2/3d Marines. *Casualties:* U.S.—17 KIA, 152 WIA; NVA/VC—58 KIA, 1 POW.

25 May–5 June: *Operation Union II. Locations:* I Corps; Quang Tin Province; Que Son Valley (Nui Loc Son Basin); Ly Ly River; Tam Ky; Vinh Huy; LZs Blue Jay, Eagle and Robin. *Type/Objective:* Search and Clear operation to follow up on *Union I.* **Union II** is in reaction to intelligence reports the 3d and 21st NVA regiments are moving back into the Que Son Valley. *Units:* USMC—1/5th Marines, 3/5th Marines; VNAF—6th ARVN Regiment, 1st ARVN Rangers Group; NVA/VC—3d and 21st NVA regiments reported in area of operations. *Events:* 26 May—"Battle of LZ Eagle." Companies L and M–3/5th Marines air assault into Eagle against elements of the 3d NVA Regiment, 2.5 miles east of Nui Loc Son outpost (near Vinh Huy). Losses: U.S.−38 KIA, 82 WIA; NVA/ VC−171 KIA (estimated). **30 May–2 June**—The 1/5th and 3/5th Marines assault a heavily fortified enemy position in the hills along the southern rim of the Que Son Valley, near the Vinh Huy village complex (5.2 miles southeast of Que Son). Losses in the battle: U.S.−73 KIA, 139 WIA; NVA/VC− 540 KIA. *Casualties:* Totals for *Union II.* U.S.−110 KIA, 241 WIA; NVA/VC− 711 KIA, 23 POWs.

26 May: U.S. sources announce casualties for the week ending 22 May reach a record high: 337 KIA and 2282 WIA.

1 June–2 July: *Operation Cimmaron.* *Locations:* I Corps; Quang Tri Province; Con Thien; Gio Linh. *Type/Objective:* Search and Destroy. *Cimmaron* is a follow-up operation to the *Prairie* series and is centered on the area five miles southwest of Con Thien. *Units:* USMC−SLF Bravo–BLT 2/3d Marines; 3/3d Marines; 1/4th Marines; 1/9th Marines; 3/9th Marines and one battalion from the 26th Marines. *Casualties:* U.S.−38 KIA, 470 WIA; NVA/ VC−245 KIA.

1 June–26 July: *Operation Coronado I. Locations:* III Corps; Long An and Gia Dinh provinces; IV Corps; Dinh Tuong and Go Cong provinces; Rung Sat Special Zone; Soi Rap River; Cho Gao Canal; Can Giouc; Dong Tam; Go Cong. *Type/Objective:* Search and Destroy operation targeted at the Cho Goa District company (VC) and providing security of the Chu Gao Canal. *Units:* USA−Mobile Riverine Force: 9th Infantry Division: 2d Bde (3/47th Inf, 4/47th Inf, 2/60th Inf); VNAF−2/46th ARVN Regiment. *Event:* **4–6 July**— "Battle of Go Cong." 3/47th Infantry

and 4/47th Infantry battle Viet Cong local force units near Vam Co (IV Corps; Go Cong Province). No American casualties. Enemy losses: 66 KIA, 62 POWs. *Casualties:* NVA/VC−478 KIA (U.S. losses not included in sources).

2–12 June: *Operation Bear Bite. Location:* I Corps; Thua Thien Province. *Type/Objective:* Amphibious and helicopter assault of the coastal "Street Without Joy" region 18 miles northeast of Hue. *Units:* USMC−SLF Alpha– BLT 1/3d Marines. *Casualties:* U.S.−3 KIA, 29 WIA; NVA/VC−21 KIA.

3 June–15 September: *Operation Cumberland. Location:* I Corps; Thua Thien Province; Ashau Valley. *Objective:* The mission of *Cumberland* is to establish a fire support base, 17 miles west of Phu Bai, to counter the enemy buildup in the Ashau Valley. *Units:* USMC−4th Marines; USA−Artillery elements. *Casualties:* Not included in sources.

5–9 June: *Operation Bluefield I. Locations:* III Corps; Binh Duong Province; Song Be River; Ap Bau Bang; Lai Khe. *Type:* Reconnaissance in Force. *Units:* USA−1st Infantry Division: 1st Bde (1/26th Inf, 1/4th Cav), 3d Bde (2/2d Inf [M], 1/16th Inf [M], 2/28th Inf); NVA/ VC−9th VC Division (273d VC Regiment) reported in area of operations. *Casualties:* U.S.−1 KIA, 2 WIA; NVA/ VC−1 KIA.

12–26 June: *Operation Billings. Locations:* III Corps; Binh Duong and Phuoc Long provinces; War Zone D; Rach Rat and Soui Hur rivers; Chi Linh; Don Luan; Xom Bo FSB Gunner II; LZ Rufe. *Type/Objective:* Search and Destroy aimed at eliminating the 271st Viet Cong Regiment and providing security for Phuoc Vinh. *Units:* USA− 1st Infantry Division: 2d Bde (2/18th Inf), 3d Bde (1/16th [M], 2/28th Inf); NVA/VC−271st Viet Cong Regiment.

Events: **14 June**—"Battle of Xom Bo I." B–1/16th Infantry (M) tangles with elements of the 1/271st VC Regiment near Xom Bo, approximately 25 miles northeast of Lai Khe. Six Americans are KIA and 16 WIA in the three-hour firefight. Sixty enemy bodies are counted. **17 June**—"Second Battle of Xom Bo." The battle begins as elements of companies A, 1/16th Infantry (M) and A,B–2/28th Infantry attack an ambush position of the 1/271st VC Regiment. Thirty Americans are KIA and 150 WIA in the short, but fierce firefight. The enemy body count is 222 KIA. *Casualties:* Totals for *Billings.* U.S.—57 KIA, 197 WIA; NVA/ VC—347 KIA, 1 POW.

13 June–26 July: *Operation Great Bend. Locations:* III Corps; Gia Dinh Province; Rung Sat Special Zone. *Objective:* Security of the Long Tau Shipping Channel. *Unit:* USA—Mobile Riverine Force, 9th Infantry Division: 2d Brigade. *Casualties:* Not included in sources.

14–22 June: *Operation Arizona. Locations:* I Corps; Quang Nam Province; An Hoa; Duc Duc. *Type/Objective:* Search and Destroy. *Arizona* is also responsible for the relocation of refugees to a camp at Duc Duc, 15 miles south of DaNang. *Units:* USMC—7th Marines. *Casualties:* Not included in source.

15 June: More than 50 enemy rockets hit the DaNang compound. Eight Americans are KIA and more than 170 WIA. Ten aircraft are destroyed and two damaged in the attack.

15–25 June: *Operation Adair. Location:* I Corps; Quang Tin Province; Thang Binh. *Type:* Cordon and Search. *Unit:* USMC—3/5th Marines. *Casualties:* U.S.—11 KIA, 41 WIA; NVA/VC— 74 KIA.

17 June–11 October: *Operation Greeley. Locations:* II Corps; Kontum Prov-ince; Poko River; Dak Seang; Dak To. *Type/Objective:* Search and Destroy. *Greeley* is part of border screening efforts begun with the *Paul Revere* series and is a complementary operation to *Francis Marion.* The specific mission of *Greeley* is to prevent an attack on and to take control of the CIDG camp at Dak To. *Units:* USA—1st Cavalry Division (24 June–24 July), 3d Bde (2/7th Cav, 5/7th Cav), 173d Airborne Brigade (1/503d Abn, 2/503d Abn, 4/503d Abn); VNAF—5th and 8th ARVN Airborne battalions, elements from the 42d ARVN Regiment; NVA/ VC—316th NVA Division (174th NVA Regiment), 24th NVA Rgt, 174th NVA Rgt, 304th Main Force Battalion (VC), Doc Lap Battalion (VC). *Events:* **22 June**—A–2/503d Airborne is attacked near Dak To by an estimated 800 soldiers of the 6/24th NVA Regiment. Seventy-six Sky Soldiers are KIA and 23 WIA before help can arrive. The enemy body count is 106. American troops entering the battleground the next day find that most of the dead were killed execution style . . . point-blank gunshots to the head. **10 July**— A–4/503d Airborne battles a well-entrenched enemy battalion southwest of Dak To. Losses for the engagement: U.S.—25 KIA, 50 WIA; NVA/VC—9 KIA. *Comment: Greeley* consolidated with *Operation MacArthur* 11 October 1967. *Casualties:* Figures as of 31 July 1967: NVA/VC—189 KIA (U.S. losses not included in sources).

18 June–2 July: *Operation Beacon Torch/Calhoun. Locations:* I Corps; Quang Nam and Quang Tin provinces; "Pagoda Valley"; Truong Giang River; Hoi An; LZs Cardinal and Wren. *Type/ Objective:* Search and Destroy mission aimed at clearing Viet Cong infiltration routes. *Unit:* USMC—SLF Bravo–BLT 2/3d Marines. *Event:* **18 June**—H–2/3d Marines makes contact with the enemy near LZ Wren. Casualties for the battle: U.S.—5 KIA, 14 WIA (the Marines suffered 43 nonbattle, heat-related casualties); NVA/VC—23 KIA. Comment: Calhoun (25 June-2 July) runs in conjunction with Beacon Torch (18 June-2 July). Casualties: U.S.—17 KIA, 111 WIA (123 nonbattle casualties). NVA/VC—115 KIA.

19–21 June: *Operation Concordia I.* Locations: III Corps; Long An Province; Soi Rap River; Van Creek; Ap Bac; Can Giouc; Rach Nui. Type: Search and Destroy. Units: USA—Mobile Riverine Force-9th Infantry Division: 2d Bde (4/47th Inf, 3/47th Inf, 2/60th Inf); VNAF—2/46th ARVN Regiment; NVA/VC—5th Nha Be Battalion (VC). Casualties: U.S.—46 KIA, 150 WIA; NVA/VC—255 KIA.

25–27 June: *Operation Maryland.* Location: I Corps; Thua Thien Province. Type: Search and Destroy. Unit: USMC—SLF Alpha-BLT 1/3d Marines. Casualties: U.S.—3 WIA; NVA/VC—7 KIA, 35 POWs.

27 June–2 July: *Operation Quicksilver.* Locations: III Corps; Long Khanh Province; War Zone D; Dong Nai River. Type: Search and Destroy. Units: USA—9th Infantry Division: 1st Bde (4/39th Inf), 3d Bde (2/39th Inf), 11th Armored Cavalry Regiment (1st Sqdn); VNAF—18th ARVN Division; NVA/VC—275th Viet Cong Regiment. Casualties: Not included in source document.

2–14 July: *Operation Buffalo.* Locations: I Corps; Quang Tri Province; DMZ; Route 561; Cam Lo; Con Thien; Dong Ha; LZs Canary and Hawk. Objective: Marine counterattack in response to NVA efforts to attack Con Thien, one of the key points in the Strong Point Obstacle System. Units: USMC—SLF Alpha-BLT 1/3d Marines, SLF Bravo-BLT 2/3d Marines, 1/9th Marines, 3/9th Marines; NVA/VC—90th NVA Regiment. Events: 2 July—B-1/9th Marines is ambushed on Route 561, 1.5 miles northeast of Con

Thien, by two battalions of NVA. Marine losses are heavy: 84 KIA, 190 WIA. 2–3 July—NVA rocket attacks on Con Thien kill 51 Marines and wound 170. Thirty-four MIAs are reported. 3 July—BLT 1/3d Marines and 3/9th Marines clash with an NVA force near Lang Son, 2.5 miles northwest of Con Thien. Losses: 15 KIA, 44 WIA. 6 July—BLT 2/3d Marines comes into heavy contact near Con Thien, killing 35 of the enemy. American losses: 5 KIA, 25 WIA. 7 July—An NVA artillery shell hits the 1/9th Marines' command post at Con Thien, killing 11. 8 July—BLT F,G-2/3d Marines engage an estimated 200 NVA regulars southwest of Con Thien. Sixteen Marines KIA and 72 WIA. Enemy body count: 157. Casualties: Totals for *Buffalo*. U.S.—159 KIA, 345 WIA; NVA/VC—1281 KIA, 2 POWs.

3–4 July: Location: I Corps; Quang Nam Province; Nong Son. Action: NVA soldiers launch an attack on South Vietnam's only producing coal mine at Nong Son. Unit: USMC—F-2/5th Marines. Casualties: U.S.—13 KIA, 43 WIA; NVA/VC—44 KIA.

5–13 July: *Operation Beaver Track.* Locations: I Corps; Quang Tri Province; DMZ; Cam Lo. Type/Objective: Search and Destroy in conjunction with *Buffalo* and *Hickory II.* Units: USMC—SLF Bravo-BLT 2/3d Marines, 1-A/3d Tank Battalion (Marines); NVA/VC—29th NVA Regiment. Event: 8 July—H-2/3d Marines finds a crashed and stripped American helicopter with NVA gear strewn around. Unfortunately a Marine sets off a boobytrap near the chopper, killing eight. Comment: *Beaver Track* absorbed into *Hickory II* on 13 July. Casualties: U.S.—16 KIA; NVA/VC—148 KIA.

6–12 July: *Operation Lake.* Location: I Corps; Quang Ngai Province; Song Ne Valley. Type/Objective: Search and Destroy. *Lake* is to provide security for engineer operations on Route 1 between Dien Truong and Sa Huynh. *Units:* USA—Task Force Oregon–101st Airborne Division: 1st Bde (1/327th Abn, A–2/17th Cav, 1 plt–C–2/34th Armor). *Casualties:* U.S.—2 KIA, 40 WIA.

8–15 July: *Operation Paddington. Locations:* III Corps; Long Khanh and Phuoc Tuy provinces; Long Giao; Nui Dat. *Units:* USA—9th Infantry Division: 1st Bde (2/39th Inf, 4/39th Inf, 2/47th Inf [M]), 11th Armored Cavalry Regiment; VNAF—VNMC; Aust—1st Australian Task Force. *Casualties:* Not included in source document.

10–14 July: *Operation Concordia II. Location:* III Corps; Long An Province. *Type:* Search and Destroy. *Units:* USA—Mobile Riverine Force–9th Infantry Division: 2d Bde (3/47th Inf, 4/47th Inf, 3/60th Inf). *Casualties:* U.S.—1 KIA, 17 WIA; NVA/VC—59 KIA, 6 POWs.

10 July–31 October: *Operation Fremont. Location:* I Corps; Thua Thien Province. *Type/Objective:* Search and Destroy. *Fremont* is to screen the western approaches to Hue and Phu Bai. *Units:* USMC—SLF Bravo–BLT 2/3d Marines, 4th Marines; NVA/VC—806th Battalion (VC). *Comment: Fremont* incorporated into *Neosho* 1 November. *Casualties:* U.S.—17 KIA, 260 WIA; NVA/VC—123 KIA.

11 July: *Locations:* III Corps; Binh Long Province; Quan Loi. *Action:* Viet Cong forces launch a ground and mortar attack in an effort to destroy the artillery and armored vehicles positioned at Quan Loi. *Units:* USA—1st Infantry Division–Task Force Dixie: 3d Bde (1/26th Inf [detached from 1st Bde], 1–A–1/4th Cav); NVA/VC—141st Viet Cong Regiment. *Casualties:* U.S.—7 KIA, 27 WIA; NVA/VC—7 KIA.

14 July: *Location:* I Corps; Quang Nam Province; DaNang. *Action:* Enemy

rocket attack on DaNang Air Base. *Units:* USMC and USAF. *Casualties:* U.S.—8 KIA, 176 WIA (10 aircraft destroyed and 40 others damaged).

14–16 July: *Operation Hickory II. Locations:* I Corps; Quang Tri Province; DMZ; "Leatherneck Square"; Cam Lo River; Cua Viet; Gio Linh. *Type/Objective:* Search and Destroy. *Hickory II* is a sweep of the southern half of the DMZ to clear the area of enemy fortifications, mortar and artillery positions. *Units:* USMC—SLF Alpha–BLT 2/3d Marines, 1/4th Marines; NVA/VC—29th NVA Regiment reported in the area. *Event:* **15 July**—The 1st Amphibious Tractor Battalion battles an enemy force four miles east of Gio Linh, killing 25 NVA. *Casualties:* Totals for *Hickory II:* U.S.—4 KIA, 90 WIA; NVA/VC—39 KIA.

16 July–31 October: *Operation Kingfisher. Locations:* I Corps; Quang Tri Province; DMZ; Ben Hai River; Ca Lu; Con Thien; Thon Cam Son. *Objective: Kingfisher's* goal is to screen enemy entry into Quang Tri Province from the north. *Units:* USMC—3/3d Marines, 2/4th Marines, 3/4th Marines, 1/9th Marines, 2/9th Marines, 3/9th Marines, 3/26th Marines. NVA/VC—324–B NVA Division, 325–C NVA Division, 90th NVA Regiment, 812th NVA Regiment. *Events:* **29 July**—Companies E,F,G,H–2/9th Marines and I–3/4th Marines fight it out with a large enemy force near Thon Cam Son, five miles northwest of Con Thien. Marine losses are 24 KIA and 251 WIA. Forty-eight enemy bodies are counted after the fight. **21 August**—An NVA battalion ambushes a Marine convoy just north of Ca Lu. Six Marines are KIA and 35 WIA. One hundred and nine NVA are reported KIA. **4 September**—Siege of Con Thien begins as Marines from companies I,M–3/4th Marines clash with a company of NVA regulars a half-mile south of Con Thien. Losses in firefight: U.S.—6 KIA, 47 WIA; NVA/VC—

38 KIA, 1 POW. **7 September**—Another Marine convoy is ambushed at the 21 August ambush site. The ensuing eight-hour firefight ends with five Marines KIA and 56 WIA. NVA losses are confirmed at 92 KIA. **7 September**—I–3/26th Marines runs into an NVA company three miles south of Con Thien. Fifty-one of the enemy are KIA. The Marines suffer 14 KIA. **10 September**—In one of the biggest battles of *Kingfisher*, the 3/26th Marines fights the 812th NVA Regiment 3.5 miles southwest of Con Thien. Losses are heavy in the four-hour firefight: U.S.—34 KIA, 192 WIA; NVA/VC—140+ KIA. **21 September**—Companies E,F,G,H—2/4th Marines engages the 90th NVA Regiment one mile east of Con Thien. Losses: U.S.—16 KIA, 118 WIA; NVA/VC—39 KIA. **25 September**—More than 1100 rounds of enemy rockets, mortars and artillery pound the *Kingfisher* area, concentrating on the base at Con Thien. Casualties are 23 KIA and 36 WIA. **14 October**—"Battle of Bastard's Bridge." NVA regulars attack the 2/4th Marines guarding a bridge south of Con Thien. Twenty-one Marines are KIA and 23 WIA. Twenty-four enemy bodies are counted the next day. *Casualties:* Totals for *Kingfisher.* U.S.—340 KIA, 1461 WIA; NVA/VC—1117 KIA, 5 POWs.

17 July–31 October: *Operation Ardmore. Locations:* I Corps; Quang Tri Province; Khe Sanh. *Type/Objective:* Search and Destroy. *Ardmore* is a follow-up operation to *Crockett. Unit:* USMC—26th Marines. *Comments: Ardmore* was redesignated as *Scotland* on 1 November 1967. *Casualties:* U.S.—10 KIA, 39 WIA; NVA/VC—113 KIA.

18 July: *Location:* III Corps; Binh Duong Province; "A–O Strike" Xon Lon. *Action:* U.S. forces encounter a Viet Cong base camp near Xon Lon, six miles northeast of Bien Hoa. *Units:* USA—1st Infantry Division: 1st Bde (1/2d Inf); NVA/VC—271st Viet Cong Regiment reported in the area. *Casualties:* U.S.—7 KIA, 28 WIA; NVA/VC—5 KIA.

20–21 July: *Operation Bear Chain. Location:* I Corps; Quang Tri and Thua Thien provinces. *Type:* Search and Destroy. *Units:* USMC—SLF Bravo–BLT 2/3d Marines, NVA/VC—806th Viet Cong Battalion. *Comment: Bear Chain* phased into *Fremont* on 21 July. *Casualties:* U.S.—11 KIA (enemy losses not included in source).

21–30 July: *Operation Beacon Guide. Location:* I Corps; Thua Thien Province; Hue. *Type/Objective:* Search and Destroy 18 miles southeast of Hue designed to maintain the pressure on VC units operating in the area. *Unit:* USMC—SLF Alpha–BLT 1/3d Marines. *Casualties:* Not included in source.

21 July–14 September: *Operation Emporia. Locations:* III Corps; Long Khanh Province; Hat Dich Secret Zone; Highway 1; Gia Ray; Xa Bang. *Type:* Road clearing and security. *Units:* USA—11th Armored Cavalry Regiment (1st and 3d squadrons); VNAF—52d ARVN Ranger Battalion; NVA/VC—275th Viet Cong Regiment, D–800 Main Force Battalion (VC). *Event:* 21 July—The 3/11th ACR is ambushed by the 2d and 3d battalions of the 275th VC Regiment and elements from the D–800 Main Force Battalion. Losses in the ensuing battle: U.S.—14 KIA, 47 WIA; NVA/VC—96 KIA, 1 POW. *Casualties:* Not included in the source document.

27–29 July: *Locations:* III Corps; Binh Duong Province; Phu Loi; Phuoc Vinh. *Action:* Viet Cong mortar and rocket attacks on U.S. bases at Phu Loi and Phuoc Vinh. *Units:* USA—1st Infantry Division; NVA/VC—271st Viet Cong Regiment. *Events:* **27 July**—The 271st VC Regiment hammers the 1st Infantry's 1st brigade base camp at Phuoc

Vinh with 73 82mm mortar rounds and 86 122mm rockets. Twelve Americans are KIA and 72 WIA. **29 July**—The 1st Infantry Division's artillery base camp at Phu Loi is hit with 200 mortar rounds and more than 40 122mm rockets that kill two and wound 63. *Casualties:* U.S.—14 KIA, 135 WIA.

28 July–1 August: *Operation Coronado II. Locations:* IV Corps; Dinh Tuong Province; Soi Rap and Vam Co rivers; Base Area 470; Ap Binh Thoi; Cam Son; Cai Lay; Dong Tam; Vinh Kim. *Type/Objective:* Search and Destroy to help provide security for the Dong Tam Base Camp. *Units:* USA—Mobile Riverine Force–9th Infantry Division: 2d Bde (3/39th Inf, 3/47th Inf, 4/47th Inf, 5/60th Inf [M], D–3/5th Cav); VNAF—7th ARVN Division, 3/VNMC, 44th ARVN Ranger Battalion, 1/6th ARVN Cavalry; NVA/VC—263d Main Force Battalion (VC), 514th Main Force Battalion (VC). *Casualties:* U.S.—9 KIA, 64 WIA; NVA/VC—73 KIA, 68 POWs.

August: *Operation Pike. Location:* I Corps; Quang Nam Province; Route 1; Hoi An. *Type:* Search and Destroy. *Units:* USMC—1/1st Marines, 3/5th Marines; NVA/VC—2d NVA Division. *Casualties:* U.S.—8 KIA, 60 WIA; NVA/VC—100 KIA, 4 POWs.

1–3 August: *Operation Kangaroo Kick. Locations:* I Corps; Quang Tri and Thua Thien provinces; O'Lau River; Hue. *Type:* Search and Destroy. *Unit:* USMC—SLF Alpha–BLT 1/3d Marines. *Comment:* **Kangaroo Kick** phased into **Fremont** on 3 August. *Casualties:* Not included in source.

1–18 August: *Operation A–O Strike. Location:* III Corps; Binh Duong Province; Phuoc Vinh. *Type:* Search and Destroy. *Units:* USA—1st Infantry Division: 1st Bde (1/26th Inf), 2d Bde (1/18th Inf, 2/18th Inf). *Casualties:* U.S.—7 KIA, 28 WIA; NVA/VC—6 KIA.

1–19 August: *Locations:* I Corps; Quang Ngai Province; Nuoc Dinh and Song Re valleys. *Type/Objective:* Reconnaissance in Force into southern Quang Ngai Province. *Units:* USA—1st Cavalry Division: 1st Bde (2/8th Cav), 2d Bde (2/12th Cav), 3d Bde (5/7th Cav). *Casualties:* U.S.—7 KIA, 44 WIA; NVA/VC—42 KIA, 2 POWs.

2–13 August: *Operation Hood River. Location:* I Corps; Quang Ngai Province; Base Areas 118 and 121. *Type/Objective:* Search and Destroy 25 miles west of Quang Ngai City. *Units:* USA—Task Force Oregon, 101st Airborne Division: 1st Bde (1/327th Inf, 2/327th Inf, 2/502d Abn), 196th Light Infantry Brigade (2/1st Inf, 3/21st Inf, 4/31st Inf); VNAF—2d ARVN Division; ROK—2d ROK Marine Brigade; NVA/VC—2d NVA Division. *Casualties:* U.S.—3 KIA, 38 WIA; NVA/VC—78 KIA, 13 POWs.

5–17 August: *Operation Coronado III. Location:* III Corps; Gia Dinh Province; Rung Sat Special Zone; Soi Rap and Vam Co rivers. *Objective:* The mission of **Coronado III** is to disrupt possible Viet Cong attack on shipping in the Long Tau Channel. *Units:* USA—Mobile Riverine Force–9th Infantry Division: 2d Bde (3/47th Inf, 4/47th Inf, 3/60th Inf). *Casualties:* Not included in sources.

7–11 August: *Operation Beacon Gate. Locations:* I Corps; Quang Nam and Quang Tin provinces; Hoi An. *Type:* Search and Destroy. *Units:* USMC—SLF Alpha–BLT 1/3d Marines; NVA/VC—V-25 Local Force Battalion (VC). *Comment:* **Beacon Gate** phased into **Cochise** on 11 August. *Casualties:* Reported in entry for **Cochise** (11–28 August).

11–28 August: *Operation Cochise. Locations:* I Corps; Quang Tin Province; Que Son Valley; Hiep Duc; Tam Ky; Thang Binh. *Type/Objective:* Search and Destroy. **Cochise** is a continuation of operations in the old *Union II* area of the Que Son Valley. *Units:* USMC— SLF Alpha–BLT 1/3d Marines, Task Force X-Ray (1/5th Marines, 3/5th Marines); VNAF—2d ARVN Division (6th ARVN Regiment), ARVN Rangers; NVA/VC—2d NVA Division, 3d NVA Regiment, 1st Viet Cong Regiment. *Casualties:* Totals for *Beacon Gate* and *Cochise.* U.S.—10 KIA, 93 WIA; NVA/ VC—156 KIA, 13 POWs.

12–21 August: *Operation Portland.* *Locations:* III Corps; Binh Long Province; Saigon River; Route QL 13; Chon Thanh; Lai Khe; Xa Thon Kai; FSBs Bravo and Whiskey. *Type:* Search and Destroy. *Units:* USA—1st Infantry Division: 1st Bde (1/26th Inf), 2d Bde (1/18th Inf), 3d Bde (2/2d Inf [M], 1/16th Inf [M], 2/28th Inf); NVA/VC—7th NVA Division, 141st NVA Regiment, 165th NVA Regiment (1600–2000 enemy troops reported in the area). *Casualties:* U.S.—0; NVA/VC—1 KIA, 23 POWs.

14 August–1 September: *Operation Benton.* *Locations:* I Corps; Quang Tin Province; Base Area 117; Chu Lai. *Type:* Search and Destroy. *Units:* USA—Task Force Oregon, 101st Airborne Division: 1st Bde (1/327th Abn, 2/327th Abn, 2/502d Abn), 196th Light Infantry Brigade (2/1st Inf, 3/21st Inf, 4/31st Inf); NVA/VC—2d NVA Division (21st NVA Regiment), 70/1st Viet Cong Regiment. *Casualties:* U.S.—41 KIA, 263 WIA; NVA/VC—397 KIA, 15 POWs.

19 August–9 September: *Operation Coronado IV.* *Locations:* III Corps; Gia Dinh and Long An provinces; IV Corps; Go Cong and Kien Hoa provinces; Rung Sat Special Zone; Ben Luc; Can Duoc; Tan Tru. *Type:* Search and Destroy. *Units:* USA—Mobile Riverine Force–9th Infantry Division: 2d Bde (3/47th Inf, 3/60th Inf), 3d Bde (3/39th Inf); NVA/VC—506th Local Force Battalion (VC). *Event:* **20 August**—"Battle of Ben Luc." 3/47th Infantry, 3/39th Infantry and the 3/60th Infantry battle

the 506th Local Force Battalion at Ben Luc, 11 miles southwest of Saigon. Losses: U.S.—6 WIA; NVA/VC—59 KIA. *Casualties:* Not included in source.

22–26 August: *Operation Waimea.* *Locations:* III Corps; Binh Duong Province; Saigon River; Rach Tra Stream; Tan Than Dong. *Type/Objectives:* Search and Destroy and jungle clearing along the Saigon River. *Wiamea* is a suboperation to *Barking Sands.* *Units:* USA—25th Infantry Division: 1st Bde (4/9th Inf, 2/14th Inf, 4/23d Inf [M]), 199th Light Infantry Brigade (4/12th Inf attached to the 25th Inf Div); VNAF— 2/7th ARVN Rgt, 4/7th ARVN Rgt. *Casualties:* Not included in source document for the individual operation.

22–27 August: *Operation Akron II.* *Location:* III Corps; Long Khanh and Phuoc Tuy provinces. *Type/Objective:* Search and Destroy. *Akron II* is a series of spoiling attacks on reported enemy buildups in southern Long Khanh and northern Phuoc Tuy provinces. *Units:* USA—9th Infantry Division: 1st Bde (2/39th Inf, 4/39th Inf, 2/47th Inf [M]); NVA/VC—274th Viet Cong Regiment. *Casualties:* Not reported in source document for the individual operation.

27 August–5 September: *Operation Belt Drive.* *Location:* I Corps; Quang Tri Province; Nhung River. *Type/Objective:* Search and Destroy aimed at spoiling communist attempts to disrupt the voting in Quang Tri City. *Units:* SLF Bravo–BLT 2/3d Marines. *Comment:* BLT 2/3d Marines participated in the 4th Marines' *Operation Liberty* 1–4 September. *Casualties:* U.S.—4 KIA, 59 WIA; NVA/VC—18 KIA.

27 August–5 September: *Operation Yazoo.* *Locations:* I Corps; Quang Nam Province; "Happy Valley"; DaNang. *Type:* Search and Destroy. *Units:* USMC—1/7th Marines. *Casualties:* Not included in source.

28 August: *Location:* I Corps; Quang Nam Province; Marble Mountain. *Action:* Enemy troops launch a 140mm rocket attack on the Marble Mountain facility. *Units:* USMC/USAF. *Casualties:* U.S.—5 KIA, 54 WIA.

31 August–1 September: *Operation Strike Force. Locations:* I Corps; Quang Ngai Province; Lang Di; Quyet Thang. *Type/Objective:* Airmobile raid to liberate U.S. and VNAF POWs. *Unit:* USA—Task Force Oregon–101st Airborne Division: 1st Bde (2/502d Abn). *Casualties:* Not included in source document.

1 September: The first AH–1G "Cobra" gunships arrive in South Vietnam.

1–6 September: *Operation Beacon Point. Location:* I Corps; Thua Thien Province; "The Street Without Joy." *Type:* Search and Destroy. *Unit:* USMC—SLF Alpha–BLT 1/3d Marines. *Casualties:* Not included in source.

1 September–23 October: *Operations Valdosta I–II. Locations:* III Corps; Long Khanh Province; La Nga River; Xuan Loc. *Objective:* Security of provincial routes during the national elections. *Units:* USA—9th Infantry Division: 1st Bde (4/39th Inf), 11th Armored Cavalry Regiment (1st, 2d and 3d squadrons); VNAF—18th ARVN Division, 43d ARVN Regiment. *Casualties:* Not included in source document for the individual operation.

1 September–17 November: *Operation Strike. Location:* III Corps; Bien Hoa Province; Long Binh. *Objective: Strike*'s mission is to prevent rocket attacks on the Bien Hoa–Long Binh complex. *Units:* USA—9th Infantry Division: 1st Bde (2/47th Inf [M]). *Comment: Strike* combined with the 199th Light Infantry's *Operation Uniontown* on 17 November. *Casualties:* Not included in source document for the individual operation.

2–9 September: *Operation Cook. Location:* I Corps; Quang Ngai Province; Base Area 121; Song Ne Valley. *Type/Objective:* Search and Destroy into northern Song Ne Valley. *Units:* USA—Task Force Oregon–101st Airborne Division: 1st Bde (1/327th Abn, 2/327th Abn, 2/502d Abn); NVA/VC—2d Viet Cong Regiment reported in area. *Casualties:* U.S.—1 KIA, 5 WIA; NVA/VC—54 KIA, 5 POWs.

4–15 September: *Operation Swift. Locations:* I Corps; Quang Nam and Quang Tin provinces; Que Son Valley; Hills 48 and 63; Chau Lam; Dong Son; Tam Ky; Thang Binh; Vinh Huy. *Objective: Swift* is to prevent enemy disruption of the national elections. *Units:* USMC—Task Force X-Ray (1/5th Marines, H–2/5th Marines, 3/5th Marines); USA—4th Infantry Division: 3d Bde (1/14th Inf; *note:* 1/14th Inf attached to USMC Task Force X-Ray); NVA/VC—2d NVA Division, 3d NVA Regiment, 1st Viet Cong Regiment. *Events:* **4 September**—"Battle of Dong Son (2)/Chau Lam." Companies D,B–1/5th Marines encounter heavy resistance near the hamlets of Dong Son (2) and Chau Lam, eight miles southwest of Thang Binh. As the fighting increases in intensity, companies K,M–3/5th Marines are sent in as reinforcements. Casualties: U.S.—54 KIA, 104 WIA; NVA/VC—130 KIA. **5–7 September**—Companies D,B–1/5th Marines again engage a large enemy force, this time at Vinh Huy, approximately 12 miles southwest of Thang Binh. Marine losses are 35 KIA and 92 WIA. Losses for the 1st Viet Cong Regiment are 61 KIA. **6 September**—"Battle of Hill 43." Companies I,K–3/5th wage a fierce battle for Hill 43, approximately nine miles southwest of Thang Binh. Losses: U.S.—34 KIA, 109 WIA; NVA/VC—88 KIA. *Casualties:* Totals for *Swift.* U.S.—127 KIA, 362 WIA; NVA/VC—517 KIA, 8 POWs.

6 September: Secretary of Defense

Robert McNamara announces plans to build a fortified barrier just south of the DMZ to prevent infiltration into South Vietnam.

6–15 September: *Operation Join Hands. Locations:* II Corps; Binh Dinh Province; Cay Giep Mountains. *Type/ Objective:* Joint U.S./ARVN amphibious and airmobile assault into the Cay Giep Mountains. *Units:* USA—1st Cavalry Division: 1st Bde (1/8th Cav), 2d Bde (1/5th Cav, 2/12th Cav); VNAF—22d ARVN Division (40th and 41st ARVN regiments), VNMC Task Force Bravo. *Casualties:* U.S.—0 KIA, 12 WIA; NVA/ VC—21 KIA, 18 POWs.

11 September–11 November: *Operation Wheeler. Locations:* I Corps; Quang Tin Province; Tam Ky; Tien Phuoc. *Type:* Search and Destroy. *Units:* USA—Task Force Oregon–23d Infantry Division (Americal) after 25 September. 196th Light Infantry Brigade (2/1st Inf, 3/21st Inf, 4/31st Inf), 4th Infantry Division: 3d Bde (1/14th Inf, 1/35th Inf), 101st Airborne Division: 1st Bde (1/327th Abn, 2/327th Abn, 2/502d Abn, A–2/17th Cav); VNAF—2d ARVN Division; NVA/VC—2d NVA Division (21st and 31st NVA regiments), 1st and 21st Main Force regiments (VC) reported in area of operations. *Events:* **7–9 October**—U.S. forces from A–2/ 502d Airborne, A–2/327th Airborne and A–1/35th Infantry fight a running three-day battle throughout Quang Tin Province. Losses: U.S.—34 KIA, 26 WIA; NVA/VC—92 KIA. **21 October**—While patrolling northwest of Tam Ky, A–2/502d Airborne receives heavy mortar and machinegun fire from an enemy force of unknown size. American losses are 7 KIA and 17 WIA. **27 October**—B–2/327th Airborne clashes with a well-entrenched NVA company 10 miles northwest of Tam Ky. Eleven Americans are KIA and 18 WIA in the six-hour battle. Enemy losses are unknown. *Comment:* **Wheeler** combined with **Wallowa** 11 November.

Casualties: Totals for **Wheeler.** U.S.—126 KIA, 498 WIA; NVA/VC— 1103 KIA, 50 POWs.

12 September–8 October: *Operation Coronado V. Locations:* IV Corps; Dinh Tuong and Kien Hoa provinces; Cam Son Secret Zone; My Tho River; Rach Ba Rai; "Snoopy's Nose"; Ban Long; Cai Be; Cai Lay; Long Trung; Vinh Kim. *Type:* Search and Destroy. *Units:* USA—Mobile Riverine Force– 9th Infantry Division: 2d Bde (3/47th Inf, 3/60th Inf), 3d Bde (2/60th Inf, 5/60th Inf); VNAF—7th ARVN Division (6th ARVN Cav, 10th ARVN Rgt), Dinh Tuong Province Regional Forces; NVA/VC—263d Main Force Battalion (VC), 514th Local Force Battalion (VC). *Events:* **12–13 September**—"Battle of Ban Long." 3/60th Infantry is ambushed approximately four miles northeast of Cai Be by a well-entrenched force from the 514th Local Force Battalion. The 3/60th is reinforced by the 5/60th Infantry during the fight. Losses: U.S.—9 KIA, 23 WIA; NVA/VC—134 KIA, 39 POWs. **15–16 September**— "Battle of Cam Son." American forces from the 2/60th Infantry, 3/60th Infantry, 5/60th Infantry and the 3/47th Infantry fight a two-day battle along the Rach Ba Rai, 2–4 miles northeast of Cai Be, against the 263d Main Force and 514th Local Force battalions. Losses: U.S.—16 KIA, 146 WIA; NVA/VC—213 KIA. *Casualties:* Total figures for *Coronado V* not included in sources. Partial totals are U.S.—26+ KIA, 50+ WIA; NVA/VC—540 KIA (estimated).

16–22 September: *Operation Ballistic Charge. Location:* I Corps; Quang Nam Province; Dai Loc. *Type/Objective:* Search and Destroy four miles southeast of Dai Loc. *Unit:* USMC— SLF Alpha–BLT 1/3d Marines. *Casualties:* Not included in source.

17–25 September: *Operation Fortress Sentry. Locations:* I Corps; Quang Tri Province; Cua Viet River; "The

Street Without Joy"; An My; Dong Ha; Gio Linh. *Type/Objective:* Search and Destroy. **Fortress Sentry** is an operation into the old **Beacon Hill/Beau Charger** area of operations and is intended to neutralize enemy forces threatening **Kingfisher**. *Unit:* USMC — SLF Bravo–BLT 2/3d Marines. *Casualties:* Not included in source.

18–23 September: *Operation Arkansas City.* *Locations:* III Corps; Long Khanh Province; Base Area 303; May Tao Secret Zone; Hat Dich; Xa Bang. *Type/Objective:* Search and Destroy into Base Area 303. *Units:* USA — 9th Infantry Division: 1st Bde (4/39th Inf, 2/47th Inf [M]), 11th Armored Cavalry Regiment (3d Sqdn); NVA/VC — 274th Viet Cong Regiment. *Casualties:* U.S. — 0; NVA/VC — 14 KIA, 1 POW.

18 September 1967–31 January 1969: *Operation Bolling/Dan Hoa.* *Locations:* II Corps; Khanh Hoa and Phu Yen provinces; Song Ba and Song Da Rang rivers; Phu Hiep; Tuy Hoa. *Type/Objective:* Search and Destroy effort to protect the rice crop. *Units:* USA — 1st Cavalry Division (17 September–14 October 1967): 1st Bde (2/8th Cav), 173d Airborne Brigade (1/503d Abn, 3/503d Abn, 4/503d Abn, D/16th Armor); VNAF — 47th ARVN Regiment; NVA/VC — 5th NVA Division (95th NVA Regiment), 30th and 85th Main Force battalions (VC). *Casualties:* NVA/VC — 715 KIA, 30+ POWs (U.S. losses not included in source).

22 September: MACV redesignates Task Force Oregon as 23d Infantry Division (Americal). The new division is based at Chu Lai (I Corps; Quang Tin Province) and initially consists of only the 196th Light Infantry Brigade. The 11th and 198th Light Infantry brigades join the Americal by the end of the year.

22–28 September: *Operation Richmond.* *Locations:* III Corps; Long Khanh Province; La Nga River; High-

way 20. *Type/Objective:* Search and Destroy to provide security for road work teams on Highway 20. *Units:* USA — 11th Armored Cavalry Regiment (3d Sqdn); VNAF — 3/5th ARVN Cavalry, 52d ARVN Rangers. *Casualties:* U.S. — 1 KIA, 5 WIA; NVA/VC — 2 KIA, 2 POWs.

23–28 September: *Operation Bluefield II.* *Locations:* III Corps; Binh Duong Province; Ap Bau Bang; Bo La. *Type/Objective:* Search and Destroy along Route 301. *Units:* USA — 1st Infantry Division: 1st Bde (1/2d Inf, 1/26th Inf, 1/28th Inf), 3d Bde (2/2d Inf [M]). *Casualties:* U.S. — 1 WIA; NVA/VC — 2 POWs.

27 September–19 November: *Operation Shenandoah II.* *Locations:* III Corps; Binh Duong and Binh Long provinces; "Thunder Road" (Highway 13); Loc Ninh; Phuoc Vinh; FSBs Caisson III South and Lorraine II; LZs David and Goliath. *Type:* Search and Destroy. **Shenandoah II** is charged with clearing and securing Highway 13. *Units:* USA — 1st Infantry Division: 1st Bde (1/2d Inf, 1/26th Inf, 1/28th Inf), 2d Bde (1/18th Inf, 1/4th Cav), 3d Bde (2/2d Inf [M], 1/16th Inf [M], 2/28th Inf); NVA/VC — 165th NVA Regiment; 271st, 272d and 273d Viet Cong regiments reported in the area of operations. *Events:* **4 October** — 1/2d Infantry battles a unit of unknown size from the 271st VC Regiment. Four Americans are KIA and 26 WIA. Enemy body count is 12. **6 October** — The 1/18th Infantry fights off two VC attacks during the night. Losses: U.S. — 2 KIA, 17 WIA; NVA/VC — 59 KIA. **17 October** — "Battle of Ong Thang." Elements of the 271st Viet Cong Regiment ambush A,D–2/28th Infantry near Ong Thang, 12.3 miles north of Lai Khe. Losses in the ambush and ensuing 11-hour firefight are high: U.S. — 70+ KIA, 114 WIA; NVA/VC — 212 KIA. **30 October** — 1/18th Infantry and two South Vietnamese CIDG companies engage elements from the 273d

VC Regiment just west of Loc Ninh. Four Americans are KIA and five WIA. Eighty-three enemy dead are reported. **7 November**—While on patrol 3.2 miles northeast of Loc Ninh, the 1/26th Infantry is attacked by troops from the 272d VC Regiment. Eighteen U.S. soldiers die in the fight. *Casualties:* Partial totals for **Shenandoah II:** U.S.—70+ KIA, 114+ WIA; NVA/VC—956 KIA.

4 October–11 November: *Operation Wallowa. Locations:* I Corps; Quang Tin Province; Chu Lai; Hiep Duc; Que Son; Tam Ky; Thanh Binh. *Objective:* The goal of **Wallowa** is to reinforce the III MAF allowing more Marines to be deployed further north and to relieve some of the pressure in southern I Corps. *Units:* USA—1st Cavalry Division: 2d Bde (5/7th Cav, B–1/9th Cav), 3d Bde (1/7th Cav, 2/12th Cav), 23rd Infantry Division (Americal): 196th Light Infantry Brigade (2/1st Inf, 1/6th Inf, 3/21st Inf, 4/31st Inf, 1/46th Inf); NVA/VC—2d NVA Division (3d and 21st NVA rgts). *Comment:* **Wallowa** merged with **Wheeler** on 11 November. *Casualties:* Totals for **Wallowa** current to 31 October. U.S.—46 KIA, 480 WIA; NVA/VC—675 KIA, 17 POWs.

11–18 October: *Operation Coronado VI. Locations:* III Corps; Gia Dinh Province; Rung Sat Special Zone; My Tho and Cua Tieu rivers. *Objective:* Security of the Long Tau Ship Channel. *Units:* USA—Mobile Riverine Force–9th Infantry Division: 2d Bde (3/47th Inf, 4/47th Inf, 3/60th Inf). *Casualties:* Not included in source.

11–20 October: *Operation Medina/ Bastion Hill. Locations:* I Corps; Quang Tri Province; Hai Lang National Forest; Base Area 101; LZs Dove and Buzzard. *Type/Objective:* Search and Destroy targeted at the enemy's Base Area 101. *Units:* USMC—1/1st Marines, 2/1st Marines, SLF Alpha–BLT 1/3d Marines; VNAF—ARVN Airborne Battalion; NVA/VC—5th and 6th NVA Regi-

ments. *Event:* **11–12 October**—"Battle of LZ Dove." The 1/1st Marines and 2/1st Marines fight an enemy force of unknown size in the Hai Lang Forest, 5.5 miles south of Quang Tri City. *Losses:* U.S.—8 KIA, 39 WIA; NVA/ VC—40 KIA. *Comment:* 1/1st Marines and 2/1st Marines (**Medina**), SLF Alpha had responsibility for **Bastion Hill.** *Casualties:* Totals for **Medina/Bastion Hill.** U.S.—35 KIA, 174 WIA; NVA/ VC—64 KIA.

12 October 1967–31 January 1969: *Operation MacArthur/Binh Tay. Locations:* II Corps; Kontum and Pleiku provinces; Hills 1338, 823 and 875; Ben Het; Dak To; Ngok Kom Leat; Plei Bo; Plei Chi Teh; Plei Pham Ngol. *Type/Objective:* Search and Destroy. The purpose of **MacArthur/Binh Tay** is to fight NVA troop and logistical buildups in the Western Highlands. *Units:* USA—4th Infantry Division: 1st Bde (1/8th Inf, 3/8th Inf, 3/12th Inf), 2d Bde (2/8th [M], 1/12th Inf, 1/22d Inf), 3d Bde (1/14th Inf, 1/35th Inf, 2/35th Inf), Task Force 22 composed of 2/8th Inf [M], 1/69th Armor and 1/10th Cav, 173d Airborne Brigade (1/503d Abn, 2/503d Abn, 4/503d Abn); VNAF—42d ARVN Regiment; 2d, 3d and 9th ARVN Airborne battalions; NVA/VC—1st NVA Division (24th, 32d and 66th NVA regiments), 17th and 174th NVA regiments. *Events:* **1 November–1 December**—"Battle of Dak To." **6–7 November**—Elements from the 3/8th Infantry, 3/12th Infantry and 4/503d Airborne clash with the 66th NVA Regiment near Ngok Kom Leat (Kontum Province), eight miles southwest of Dak To. *Losses:* U.S.—15 KIA, 48 KIA; NVA/VC—117 KIA (estimated), 1 POW. **13 November**—B-2/ 503d Airborne battles the 3/174th NVA Regiment. **15 November**—An enemy mortar attack on the Dak To base camp ignites the ammunition dump. **17 November**—The battle for Hill 875 begins in Kontum Province as 2/503d Airborne takes up positions 12 miles west of Dak To. The Sky Soldiers are squared-off against the 17th NVA Regiment. **19 November**—A U.S. fighter-bomber accidentally releases a 500-lb. bomb within the friendly forces perimeter, killing 42 and wounding 45 others. **23 November**—The final assault on Hill 875. Soldiers of the 4/503d Airborne and the 1/12th Infantry reach the crest of the hill only to find that the majority of the enemy soldiers had already gone. This was a common occurrence in Vietnam. When a U.S. unit located a well-entrenched enemy force, they would call in air strikes. However, the U.S. rules of engagement called for the friendly forces to be withdrawn well out of range of the bombs and resulting shrapnel. As a result of the loosening-up of the American perimeter, the enemy unit was able to escape the battlefield. Losses in the battle for Hill 875: U.S.—158 KIA, 402 WIA; NVA/VC—1500 KIA (estimated). *Casualties:* Figures for American losses for the entire operation not included in sources. Total NVA/VC casualties placed at 5731 KIA. U.S. losses in the "Battle of Dak To" (1 November–1 December) are 192 KIA, 642 WIA.

17–18 October: *Operation Formation Leader. Locations:* I Corps; Thua Thien Province; Phu Loc; Vinh Loc. *Type/Objective:* Area Control operation used to help stabilize the Thua Thien coastal area prior to the Vietnamese National Assembly election. *Unit:* USMC—SLF Bravo–BLT 2/3d Marines. *Casualties:* Not included in source.

20 October: The 4/3d Infantry (The Old Guard) of the 11th Infantry Brigade, 23d Infantry Division (Americal), arrives in South Vietnam. The battalion is stationed at Duc Pho (I Corps; Quang Ngai Province).

20 October 1967–20 January 1968: *Operation Osceola. Location:* I Corps; Quang Tri Province; Hai Lang Forest. *Type:* Search and Destroy. *Units:* USMC—1st Marines, BLT 1/3d Marines, 2/4th Marines. *Casualties:* U.S.—17 KIA, 162 WIA; NVA/VC—76 KIA.

21 October: The 198th Light Infantry Brigade arrives in South Vietnam. The Brigade is assigned to the 23d Infantry Division (Americal) and is stationed at Duc Pho (I Corps; Quang Ngai Province).

22 October: The 1/6th Infantry (The Regulars) and the 1/46th Infantry (The Professionals) of the 198th Light Infantry Brigade, 23d Infantry Division (Americal), arrive in South Vietnam. The battalions are stationed at Duc Pho (I Corps; Quang Ngai Province).

23 October: The 3/506th Airborne (Currahee) of the 101st Airborne Division arrives in South Vietnam. The battalion is initially stationed at Phan Rang (II Corps; Ninh Thuan Province).

23 October: The 3/503d Airborne (The Rock Regiment) of 173d Airborne Brigade arrives in South Vietnam. The battalion splits its initial posting between Bien Hoa (III Corps; Bien Hoa Province) and Tuy Hoa (II Corps; Phu Yen Province).

24 October–4 November: *Operation Knox. Location:* I Corps; Thua Thien Province; Phu Loc. *Type/Objective:* Search and Destroy effort aimed at keeping the enemy out of the DaNang rocket belt. *Units:* USMC—SLF Bravo–BLT 2/3d Marines, 7th Marines. *Casualties:* U.S.—2 KIA, 15 WIA; NVA/VC—losses not included in source.

26 October–4 November: *Operation Granite. Location:* I Corps; Quang Tri Province; Hai Lang Forest; Base Area 114. *Type:* Search and Destroy. *Units:* USMC—SLF Alpha–BLT 1/3d Marines, 1/4th Marines. *Casualties:* U.S.—3 KIA, 24 WIA; NVA/VC—17 KIA.

27–29 October: *Operation Coronado VIII. Locations:* III Corps; Gia Dinh

Province; Rung Sat Special Zone; Nhon Trach. *Type:* Search and Destroy. *Units:* USA — Mobile Riverine Force– 9th Infantry Division: 2d Bde (3/47th Inf, 4/47th Inf, 3/60th Inf, Royal Thai Regiment. *Casualties:* Not included in sources.

November: The monsoon (rainy) season begins in the northern provinces and ends in the south.

1 November 1967–20 January 1968: *Operation Lancaster. Locations:* I Corps; Quang Tri Province; "The Rockpile"; Camp Carroll; Ca Lu. *Type/Objective:* Search and Destroy into the old *Kingfisher* operational area. *Units:* USMC — 3d Marines, 9th Marines (2/9th Marines). *Casualties:* U.S. — 27 KIA, 106 WIA; NVA/VC — 46 KIA.

1 November 1967–20 January 1968: *Operation Neosho. Location:* I Corps; Thua Thien Province; Hue. *Objective: Neosho* replaces *Fremont* and has the responsibility of screening the approaches to Hue City. *Units:* USMC — 4th Marines. *Casualties:* U.S. — 12 KIA, 73 WIA; NVA/VC — 78 KIA.

1 November 1967–21 January 1968: *Operation Coronado IX. Locations:* IV Corps; Dinh Tuong and Kien Phong provinces; Cam Son Secret Area; My Tho River; Kinh Xong Canal; Ap Bac; Dong Tam. *Type:* Search and Destroy. *Units:* USA — Mobile Riverine Force– 9th Infantry Division: 2d Bde (3/47th Inf, 4/47th Inf, 3/60th Inf), 3d Bde (3/39th Inf, 2/60th Inf, 5/60th Inf [M]); VNAF — 7th and 9th ARVN divisions, 5/VNMC; NVA/VC — 261st, 263d and Main Force battalions (VC), 267th, 502d and 514th Local Force battalions (VC). *Events:* **1 November** — Viet Cong sappers mine the LST USS *Westchester County* as she lay at anchor on the My Tho River. The blast kills 25 and wounds 27, and four Americans are listed as MIA. **16–18 November** — An Allied force consisting of all operational

elements engages enemy troops along the Dinh Tuong and Kien Phong Provincial border. Casualties in the two-day fight: Allied — 26 KIA, 155 WIA; NVA/ VC — 178 KIA, 50 POWs. **4–5 December** — "Battle of Rach Ruong Canal." While on a Search and Destroy patrol in western Dinh Tuong Province, the 3/47th Infantry, 4/47th Infantry and the 5/VNMC engage the 267th and 502d Viet Cong battalions. Casualties in the fight: U.S. — 9 KIA, 89 WIA; VNAF — 40 KIA, 107 WIA; NVA/VC — 266 KIA. **10–12 January 1968** — Units from the MRF: 4/47th Infantry and 3/60th Infantry meet the 261st Viet Cong Regiment in the Cai Be District of Dinh Tuong Province. Losses: U.S. — 18 KIA, 50 KIA; NVA/VC — 47 KIA. *Casualties:* Totals for *Coronado IX.* Allied — 76 KIA, 374 WIA; NVA/VC — 434 KIA.

1 November 1967–28 February 1968: *Operation Kentucky. Locations:* I Corps; Quang Tri Province; "Leatherneck Square"; Cam Lo; Con Thien; Dong Ha; Gio Linh. *Objective: Kentucky* is a series of operations designed to prevent enemy interference with the construction of Strong Point A-3, part of the Strong Point Obstacle System south of the DMZ. *Units:* USMC — SLF Alpha–BLT 1/3d Marines, 1/4th Marines, 1/9th Marines, 2/9th Marines, 3/9th Marines; NVA/VC — Elements of the 324–B and 325–C divisions. *Event:* **30 November** — The 2/9th Marines engages an NVA company–sized force in bunkers 2.5 miles south of Con Thien. Taking the bunkers costs the Marines 15 KIA and 53 WIA. Forty-one enemy bodies are found. *Casualties:* Totals for *Kentucky.* U.S. — 478 KIA, 2698 WIA; NVA/VC — 3921 KIA.

1 November 1967–31 March 1968: *Operation Scotland. Locations:* I Corps; Quang Tri Province; Huong Hoa District; Hills 863, 881 North and 881 South; Khe Sanh Combat Base. *Type/ Objective:* Search and Destroy operation to help support and defend the base at Khe Sanh. *Units:* USMC—1/9th Marines, 1/26th Marines, 2/26th Marines, 3/26th Marines; NVA/VC—325-C NVA Division (95th and 101st NVA regiments), 304th NVA Division (66th NVA Regiment). *Events:* **19 January**—The 77-day siege of Khe Sanh begins. 1–3/26th Marines comes under heavy fire near Hill 881 North. *Losses:* U.S.—8 KIA, 71 WIA; NVA/VC—135 KIA. **20 January**—K-3/26th Marines defends Hill 861 from an NVA assault. The Marines, often resorting to hand to hand combat, manage to hold the hill. Losses: U.S.—7 KIA, 103 WIA; NVA/VC—135 KIA. **21 January**—Khe Sanh Combat Base is shelled, blowing up the Marines' ammo dump. **22 January**—The 1/9th Marines are flown in to reinforce Khe Sanh. **27 January**—The 37th ARVN Ranger Battalion adds to the reinforcements at Khe Sanh. **5 February**—Two NVA companies from the 325-C Division try to take Hill 861A. E-2/26th Marines fights off the attack with a mixture of heroic hand to hand combat and firepower. Losses: U.S.—7 KIA, 35 WIA; NVA/VC—109+ KIA. **7 February**—A battalion-sized force from the 66th NVA Regiment, and supported by 10–12 Soviet PT-76 tanks, attacks and overruns the Lang Vei Special Forces Camp about five miles southwest of the Khe Sanh Combat Base. Losses in the attack: U.S.—10 KIA; CIDG/Allied—200+ KIA, 75 WIA; NVA/VC—200 KIA. **8 February**—The 101-D NVA Regiment attacks companies A,D-1/9th Marines on Hill 64. The Marines fight off the human wave attacks, killing 150 NVA. American losses are 24 KIA and 29 WIA. **23 February**—The base at Khe Sanh receives more than 1300 incoming rounds of enemy fire in a 24-hour period. **25 February**—The 1st and 2d squads of 3d platoon—B-1/26th Marines are ambushed south of the Khe Sanh Combat Base. Twenty-two Marines are KIA and 21 WIA. **6 March**—A U.S. Air Force C-123 is shot down east of the Khe Sanh runway, killing 48. **24**

March—A patrol from A–1/9th Marines assaults a series of enemy bunkers approximately 1.5 miles west of the Khe Sanh airstrip. Losses: U.S.—5 KIA, 14 WIA; NVA/VC—31 KIA. **30 March**—B–1/26th Marines attacks a fortified enemy position south of Khe Sanh, killing 115 NVA. The Marines lose nine KIA. *Casualties:* Totals for *Scotland.* U.S.—205 KIA, 1668 WIA; NVA/VC—1602 KIA, 7 POWs. (The Marines and Air Force estimate an additional 10,000–15,000 NVA KIA due to the massive bombings around Khe Sanh during the siege.)

3 November 1967–5 January 1968: *Operation Santa Fe. Locations:* III Corps; Binh Tuy, Long Khanh and Phuoc Tuy provinces; May Tao Secret Zone; Route 20; Gia Ray; Xuan Loc; FSB Wildcat. *Type:* Reconnaissance in Force. *Units:* USA—9th Infantry Division: 1st Bde (2/39th Inf, 4/39th Inf, 2/47th Inf [M]), 11th Armored Cavalry Regiment (1st, 2d and 3d squadrons); VNAF—18th ARVN Division; NVA/VC—5th Viet Cong Division, 275th VC Rgt; Aust—1st Australian Task Force. *Casualties:* Not included in source document.

5 November 1967–9 December 1968: *Operation Napoleon/Saline. Locations:* I Corps; Quang Tri Province; Cua Viet River; Dong Ha; Ha Loi Tay. *Objective: Napoleon/Saline* is to provide security for the Cua Viet River and to keep the lines of communication open to Dong Ha. *Units:* USMC—1/1st Marines, 2/4th Marines, 1st Amphibious Tractor Battalion. *Event:* **10–11 December 1967**—The 1st Amphibious Tractor Battalion and F-2/4th Marines battle enemy troops near Gio Linh at Ha Loi Tay, 1.5 miles north of the Cua Viet River. Losses: U.S.—1 KIA, 20 WIA; NVA/VC—54 KIA. *Comment: Napoleon* begun on 5 November 1967, *Saline* begun 30 January 1968 and then combined 29 February 1968. *Casualties:* Totals for *Napoleon/Saline.*

U.S.—395 KIA, 1680 WIA; NVA/VC—
3495 KIA.

6–17 November: *Operation Essex.*
Locations: I Corps; Quang Nam Province; "Antenna Valley"; An Hoa; Ap Bon. *Type/Objective:* Search and Destroy six miles south of An Hoa. *Essex* is a complementary operation to the Army's *Wheeler/Wallowa.* It is the Marines' intention to drive the NVA from the *Essex* area of operations into the Que Son Valley and forces from the 23d Infantry Division (Americal). *Units:* USMC—2/5th Marines; NVA/VC—2d NVA Division (2d NVA Regiment). *Event:* 6 November—Companies F,H–2/5th Marines assault the village of Ap Bon (2). Marine losses are 16 KIA and 37 WIA. *Casualties:* U.S.—37 KIA, 122 WIA; NVA/VC—72 KIA.

11–30 November: *Operation Rose.*
Locations: II Corps; Binh Thuan and Ninh Thuan provinces; Secret Base 35. *Type/Objective:* Search and Destroy along Highway QL 1 to provide security for work details. *Units:* USA—101st Airborne Division: 1st Bde (3/506th Abn); VNAF—3/45th ARVN Regiment; NVA/VC—112th Local Force Company (VC), C–270 Local Force Company (VC). *Casualties:* U.S.—9 WIA; NVA/VC—8 KIA.

11 November 1967–11 November 1968: *Operation Wheeler/Wallowa.*
Locations: I Corps; Quang Nam and Quang Tin provinces; Que Son Valley; Nui Hoac Ridge; Hiep Duc; FSB Center; LZs Baldy, Cacti and West. *Type/Objective:* Search and Destroy operations to clear the enemy out of Quang Nam and Quang Tin provinces, with special emphasis on the Que Son Valley. *Units:* USA—1st Cavalry Division: 2d Bde (5/7th Cav), 3d Bde (1/7th Cav, 2/12th Cav), 23d Infantry Division (Americal): 196th Light Infantry Brigade (2/1st Inf, 3/21st Inf, 4/31st Inf), 198th Light Infantry Brigade (1/6th Inf, 1/46th Inf, 1/1st Cav), 101st Airborne

Division: 1st Bde (1/327th Abn, 2/327th Abn, 2/502d Abn, A–2/17th Cav); NVA/VC—2d NVA Division (3d and 31st NVA rgts). *Events:* 3 January—Units from the 196th Light Infantry Brigade encounter soldiers from the 2d NVA Division near Hiep Duc (Quang Tin Province). Eighteen Americans are KIA and 100 WIA. 9 February 1968—The 1/14th Infantry and 1/35th Infantry (3d Bde/4th Infantry Division attached to the 23d Infantry Division) meet the 21st NVA Regiment near Go Noi Island, 12 miles south of DaNang. More than 230 of the enemy are KIA. *Comment:* *Wheeler/Wallowa* is a combination of the 1st Cavalry's *Wallowa* (4 October–11 November) and the 23d Infantry Division's *Wheeler* (11 September–11 November). *Casualties:* U.S.—682 KIA, 3995 WIA; NVA/VC—10,008 KIA, 184 POWs.

13 November: MACV releases "adjusted" figures of NVA/VC troop strength that are minus more than 200,000 militia and support troops. This is a high-level compromise so as not to spoil the propagated image that the United States is winning the war and that the enemy could not continue to increase in strength.

13–30 November: *Operation Foster/ Badger Hunt. Locations:* I Corps; Quang Nam Province; Song Thu Bon River; An Hoa; Dai Loc; Duc Duc; Hiep Duc. *Type/Objective:* Search and Destroy 15 miles southwest of DaNang in retaliation for VC raids on Dai Loc and Duc Duc. *Foster/Badger Hunt* is also to prevent enemy infiltration into the DaNang rocket belt. *Units:* USMC—3/7th Marines (*Foster*), SLF Bravo–BLT 2/3d Marines (*Badger Hunt*); NVA/VC—R–20 and V–25 battalions (VC), Q–13 Viet Cong Company. *Casualties:* U.S.—25 KIA, 137 WIA; NVA/VC—125 KIA, 8 POWs.

16–24 November: *Operation Kien Giang 9-1. Locations:* IV Corps; Dinh

Tuong and Kien Phuong provinces; Cam Son Secret Zone; Base Areas 470 and 471. *Type:* Search and Destroy. *Units:* USA—Mobile Riverine Force– 9th Infantry Division: 2d Bde (3/47th Inf, 4/47th Inf, 3/60th Inf); VNAF—7th and 9th ARVN divisions, 5/VNMC; NVA/VC—263d Main Force Battalion (VC), 514th Local Force Battalion (VC). *Casualties:* U.S.—12 KIA, 122 WIA; NVA/VC—21 KIA, 5 POWs.

18 November: The 2d and 3d brigades of the 101st Airborne Division officially arrive in South Vietnam. The brigades are initially stationed at Bien Hoa (III Corps; Bien Hoa Province).

18 November–23 December: *Operation Atlanta. Locations:* III Corps; Binh Duong Province; "Iron Triangle"; "The Trapezoid"; An Thuan; Phu An. *Type:* Search and Destroy. *Units:* USA—25th Infantry Division: 2d Bde (1/27th Inf, 2/27th Inf, 1/5th Inf [M]). *Casualties:* Not included in source documents.

24–27 November: *Operation Ballistic Arch. Locations:* I Corps; Quang Tri Province; Mai Xa Thi. *Type/Objective:* Search and Destroy four miles south of the DMZ. *Units:* USMC—SLF Alpha– BLT 1/3d Marines. *Comment:* Bogus intelligence information sends the Marines on a "wild goose chase" through an already pacified area. *Casualties:* Not included in source.

29 November: After months of doubt and frustration, Secretary of Defense McNamara resigns to become president of the World Bank. McNamara is replaced in January 1968 by a longtime associate of President Johnson's, Clark Clifford.

December: *Operation Pitt. Location:* I Corps; Quang Nam Province; Da-Nang. *Type/Objective:* Search and Destroy to prevent enemy infiltration into the DaNang area. *Units:* USMC—5th

and 7th Marines. *Casualties:* Not included in source.

1–17 December: *Operation Uniontown/Strike. Locations:* III Corps; Binh Long Province; FSB Nashua. *Objective:* The mission of *Uniontown/Strike* is to prevent rocket and mortar attacks on the Bien Hoa–Long Binh complex. *Units:* USA—9th Infantry Division: 1st Bde (2/39th Inf, 4/39th Inf, 2/47th Inf [M]), 199th Light Infantry Brigade (2/3d Inf, 3/7th Inf, 4/12th Inf); NVA/VC— Dong Nai Regiment (VC). *Event:* 6 December—FSB Nashua, base camp for the 4/12th Infantry, is mortared (wounding three U.S. soldiers). A reaction force on a Search and Destroy patrol to the southeast of the base meets heavy resistance from an estimated enemy battalion. Losses in the battle are high: U.S.—25 KIA, 82 WIA; NVA/VC—67 KIA. *Casualties:* Not included in source documents for the individual operation.

1 December 1967–8 January 1968: *Operation Klamath Falls. Locations:* II Corps; Binh Thuan and Lam Dong provinces; Song Mao and Song Nga rivers; Bao Loc; Di Linh; Phan Rang; Phan Thiet. *Type/Objective:* Search and Destroy aimed at eliminating the headquarters of the enemy's MR-6 (Military Region 6) and all enemy forces in the area of operations. *Units:* USA—1st Cavalry Division: 3d Bde (2/7th Cav), 101st Airborne Division: 1st Bde (1/327th Abn, 2/327th Abn, 2/502d Abn, 3/506th Inf); VNAF—2/44th ARVN Rgt, 3/44th ARVN Rgt, 4/44th ARVN Rgt, 11th ARVN Ranger Bn; NVA/VC—145th, 1865th, 482d and 840th Main Force battalions (VC). *Casualties:* U.S.—25 KIA, 130 WIA; NVA/VC—156 KIA, 8 POWs.

8 December 1967–24 February 1968: *Operation Yellowstone. Locations:* III Corps; Tay Ninh Province; War Zone C; Bo Tuc; Katum; Soui Cat; Soui Tre; FSB Beauregard; FSB Burt.

Type: Search and Destroy. *Units:* USA—25th Infantry Division: 1st Bde (4/9th Inf, 2/14th Inf, 4/23d Inf [M]), 2d Bde (1/27th Inf, 2/27th Inf, 1/5th Inf [M]), 3d Bde (2/12th Inf, 2/22d Inf [M]); NVA/VC—141st NVA Regiment, 271st and 272d Viet Cong regiments. *Events:* **20 December**—NVA troops of the 2d and 3d battalions of the 141st NVA Regiment attack the 4/9th Infantry at FSB Beauregard. The defenders fight off the attack, killing 40 NVA. American losses are 6 KIA and 22 WIA. **1 January 1968**—Elements from the 271st and 272d Viet Cong regiments attack the 3d Brigade/25th Infantry Division's base at FSB Burt. Losses in the bitter fight: U.S.—21 KIA, 152 WIA; NVA/VC—400 KIA, 9 POWs. *Casualties:* Totals for *Yellowstone.* U.S.—137 KIA, 1085 WIA; NVA/VC—1170 KIA, 182 POWs.

8 December 1967–11 March 1968: *Operation Saratoga. Locations:* III Corps; Binh Duong; Gia Dinh, Hau Nghia and Long An provinces; "Iron Triangle"; Filhol Plantation; Cu Chi; Dau Tieng; Trung Lap; FSBs Bowie, Crockett, Logan I–II, Scarlett and Wainwright. *Type/Objective:* Search and Destroy. *Saratoga* is a follow-up operation to *Kole Kole. Units:* USA—1st Infantry Division: 1st Bde (1/2d Inf), 25th Infantry Division: 1st Bde (4/9th Inf, 2/14th Inf, C–4/23d Inf [M], D–3/17th Cav), 2d Bde (1/5th Inf [M], 1/27th Inf, 2/27th Inf, 2/34th Armor), 3d Bde (2/12th Inf, 2/22d Inf, 3/22d Inf, A–3/4th Cav); VNAF—5th and 25th ARVN divisions, 5th ARVN Ranger Group; NVA/VC—101st NVA Regiment, 2d Local Force Battalion (VC), 7th Cu Chi Local Force Battalion (VC), 269th Local Force Battalion (VC), NVA/VC D–14 Local Force Battalion. *Events:* **21 December**—A–2/34th Armor battles an enemy force of unknown size near Bao Dung, 13 miles southwest of Lai Khe. Losses in the fight: U.S.—4 KIA, 16 WIA (two tanks destroyed); NVA/VC—29 KIA. **4–5 January**—The 1/27th

Infantry assaults enemy positions near Trung An and Ap Nha, 12 miles southwest of Lai Khe. Losses: U.S.—10 KIA, 35 WIA; NVA/VC—89 KIA. *Note:* Some American casualties are the result of A–1/27th Infantry being accidentally hit with friendly air support: 4 KIA, 20 WIA. **21 January**—Companies A,C–4/23d Infantry (M) clash with an enemy force near Ap Tra (Binh Duong Province), 12 miles southwest of Lai Khe. Losses in the action: U.S.—3 KIA, 12 WIA; NVA/VC—30 KIA. **24 January**—While conducting a reconnaissance in force 11 miles southwest of Lai Khe, near Xa Goc Chang, companies B,C–4/23d Infantry (M) tangle with an unknown number of VC in a 90-minute firefight. U.S.—5 KIA, 15 WIA; NVA/VC—22 KIA. **31 January**—While on patrol near Hoc Mon, five miles northwest of Cu Chi, B–1/27th Infantry engages a Viet Cong force. Losses: U.S.—2 KIA, 17 WIA; NVA/VC—9 KIA. **31 January**—Company C–3/4th Cavalry is ambushed outside Gate 051 of Tan Son Nhut Airbase. Airbase Security Troops D and B reinforce the ambushed unit. Losses: U.S.—14 KIA, 64 WIA; NVA/VC—309 KIA, 24 POWs. **9 February**—2/12th Infantry clashes with a VC unit while patrolling along Highway 8A, two miles south of Cu Chi. Eight Americans are KIA and 15 WIA in the day-long battle. Nine VC bodies are accounted for. **13 February**—D–4/23d Infantry (M) withstands a fierce mortar and RPG attack in the Gia Dinh area, approximately four miles southeast of Cu Chi. Losses: 4 KIA, 34 WIA. Enemy losses due to tactical air support and artillery are unknown. *Casualties:* Totals for *Saratoga.* U.S.—392 KIA, 2047 WIA; NVA/VC—3836 KIA, 581 POWs.

16 December: The 3/187th Infantry (Rakkasans), 1/501st Infantry, 2/501st Infantry, 1/502d Infantry, 1/506th Infantry and the 2/506th Infantry (Currahee) of the 101st Airborne Division arrive in South Vietnam. The battalions are stationed as follows: 3/187th, 1/506th and 2/506th at Phuoc Vinh (III Corps, Binh Duong Province), 1/501st, 2/501st and 1/502d at Cu Chi (III Corps; Hau Nghia Province).

17–31 December: *Operation Camden. Locations:* III Corps; Binh Duong, Hau Nghia and Tay Ninh provinces; Boi Loi Forest; Ho Ho Woods; "The Trapezoid." *Type:* Search and Destroy. *Units:* USA—25th Infantry Division: (1/5th Inf [M], 1/27th Inf, 2/27th Inf), 3d Bde (2/12th Inf, 2/22d Inf [M], 3/22d Inf); NVA/VC—101st NVA Regiment. *Casualties:* Totals for *Camden.* U.S.— 27 KIA, 118 WIA; NVA/VC—109 KIA, 4 POWs.

17 December 1967–8 March 1968: *Operation Uniontown. Locations:* III Corps; Bien Hoa Province; War Zone D. *Objective:* Prevention of rocket and mortar attacks on the Bien Hoa–Long Binh complex. *Units:* USA—199th Light Infantry Brigade (2/3d Inf, 3/7th Inf, 4/12th Inf); NVA/VC—Dong Nai Regiment (VC). *Casualties:* NVA/VC— 922 KIA (U.S. losses not included in source document for the individual operation).

18 December: The 1/20th Infantry (Syke's Regulars) of the 11th Light Infantry Brigade, 23d Infantry Division (Americal), arrives in South Vietnam. The battalion is stationed at Duc Pho (I Corps; Quang Ngai Province).

18 December 1967–12 January 1968: *Operation Manchester. Locations:* III Corps; Bien Hoa Province; FSB Keane. *Type/Objective:* Search and Destroy charged with the security of Bien Hoa/Long Binh. *Units:* USA— 199th Light Infantry Brigade (3/7th Inf). *Casualties:* U.S.—28 WIA; NVA/ VC—27 KIA.

19 December: The 11th Light Infantry Brigade, part of the 23rd Infantry Division (Americal), officially arrives in

South Vietnam. The Brigade is stationed at Duc Pho (I Corps; Quang Ngai Province).

19 December: The 3/1st Infantry of the 11th Light Infantry Brigade, 23d Infantry Division (Americal), arrives in South Vietnam. The battalion is stationed at Duc Pho (I Corps; Quang Ngai Province).

19 December 1967–10 June 1968: *Operation Muscatine. Locations:* I Corps; Quang Ngai Province; Binh Son; Duc Pho; Son Tinh. *Type/Objective:* Search and Destroy. The goals of *Muscatine* are the relief of the ROK 2d Marine Brigade and the pacification of Quang Ngai Province. *Units:* USA—4th Infantry Division: 3d Bde (2/12th Inf, 1/14th Inf, 2/22d Inf, 3/22d Inf), 23d Infantry Division (Americal), 11th Light Infantry Brigade (3/1st Inf, 4/3d Inf, 1/20th Inf, 4/21st Inf), 198th Light Infantry Brigade (1/6th Inf, 1/46th Inf, 5/46th Inf, 1/52d Inf); VNAF—2d ARVN Division. *Event:* **16 March 1968**—In the most notorious and well-publicized atrocity committed by American troops during the war, a platoon of C–1/20th Infantry (11th Infantry Brigade/23d Infantry Division [Americal]) attacks the village of Son My (4)... better known as My Lai. The soldiers, led by Lt. William Calley, kill between 200 and 500 unarmed civilians. My Lai is located in I Corps, Quang Ngai Province, approximately six miles northeast of Quang Ngai City. *Casualties:* Totals for *Muscatine.* U.S.— 186 KIA, 417 WIA; NVA/VC—1129 KIA.

21–24 December: *Operation Fortress Ridge. Locations:* I Corps; Quang Tri Province; Cua Viet River; Con Thien; Giem Ha Trung; Gio Linh; Ha Loi Tay. *Type/Objective:* Search and Destroy. *Fortress Ridge* is basically a clearing operation in the old *Kentucky* area of operations, 3.5 miles south of the DMZ. *Units:* USMC—SLF Bravo–BLT 3/1st

Marines; NVA/VC—716th and 803d NVA regiments and the K–400 Local Force Company (VC) reported in the area of operations. *Casualties:* U.S.—10 KIA, 28 WIA; NVA/VC—10 KIA.

21 December 1967–21 January 1968: Operation Fargo. *Locations:* III Corps; Binh Long and Tay Ninh provinces; Loc Ninh. *Type:* Reconnaissance in Force. *Units:* USA—11th Armored Cavalry Regiment; NVA/VC—7th NVA Light Infantry Division, 9th VC Light Infantry Division (271st, 272d and 273d VC regiments). *Casualties:* Not included in source document.

26 December 1967–2 January 1968: Operation Badger Tooth. *Locations:* I Corps; Quang Tri and Thua Thien provinces; Ap Phuoc Phu; Tho Trung An; Thom Tham Khe; LZ Finch. *Type/ Objective:* Combined amphibious and helicopter assault into the "Street Without Joy" area near the Quang Tri–Thua Thien border. *Units:* USMC—SLF Bravo–BLT 3/1st Marines; NVA/VC—716th NVA Regiment (116th NVA Bn). *Event:* **27–28** December—"Battle of Thom Tham Khe." The Marines of companies I,K,L and M–3/1st Marines clash with the 116th NVA Battalion-

in coastal villages of Thom Tham Khe and Thon Trung An. Losses in the grueling battle: U.S.—48 KIA, 87 WIA; NVA/VC—100+ KIA. *Casualties:* Complete totals for *Badger Tooth* not included in sources. Partial figures: U.S.—48+ KIA, 87+ WIA; NVA/VC—140+ KIA.

31 December: There are now more than 480,000 U.S. personnel in South Vietnam, an increase of 100,000 for the year. U.S. ground forces end the year in the following strengths: Army—331,000, Marines—78,000; American losses for the year: 9353 KIA, 62,024 WIA. Another 328 U.S. aircraft were lost over North Vietnam in 1967, bringing the total number of planes lost or shot down to 779 since the *Rolling Thunder* program began. Total American losses in Vietnam since 1959: 16,021 KIA, 107, 407 WIA; VNAF strength at the end of the year: 800,000; VNAF losses for the year: 11,135 KIA; total VNAF KIA since 1965: 62,428; estimated NVA/VC strength at the end of 1967: 500,000; estimated NVA/VC losses for the year: 90,400 KIA; estimated NVA/VC losses since 1965: 186,616 KIA.

1968

As of 1 January 1968, there are now more than 480,000 American personnel in the Southeast Asia theater: Army—332,000; Navy—22,000; Marines—78,000; Air Force—56,000. Combined VNAF strength is estimated at 800,000 ARVN, Regional Forces/Popular Forces and militia. NVA/VC strength is estimated at 500,000 regular, main force and local guerilla troops.

January: The 27th Marines (1st Marine Division) arrives in South Vietnam. The regiment is stationed at DaNang (I Corps; Quang Nam Province).

11–21 January: *Operation Akron V. Locations:* III Corps; Bien Hoa Province; Base Area 303; Binh Son; Hat Dich; Long Thanh. *Type/Objective:* Search and Destroy/Reconnaissance in Force into Base Area 303. *Units:* USA—9th Infantry Division: 1st Bde (2/39th Inf, 4/39th Inf, 2/47th Inf [M], 3/5th Cav); NVA/VC—274th Main Force Regiment (VC). *Casualties:* U.S.—8 KIA, 84 WIA; NVA/VC— 39 KIA.

16 January–9 February: *Operation San Angelo. Locations:* II Corps; Phuoc Long and Quang Duc provinces; Bu Chirr Phuoc; Bu Blim; Bu Mia Gap; Song Be. *Type/Objective:* Search and Destroy. The purpose of **San Angelo** is to establish blocking positions along the Cambodian border during the TET truce period. *Units:* USA—101st Airborne Division: 1st Bde (1/327th Abn,

2/327th Abn, 2/502d Abn, 3/506th Inf); VNAF—2/9th ARVN Regiment, 31st Ranger Battalion. *Casualties:* As of 31 January 1968: U.S.—11 KIA, 59 WIA; NVA/VC—43 KIA.

18 January–13 February: *Operation Coronado X. Locations:* IV Corps; Dinh Tuong and Vinh Long provinces; Cai Be; Cai Lay; My Tho. *Type/Objective:* Search and Destroy. **Coronado** X is a reaction operation to drive the enemy from the My Tho/Vinh Long area. *Units:* USA—Mobile Riverine Force–9th Infantry Division: 2d Bde (3/47th Inf, 4/47th Inf, 3/60th Inf); NVA/VC—263d Main Force Battalion (VC), 514th Provincial Battalion (VC). *Casualties:* Not included in source document for the individual operation.

20 January 1968–31 January 1969: *Operation McLain. Location:* II Corps; Binh Thuan Province. *Type/Objective:* Reconnaissance in Force operation in support of pacification efforts in Binh Thuan Province. *Units:* USA—173d Airborne Brigade (3/503d Abn). *Casualties:*

NVA/VC—1042 KIA (U.S. losses not included in source document for the individual operation).

21–24 January: *Operation Neosho II.* *Location:* I Corps; Thua Thien Province. *Type/Objective:* Clearing operation to provide cover for the 1st Cavalry Division's arrival at Camp Evans, 15 miles northwest of Hue. *Units:* USMC—1st Marines. *Casualties:* U.S.—4 WIA; NVA/VC—1 KIA.

21–30 January: *Operation Attala/ Casey.* *Location:* III Corps; Binh Duong Province. *Type:* Reconnaissance in Force. *Units:* USA—1st Infantry Division: 1st Bde (1/2d Inf, 1/26th Inf, 1/28th Inf), 101st Airborne Division: 2d Bde (1/501st Inf, 2/501st Inf, 1/502d Inf), 11th Armored Cavalry Regiment (1st and 2d squadrons); NVA/VC—7th NVA Division (165th NVA Regiment). *Casualties:* Not included in source document for the individual operation.

21 January–16 February: *Operation Osceola II.* *Locations:* I Corps; Quang Tri Province; Hai Lang Forest. *Type/ Objective:* Search and Destroy. This operation is a continuation of *Osceola I.* *Units:* USMC—4th Marines. *Casualties:* U.S.—2 KIA, 46 WIA; NVA/VC—24 KIA.

21 January–23 November: *Operation Lancaster II.* *Locations:* I Corps; Quang Tri Province; "The Rockpile"; Ca Lu; Camp Carroll. *Type/Objective:* Search and Clear operation near Ca Lu, 21 miles west of Quang Tri City. *Units:* USMC—2/9th Marines, 3/9th Marines. *Casualties:* U.S.—359 KIA, 1713 WIA; NVA/VC—1801 KIA.

22–26 January: *Operation Ballistic Armor.* *Location:* I Corps; Thua Thien Province. *Type/Objective:* Clearing operation 15 miles northwest of Hue in support of the 1st Cavalry Division's move to Camp Evans. *Unit:* USMC—

SLF–BLT 2/4th Marines. *Casualties:* U.S.—3 WIA; NVA/VC—6 KIA.

22 January–29 February: *Operation Pershing II.* *Location:* II Corps; Binh Dinh Province. *Type/Objective:* Clearing and Pacification of Binh Dinh Dinh. A continuation of **Pershing I.** *Units:* USA—1st Cavalry Division; NVA/VC—610th NVA Division. *Casualties:* NVA/VC—614 KIA (U.S. losses not included in source).

22 January–31 March: *Operation Jeb Stuart.* *Locations:* I Corps; Quang Tri and Thua Thien provinces; Ba Long Valley; Thach Hon River, Base Areas 101 and 114; Hue; Quang Tri City; Camp Evans. *Type/Objective:* Search and Destroy operation aimed at enemy Base Areas 101 and 114. One of the primary goals of *Jeb Stuart* is the reinforcement of the Marines in I Corps. *Units:* USA—1st Cavalry Division: 1st Bde (2/8th Cav), 2d Bde (5/7th Cav), 3d Bde (2/12th Cav), 101st Airborne Division: 2d Bde (1/501st Inf, 2/501st Inf); NVA/VC—2d NVA Division, 325–B NVA Division (5th, 6th, 7th, 9th and 812th NVA rgts). *Event:* **31 January–1 February**—"Battle of Quang Tri." The NVA attack the provincial capital of Quang Tri as part of the 1968 *TET Offensive.* A combined force of the 1st Cavalry's 1/5th Cavalry, 1/12th Cavalry, 1st ARVN Regiment and the 9th ARVN Airborne Battalion battles elements from the 812th NVA Regiment, the 10th NVA Sapper Battalion, the K–4 and K–8 battalions. More than 875 NVA are reported KIA and 100 captured. *Casualties:* Totals for *Jeb Stuart.* U.S.—291 KIA, 1735 WIA, 24 MIA; NVA/VC—3268 KIA, 119 POWs.

23–26 January: *Operation Badger Catch.* *Locations:* I Corps; Quang Tri Province; Cua Viet River; My Loc. *Type/Objective:* Search and Destroy to clear north banks of the Cua Viet River and prevent enemy interdiction of river traffic. *Units:* USMC—BLT 3/1st Marines; NVA/VC—803d NVA Regiment.

Casualties: U.S.—13 KIA, 49 WIA; NVA/VC—10 KIA.

27 January: *Operation Fortress Attack. Location:* I Corps; Quang Tri Province; Cam Lo. *Type:* Helicopter assault west of Dong Ha. *Unit:* USMC— BLT 2/4th Marines. *Casualties:* None reported.

31 January–7 March: *The TET Offensive. Locations:* Attacks launched in all four corps areas. *Objective:* The communist leadership hoped to bring about a quick end to the war by launching an all-out offensive against the cities, hoping to trigger a massive uprising of southern sympathizers who would join forces with the communists and topple the Thieu-Ky government and drive the Americans out of Vietnam. The communists were well aware 1968 was an election year in the United States and what impact an attack of this nature would have on American public opinion. *Events:* 31 January—The *TET Offensive* begins as communist forces attack cities and allied installations throughout the country. Thirty-six of the 44 provincial capitals, five of six autonomous cities and 23 major bases and airfields are attacked on the first night of the Vietnamese holiday season. *Note:* Other events listed under individual operational entries. *Casualties:* Totals for *TET.* U.S.—1536 KIA, 7764 WIA, 11 MIA; VNAF—2788 KIA, 8299 WIA, 587 MIA; NVA/VC—45,000 KIA (estimated), 6991 POWs.

1 February–10 March: *Operation LAM SON-68. Locations:* III Corps; Binh Duong Province; An My; Lai Khe; Phu Loi; Tan Phuoc Khanh. *Type/Objective:* Search and Destroy in support of the Vietnamese government's (GVN) Revolutionary Development Program. *Units:* USA—1st Infantry Division: 1st Bde (1/28th Inf, 1/4th Cav), 2d Bde (2/16th Inf, 1/18th Inf, 2/18th Inf), 3d Bde (2/2d Inf [M], 1/16th Inf [M]); NVA/VC—273d VC Regiment, Dong

Nai Regiment (VC). *Events:* 1 February—Companies A,D-1/28th Infantry and A-2/16th Infantry battle the 273d Viet Cong Regiment near An My, 13.5 miles southwest of Lai Khe. Losses: U.S.—5 KIA, 32 WIA; NVA/VC—197 KIA. 7 February—While conducting a reconnaissance in force operation 10 miles northwest of Phu Loi, C-2/18th Infantry, A-2/16th Infantry, B-1/4th Cavalry and I-3/11th ACR clash with a VC force of unknown size. Three Americans are KIA and 29 WIA. The enemy body count is 42. 20 February—C-1/28th Infantry engages a VC force of unknown size near Thu Duc, three miles north of Saigon. Casualties are high in the brief skirmish: U.S.—19 KIA, 11 WIA; NVA/VC—123 KIA. *Casualties:* Totals for *LAM SON-68.* U.S.—74 KIA, 273 WIA; NVA/VC—1235 KIA, 46 POWs.

1 February–23 March: *Operation Adairsville. Locations:* III Corps; Bien Hoa and Binh Duong provinces; FSB Buffalo. *Type/Objective:* Reconnaissance in Force operation. *Adairsville* is to provide security for the Saigon/Long Binh–Bien Hoa area in wake of the *TET Offensive. Units:* USA—11th Armored Cavalry Regiment (1st, 2d and 3d squadrons); VNAF—1/18th ARVN Regiment; NVA/VC—5th Viet Cong Division (274th Viet Cong Regiment, 267th and 296th Main Force [VC] battalions) reported in area of operations. *Casualties:* Not reported in source document.

2 February–2 March: *Operation Hue City. Locations:* I Corps; Thua Thien Province; Perfume River; Hue; The Citadel. *Objective:* The retaking of Hue during the *TET Offensive. Units:* USA—1st Cavalry Division: 2d Bde (5/7th Cav), 3d Bde (1/7th Cav, 2/7th Cav, 2/12th Cav), 101st Airborne Division: 2d Bde (1/501st Inf, 2/501st Inf); USMC—1st and 5th Marines; VNAF—4/2d ARVN Regiment, 3d ARVN Regiment, 9th ARVN Airborne Battalion,

7/ARVN Armored Cavalry Regiment; NVA/VC—4th NVA Rgt (804th Sapper Battalion), 6th NVA Rgt (800th, 802d and 806th bns), 12th Viet Cong Battalion, K-4 Battalion. *Casualties:* U.S.—119 KIA, 961 WIA; VNAF—363 KIA, 1242 WIA; NVA/VC—5000 KIA (estimated), 15 POWs; Civilians—5800 KIA/MIA, 116,000 homeless.

6–9 February: *Operation Miracle. Location:* I Corps; Quang Nam Province. *Units:* USA—23d Infantry Division (American), 198th Light Infantry Brigade (1/6th Inf); NVA/VC—2d NVA Division (elements). *Casualties:* Not included in source document.

7–8 February: *Battle of Lang Vei. Location:* I Corps; Quang Tri Province; Xe Pone River; Highway 9; Lang Troai. *Action:* NVA attack on U.S. Special Forces Camp at Lang Vei, five miles west of Khe Sanh. *Units:* USA—Special Forces Detachment A-101; VNAF—ARVN Special Forces (LLDB); Allies—33d Royal Thai Battalion, Mobile Strike Force (Hre Tribesmen), 1 Company of Bru CIDG; NVA/VC—66th NVA Regiment with armored support. *Casualties:* U.S.—10 KIA, 11 WIA; Allies—200 KIA/MIA, 75 WIA; NVA/VC—200 KIA (estimated).

9 February: *Location:* I Corps; Quang Nam Province; Hoi An. *Action: TET Offensive*-related battle with an enemy force estimated at 250–300 strong near Hoi An 10 miles southeast of DaNang. *Units:* USA—4th Infantry Division: 3d Bde (C-1/35th Inf). *Casualties:* U.S.—10 KIA, 33 WIA; NVA/VC—200 KIA (estimated).

10 February: The 1/52d Infantry (The Ready Rifles) arrives in South Vietnam. The 1/52d is part of the 198th Light Infantry Brigade, 23d Infantry Division (American). The battalion is stationed at Chu Lai (I Corps; Quang Tin Province).

13 February–6 March: *Operation*

Coronado XI. Locations: IV Corps; Ba Xuyen and Phong Dinh provinces; Bassac and My Tho rivers; Kinh Lai Hieu Canal; Cu Lao May Island; Cai Rang; Can Tho; Hiep Hung; Phung Hiep. *Type/Objective:* Search and Destroy. *Coronado XI* is a combined Riverine/Airmobile operation designed to relieve pressure on Can Tho, locate and engage VC units in the area and locate and destroy the Viet Cong Military Region III Headquarters. *Units:* USA—Mobile Riverine Force–9th Infantry Division: 2d Bde (3/47th Inf, 3/60th Inf); VNAF—9th and 21st ARVN divisions; NVA/VC—303d and 306th Main Force battalions (VC), Tay Do Battalion (VC), U-Minh 10th Battalion (VC). *Casualties:* Not included in source material.

17 February: The 2/505th Airborne (Panthers) of the 3d Brigade/82d Airborne Division arrives in South Vietnam. The battalion is initially stationed at Hue (I Corps; Thua Thien Province).

18 February: The 3d Brigade/82d Airborne Division officially arrives in South Vietnam. The brigade is stationed at Hue–Phu Bai (I Corps; Thua Thien Province). Also arriving with the 3d Brigade headquarters is the 1/508th Airborne. The battalion is stationed at Hue (I Corps; Thua Thien Province).

24 February: The 1/505th Airborne (Panthers) of the 3d Brigade/82d Airborne Division arrives in South Vietnam. The battalion is stationed at Hue (I Corps; Thua Thien Province).

26 February–12 September: *Operation Houston. Locations:* I Corps; Quang Nam and Thua Thien provinces; Hai Van Pass; Phu Loc. *Objective: Houston* is assigned the responsibility for keeping Highway 1 open and providing security for details working on the railroad between Hue and DaNang. *Units:* USMC—2/3d Marines, 3/5th Marines, 26th Marines. *Casualties:* Totals for *Houston.* U.S.—121 KIA, 848 WIA; NVA/VC—702 KIA.

28 February: General Earle Wheeler, Chairman of the Joint Chiefs of Staff, returns from a conference in South Vietnam and passes on COMUSMACV Westmoreland's request for an additional 206,000 troops. Westmoreland feels that with the extra manpower, he could seize the initiative in the war once more . . . perhaps even launch incursions into Laos and Cambodia.

7 March–30 July: *Operation Truong Cong Dinh. Locations:* IV Corps; Dinh Tuong; Kien Hoa; Kien Tuong, Vinh Binh and Vinh Long provinces; Cai Lay; Long Dinh; Mo Cay; My Tho; Xon Xhua. *Type/Objective:* Search and Destroy to provide security for Highway 4 and My Tho. *Units:* USA—9th Infantry Division: 1st Bde (2/39th Inf, 2/47th Inf [M]), 2d Brigade–Mobile Riverine Force (3/47th Inf, 4/47th Inf, 3/60th Inf), 3d Bde (4/39th Inf); VNAF—7th ARVN Division; NVA/VC—514th and 516th Main Force battalions (VC), 261-A and 261-B battalions (VC). *Comment: Truong Cong Dinh* combined with *Operation Duong Cua Dan (People's Road)* 21 May. *Casualties:* Totals for *Truong Cong Dinh/Duong Cua Dan.* U.S.—197 KIA, 1094 WIA; NVA/VC—2246 KIA, 134 POWs.

8 March–17 May: *Operations Carentan I–II. Locations:* I Corps; Quang Tri and Thua Thien provinces; Song Bo River; Col Co Beach; Hue; Phuoc Yen; Van Xa Lang; Xom Dong; FSB Hardcore; LZs Devil, Detroit, Geronimo, Pinky. *Type/Objective: Carentan I–II* combines Search and Destroy, Cordon and Search and Reconnaissance in Force operations into the lowlands of Quang Tri and Thua Thien provinces. *Note: Carentan I* (8–30 March) and *Carentan II* (1 April–17 May). *Units:* USA—23d Infantry Division (Americal), 198th Light Infantry Brigade (2/1st Infantry), 3d Brigade/82d Airborne Division (1/505th Abn, 2/505th Abn, 1/508th Abn), 101st Airborne Division: 1st Bde (2/327th Abn, 2/17th Cav), 2d Bde (1/501st Inf, 2/501st Inf, 1/502d Inf); VNAF—1st ARVN Division; NVA/ VC—324–B NVA Division (90th, 803d and 812th NVA regiments), 4th NVA Regiment. *Events:* **10 April**—"Battle of Thon Phuoc Dien." Companies A,B,D–2/501st Infantry (101st Abn Div) encounter an estimated six battalions from the 812th NVA Regiment near the small village of Thon Phuoc Dien, 12 miles southeast of Quang Tri City. Seven Americans are KIA and 35 WIA in the firefight. Enemy losses are reported at 66 KIA. **28 April–4 May**—While conducting a Cordon and Search of the villages of Thon Duong Son and Phuoc Yen, several elements of the 101st Airborne Division clash with a strong enemy force four miles northwest of Hue. Involved in the action are B,D–2/501st Infantry, 1/502d Infantry, 2/1st Infantry, 2/17th Cavalry and the 2/327th Airborne versus the 8/90th NVA Regiment. Losses in the fight: U.S.—6 KIA, 43 WIA; NVA/VC—314 KIA, 107 POWs. **1 May**—The 2/17th Cavalry battles a reinforced company of NVA soldiers 13 miles northwest of Hue. Losses: U.S.—2 KIA, 26 WIA; NVA/VC—82 KIA. **5–6 May**—"Battle of La Chu." While conducting a Cordon and Search of La Chu, three miles northwest of Hue, companies A,D–1/501st Infantry, A,C–2/501st Infantry, 2/17th Cavalry and C–2/34th Armor engage an NVA force of unknown size. Losses: U.S.—1 KIA, 18 WIA; NVA/VC—55 KIA. *Casualties:* Totals for *Carentan I–II.* U.S.—193 KIA, 1190 WIA, 11 MIA; NVA/VC—1892 KIA, 69 POWs.

10 March: The *New York Times* breaks the story of General Westmoreland's appeal for 206,000 more troops. Antiwar sentiment in the United States intensifies. The American public has been told that we are winning the war, yet the enemy musters enough strength to launch the massive *TET Offensive* and Westmoreland is calling for reinforcements.

11 March–7 April: *Operation Wilderness. Locations:* III Corps; Binh Duong and Tay Ninh provinces; Dau Tieng; FSB St. Barbara. *Type/Objective:* Search and Destroy. *Wilderness* is a complementary operation to *Yellowstone* and is to provide security for the Tay Ninh Base Camp. *Units:* USA—25th Infantry Division: 1st Bde (4/9th Inf, 2/14th Inf, 4/23d Inf [M]), 3d Bde (2/12th Inf), 199th Light Infantry Brigade (3/7th Inf, 4/12th Inf). *Casualties:* Totals for *Wilderness.* U.S.—26 KIA, 155 WIA; NVA/VC—274 KIA, 4 POWs.

11 March–7 April: *Operation Quyet Thang (Resolve to Win). Locations:* III Corps; Binh Duong; Gia Dinh and Hau Nghia provinces; Capital Military District; Ho Bo Woods; Ben Cat; Chau Thanh; Cu Chi; Di An; Hoc Mon; Lai Thieu; Tan Binh. *Type/Objective:* Clearing operation. Post-*TET* sweep to secure the immediate Saigon area, and the mopping up of pockets of rebels. *Units:* USA—1st Infantry Division: 1st Bde (1/2d Inf, 1/26th Inf, 1/28th Inf), 2d Bde (2/16th Inf, 2/18th Inf), 3d Bde (2/2d Inf [M], 1/16th Inf [M], 2/28th Inf), 9th Infantry Division: 1st Bde (2/39th Inf, 2/47th Inf), 3d Bde (3/39th Inf, 4/39th Inf, 2/60th Inf, 5/60th Inf), 25th Infantry Division: 1st Bde (2/14th Inf, 4/23d Inf [M]), 2d Bde (1/5th Inf [M], 1/27th Inf, 2/27th Inf), 3d Bde (2/12th Inf, 1/14th Inf, 2/22d Inf [M]); VNAF— 5th and 25th ARVN divisions, VNMC; NVA/VC—273d Viet Cong Regiment, 7th Cu Chi Battalion. *Events:* **24 March**—2/14th Infantry (25th Inf Div) battles 400 members of the 7th Cu Chi Battalion (VC) near Sa Nho, eight miles northwest of Cu Chi. Sixty-six NVA/VC reported KIA, two captured. **25 March**—4/23d Infantry (M) and 2/34th Armor engage an enemy force of unknown size near Trang Bang, approximately eight miles northwest of Cu

Chi. A reported 111 of the enemy are KIA and two are captured. *Comment:* Involving some 50,000 Allied troops, including 22 U.S. combat battalions, *Quyet Thang* is the largest operation of the Vietnam War to date. *Casualties:* Totals for U.S. losses in *Quyet Thang* are incomplete. 1st Infantry Division— 29 KIA, 332 WIA; 25th Infantry Division—50 KIA, 396 WIA; 9th Infantry Division—not included in source document; NVA/VC—3387 KIA, 36 POWs.

13–26 March: *Operation Worth. Location:* I Corps; Quang Nam Province, operational area 15 miles southwest of DaNang. *Units:* USA—1st Cavalry Division (3/5th Cav); USMC—1/7th Marines, 2/7th Marines. *Casualties:* U.S.— 27 KIA, 89 WIA; NVA/VC—167 KIA.

16–22 March: *Operation Box Springs. Locations:* III Corps; Binh Duong Province; War Zone D; Phuoc Vinh. *Type/ Objective:* Combination of Search and Clear and Reconnaissance in Force in western War Zone D. *Units:* USA— 101st Airborne Division: 3d Bde (3/187th Inf). *Casualties:* U.S.—16 KIA, 62 WIA; NVA/VC—147 KIA.

17 March–30 July: *Operation Duong Cua Dan (People's Road). Locations:* IV Corps; Dinh Tuong and Kien Tuong provinces. *Objective:* To provide security for engineers at work on Route 4, one of the main routes between Saigon and the Delta. *Units:* USA—9th Infantry Division; VNAF—7th ARVN Division. *Comment: Duong Cua Dan* combined with *Truong Cong Dinh* 23 May. *Casualties:* Totals for *Duong Cua Dan.* U.S.—28 KIA, 205 WIA, 1 MIA; NVA/ VC—231 KIA. Totals for combined operations: U.S.—225 KIA, 1299 WIA, 1 MIA; NVA/VC—2477 KIA, 178 WIA.

21 March–7 April: *Operation Alcorn Cove. Locations:* III Corps; Bien Hoa, Hau Nghia and Long Khanh provinces; Gia Ray Rock Quarry; Blackhorse Base Camp. *Type/Objective:* Reconnaissance

March : 1968 71

in Force. *Alcorn Cove* is a continuation of security operations in the Long Binh–Bien Hoa complex area. *Units:* USA—11th Armored Cavalry Regiment (1st, 2d and 3d squadrons); VNAF—18th and 25th ARVN divisions; NVA/VC—267th, 269th and 274th Main Force battalions (VC). *Events:* 28 March—Troops L,M-3/11th ACR and ARVN elements battle the 1/272d Viet Cong in Hau Nghia Province. Losses: U.S.—2 KIA, 4 WIA; ARVN—2 WIA; NVA/VC—57 KIA. 11 April—I-3/11th ACR and 2/49th ARVN Regiment clash with an enemy force of unknown size east of Kiem Chong (Hau Nghia Province). Two Americans are KIA, four WIA. The enemy body count is 73. *Casualties:* Totals for *Alcorn Cove* not included in source documents.

25 March: Secretary of Defense Clark Clifford tells President Johnson that the war in Vietnam is a "real loser." In response, Johnson convenes a special panel to discuss his alternatives in the war. After two days of deliberation the panel advises against any further troop increases and recommends that the administration seek a negotiated peace. Johnson is reported as being extremely upset at the conclusions reached.

30 March 1968–31 January 1969: *Operation Cochise Green/Dan Sinh. Locations:* II Corps; Binh Dinh Province; Kron River; Soui Ca Valley; Vinh Thanh Mountains; Bong Son; Truong Lam; LZs Dog, English and Uplift. *Type:* Search and Destroy—Pacification. *Units:* USA—4th Infantry Division: 3d Bde (1/14th Inf, 1/35th Inf, 2/35th, 1/50th Inf [M]), 23d Infantry Division (Americal)—elements, 173d Airborne Brigade (1/503d Abn, 2/503d Abn); VNAF—22d ARVN Division (40th and 41st ARVN regiments); NVA/VC—3d NVA Division (2d, 18th and 22d NVA regiments). *Events:* 5 May—Company A-2/503d is ambushed by a platoon of enemy troops south of Gia An, approximately nine miles northeast

of Bong Son. Eight Sky Soldiers are WIA in the firefight. Thirteen NVA/VC bodies are found. **5 May**—Companies A,C-1/50th Infantry (M) and B-1/69th Armor engage an estimated two NVA battalions near My Duc, three miles south of Bong Son. Losses: U.S.—6 KIA, 50 WIA, 9 MIA; NVA/VC—100 KIA. **7 May**—The overnight position of companies B,C-1/50th Infantry (M) near the Dam Tra-O Lake, approximately 10 miles southeast of Bong Son, is rocketed killing seven and wounding 43 others. Enemy losses in the attack are reported at 18 KIA. **11 May**—B,C-1/50th Infantry (M) confronts an estimated NVA battalion near Loc Son, 13 miles southeast of Bong Son. Losses: U.S.—3 KIA, 33 WIA; NVA/VC—60 KIA. **22 September–6 October**—"Battle of Soui Ca Valley." Elements from the 41st ARVN Regiment and the 1/503d Airborne engage the 7 and 8/18th NVA Regiment in the Soui Ca Valley, approximately 20 miles south of Bong Son. A reported 197 NVA/VC are KIA. *Casualties:* Totals for *Cochise Green/Dan Sinh.* U.S.—114 KIA, 187 WIA (current as of 31 October 1968); NVA/VC—929 KIA, 25 POWs (total).

31 March: There are now 50 U.S. combat battalions operating in I Corps accounting for 170,000 troops—an increase of 30,000 in the last three months.

31 March: The 5/46th Infantry (The Professionals) of the 198th Light Infantry Brigade/23d Infantry Division (American) arrives in South Vietnam. The battalion is initially stationed at Chu Lai (I Corps; Quang Tin Province).

31 March: In the execution seen around the world, Chief of the South Vietnamese National Police, General Nguyen Ngoc Loan, shoots a VC suspect in the head at point-blank range. News cameras record the incident and the pictures become the most "famous" of the war.

31 March: President Johnson announces a unilateral halt of the bombing of North Vietnam. In his televised address, the President says only the area immediately north of the DMZ will continue to be bombed to try and insure the safety of American soldiers in I Corps. Johnson also announces his withdrawal from the 1968 Presidential election. The North Vietnamese use the period of decreased bombings to rebuild roads, bridges and other supply lines. Troop infiltrations into South Vietnam also dramatically increase.

1–15 April: *Operation Pegasus. Locations:* I Corps; Quang Tri Province; Ca Lu; Khe Sanh; LZs Cales, Snapper, Stud, Thor, Tom, Wharton. *Objective:* The relief of Khe Sanh Combat Base. *Units:* USA—1st Cavalry Division: 1st Bde (1/8th Cav, 2/8th Cav, 1/12th Cav), 2d Bde (1/5th Cav, 2/5th Cav, 5/7th Cav), 3d Bde (1/7th Cav, 2/7th Cav, 2/12th Cav); USMC—2/1st Marines, 2/3d Marines, 1/9th Marines, 1/26th Marines, 2/26th Marines, 3/26th Marines; VNAF—3d, 6th and 8th ARVN Airborne battalions; NVA/VC—66th NVA Regiment. *Events:* 4 April—The 1/9th Marines drives elements of the 66th NVA Regiment off Hill 471, two miles south of Khe Sanh. 5 April—Elements of the 26th Marines kill 122 of the enemy while repelling an NVA attempt to retake Hill 471. 6 April—The 1/5th Cavalry battles NVA elements holed up in the abandoned French fort about three miles south of the Khe Sanh Combat Base. 8 April—The Khe Sanh Combat Base is formally relieved by elements of the 1st Cav, ending the 77-day siege. 14 April—In the final battle of *Pegasus*, the 3/26th Marines clashes with an enemy force between Hills 881 North and 881 South. Losses: U.S.—6 KIA; NVA/VC—106 KIA. *Comment:* By 27 June, the evacuation of Khe Sanh has begun . . . by 5 July the base has been deactivated and torn down. *Casualties:* Totals for *Pegasus.* U.S.—92 KIA, 667 WIA, 5 MIA;

VNAF—33 KIA, 187 WIA; NVA/VC—1044 KIA, 9 POWs.

6–9 April: *Operation Weatherford. Location:* III Corps; Binh Long Province; Chon Thanh. *Type:* Reconnaissance in Force. *Units:* USA—1st Infantry Division: 1st Bde (1/26th Inf), 3d Bde (1/16th Inf [M]); NVA/VC—7th NVA Division (165th NVA Regiment) reported in area of operations. *Casualties:* U.S.—3 WIA; NVA/VC—7 KIA.

7 April: The 5/12th Infantry of the 199th Light Infantry Brigade arrives in South Vietnam. The battalion is stationed at Gao Hi Nai (III Corps).

8 April–31 May: *Operation Toan Thang (Complete Victory). Locations:* III Corps; Bien Hoa, Binh Duong, Hau Nghia, Long An and Long Khanh provinces; War Zone C; Capital Military District; Michelin Plantation; Bien Hoa; Cu Chi; Dau Tieng; Di An; Long Binh; Phu Loi; Saigon; FSBs Maury and Pike IV. *Type/Objective:* Search and Clear. *Toan Thang* is the first of a series of massive operations combining the assets and operations of ARVN's III Corps and the Americans' II Field Force. The purpose of *Toan Thang* is to maintain the post–*TET* pressure on the enemy and drive all remaining NVA/VC troops from III Corps and the Saigon area. *Units:* USA—1st Infantry Division: 1st Bde (1/2d Inf, 1/26th Inf, 1/28th Inf), 2d Bde (2/16th Inf, 2/18th Inf), 3d Bde (2/2d Inf [M], 1/16th Inf [M], 2/28th Inf), 9th Infantry Division: 1st Bde (2/39th Inf, 2/47th Inf, 2/60th Inf), 2d Bde (3/47th Inf, 4/47th Inf, 3/60th Inf), 3d Bde (6/31st Inf, 3/39th Inf, 4/39th Inf, 5/60th Inf [M]), 25th Infantry Division: 1st Bde (4/9th Inf, 2/14th Inf, 4/23d Inf [M]), 2d Bde (1/5th Inf [M], 1/27th Inf, 2/27th Inf), 3d Bde (2/12th Inf, 1/14th Inf, 2/22d Inf, 2/34th Armor), 101st Airborne Division: 3d Bde (3/187th Inf, 1/506th Inf, 2/506th Inf), 199th Light Infantry Brigade (2/3d Inf, 3/7th Inf, 4/12th Inf, 5/12th Inf),

11th Armored Cavalry Regiment (1st, 2d and 3d squadrons). *Note:* A total of 42 U.S. combat battalions participate at one time or another in *Toan Thang.* VNAF—Elements from the 5th, 7th, 9th, 18th and 25th ARVN divisions. A total of 37 ARVN combat battalions participate in *Toan Thang;* NVA/VC— 7th NVA Division (141st and 165th NVA rgts), 9th NVA Division (273d VC Rgt), 5th Viet Cong Division (274th and 275th VC rgts). *Events:* 11 April—The 3/22d Infantry and 2/22d Infantry (M) (25th Inf Div) engage a multibattalion enemy force 13 miles north of Dau Tieng. Sixteen Americans are KIA and 47 WIA in the firefight. The enemy loses a reported 155 KIA. 13 April— While conducting a Reconnaissance in Force 10 miles northwest of Dau Tieng, 2/22d Infantry (M) (25th Inf Div) battle an enemy force of unknown size. Losses: U.S.—6 KIA, 46 WIA; NVA/ VC—36 KIA. 3–4 May—Companies D,B–1/18th Infantry (1st Inf Div), battle elements of the 5th VC Division north of Di An. The U.S. forces kill 260 and capture five of the enemy. 5–6 May— "Battle of Xom Moi." B–1/4th Cavalry and B–1/18th Infantry (1st Inf Div) engage the 165th NVA Regiment near Xom Moi, 1.6 miles south of Phu Loi. Losses in the battle: U.S.—5 KIA, 21 WIA; NVA/VC—440 KIA. 7 May— Elements of the 25th Infantry Division trap an estimated 400–500 enemy troops in a large swampy area five miles south of Cu Chi. The 25th Infantry reports 285 enemy KIAs. 9 May—The 4/23d Infantry (M) (25th Inf Div) and I–3/11th ACR clash with a force of unknown size near FSB Maury, four miles north of Cu Chi. Losses: U.S.—9 KIA, 68 WIA; NVA/VC—14 KIA, 1 POW. 12 May—Ninety-eight VC are KIA when a battalion from the 272d Viet Cong Regiment attacks FSB Pike IV, just west of Saigon. Defending the base are the 25th Infantry Division's 4/9th Infantry, 1/8th Artillery, 3/13th Artillery and 6/77th Artillery. 13 May—Enemy sappers attack a communications sta-

tion atop Nui Ba Den Mountain (Tay Ninh Province). Nineteen Americans are KIA in the attack. Twenty-five of the enemy are reported KIA. *Casualties:* Totals for *Toan Thang* are incomplete. Total U.S. losses are not included in source documents: Partial figures: 1st Infantry Division: Total— 118 KIA, 682 WIA; 9th Infantry Division: Total—90 KIA, 528 WIA, 1 MIA; 25th Infantry Division (as of 30 April): 87 KIA, 534 WIA; U.S.—295+ KIA, 1744+ WIA; NVA/VC—3542 KIA (reported).

8 April: The 6/31st Infantry (Polar Bears–Bearcats) of the 9th Infantry Division arrives in South Vietnam. The battalion is stationed at Binh Chanh (III Corps; Long An Province).

8 April–11 November: *Operation Burlington Trail. Locations:* I Corps; Quang Tin Province; "Hawk Hill"; Tam Ky; Tien Phuoc; LZs Pleasantville, Professional and Young. *Objective:* As a companion operation to *Wheeler/ Wallowa, Burlington Trail* is a sweep of the Quang Nam/Quang Tin border area. *Units:* USA—23d Infantry Division (Americal): 11th Light Infantry Brigade (1/20th Inf), 196th Light Infantry Brigade (2/1st Inf), 198th Light Infantry Brigade (1/6th Inf, 1/46th Inf, 1/1st Cav); VNAF—2d ARVN Division (6th ARVN Regiment); NVA/VC—2d NVA Division. *Casualties:* U.S.—129 KIA, 965 WIA; NVA/VC—1931 KIA.

9–19 April: *Operation Norfolk Victory. Locations:* I Corps; Quang Ngai Province; Song Ve Valley; Base Area 121; Nghia Hanh; Tu Nghia. *Objective:* Prevention of enemy massing for an attack on Quang Ngai City and to neutralize Base Area 121. *Units:* USA—23d Infantry Division (Americal): 11th Light Infantry Brigade (3/1st Inf, 4/3d Inf, 1/20th Inf); VNAF—4/4th ARVN Regiment, 1/4th ARVN Cavalry. *Casualties:* U.S.—6 KIA, 33 WIA; NVA/VC—45 KIA, 2 POWs.

14 April: The 4/21st Infantry (Gimlet) arrives in South Vietnam. The 4/21st is part of the 11th Light Infantry Brigade/ 23d Infantry Division (Americal). The battalion is stationed at Duc Pho (I Corps; Quang Ngai Province).

15 April 1968–28 February 1969: *Operation Scotland II. Locations:* I Corps; Quang Tri Province; Ca Lu; Daido; Dong Ha; Khe Sanh. *Type/Objective:* Search and Destroy. *Scotland II* is a continuation of *Scotland I* and is also a follow-up to the recently terminated *Pegasus. Units:* USA—1st Cavalry Division: 3d Bde (elements); USMC— 1/1st Marines, 2/1st Marines, 1/3d Marines, 2/4th Marines, 3/4th Marines; VNAF—2d ARVN Regiment; NVA/ VC—304th and 320th NVA divisions. *Event:* 29 April–4 May—"Battle of Dong Ha." The battle develops as an estimated 8000 troops of the 320th NVA Division attempt to take the 3d Marine Division's headquarters at Dong Ha. The defenders consist of Task Force Robbie: 2/4th Marines and 1/3d Marines assisted by the 2d ARVN Regiment. The heaviest fighting occurs near the village of Daido, 1.5 miles northeast of Dong Ha. American losses in the battle: 68 KIA, 323 WIA. *Casualties:* Totals for *Scotland II.* U.S.—435 KIA, 2395 WIA; NVA/VC—3304 KIA, 64 POWs.

19 April–17 May: *Operation Delaware/Lam Son–216. Locations:* I Corps; Quang Tri and Thua Thien provinces; Ashau Valley; Pac Nhe Valley; Rao Loa River; "Punchbowl"; A Loui; Ta Bat; FSB Bastogne; LZs Cecile, Pepper, Stallion, Tiger and Vicky. *Type/Objective:* Reconnaissance in Force. *Delaware* is an airmobile raid into the enemy stronghold of the Ashau Valley. The goal is to exploit the enemy defeat in *Pegasus* and take advantage of enemy troops massed in the area. A secondary purpose of *Delaware* is to prevent another attack on Hue. *Units:* USA—1st Cavalry Division: 1st Bde

(1/8th Cav, 2/8th Cav, 1/12th Cav), 2d Bde (1/5th Cav, 5/7th Cav, 1/9th Cav), 3d Bde (1/7th Cav, 2/7th Cav), 23d Infantry Division (Americal), 196th Light Infantry Brigade (2/1st Inf, 3/21st Inf, 4/31st Inf), 101st Airborne Division: 1st Bde (1/327th Abn, 2/327th Abn, 2/502d Abn); VNAF—1st ARVN Division (3d ARVN Regiment, 6th ARVN Airborne Battalion). *Casualties:* Totals for *Delaware/Lam Son–216.* U.S.—142 KIA, 731 WIA, 47 MIA; NVA/VC—869 KIA.

May: The monsoon (rainy) season begins in the southern provinces and ends in the north.

1 May–17 December: *Operation Kudzu. Locations:* IV Corps; Dinh Tuong Province; Dong Tam. *Objective:* Providing security for the Dong Tam area. *Units:* USA—9th Infantry Division–Task Force Funston: 2d Bde (3/47th Inf, 4/47th Inf, 3/60th Inf); NVA/VC—1st Viet Cong Regiment (261-A, 261-B and 267-B battalions). *Casualties:* U.S.—28 KIA, 336 WIA; NVA/VC—187 KIA, 41 POWs.

3 May: The United States and North Vietnam announce plans to begin formal peace talks. The negotiations are tentatively scheduled to begin on or near 10 May in Paris.

4 May–24 August: *Operation Allen Brook. Locations:* I Corps; Quang Nam Province; Ky Lam River; Go Noi Island; "Dodge City"; An Hoa; Cu Ban; Le Bac; Thu Bon. *Type:* Search and Destroy. *Units:* USMC—1/7th Marines, 2/7th Marines, 1/26th Marines, 1/27th Marines; NVA/VC—308th NVA Division (36th and 38th NVA rgts). *Casualties:* U.S.—172 KIA, 1124 WIA; NVA/VC— 1917 KIA.

5 May: The second *TET Offensive*, or *Mini TET*, begins throughout the country. Although not as fierce or widespread as the 31 January attack, 152 Americans die in just eight days of fighting.

9–17 May: *Operation Concordia Square. Location:* I Corps; Quang Tri Province. *Units:* USA—1st Cavalry Division (elements). *Casualties:* U.S.— 28 KIA, 116 WIA; NVA/VC—349 KIA.

10–12 May: *Operation Golden Valley. Location:* I Corps; Quang Tin Province; Kham Duc. *Objective:* Evacuation of approximately 1400 personnel from the Kham Duc Special Forces Camp, 60 miles west of Chu Lai. *Units:* USA— 23d Infantry Division (Americal): 196th Light Infantry Brigade (2/1st Inf), 198th Light Infantry Brigade (A–1/46th Inf); NVA/VC—2d NVA Division (elements). *Event:* **12 May**—"Battle of Kham Duc." Elements from the 2d NVA Division attack the U.S. Special Forces Camp at Kham Duc. The defenders, 2/1st Infantry, A–1/46th Infantry, kill more than 300 NVA. At least 20 Americans are KIA. Also during the attack, an evacuation plane carrying 150 civilians is hit and shot down by enemy fire killing all aboard. *Casualties:* Totals for *Golden Valley.* U.S.—20+ KIA, 116 WIA, 21 MIA; NVA/VC—345 KIA.

13 May: The Paris peace talks begin at the Majestic Hotel, site of the Viet Minh/French negotiations. The talks turn out to be part of the overall North Vietnamese strategy—the talk/fight element of revolutionary warfare. Give your opponent hope, but continue to fight and ultimately dishearten the enemy.

17 May–3 November: *Operation Jeb Stuart III. Locations:* I Corps; Quang Tri and Thua Thien provinces; Ba Long Valley; Base Areas 101 and 114; Binh An; LZs Anne, Betty, Hardcore and Sharon. *Type:* Search and Destroy–Cordon and Search. This operation is a continuation of the *Jeb Stuart* series of rice denial and cordons missions. *Units:* USA—1st Cavalry Division: 1st Bde (1/8th Cav, 3/5th Cav), 2d Bde (1/5th Cav, 2/5th Cav, 1/9th Cav); VNAF—1st and 3d ARVN regiments; NVA/VC—814th

NVA Battalion. *Event:* **27–30 June**— "Battle of Binh An." 3/5th Cavalry traps the 814th NVA Battalion in the village of Binh An, eight miles east of Quang Tri City. During the fight the 3/5th Cavalry is joined by D–1/9th Cavalry, D–1/5th Cavalry and C–2/5th Cavalry. Losses: U.S.—3 KIA; NVA/VC—233 KIA, 44 POWs. *Casualties:* Totals for *Jeb Stuart III.* U.S.—212 KIA, 1512 WIA; NVA/VC—2016 KIA, 251 POWs.

17 May 1968–28 February 1969: *Operation Nevada Eagle. Locations:* I Corps; Thua Thien Province; Ashau Valley; Dong Gi Tay; Le Xa Dong; Trung Phuong; Vinh Phu. *Type/Objective:* Reconnaissance in Force–Cordon and Search aimed at supporting government pacification and rice denial programs. *Units:* USA—3d Brigade/82d Airborne Division (1/505th Abn, 2/505th Abn, 1/508th Abn), 101st Airborne Division: 1st Bde (1/327th Abn, 2/327th Abn, 2/502d Abn), 2d Bde (1/501st Inf, 2/501st Inf, 1/502d Inf), 3d Bde (1/506th Inf, 2/506th Inf, 3/187th Inf); VNAF— 1st ARVN Division. *Events:* **19 May**— A–2/327th Airborne engages in a day-long firefight with an estimated NVA company 15 miles southwest of Hue. Casualties: U.S.—6 KIA, 19 WIA; NVA/ VC—24 KIA. **20–21 May**—Companies B–1/501st Infantry, C–2/501st Infantry and D–1/502d Infantry clash with an NVA company while conducting a Cordon and Search of Dong Gi Tay, five miles east of Hue. Twelve Screaming Eagles are wounded. Enemy losses are reported at 62 KIA. **21 May**—Thirteen U.S. soldiers are KIA and 53 WIA when NVA elements launch a ground and mortar attack on a 101st Airborne Division base camp five miles southeast of Hue. The defenders report killing 54 of the enemy and capturing two prisoners. **30–31 May**—2/17th Cavalry, C,B–1/ 501st Infantry and 3/3d ARVN Regiment conduct a Cordon and Search of Le Xa Dong, seven miles east of Hue. Losses: U.S.—6 WIA; NVA/VC—142 KIA, 46 POWs. **1–4 June**—"Trung

Phuong–Vinh Phu Cordon." Companies B–2/501st Infantry, B–1/501st Infantry and troops A,B–2/17th Cavalry and 1st ARVN Division elements conduct a Cordon and Search 10 miles east of Hue. Losses: U.S.—5 KIA, 36 WIA; NVA/VC—104 KIA, 56 POWs. *Casualties:* Totals for *Nevada Eagle.* U.S.—175 KIA, 1161 WIA; NVA/VC—3299 KIA, 853 POWs.

18 May–23 October: *Operation Mameluke Thrust. Locations:* I Corps; Quang Nam Province; "Happy Valley"; An Hoa; Thu Bon; Vu Gia. *Objective: Mameluke Thrust* is a companion operation to *Allen Brook. Units:* USMC— 2/5th Marines, 3/5th Marines, 2/7th Marines, 1st Marine Recon Battalion; NVA/VC—308th NVA Division (31st NVA Regiment). *Casualties:* U.S.—267 KIA, 1730 WIA; NVA/VC—2728 KIA.

25 May–4 June: Enemy forces launch their last major offensive of the year (*TET III*). More than 700 U.S. soldiers and Marines are KIA in various firefights, attacks and ambushes.

28 May–19 June: *Operation Robin North/Robin South. Locations:* I Corps; Quang Tri Province; FSBs Loon and Robin Torch. *Type/Objective:* Search and Destroy. In *Robin North/Robin South* the Marines use airmobile tactics to prevent an attack on Khe Sanh and northern Quang Tri Province. *Units:* USMC—Task Force Hotel: 1/1st Marines, 2/3d Marines, 1/4th Marines, 2/4th Marines, 3/4th Marines, 3/9th Marines; NVA/VC—308th NVA Division (88th and 102d NVA regiments). *Casualties:* NVA/VC—725 KIA (U.S. losses not included in source material).

1 June 1968–16 February 1969: *Operation Toan Thang II. Locations:* III Corps; Bien Hoa, Binh Duong, Binh Long, Hau Nghia, Long An, Long Khanh and Tay Ninh provinces; War Zone C; Capital Military District; "The Catcher's Mitt"; "The Fish Hook"; "The

Trapezoid"; Loc Ninh; Nha Be; FSBs Cantigny, Crockett, Julie, Junction City, Mahone, Mole City, Pershing and Reed. *Type/Objective:* Clearing operation. *Toan Thang II* is a continuation of post–*TET Offensive* operations throughout III Corps to maintain pressure on the communists. *Units:* USA—1st Cavalry Division: 2d Bde (2/7th Cav, 5/7th Cav), 1st Infantry Division: 1st Bde (1/2d Inf, 1/26th Inf, 1/28th Inf), 2d Bde (2/16th Inf, 1/18th Inf, 2/18th Inf), 3d Bde (2/2d Inf [M], 1/16th Inf [M], 2/18th Inf), 9th Infantry Division: 1st Bde (2/39th Inf, 2/60th Inf), 2d Bde (2/47th Inf, 3/47th Inf, 4/47th Inf, 3/60th Inf), 3d Bde (3/39th Inf, 4/39th Inf, 5/60th Inf [M]), 25th Infantry Division: 1st Bde (4/9th Inf, 2/14th Inf, 4/23d Inf [M]), 2d Bde (1/5th Inf [M], 1/27th Inf, 2/27th Inf), 3d Bde (2/12th Inf, 1/14th Inf, 2/22d Inf [M], 3/22d Inf), 3d Brigade/82d Airborne Division (1/505th Abn, 2/505th Abn), 101st Airborne Division (elements), 11th Armored Cavalry Regiment (elements), 199th Light Infantry Brigade (2/3d Inf, 3/7th Inf, 4/12th Inf, 5/12th Inf); VNAF—5th, 7th, 9th, 18th and 25th ARVN divisions (a total of 37 VNAF battalions participate in *Toan Thang II*); NVA/VC—7th NVA Division (32d, 33d, 101st, 141st and 165th NVA regiments), 5th Viet Cong Division (Dong Regiment). *Events:* **4 July**—A base camp for the U.S. 25th Infantry Division's 3/22d Infantry at Dau Tieng (Binh Duong Province) is attacked by an enemy force of unknown size. Five Americans are KIA and 55 WIA. The enemy body count is 16. **8 August**—Soldiers of the U.S. 9th Infantry Division and ARVN troops accidentally open fire on each other at the village of Cai Rang (near My Tho, IV Corps; Ding Tuong Province). Seventy-two villagers are KIA and 204 are WIA in the cross fire. **11 August**—The 2/16th Infantry (1st Inf Div) clashes with elements of the Viet Cong's Dong Nai Regiment southeast of Lai Khe (Binh Duong Province). Losses: U.S.—6 KIA, 18 WIA; NVA/VC—6 KIA. **12 August**—

One hundred and four VC are KIA as the 2/39th Infantry (9th Inf Div) engages an enemy battalion approximately 20 miles south of Saigon at Can Duoc (III Corps; Long An Province). **19 August** — Troops F,G,H–2/11th ACR battle the 165th NVA Regiment in the Quan Loi–An Loc area of Binh Long Province. Losses: U.S. – 4 KIA, 24 WIA; NVA/VC – 18 KIA, 20 POWs. **19 August** — An estimated enemy force of division size attacks U.S. 25th Infantry Division positions near Tay Ninh City. Twenty Americans are KIA and 86 WIA in the assault. **21–23 August** — While conducting a Reconnaissance in Force near Loc Ninh (III Corps; Binh Long Province), 2/11th ACR and 1/2d Infantry (1st Inf Div) confront units from the 141st NVA Regiment. Losses: U.S. – 8 KIA, 55 WIA; NVA/VC – 85 KIA, 1 POW. **4–6 September** — Elements from the 9th Infantry Division: 2/39th Infantry, 2/60th Infantry and 5/60th Infantry (M), fight a two-day battle against an estimated VC battalion near Can Giouc (III Corps; Long An Province), 11 miles south of Saigon. Enemy losses are reported at 131 KIA and 12 POWs. **26 October** — Communist forces launch a large mortar and ground attack on FSB Julie, eight miles west of An Loc (III Corps; Binh Long Province). Julie is defended by 400 men of the 1st Infantry Division's 1/2d Infantry. Losses in the attack: U.S. – 8 KIA, 33 WIA; NVA/VC – 80 KIA. **1 November** — The 2/28th Infantry (1st Inf Div) and B–1/4th Cavalry (1st Inf Div) are pounded by mortars, rockets and a ground attack at FSB Rita, 13 miles southwest of An Loc, near the Tay Ninh–Binh Long border. Losses: U.S. – 12 KIA, 54 WIA; NVA/VC – 27 KIA. **8 November** — A–2/22d Infantry (M) engages an enemy force of unknown size in the Bao Don area of the Boi Loi Forest (Tay Ninh Province). Losses: U.S. – 4 KIA, 4 WIA; NVA/VC – 15 KIA. **20 November** — FSB Cantigny, approximately 20 miles north of Saigon, is attacked by an estimated VC company. The defenders, 2/28th Infantry (1st Inf Div), kill 13 of the enemy, losing four KIA and 16 WIA. **23 November** — C–4/9th Infantry (25th Inf Div) battles an enemy force of unknown size in the Boi Loi Forest, near Truong Mit (Tay Ninh Province) 17 miles northwest of Trang Bang. Losses: U.S. – 15 KIA, 20 WIA; NVA/VC – 6 KIA. **27 November** — Companies A–2/22d Infantry (M) and A,B–4/9th Infantry (25th Inf Div) battle a VC battalion near the Cau Khoi Rubber Plantation, three miles southeast of Tay Ninh City (Tay Ninh Province). Losses: U.S. – 18 KIA, 36 WIA; NVA/VC – 7 KIA (confirmed). **30 November** — Six Americans are KIA and six WIA as A–1/27th Infantry (25th Inf Div) battles an enemy unit of unknown size near Thanh An (III Corps; Binh Duong Province). **1 December** — 2/28th Infantry (1st Inf Div) engages elements of the 2d Local Force Battalion (VC) and the 273d VC Regiment near FSB Junction City, approximately seven miles south of Lai Khe (III Corps; Binh Duong Province). Losses: U.S. – 1 KIA, 36 WIA; NVA/VC – 44 KIA. **3 December** — "Battle of LZ Eleanor." The 116 men of company D–2/7th Cavalry (1st Cav Div) are ambushed by an estimated 400 NVA regulars at LZ Eleanor, 17 miles northwest of Phuoc Vinh (III Corps; Binh Long Province). Twenty-four cavalrymen are KIA and 51 WIA in the five-hour firefight. **18 December** — FSB Pershing (III Corps; Hau Nghia Province) is mortared, wounding 21 men of the 2/12th Infantry (25th Inf Div). **22 December** — "Battle of FSB Mole City." Companies B,C–4/9th Infantry (25th Inf Div) repel a determined assault on the fire base by the 272d Viet Cong Regiment, nine miles south of Tay Ninh City (III Corps; Tay Ninh Province). Losses for the attack: U.S. – 17 KIA, 34 WIA; NVA/VC – 103 KIA. **14 January 1969** — Companies A,B–2/22d Infantry (M) (25th Inf Div) clash with an enemy force of unknown size near the Cau Khoi Rubber Plantation, 3 miles southeast of Tay Ninh City

(III Corps; Tay Ninh Province). Losses—U.S.—6 KIA, 9 WIA; NVA/VC—122 KIA. *Casualties:* Totals for *Toan Thang II* are incomplete, partial figures. 1st Cavalry Division—279 KIA, 1711 WIA; 1st Infantry Division—394 KIA, 2800 WIA; 9th Infantry Division—216 KIA, 1308 WIA; Totals—889 KIA, 5819 WIA. Figures for 25th Infantry and 101st Airborne divisions, 3d Bde/82d Airborne Division, 199th Light Infantry Brigade and 11th Armored Cavalry Regiment not included in source documents. NVA/VC losses also reflect only those losses inflicted by the 1st Cavalry, 1st Infantry, 9th Infantry divisions: 8617 KIA, 490 WIA.

7–14 June: *Operation Swift Saber. Location:* I Corps; Quang Nam Province. *Objective:* Operation into area 10 miles northwest of DaNang. *Units:* USMC—BLT 3/1st Marines. *Casualties:* U.S.—3 KIA; NVA/VC—1 KIA.

10 June: COMUSMACV General William C. Westmoreland turns over his command to General Creighton Abrams. Westmoreland is promoted to Army Chief of Staff. Abrams is basically told not to try to win the war, but rather to hold onto what territory they presently hold, keep casualties to a minimum and prepare for the gradual withdrawal of U.S. forces and the turning of the war to the Vietnamese ... "Vietnamization."

19–29 June: *Operation Chattachoochee Swamp. Locations:* I Corps; Quang Ngai Province; Base Area 121; Duc Pho; Ha Thanh. *Type/Objective:* Search and Destroy aimed at neutralizing enemy units in the vicinity of Base Area 121. *Units:* USA—23d Infantry Division (Americal), 11th Light Infantry Brigade (3/1st Inf); VNAF—2d ARVN Division (1/4th ARVN, 2/4th ARVN, 4/4th ARVN regiments); NVA/VC—81st Local Force Battalion (VC). *Casualties:* U.S.—2 KIA, 18 WIA; NVA/VC—23 KIA.

20 June–3 July: *Operation Vance Canyon. Locations:* I Corps; Quang Ngai Province; Base Areas 114 and 120; Chu Lai; Tra Bong; LZ Gator. *Type/Objective:* Search and Destroy into enemy Base Areas 114 and 120. *Units:* USA—23d Infantry Division (Americal): 198th Light Infantry Brigade (1/52d Inf, 5/46th Inf). *Casualties:* U.S.—5 KIA, 14 WIA; NVA/VC—6 KIA.

27 June: The Khe Sanh Combat Base is razed and abandoned.

6 July–4 August: *Operation Pocahontas Forest. Locations:* I Corps; Quang Nam Province; Phuoc Chau Valley ("Antenna Valley"); Ap Bon; Ap Hai; Hiep Duc; LZ West. *Type:* Search and Destroy. *Units:* USA—23d Infantry Division (Americal): 11th Light Infantry Brigade (4/3d Inf, 4/21st Inf), 196th Light Infantry Brigade (4/31st Inf); VNAF—2/5th ARVN, 3/5th ARVN, 4/5th ARVN); NVA/VC—2d NVA Division–elements, 1st Main Force Regiment (VC). *Casualties:* U.S.—4 KIA, 58 WIA; VNAF—2 KIA, 6 WIA; NVA/VC—96 KIA.

9–16 July: *Operation Eager Yankee. Location:* I Corps; Thua Thien Province. *Units:* USMC—BLT 2/7th Marines. *Casualties:* U.S.—8 KIA, 50 WIA; NVA/VC—9 KIA.

23–24 July: *Operation Swift Play. Location:* I Corps; Quang Nam Province. *Units:* USMC—BLT 2/7th Marines. *Casualties:* None reported.

24 July: Task Force South is organized in South Vietnam. The force is comprised of various assets: 3/503d Abn (173d Airborne Brigade) and 3/506th Infantry (101st Airborne Division) in addition to support, aviation and artillery units. Task Force South is stationed at Dalat (II Corps; Tuyen Duc Province) and Phan Thiet (II Corps; Binh Thuan Province).

25 July: The 1st Brigade/5th Infantry Division (M) officially arrives in South Vietnam. The brigade is stationed at Quang Tri (I Corps; Quang Tri Province).

27 July: The 1/61st Infantry (M) of the 1st Brigade/5th Infantry Division (M) arrives in South Vietnam. The battalion is stationed at Cam Lo (I Corps; Quang Tri Province).

28 July: The 1/11th Infantry of the 1st Brigade/5th Infantry Division (M) arrives in South Vietnam. The battalion is stationed at Cam Lo (I Corps; Quang Tri Province).

4–20 August: *Operation Somerset Plain/Lam Son-246. Locations:* I Corps; Thua Thien Province; Ashau Valley; A Loui; Ta Bat; FSBs Bastogne, Berchtesgaden, Birmingham, Eagle's Nest, Georgia, Son and Veghel. *Type/Objective:* Search and Destroy effort aimed at eliminating NVA troops trying to re-enter the Ashau Valley after *Delaware. Units:* USA — Task Force 1: 1st Cavalry Division (B-1/9th Cav), 3d Brigade/82d Airborne Division (C-1/505th Abn), 101st Airborne Division: 1st Bde (1/327th Abn, 2/327th Abn), 2d Bde (D-1/501st Inf, C-1/502d Inf, D-1/502d Inf); VNAF — 1st ARVN Division (2/1st ARVN, 3/1st ARVN); NVA/VC — Two NVA regiments reported in area of operations. *Event:* **10 August** — A USAF F-100 Super Sabre accidentally strafes troops of the 101st Airborne near FSB Bastogne. Seven Americans are KIA and 54 WIA in the mistaken attack. *Casualties:* Totals for *Somerset Plain/Lam Son-246.* U.S. — 19 KIA, 104 WIA, 2 MIA; VNAF — 15 KIA, 57 WIA, 2 MIA; NVA/VC — 171 KIA, 4 POWs.

4 August 1968–31 December 1969: *Operation Quyet Chien. Location:* IV Corps; Kien Giang Province; U Minh Forest. *Type:* Search and Destroy. *Units:* USA — 9th Infantry Division: 1st Bde (6/31st Inf), Mobile Riverine Force — 2d Brigade (3/47th Inf, 4/47th Inf), 3d Bde (5/60th [M]); VNAF — 5/VNMC. *Comment: Quyet Chien* became a part of *Speedy Express* on 1 December. *Casualties:* U.S. — 131 KIA, 997 WIA; NVA/VC — 2248 KIA, 191 POWs.

8–9 August: *Operation An Truyen. Locations:* I Corps; Thua Thien Province; An Truyen; Ap Trieu Son; Hue. *Type:* Cordon and Search. *Units:* USA — 101st Airborne Division: 2d Bde (A,B,C-1/501st Inf); VNAF — Various elements of National Police Field Force, Regional and Popular Force troops. *Casualties:* U.S. — 0; NVA/VC — 43 KIA, 23 POWs.

17 August: The United States Department of Defense reports that since February 1965, American aircraft have flown 117,000 missions over North Vietnam. Total ordnance delivered on North Vietnamese targets is said to be 2,581,876 tons. The infiltration continues.

18 August: *Location:* I Corps; Quang Tin Province; Song Chang Valley ("AK Valley"). *Action:* American troops are ambushed while trying to retrieve bodies from previous day's ambush. *Units:* USA — 23d Infantry Division (American): 196th Light Infantry Brigade (B,D-4/31st Inf); NVA/VC — 2d NVA Division (elements). *Casualties:* U.S. — 15 KIA, 41 WIA.

18–21 August: *Operation Proud Hunter. Location:* I Corps; Quang Tri Province; Cua Viet River. *Unit:* USMC — BLT 2/26th Marines. *Casualties:* None reported.

20 August: *Location:* I Corps; Quang Tin Province; Song Chang Valley ("AK Valley"). *Action:* NVA ambush. *Unit:* USA — 23d Infantry Division (Americal): 196th Light Infantry Brigade (B-3/21st Inf). *Casualties:* U.S. — 5 KIA, 24 WIA.

22 August: *Location:* I Corps; Quang Tin Province; Song Chang Valley ("AK Valley"). *Action:* NVA ambush. *Units:* USA—23d Infantry Division (Americal): 196th Light Infantry Brigade (C–2/1st Inf, A–4/31st Inf). *Casualties:* U.S.—4 KIA, 4 WIA.

23 August–19 September: *Operation Swift Pursuit. Location:* I Corps; Quang Tri Province. *Units:* USMC—BLT 2/26th Marines. *Casualties:* None reported.

26 August: *Location:* I Corps; Quang Nam Province; Que Son Valley ("Death Valley"). *Action:* NVA ambush. *Unit:* USA—23d Infantry Division (Americal): 196th Light Infantry Brigade (C–4/31st Inf).

September: The 27th Marines (of the 5th Marine Division, attached to the 1st Marine Division) leaves South Vietnam.

September: *Operation Homestead. Location:* IV Corps; Kien Hoa Province. *Type:* Search and Destroy. *Units:* USA—Mobile Riverine Force–9th Infantry Division: 2d Bde (3/47th Inf, 4/47th Inf, 3/60th Inf). *Casualties:* Not included in source for the individual operation.

4–24 September: *Operation Champagne Grove. Locations:* I Corps; Quang Ngai Province; Song Re Valley; Base Area 121; Ha Thanh; LZs Bronco, Dottie and Gator. *Type:* Search and Destroy. *Units:* USA—23d Infantry Division (Americal): 11th Light Infantry Brigade (3/1st Inf, 4/3d Inf, 1/20th Inf, 4/21st Inf, 1/1st Cav), 198th Light Infantry Brigade (1/46th Inf); VNAF—2d ARVN Division (elements); NVA/VC—3d NVA Division, 2d Main Force Regiment (VC). *Event:* **13 September**—Companies A–4/3d Infantry, B–1/46th Infantry and A,B–1/1st Cavalry battle a force of unknown size from the 2d Main Force Regiment three miles northwest of Quang Ngai City. Sixty-one of the

enemy are reported KIA. *Casualties:* Totals for *Champagne Grove.* U.S.—43 KIA, 172 WIA; NVA/VC—378 KIA.

10–20 September: *Operation Vinh Loc. Locations:* I Corps; Thua Thien Province; Vinh Loc Island; Co Col Beach. *Type/Objective:* Cordon and Search. **Vinh Loc** is a "soft cordon" of Vinh Loc Island, 15 miles east of Hue. *Units:* USA—101st Airborne Division: 2d Bde (1/501st Inf); VNAF—54th ARVN Regiment, 7th ARVN Cavalry. *Comment:* Captured Viet Cong tell their interrogators that more than 80 percent of the communist infrastructure on Vinh Loc Island was wiped out during the operation. *Casualties:* Totals for **Vinh Loc.** U.S.—2 KIA, 9 WIA; NVA/VC—154 KIA, 126 POWs.

11 September–7 November: *Operation Comanche Falls. Location:* I Corps; Quang Tri Province. *Units:* USA—1st Cavalry Division. *Casualties:* U.S.—22 KIA, 50 KIA; NVA/VC—107 KIA.

13 September–1 October: *Location:* I Corps; Quang Tri Province; DMZ; Ben Hai River. *Action:* U.S. forces launch a preemptive strike into the DMZ. *Units:* USA—1st Brigade/5th Infantry Division (1/11th Inf, 1/61st Inf [M]); USMC—elements; VNAF—2/2d ARVN Regiment; NVA/VC—320th NVA Division. *Casualties:* U.S.—65 KIA, 77 WIA.

16 September: *Operation Golden Sword. Location:* III Corps. *Units:* USA—3d Brigade/82d Airborne Division (1/508th Abn), 101st Airborne Division: 3d Bde (3/187th Inf, 1/506th Inf, 2/506th Inf). *Casualties:* Not included in sources for the individual operation.

27 September–10 October: *Operation Phu Vang. Locations:* I Corps; Thua Thien Province; Huong Thuy; Phu Vang. *Type/Objective:* Search and Destroy–Cordon and Search of Phu Vang District, eight miles southeast of

Hue. *Units:* USA—101st Airborne Division: 2d Bde (B,C–1/501st Inf, 2/17th Cav); VNAF—2/54th ARVN Regiment. *Casualties:* NVA/VC—96 KIA, 174 POWs (U.S. losses not included in source).

2–9 October: *Operation Dukes Glade.* *Locations:* I Corps; Quang Nam Province; Nui Mat and Nui Ve Dop mountains. *Type:* Search and Destroy. *Units:* USA—23d Infantry Division (Americal): 11th Light Infantry Brigade (4/21st Inf). *Casualties:* U.S.—1 KIA, 3 WIA; NVA/VC—20 KIA.

4 October: The U.S. Marines reopen the Khe Sanh Combat Base to establish an artillery position to support ongoing operations in the area.

6–19 October: *Operation Maui Peak.* *Locations:* I Corps; Quang Nam Province; Vu Gia Valley; Hill 163; LZs Sparrow and Vulture. *Objective:* Relief of the Thuong Duc Special Forces Camp, approximately 20 miles southwest of DaNang. *Units:* USMC—2/5th Marines, 3/5th Marines, 2/7th Marines; VNAF—1/51st ARVN Rgt, 2/51st ARVN Rgt. *Casualties:* U.S.—28 KIA, 100 WIA; NVA/VC—353 KIA.

7–12 October: *Operation Logan Field.* *Location:* I Corps; Quang Ngai Province; Cape Batangan. *Type/Objectives:* Search and Destroy into area northeast of Quang Ngai City. *Units:* USA—23d Infantry Division (Americal), 11th Light Infantry Brigade (1/20th Inf); NVA/VC—48th Local Force Battalion (VC). *Casualties:* U.S.—13 KIA, 66 WIA; NVA/VC—14 KIA.

14 October: United States Department of Defense sources disclose that the Army and Marine Corps will be sending approximately 24,000 men back to Vietnam for involuntary second tours. The reasons cited are the length of the war and the high turnover of personnel,

especially experienced officers, resulting from the 12-month tours of duty.

18–19 October: *Operation Dale Common.* *Locations:* I Corps; Quang Ngai Province; Song Ve Valley; Mo Duc; LZ Bulldog. *Type:* Search and Destroy. *Units:* USA—23d Infantry Division (Americal): 11th Light Infantry Brigade (3/1st Inf). *Casualties:* U.S.—3 WIA; NVA/VC—23 KIA.

23–25 October: *Operation Rich.* *Location:* I Corps; Quang Tri Province; DMZ. *Type:* Search and Destroy. *Units:* USA—1st Brigade/5th Infantry Division (1/61st [M], B–1/77th Armor). *Casualties:* U.S.—8 KIA, 16 WIA; NVA/VC—308 KIA.

24 October–6 December: *Operation Henderson Hill.* *Location:* I Corps; Quang Nam Province. *Type/Objective:* Search and Clear. **Henderson Hill** is a follow-up to **Mameluke Thrust.** *Units:* USMC—5th Marines; NVA/VC—2d NVA Division. *Casualties:* U.S.—35 KIA, 231 WIA; NVA/VC—700 KIA.

25 October–2 November: *Operation Vernon Lake I.* *Locations:* I Corps; Quang Ngai Province; Song Ve Valley; LZs Bulldog, Buff and Dancer. *Type/Objective:* Search and Destroy to exploit B–52 strikes in the area. *Units:* USA—23d Infantry Division (Americal): 11th Light Infantry Brigade (3/1st Inf, 4/3d Inf); NVA/VC—3d NVA Division (elements), 2d Main Force Regiment (VC). *Casualties:* U.S.—1 KIA, 7 WIA; NVA/VC—93 KIA.

25 October–6 November: *Operations Phu Vang II-III.* *Locations:* I Corps; Thua Thien Province; Huong Thuy; Phu Thu; Phu Vang. *Type/Objective:* Combined Search and Destroy and Cordon and Search of area east and southeast of Hue. *Units:* USA—101st Airborne Division: 2d Bde (1/501st Inf); VNAF—54th ARVN Regiment (elements). *Casualties:* U.S.—5 KIA; NVA/VC—55 KIA, 67 POWs.

25 October–16 November: *Operation Eager Hunter/Garrard Bay.* Location: I Corps; Quang Nam Province. Type/Objective: *Eager Hunter/ Garrard Bay* is a series of Cordon and Search operations in the villages southeast of DaNang. Units: USMC – 2/1st Marines, BLT 2/26th Marines. Casualties: U.S. – 7 KIA, 44 WIA; NVA/ VC – 19 KIA.

28 October–15 November: *Operation Liberty Canyon.* Locations: I Corps; Thua Thien Province; III Corps; Binh Duong Province; Camp Evans; Phuoc Vinh. Type/Objective: *Liberty Canyon* is a logistic and strategic repositioning of the 1st Cavalry Division from Camp Evans in Thua Thien to Phuoc Vinh in Binh Duong.

31 October: President Lyndon Johnson orders all bombing of North Vietnam stopped. However, bombing of the Ho Chi Minh Trail in Laos will be tripled in an effort to stem the expected increase in enemy efforts at infiltration and resupply. After three years and nine months, *Rolling Thunder* ends. The statistics are impressive, if not the results: 304,000 tactical air sorties flown. Two thousand three hundred eighty-two B–52 sorties alone dropped 643,000 tons of bombs on North Vietnam.

November: The monsoon (rainy) season begins in the north and ends in the south.

November: *Operation Phoenix* begins. *Phoenix* is a covert attempt at infiltrating, identifying and destroying the Viet Cong infrastructure in South Vietnam.

1 November: Location: IV Corps; Dinh Tuong Province; My Tho River. Action: A Viet Cong demolitions team detonates two mines on the hull of the USS *Westchester County* as she lies at anchor with other ships of Mobile Riverine Group Alpha. Casualties: U.S. – 25 KIA, 27 WIA, 4 MIA.

2–7 November: *Operation Comanche Falls III.* Locations: I Corps; Thua Thien Province; My Chon River; Thon My Chon. Type/Objective: Search and Clear. Combined U.S./ARVN sweep of area from Thon My Chon, east to the coast, approximately 20 miles northwest of Hue. Units: USA – 1st Cavalry Division: 1st Bde (2/5th Cav, 3/5th Cav), 2d Bde (1/5th Cav); VNAF – 1st ARVN Division (1st ARVN Regiment). Casualties: U.S. – 20 KIA, 57 KIA, 2 MIA; VNAF – 21 KIA, 102 WIA; NVA/ VC – 424 KIA, 37 POWs.

2 November 1968–28 February 1969: *Operation Vernon Lake II.* Locations: I Corps; Quang Ngai Province; Da Vach Mountains; Song Re and Song Ve valleys; Song Tam Rao River. Type: Search and Destroy. Units: USA – 23d Infantry Division (American): 11th Light Infantry Brigade (3/1st Inf, 4/21st Inf); NVA/VC – 3d NVA Division (2d NVA Regiment). Casualties: U.S. – 23 KIA, 158 WIA; NVA/VC – 455 KIA, 8 POWs.

7 November 1968–2 April 1969: *Operation Sheridan Sabre.* Locations: III Corps; Binh Long, Phuoc Long and Tay Ninh provinces; War Zones C and D; "Adam's Road"; "Serge's Jungle Highway"; An Loc (Hon Quan); Katum; Thien Ngon; LZs Beverly Ann, Cindy, Jill, Liz, Michael, Mustang, St. Barbara and White. Type/Objective: Search and Destroy. *Sheridan Sabre* is a screening operation designed to prevent NVA infiltration from Cambodia. Units: USA – 1st Cavalry Division: 1st Bde (2/5th Cavalry), 2d Bde (1/5th Cav, 2/7th Cav), 3d Bde (1/7th Cav, 5/7th Cav, 2/12th Cav), 11th Armored Cavalry Regiment (B–1/11th ACR); VNAF – 36th and 52d ARVN Ranger battalions. Events: **16 November** – Companies B,E–1/7th Cavalry are attacked by an estimated company of enemy soldiers west of

Katum (Tay Ninh Province). American casualties in the day-long fight are 11 WIA. Thirty-seven enemy bodies are counted after the battle. **25 November** — B/7th Cavalry clashes with an enemy force of unknown size southwest of Thien Ngon (Tay Ninh Province). Losses: U.S. — 5 KIA, 13 WIA; NVA/VC — 52 KIA. **3 December** — D-2/7th Cavalry conducts an air assault near An Loc and is hit by heavy rocket, mortar and .50 cal machine gun fire. Five hours of ground attacks by an estimated battalion-sized force are finally repulsed by the cavalrymen. American losses are 24 KIA, 52 WIA and one MIA. Enemy losses are unknown. **9 December** — While conducting a Reconnaissance in Force southwest of An Loc, A-5/7th Cavalry and C-1/11th ACR engage an estimated company-sized enemy force. Losses in the five-hour firefight: U.S. — 14 KIA, 17 WIA; NVA/VC — 93 KIA. **8 March** — Enemy forces attack LZ Grant, approximately 17 miles northeast of Tay Ninh City (Tay Ninh Province). The defenders, 2/12th Cavalry kill a reported 157 NVA/VC. American losses: 13 KIA, 39 WIA. *Casualties:* Casualty figures are current only to 31 January 1969. U.S. — 219 KIA, 1387 WIA, 6 MIA; NVA/VC — 2898 KIA, 53 POWs.

10–17 November: *Operation Daring Endeavor. Locations:* I Corps; Quang Nam and Quang Tin provinces; Cua Dai River; Barrier Island; Hoi An. *Type/Objective:* Search and Destroy in area approximately 17 miles southeast of DaNang. *Units:* USA — 23d Infantry Division (Americal)–(B,C-1/1st Cav, B/8th Cav); USMC — BLT 2/7th Marines. *Casualties:* U.S. — 1 KIA, 35 WIA; NVA/VC — 33 KIA.

10–18 November: *Troui Bridge Cordon. Location:* I Corps; Thua Thien Province; Troui Bridge. *Type:* Cordon and Search. *Units:* USA — 101st Airborne Division: 1st Bde (1/327th Abn); VNAF — 7th ARVN Armored Cavalry,

National Police Field Force (elements). *Casualties:* NVA/VC — 10 KIA, 23 POWs (U.S. losses not included in source document).

15 November: U.S. reconnaissance pilots report enemy activity in and around the DMZ has quadrupled since the 31 October bombing halt.

17–23 November: *Location:* I Corps; Quang Nam Province; Nui Chom Mountains. *Action:* "Battle of Nui Chom Mountain." Americal troops battle the enemy in the mountains approximately 4.5 miles northwest of Hiep Duc. *Units:* USA — 23d Infantry Division (Americal): 196th Light Infantry Brigade (4/31st Inf), 198th Light Infantry Brigade (5/46th Inf). *Casualties:* U.S. — 4 KIA, 33 WIA; NVA/VC — 66 KIA.

18 November–7 December: *Operation Nam Hoa I. Locations:* I Corps; Thua Thien Province; Leech Island; Nui Ke; Nam Hoa; FSBs Panther I, II and III. *Type:* Search and Destroy. *Units:* USA — 101st Airborne Division: 2d Bde (2/501st Inf); VNAF — 3d ARVN Regiment; NVA/VC — 5th NVA Regiment. *Casualties:* Allied — 6 KIA, 39 WIA; NVA/VC — 78 KIA.

20 November–9 December: *Operation Swift Move. Location:* I Corps; Quang Nam Province. *Objective: Swift Move* is a companion operation to *Meade River,* and later becomes part of that operation. *Unit:* USMC — 2/7th Marines. *Casualties:* Not included in source for the individual operation.

20 November–9 December: *Operation Meade River. Locations:* I Corps; Quang Nam Province; Ky Lam and La Tho rivers; Hill 55; "Dodge City"; Dien Ban. *Type/Objective:* Cordon and Search operations in conjunction with the *Le Loi* or "accelerated pacification" program. *Units:* USMC — 1/1st Marines, 2/1st Marines, 2/5th Marines, 3/5th

Marines, 1/7th Marines, 2/26th Marines, 3/26th Marines (5000 Marines participate in **Meade River**); NVA/VC—36th and 38th NVA regiments (1000 NVA/VC estimated in area of operations). *Casualties:* U.S.—107 KIA, 385 WIA; NVA/VC—841 KIA, 182 POWs.

28 November 1968-27 January 1969: *Operation Dawson River. Location:* I Corps; Quang Tri Province. *Units*—USMC—3d Marine Division (elements). *Casualties:* U.S.—3 KIA, 50 WIA; NVA/VC—86 KIA.

1 December 1968-31 May 1969: *Operation Speedy Express. Location:* IV Corps; Dinh Tuong Province; My Tho River. *Type/Objective:* Search and Destroy. *Speedy Express* is a suboperation of *Quyet Thang* and is charged with the security of the Dong Tam area. *Units:* USA—9th Infantry Division: 1st Bde (2/39th Inf, 4/39th Inf, 6/31st Inf), Mobile Riverine Force: 2d Bde (3/47th Inf, 4/47th Inf, 3/60th Inf), 3d Bde (3/39th Inf). *Casualties:* Casualty figures for *Speedy Express* are current only to 31 January 1969. U.S.—40 KIA, 312 WIA; NVA/VC—10,899 KIA.

2 December 1968-28 February 1969: *Operation Hardin Falls. Locations:* I Corps; Quang Tin Province; Thang Binh; FSB Fiddler's Green. *Type/Objectives:* Search and Destroy in support of pacification efforts in Quang Tin. *Units:* USA—23d Infantry Division (American)–(1/1st Cav); NVA/VC—V–15 and 78th Local Force companies (VC). *Casualties:* U.S.—1 KIA, 14 WIA; NVA/VC—78 KIA.

7 December 1968-8 March 1969: *Operation Taylor Common. Locations:* I Corps; Quang Nam Province; An Hoa Basin; "Arizona Territory"; Nong Son; Thuong Duc. *Type/Objective:* Search and Clear/Destroy of An Hoa Basin, seeking enemy Base Area 112, approximately 23 miles southwest of DaNang.

Units: USMC—Task Force Yankee (1/3d Marines, 3/3d Marines, 5th Marines); VNAF—1st ARVN Ranger Group; NVA/VC—21st and 141st NVA regiments. *Casualties:* U.S.—151 KIA, 1324 WIA; NVA/VC—1398 KIA, 29 POWs.

11 December 1968-4 January 1969: *Operation Phu Vang IV. Locations:* I Corps; Thua Thien Province; Huong Thuy; Phu Thu; Phu Vang. *Type/Objective:* Cordon and Search operations aimed at preventing local VC and main force units from regrouping in area east and southeast of Hue. *Units:* USA—101st Airborne Division: 2d Bde (1/501st Inf); VNAF—54th ARVN Regiment. *Casualties:* U.S.—2 KIA, 12 WIA; NVA/VC—75 KIA, 99 POWs.

15 December 1968-5 January 1969: *Operations Valiant Hunt I-II. Location:* I Corps; Quang Nam Province; Hoi An. *Objective:* Area approximately 17 miles southeast of DaNang. *Units:* USMC—BLT 2/26th Marines. *Casualties:* U.S.—3 KIA, 19 WIA; NVA/VC—33 KIA.

15 December 1968-17 January 1969: *Operation Navajo Warhorse I. Locations:* III Corps; Hau Nghia and Kien Tuong provinces; LZs Clare, Ray and Tracy. *Type/Objective:* Screening Operation along Cambodian border to prevent enemy infiltration and resupply. *Units:* USA—1st Cavalry Division: 1st Bde (1/8th Cav), 2d Bde (2/8th Cav), 3d Bde (2/12th Cav). *Casualties:* Not included in sources.

15 December 1968-28 February 1969: *Operation Fayette Canyon. Locations:* I Corps; Quang Nam Province; "Antenna Valley"; Nui Mat Rang Mountains. *Type/Objective:* Reconnaissance in Force–Search and Destroy campaign to locate and eliminate enemy base camps and staging areas. *Fayette Canyon* is a companion operation to the Marines' *Taylor Common. Units:* USA—

23d Infantry Division (Americal)–196th Light Infantry Brigade (2/1st Inf); NVA/VC—NVA 2d Division (1st Main Force Rgt (VC). *Casualties:* U.S.—2 KIA, 17 WIA; NVA/VC—327 KIA, 4 POWs.

16–24 December: *Operation Rawlins Valley. Locations:* I Corps; Thua Thien Province; Nam Hoa. *Type/Objective:* Reconnaissance in Force operation in Nam Hoa District, approximately 10 miles south of Hue. *Units:* USA—101st Airborne Division: 3d Bde (3/187th Inf, 1/506th Inf); VNAF—3d ARVN Regiment; NVA/VC—6th NVA Regiment. *Casualties:* Totals for *Rawlins Valley,* NVA/VC—8 KIA (U.S. losses not included in source document for the individual operation).

31 December 1968–13 January 1969: *Operation Todd Forest. Location:* I Corps; Thua Thien Province; Nam Hoa. *Type/Objective:* Reconnaissance in Force into area 10 miles south of Hue. *Units:* USA—101st Airborne Division: 3d Bde (1/506th Inf); VNAF—1st ARVN Regiment. *Casualties:* Allied—2 WIA; NVA/VC—12 KIA.

31 December: There are now more than 530,000 U.S. personnel in South Vietnam. U.S. ground forces end the year in the following strengths: Army—359,313, Marines—80,716; American losses for the year: 14,314 KIA, 100,088 WIA; total American losses in Vietnam since 1959: 30,610 KIA, 207,495 WIA; VNAF strength at the end of 1968: 820,000; VNAF losses for the year: 20,482 KIA; total VNAF losses since 1965: 88,343 KIA; estimated NVA/VC strength at the end of 1968: 240,000+; estimated NVA/VC losses for the year: 35,774 KIA, 6991 POWs; estimated NVA/VC losses since 1961: 439,000 KIA.

1969

The year begins with more than 530,000 U.S. soldiers, Marines and airmen stationed in South Vietnam and Thailand. VNAF strength is placed at 820,000. Opposing the Allied forces are more than 240,000 North Vietnamese and Viet Cong.

1 January–31 August: *Operation Rice Farmer.* *Location:* III and IV Corps. *Units:* USA—9th Infantry Division; VNAF—5th ARVN Regiment. *Casualties:* NVA/VC—1869 KIA (U.S. losses not included in sources for the individual operation).

1 January–31 December: *Operation Quyet Thang. Locations:* IV Corps; Co Cong, Dinh Tuong; Kien Hoa and Kien Phong provinces; My Tho River; Ap Phuoc Hau; Dong Tam. *Type:* Search and Clear; Pacification. *Units:* USA—9th Infantry Division: 1st Bde (2/39th Inf, 4/39th Inf, 6/31st Inf), Mobile Riverine Force: 2d Bde (3/47th Inf, 4/47th Inf, 3/60th Inf), 3d Bde (3/39th Inf); VNAF—7th, 9th and 21st ARVN divisions; NVA/VC—1st Dong Thap Regiment (261st and 514th Local Force [VC] battalions), 2d Dong Thap Regiment (263d and 267th Main Force [VC] battalions). *Events:* 9–10 May—While conducting a sweep 35 miles northwest of Can Giouc (IV Corps–Dinh Tuong Province), 2/39th Infantry, 4/39th Infantry and the 12th ARVN Regiment tangle with an enemy force of unknown size. Losses: U.S.—4 KIA, 8 WIA; NVA/VC—52 KIA. 21–22 May—Companies A,B,C–4/39th Infantry and B–3/17th Cavalry encircle an enemy force near Can Giouc, 35 miles northwest of Dong Tam (Dinh Tuong Province). U.S. forces kill a reported 117 of the enemy. Four Americans are WIA. *Casualties:* Totals for *Quyet Thang.* NVA/VC—37,874 KIA, 500+ POWs; U.S. losses current only to 30 April: 178 KIA, 1836 WIA.

2 January: The Paris Peace Talks stall due to a controversy over the shape of the conference table.

6 January–5 February: *Operation Platte Canyon. Locations:* I Corps; Thua Thien Province; Ruong Ruong Valley; "Elephant Valley"; Hai Van Pass; FSBs Cutlass, Dagger and Quick. *Type:* Reconnaissance in Force. *Units:* USA—101st Airborne Division: 1st Bde (1/327th Abn, 2/327th Abn, 2/502d Abn); VNAF—5th ARVN Regiment, 7th ARVN Cavalry Task Force; NVA/VC—4th NVA Regiment. *Casualties:*

Allied—10 KIA, 19 WIA; NVA/VC—80 KIA, 10 POWs.

13 January–9 February: *Operation Bold Mariner.* *Locations:* I Corps; Quang Ngai Province; Batangan Peninsula; Van Tuong. *Type/Objective:* Cordon and Search and sweeping operation in old *Starlite* area of the Batangan Peninsula. *Units:* USMC—SLF Alpha BLT–2/26th Marines, SLF Bravo BLT–3/26th Marines; VNAF—2d ARVN Division; NVA/VC—38th Main Force (VC) Regiment, 48th Local Force (VC) Battalion. *Comment:* **Bold Mariner** is the largest amphibious assault of the Vietnam War. *Casualties:* U.S.—5 KIA, 32 WIA; NVA/VC—60 KIA, 26 POWs.

13 January–21 July: *Operation Russell Beach.* *Locations:* I Corps; Quang Ngai Province; Batangan Peninsula; Quang Ngai City; LZ Minuteman. *Type/Objective:* Combined Search and Destroy/Cordon and Search operation. *Russell Beach* is a complementary operation to **Bold Mariner.** *Units:* USA— 23d Infantry Division (American)–11th Light Infantry Brigade (4/3d Inf), 196th Light Infantry Brigade (5/46th Inf); USMC—SLF Alpha BLT–2/26th Marines, SLF Bravo–3/26th Marines; VNAF—2d ARVN Division (6th ARVN Regiment); NVA/VC—3d NVA Division (22d NVA Regiment), 38th and 48th Local Force (VC) battalions. *Comment:* During the course of **Russell Beach** and **Bold Mariner,** more than 12,000 civilians are checked out and relocated off the Batangan Peninsula to the Quang Ngai City area. *Casualties:* Combined USA/USMC totals. 56 KIA, 268 WIA; NVA/VC—158 KIA, 104 POWs.

17 January–29 March: *Operation Navajo Warhorse II.* *Locations:* III Corps; Hau Nghia, Kien Tuong and Tay Ninh provinces; LZs Clare, Ray and Tracy. *Type/Objective:* Navajo Warhorse II is a continuation of the 1st Cavalry's screening of the Cambodian

border area. *Units:* USA—1st Cavalry Division: 1st Bde (2/5th Cav), 2d Bde (1/5th Cav, 2/8th Cav), 3d Bde (2/12th Cav). *Event:* 9 March—Company B–2/5th Cavalry encounters an enemy force of unknown size near the Tay Ninh– Hau Nghia provincial border. Losses: U.S.—14 KIA, 31 WIA; NVA/VC—36 KIA. *Casualties:* Totals for **Navajo Warhorse II** not included in source material.

22–25 January: *Operation Dawson River South.* *Locations:* I Corps; Quang Tri Province; Da Krong Valley; Hills 1224 (Tam Boi) and 1228 (Co A Nong– "Tiger Mountain"); Ca Lu; Vandergrift Combat Base; FSBs Cunningham, Henderson, Jack, Shiloh and Tun Tavern. *Type/Objective:* Search and Destroy into enemy staging area 30 miles west of Hue. *Units:* USMC—Task Force Hotel–1/9th Marines, 2/9th Marines, 3/9th Marines; NVA/VC—6th and 9th NVA regiments. *Comment:* **Dawson River South** renamed **Dewey Canyon.**

22 January–19 March: *Operation Dewey Canyon.* *Locations:* I Corps; Quang Tri and Thua Thien provinces; Ashau and Da Krong valleys; Base Area 611; Ca Lu; Vandergrift Combat Base; FSBs Cunningham, Erskine, Henderson, Razor, Riley, Shiloh and Tun Tavern. *Type/Objective:* Search and Destroy into Base Area 611 and the Da Krong Valley (southwest corner of Quang Tri Province). The purpose of **Dewey Canyon** is to disrupt enemy logistic and base areas threatening Hue. *Units:* USMC—Task Force Hotel–1/9th Marines, 2/9th Marines, 3/9th Marines; NVA/VC—6th and 9th NVA regiments, 65th NVA Artillery Regiment. *Comment:* **Dewey Canyon** is the first major operation for 3d Marine Division commander, Major General Raymond Davis. Davis brings to the Marines a more progressive style; making more use of the airmobile concept. His style of combat produces operations that are more carefully scouted, planned and executed—*Dewey Canyon* is an example. Davis uses a very "linear" style: Recon the area thoroughly; establish fire support bases and logistical support; initiate Search and Destroy patrols up to battalion size out to the limits of artillery coverage; recon a new forward area of operations; establish new fire bases and repeat the process until the operational objectives are met. *Events:* 2 February—FSB Cunningham is hit with an artillery barrage killing five and wounding five others. 5 February—Company G–2/9th Marines is ambushed by an estimated 30 NVA. Five Marines are KIA and 18 WIA. 17 February—Company G–2/9th Marines fights a daylong battle with an estimated NVA company. Losses in the fight: U.S.—5 KIA, 12 WIA; NVA/VC—39 KIA. 18 February—Enemy sappers attack FSB Cunningham, 25 miles south of Vandegrift Combat Base. Four Marines are KIA and 46 WIA. 22 February—A–1/9th Marines are involved in heavy combat near the Laotian border at La Hang, 30 miles southwest of Vandegrift Combat Base. The Marines kill a reported 105 of the enemy while losing 11 KIA and 72 WIA. 24 February–3 March—Companies E,F, and H–2/9th Marines foray into Laos along Route 922. The cross-border action kills 48 NVA. Marine losses are eight KIA and 33 WIA. *Casualties:* Totals for *Dewey Canyon.* U.S.—130 KIA, 920 WIA; NVA/VC—1617 KIA, 5 POWs.

24 January–9 February: *Operation Sherman Peak. Locations:* I Corps; Thua Thien Province; Ashau Valley; Rao Nai River; Route 547; FSB Veghel. *Type:* Reconnaissance in Force. *Units:* USA—101st Airborne Division: 2d Bde (1/501st Inf, 2/501st Inf, 1/502d Inf); VNAF—3/3d ARVN Regiment. *Casualties:* NVA/VC—1 KIA (U.S. losses not included in source document for the individual operation).

24 January–28 February: *Opera-*

tion Ohio Rapids. Locations: I Corps; Thua Thien Province; Base Area 101; O'Lau River. *Type:* Reconnaissance in Force. *Units:* USA—101st Airborne Division: 3d Bde (3/187th Inf, 1/506th Inf, 2/506th Inf); VNAF—1st ARVN Regiment; NVA/VC—6th NVA Regiment. *Casualties:* U.S.—6 KIA, 6 WIA; NVA/VC—102 KIA, 5 POWs.

27 January–7 February: *Operation Linn River. Locations:* I Corps; Quang Nam Province; Go Noi Island; Chau Son (1); LZs Hawk and Owl. *Type:* Cordon and Search. *Units:* USMC—7th Marines, BLT–2/26th Marines. *Casualties:* U.S.—9 KIA, 46 WIA; NVA/VC—58 KIA, 3 POWs.

1 February (begins): *Operation Dan Quyen/Hines. Locations:* II Corps; Binh Dinh, Kontum and Pleiku provinces; Dak Payou and Plei Trap valleys; Base Area 226; Ben Het; Polei Kleng; Suoi Doi; LZs Suzie and Toughie. *Type/Objective:* Search and Destroy in support of pacification programs and the disruption of enemy infiltration routes. *Units:* USA—4th Infantry Division: 1st Bde (1/8th Inf, 3/8th Inf, 3/12th Inf), 2d Bde (2/8th Inf [M], 1/12th Inf, 1/22d Inf, 1/10th Cav), 3d Bde (1/14th Inf, 1/35th Inf); VNAF—22d ARVN Division (3d ARVN Regiment); NVA/VC—3d NVA Division (18th, 24th, 28th, 66th and 95–B NVA regiments). *Casualties:* Current only to 31 January 1970: NVA/VC—306 KIA (U.S. losses not included in source for the individual operation).

1–3 February: *Operation Darby March I. Location:* II Corps; Phu Yen Province; An Nghiep. *Objective:* The purpose of *Darby March I* is the support of pacification efforts in Phu Yen Province. *Units:* USA—173d Airborne Brigade (4/503d Abn–D/16th Armor); ROK—26th ROK Regiment. *Casualties:* Totals for *Darby March I.* U.S.—4 WIA; NVA/VC—8 KIA.

1–7 February: *Operation Darby Trail I. Locations:* II Corps; Binh Dinh Province; Bong Song Plains; Base Area 225. *Type/Objective:* Search and Destroy aimed at finding and eliminating enemy Base Area 225. *Units:* USA—173d Airborne Brigade (2/503d Abn); VNAF—40th ARVN Regiment, 2/14th ARVN APC Troop; NVA/VC—3d NVA Division (2d NVA Regiment). *Casualties:* U.S.—1 WIA; NVA/VC—4 KIA.

1 February–3 March: *Operation Darby Crest I. Locations:* II Corps; Binh Dinh Province; "Crescent Plains"; Hoai An. *Type/Objective:* Search and Destroy with the mission of breaking up enemy food collection efforts. *Units:* USA—173d Airborne Brigade (1/503d Abn); VNAF—40th ARVN Regiment (elements); NVA/VC—18th NVA Regiment (elements), D-22 Hoai An District Company (VC). *Casualties:* Totals for *Darby Crest I.* U.S.—1 KIA, 6 WIA; VNAF—1 KIA, 1 WIA; NVA/VC—48 KIA, 1 POW.

4–12 February: *Operation Strangler I. Location:* III Corps; Long An Province; Hung Long (3). *Type/Objective:* Cordon and Search of pro–VC village prior to 1969 *TET Offensive. Strangler I* is officially part of the *Toan Thang* series of operations. *Units:* USA—199th Light Infantry Brigade (2/3d Inf, B,C–3/7th Inf, B–5/12th Inf); VNAF—30th and 33d ARVN Ranger battalions; NVA/VC—9th VC Division (elements). *Casualties:* Not included in source document for the individual operation.

8 February–6 March: *Operation Darby March II. Location:* II Corps; Phu Yen Province. *Objective:* Offensive operations in support of pacification efforts in Phu Yen Province. *Units:* USA—173d Airborne Brigade (4/503d Abn); VNAF—47th ARVN Regiment. *Event:* **25 February**—A–4/503d Airborne is ambushed by an enemy force of unknown size 17 miles northwest of Tuy Hoa. Seven Sky Soldiers are KIA

and 10 WIA in the ambush. *Casualties:* Totals for *Darby March II.* U.S.—7 KIA, 27 WIA; NVA/VC—25 KIA.

10–16 February: *Operation Defiant Measure. Location:* I Corps; Quang Tin Province; Hoi An. *Type:* Search and Destroy. *Units:* USMC—BLT–2/26th Marines, 3/26th Marines; VNAF—1st ARVN Ranger Group. *Casualties:* None reported.

12–16 February: *Operation Strangler II. Locations:* III Corps; Long An Province; Binh Chanh; Tan Nhut (2). *Type/Objective:* Cordon and Search of pro–VC village. *Strangler II* is a part of the continuing *Toan Thang* series of operations. *Units:* USA—199th Light Infantry Brigade (2/3d Inf, C,D–4/12th Inf, A,D–5/12th Inf); VNAF—Regional Forces (RF) elements; NVA/VC—9th VC Division (elements). *Casualties:* Not included in source document for the individual operation.

17 February–31 October: *Operation Toan Thang III. Locations:* III Corps; Binh Duong, Binh Long, Hau Nghia, Long An, Long Khanh, Phuoc Long and Tay Ninh provinces; War Zones C and D; "Iron Triangle"; "Straight-Edge Woods"; "The Trapezoid"; Boi Loi Forest; Michelin Plantation; An Dien; An Loc; Chanh Luu; Dau Tieng; Dong Xoai; Lai Khe; Loc Ninh; Quan Loi; Song Be; FSBs All American, Aspen, Buttons, Caldwell, Chamberlain, Don, Frontier City, Gela, Mary, O'Keefe, Sidewinder and Thunder IV. *Type/Objective:* Multiple Search and Destroy operations throughout III Corps in an effort to maintain pressure on the enemy following the 1968 *TET Offensive. Units:* USA—1st Cavalry Division: 2d Bde (5/7th Cav, 1/8th Cav, 2/12th Cav), 1st Infantry Division: 1st Bde (1/2d Inf, 1/26th Inf, 1/28th Inf), 2d Bde (2/16th Inf, 1/18th Inf, 2/18th Inf, 1/4th Cav), 3d Bde (2/2d Inf [M], 1/16th Inf [M], 2/28th Inf), 9th Infantry Division: 1st Bde (6/31st Inf), 2d Bde (2/47th Inf

[M]), 3d Bde (2/60th Inf, 5/60th Inf [M]), 25th Infantry Division: 1st Bde (4/9th Inf, 2/14th Inf, 4/23d Inf [M]), 2d Bde (1/5th Inf [M], 1/27th Inf, 2/27th Inf), 3d Bde (2/12th Inf, 2/22d Inf [M], 3/22d Inf), 3d Bde/82d Airborne Division (1/505th Abn, 2/505th Abn, 1/508th Abn), 11th Armored Cavalry Regiment, 199th Light Infantry Brigade (2/3d Inf, 3/7th Inf, 4/12th Inf, 5/12th Inf); VNAF — 5th, 7th, 9th and 18th ARVN Divisions (7th, 8th, 9th and 50th ARVN regiments), 15th ARVN Cavalry Regiment; NVA/VC — 1st NVA Division (18–B, 95–C and 101–D NVA regiments), 7th NVA Division (141st and 165th NVA regiments), 5th Viet Cong Division (95th, 174th and 275th VC regiments), 9th Viet Cong Division (88th, 271st and 272d VC regiments). *Events:* 25 February — An estimated 40 enemy sappers attack the 25th Infantry Division Base Camp at Cu Chi (Hau Nghai Province). Thirty-eight Americans are KIA and 14 CH–47 "Chinook" helicopters are destroyed in the attack. The enemy body count is 13. 13 April — A–1/11th ACR, C–1/8th Cavalry and D–2/12th Cavalry battle an entrenched force of unknown size northwest of Dau Tieng in Tay Ninh Province. Losses in the fight: U.S. — 14 KIA, 16 WIA; NVA/VC — 11 KIA. 15 April — An estimated two NVA battalions attack the 2/27th Infantry (25th Inf Div) at FSB Diamond III, about 20 miles southwest of Tay Ninh City. Losses: U.S. — 13 KIA; NVA/VC — 190 KIA. 26 April — An NVA force of unknown size attacks FSB Frontier City, 13 miles south of Tay Ninh City. The defenders, C–4/9th Infantry (25th Inf Div), suffer only one WIA in the attack, and report an enemy body count of 213. 9–10 May — Companies C–2/22d Infantry (M) and D–1/27th Infantry (25th Inf Div) encounter between 200–400 soldiers of the 101st NVA Regiment near Xom Tra Ginh, approximately 6.5 miles west of Dau Tieng (Binh Duong Province). Losses in the battle: U.S. — 2 KIA, 9 WIA; NVA/VC — 115 KIA, 2 POWs. 12 May —

An NVA force of unknown size launches a mortar and ground attack on FSB Gela. The defenders, 1/28th Infantry (1st Inf Div) kill 41 of the enemy. American losses are three KIA and 20 WIA. 12–13 May — Companies B,C,D–2/60th Infantry, B and D–5/60th Infantry (M), B–3/17th Cavalry (all of the 9th Inf Div) with ARVN support engage NVA/VC troops near Thu Thua (Long An Province), approximately 16 miles northwest of My Tho. Losses: U.S. — 4 KIA, 37 WIA; NVA/VC — 91 KIA, 6 POWs. 21 May — Elements of the 7th NVA Division ambush a U.S. supply convoy near Ap Bau Bang (Binh Long Province), approximately five miles north of Lai Khe. The convoy is defended by B–2/2d Infantry (M) and C–1/4th Cavalry (1st Inf Div). Casualties: U.S. — 4 KIA, 15 WIA; NVA/VC — 8 KIA. 6 June — While counterattacking in response to an attack on FSB Thunder IV, B–2/2d Infantry (M) (1st Inf Div), encounters a company-sized enemy force 10 miles south of Loc Ninh (Binh Long Province). Four Americans are KIA and 14 WIA in the clash. An enemy body count of 78 is reported. 7 June — Company C–2/2d Infantry (M) (1st Inf Div) and 2/11th ACR engage an enemy force of unknown size in a five-hour firefight near An Loc (Binh Long Province). Losses: U.S. — 4 KIA, 26 WIA; NVA/VC — 96 KIA. 3 July — Company D–2/3d Infantry (199th LIB) is attacked by an enemy force of unknown size near Blackhorse Base Camp (Long Khanh Province). Nine Americans are KIA and 19 WIA in the attack. Enemy losses are unknown. 9 July — While escorting a convoy on QL 13 north of An Loc (Binh Long Province), 2/11th ACR is ambushed by an estimated two battalions of NVA. Losses in the attack: U.S. — 4 KIA, 15 WIA; NVA/VC — 23 KIA, 1 POW. 19 July — The 1/5th Infantry (M) and B–2/14th Infantry (25th Inf Div) launch an airmobile raid into a suspected enemy base area near Tu Duon (Hau Nghia Province). No American losses reported; however, the attackers report killing 54 and capturing 10 enemy soldiers. **1–10 August** — Enemy mines and booby traps throughout the area of operations kill five Americans and wound 86. **12 August** — NVA/VC troops attack two U.S. bases. The 3d Brigade/1st Cavalry Division HQ at Quan Loi, four miles northeast of An Loc is attacked by elements of the 88th NVA, 271st and 272d VC regiments. Losses: U.S. — 8 KIA, 63 WIA; NVA/VC — 48 KIA. Meanwhile, 20 miles west of An Loc, the 1st Cav's 2/8th Cavalry at FSB Becky is attacked by rockets and a large ground assault from the 1st NVA Division's 18–B Regiment. Losses: U.S. — 13 KIA, 46 WIA; NVA/VC — 101 KIA. Total casualties in the two attacks: U.S. — 21 KIA, 96 WIA; NVA/VC — 149 KIA. **12 August:** NVA forces launch attacks on 11th ACR positions near Loc Ninh (Binh Long Province). The 7/209th NVA Regiment of the 7th NVA Division assaults FSBs Kelly and Jon, while the K–2 Battalion of the 9th VC Division attacks FSBs Aspen and Sidewinder. Total casualties in the two attacks: U.S. — 11 KIA, 98 WIA; VNAF — 44 KIA, 37 WIA; NVA/VC — 224 KIA, 4 POWs. **5 September** — The 1st Plt–A–1/16th Infantry (M) (1st Inf Div) is ambushed four miles south of An Loc (Binh Long Province) by an unidentified company-sized force. The platoon is reinforced by A,C–1/16th Infantry (M). Losses: U.S. — 2 KIA, 68 WIA; NVA/VC — 63 KIA. **6 September** — B–1/11th ACR battles a company-sized force three miles west of Loc Ninh (Binh Long Province). Losses in the firefight: U.S. — 2 KIA, 30 WIA; NVA/VC — 32 KIA, 5 POWs. *Casualties:* Totals for *Toan Thang III.* Casualty figures for American forces are incomplete and are as follows. 1st Infantry Division — 386 KIA, 2320 WIA; 9th Infantry Division — 22 KIA, 378 WIA; 25th Infantry Division — 478 KIA, 1107 WIA; totals — 886 KIA, 3805 WIA. Figures for the 1st Cavalry Division, 3d Bde/82d Airborne Division, 199th Light Infantry Brigade and 11th

ACR not included in source documents. Total enemy losses in *Toan Thang III.* NVA/VC — 12,051 KIA, 406+ POWs.

23 February: *"Post TET"–1969 Offensive* begins throughout South Vietnam. In III Corps alone, 100 U.S. soldiers die in the first day of fighting. Within two weeks 789 Americans are dead and another 4287 wounded.

25 February: *Location:* I Corps; Quang Tri Province, *Scotland II* Area of Operations; FSB Neville. *Action:* NVA troops attack Marine positions at FSB Neville. *Units:* USMC — H–2/4th Marines; NVA/VC — 246th NVA Regiment (sapper units). *Casualties:* U.S. — 11 KIA, 29 WIA; NVA/VC — 36 KIA.

25 February: *Location:* I Corps; Quang Tri Province; *Scotland II* Operational Area; FSB Russell. *Action:* NVA forces launch 200–man "human wave" suicide attacks on Marine positions at FSB Russell. *Units:* USMC — E,F,K and H/12th Marines; NVA/VC — 27th NVA Regiment. *Casualties:* U.S. — 26 KIA, 77 WIA; NVA/VC — 56 KIA.

25 February: Formal truce negotiations begin in Paris.

26 February: *Locations:* IV Corps; Kien Hoa Province; Rach An Binh; Mo Cay. *Action:* U.S. troops ambush a Viet Cong waterborne convoy approximately 20 miles south of My Tho. *Units:* USA — Mobile Riverine Force–9th Infantry Division: 2d Bde (3/60th Inf). *Casualties:* U.S. — none; NVA/VC — 21 KIA.

26 February–3 March: *Operation Spokane Rapids. Locations:* I Corps; Thua Thien Province; Ta Trach River; Nam Hoa District; FSBs Normandy and Spear. *Type:* Reconnaissance in Force. *Units:* USA — 101st Airborne Division: 1st Bde (2/502d Abn), 3d Bde (3/187th Inf); NVA/VC — 5th NVA Regiment. *Casualties:* Totals for

Spokane Rapids. U.S.—3 KIA, 11 WIA; NVA/VC—9 KIA, 2 POWs.

27 February–8 May: *Operation Purple Martin. Locations:* I Corps; Quang Tri Province; Cam Lo Valley; Hill 1308; Vandergrift Combat Base; "The Rockpile"; FSBs Argonne, Neville and Russell; LZs Catapult, Mack and Sierra. *Type/Objective:* Search and Destroy aimed at driving the enemy back across the DMZ. *Units:* USMC—1/4th Marines, 2/4th Marines, 3/4th Marines; NVA/VC—246th NVA Regiment. *Events:* 11–14 March—G-2/4th Marines assaults enemy positions near LZ Catapult, three miles north of FSB Neville. Losses in the three-day battle: U.S.—4 KIA, 13 WIA; NVA/VC—24 KIA. 13 March—Company M-3/4th Marines clashes with an estimated NVA platoon on a hill called "Sierra North." Losses: U.S.—10 KIA, 35 WIA; NVA/VC—23 KIA. 20 March—"Battle of FSB Argonne." Marine forces from 1/4th Marines battle NVA soldiers for control of abandoned FSB Argonne. Six Americans are KIA and 11 WIA. The enemy body count is 15. *Casualties:* U.S.—79 KIA, 268 WIA; NVA/VC—347 KIA, 4 POWs.

28 February–3 March: *Locations:* I Corps; Quang Tri Province; Cam Lo River; Con Thien; Quat Xa; LZ Sharon. *Action:* "Battle of Cam Hung." *Units:* USA—1st Brigade/5th Infantry Division (M): 1/61st Inf (M), 3/5th Cav; USMC—3/3d Marines (one platoon); NVA/VC—27th NVA Regiment. *Events:* 28 February—The hamlet of Quat Xa is mortared by the enemy. Intelligence estimates Cam Hung as the source of the fire and 3d Plt–B-3/5th Cavalry is sent to investigate. The platoon is then hit by an estimated NVA company. The remainder of B Company and C-3/5th Cavalry and one platoon of Marines (3/3d Marines) are sent as reinforcements. Losses for Day 1 at the Battle of Cam Hung: U.S.—1 KIA, 9 WIA; NVA/VC—60 KIA. 1 March—A-4/12th Cavalry

and B-1/61st Infantry (M) join the battle as enemy contact flares up again near the village of Cam Hung. Two Americans are KIA and 25 WIA. The enemy body count is reported at 17. *Casualties:* Totals for the Battle of Cam Hung. U.S.—3 KIA, 35 WIA; NVA/VC—118 KIA.

1–10 March: *Operation Eager Pursuit I. Locations:* I Corps; Quang Nam Province; Go Noi Island. *Units:* USMC—2/7th Marines, 1/26th Marines, BLT–2/26th Marines; VNAF—51st ARVN Regiment. *Casualties:* U.S.—5 KIA, 60 WIA; NVA/VC—9 KIA, 2 POWs.

1 March–14 April: *Operation Wayne Grey. Location:* II Corps; Kontum Province. *Unit:* USA—4th Infantry Division. *Casualties:* NVA/VC—608 KIA (U.S. losses not included in source document for the individual operation).

1 March–8 May: *Operation Massachusetts Striker. Locations:* I Corps; Thua Thien Province; Ashau Valley; Dong Tre Gong; FSBs Fury, Veghel and Whip. *Type/Objective:* Search and Destroy. *Massachusetts Striker's* mission is to prevent the enemy from massing in the Ashau Valley and to disrupt their logistical capabilities. The operation is a prelude to the upcoming *Apache Snow. Units:* USA—101st Airborne Division: 1st Bde (2/327th Abn), 2d Bde (1/501st Inf, 2/501st Inf, 1/502d Inf); VNAF—2/3rd ARVN Regiment, 3/3d ARVN Regiment; NVA/VC—816th NVA Battalion. *Event:* 17–20 April—"Battle of Bloody Ridge (Dong A Tay)." Companies A,B-1/502d Infantry battle the 816th NVA Battalion on a mountain six miles east of Ta Bat. Heavy casualties inspire the name "Bloody Ridge." Losses in the fight: U.S.—35 KIA, 100+ WIA; NVA/VC—86 KIA. *Casualties:* Totals for *Massachusetts Striker.* NVA/VC—176 KIA, 2 POWs (U.S. losses not included in sources).

1 March–14 August: *Operation Kentucky Jumper. Locations:* I Corps; Thua

Thien Province; Base Area 611; Phu Loc District; FSB Tomahawk. *Type/Objective:* Search and Destroy. *Kentucky Jumper* is essentially a continuation of *Nevada Eagle* and is charged with eliminating enemy base areas, lines of communication and infiltration routes. *Units:* USA—101st Airborne Division: 2d Bde (1/501st Inf, 2/501st Inf, 1/502d Inf), 3d Bde (3/187th Inf, 1/506th Inf, 2/506th Inf); VNAF—1st ARVN Division; NVA/VC—4th, 6th, 9th and 29th NVA regiments. *Events:* **23 April–5 May**—"Battle of Dong Ngai Mountain." While following up on an intelligence report on Dong Ngai Mountain, approximately seven miles northeast of Ta Bat, the 2/17th Cavalry's aero-rifle platoon is hit hard by NVA troops. Companies A,B,D–3/187th Infantry are sent as reinforcements. Losses for the Battle of Dong Ngai: U.S.—45+ KIA, 54+ WIA; NVA/VC—100+ KIA. **19 June**—The 72d Sapper Company/4th NVA Regiment attacks FSB Tomahawk, approximately 24 miles south of Hue. The defenders, 1st Plt C–2/501st Infantry and C–1/138th Artillery, repel the attack killing 17 NVA. American losses are 13 KIA and 40 WIA. *Casualties:* Totals for *Kentucky Jumper.* NVA/VC—1675 KIA, 41 POWs (U.S. losses not included in source documents for the individual operation).

10–27 March: *Operation Eager Pursuit II. Location:* I Corps; Quang Nam Province; Go Noi Island. *Units:* USMC—2/7th Marines, BLT–1/26th Marines, 2/26th Marines; VNAF—51st ARVN Regiment. *Casualties:* Not included in source.

12–14 March: *Operation Lulu. Locations:* III Corps; Long An Province; Loc Trung; Long Thoi; Long Thuong. *Type:* Search and Clear. *Units:* USA—9th Infantry Division (elements), 199th Light Infantry Brigade (D–2/3d Inf, A–3/7th Inf, B–4/12th Inf, D–5/12th Inf); VNAF—46th ARVN Regiment, 5th ARVN Ranger Group. *Casualties:* Not

included in source document for the individual operation.

14–16 March: *Operation Twinkletoes. Location:* III Corps; Binh Duong Province; Phuoc Vinh. *Type/Objective:* Search and Destroy. The mission of *Twinkletoes* is to eliminate the enemy's Sub–Region 5 Headquarters, believed to be south of Phuoc Vinh. *Unit:* USA—11th Armored Cavalry Regiment. *Casualties:* NVA/VC—23 KIA (U.S. losses not included in source document).

15 March–2 May: *Operation Maine Crag. Locations:* I Corps; Quang Tri Province; "The Vietnam Salient"; Route 926; Ca Lu; Lang Vei; Trung Thuan; LZs Alpine, Hanoi, Paris, Saigon, Sparrow and Torch. *Type/Objective:* Search and Clear. *Maine Crag,* conducted in the southwest corner of Quang Tri, is a complementary operation to *Dewey Canyon. Units:* USA—1st Brigade/5th Infantry Division (M): Task Force Remagen (B–1/61st Inf [M], C–1/77th Armor); USMC—1/3d Marines, 2/3d Marines; VNAF—2d ARVN Regiment, 7th ARVN Cavalry; NVA/VC—304th NVA Division (9th and 57th NVA regiments). *Events:* **25 April**—An estimated NVA battalion attacks the 2/7th ARVN Cavalry, killing eight and wounding 40. American losses in the battle: two KIA and two WIA. **28 April**—The 9/57th NVA Regiment attacks Company A–1/61st Infantry (M) southwest of Ca Lu, near Trung Thuan. Losses: U.S.—5 KIA, 35 WIA; NVA/VC—34 KIA. *Casualties:* Totals for *Maine Crag.* U.S.—17 KIA, 104 WIA; NVA/VC—207 KIA.

17–24 March: *Operation Atlas Wedge. Locations:* III Corps; Binh Duong and Tay Ninh provinces; War Zone C; Michelin Plantation; Dau Tieng; FSBs Doc and Holiday Inn. *Type/Objective:* Search and Destroy. *Atlas Wedge* is meant to prevent the 7th NVA Division from infiltrating toward Saigon through the Michelin

Rubber Plantation. *Units:* USA—1st Cavalry Division (1/5th Cav), 1st Infantry Division: 1st Bde (1/28th Inf, 1/4th Cav), 2d Bde (1/18th Inf), 3d Bde (2/28th Inf), 11th Armored Cavalry Regiment (1st and 3d squadrons); NVA/VC—7th NVA Division (320th NVA Regiment). *Events:* **20 March**—Heavy fighting erupts in the Michelin Plantation involving Troops L,M–3/11th ACR and A–1/5th Cavalry. Losses in the day's battle: U.S.—1 KIA, 12 WIA; NVA/VC—72 KIA. **30 March**—1/4th Cavalry battles well-entrenched NVA soldiers in the Michelin Plantation throughout the day with heavy losses on both sides: U.S.—12 KIA, 19 WIA; NVA/VC—79 KIA, 2 POWs. *Casualties:* Totals for **Atlas Wedge.** NVA/VC—335 KIA, 1 POW. U.S. losses are incomplete. Source documents included losses for the 1st Infantry Division only: 20 KIA, 100 WIA. 1st Cavalry and 11th ACR losses not reported in sources for the individual operation.

18 March: The covert and illegal bombing of Cambodia begins. Codenamed *Operation Menu,* the bombings last 14 months as B–52s pound NVA staging areas and troop concentrations across the border.

18 March 1969 (begins): *Operation Geneva Park. Locations:* I Corps; Quang Ngai and Quang Tin provinces; Ho Cong and Nui Luoi mountains; Song Tra Khuc River; "The Horseshoe"; LZs Bayonet, Fat City, Gator and Stinson. *Type/Objective:* Search and Destroy. The goal of **Geneva Park** is the prevention of attacks on Chu Lai and Quang Ngai City and to secure major lines of communications. *Units:* USA—23d Infantry Division (American): (4/3d Inf, 1/6th Inf, 3/21st Inf, 5/46th Inf, 1/52d Inf); VNAF—2d ARVN Division (6th ARVN Regiment); NVA/VC—78th and 409th Main Force (VC) Rocket battalions. *Events:* **1 February 1970**—A–1/52d Infantry is mortared at LZ Stinson. One American is

KIA and 12 WIA. **22 February 1970**—Eleven troopers of the 17th Cavalry are hit by a 1000-lb. bomb rigged as a mine. Five Americans are KIA and one WIA. **5 August 1970**—C–1/52d Infantry is ambushed by enemy troops who detonate two claymore mines 10 miles west of Chu Lai (Quang Tin Province). Losses: 2 KIA, 9 WIA. *Casualties:* Totals for **Geneva Park** are current only to 31 October 1970. U.S.—166 KIA, 1138 WIA; NVA/VC—1714 KIA, 37 POWs.

18 March 1969 (begins): *Operation Frederick Hill. Locations:* I Corps; Quang Nam and Quang Tin provinces; Hiep Duc, Que Son and "Antenna" valleys; "Pineapple Forest"; Barrier Island; Truang Giang Channel; FSBs Hawk Hill and West. *Type/Objective:* Search and Destroy into the highlands of Quang Nam and Quang Tin. The secondary mission of **Frederick Hill** is to secure the population centers along the coastal plain. *Units:* USA—23d Infantry Division (American): 2/1st Inf, 3/21st Inf, 4/31st Inf, 1/46th Inf, 1/1st Cav; USMC—2/7th Marines; VNAF—2d ARVN Division (5th ARVN Regiment); NVA/VC—2d NVA Division (4000 NVA reported in the area of operations). *Events:* **11 June 1969**—Elements of the 2d NVA Division's 35th Sapper Battalion attack LZ East killing 16 Americans and wounding 33. Enemy losses are 27 KIA. **12 August 1969**—An enemy force of unknown size attacks C–1/1st Cavalry and A–3/16th Artillery at FSB Hawk Hill. Losses in the assault: U.S.—7 KIA, 51 WIA; NVA/VC—13 KIA. **18 August 1969**—Companies B,D–4/31st Infantry each battle an enemy force of unknown size east of Hiep Duc (Quang Tin Province). American losses in the day's fighting: 13 KIA and 48 WIA. **19–20 August 1969**—A–3/21st Infantry air assaults into the site of a helicopter crash near An Lam (3), seven miles east of Hiep Duc, to recover the bodies of the dead Americans. They meet heavy resistance and are not able to retrieve the bodies until

24 August. Losses in the fight: U.S.—6 KIA, 10 WIA; NVA/VC—20 KIA. **28 August 1969**—The 2/7th Marines comes under heavy fire 31 miles south of DaNang (Quang Nam Province). Thirteen Marines are KIA, 42 WIA. **6–7 January 1970**—A–1/1st Cavalry, D–3/21st Infantry, F/17th Cavalry and 3/4th ARVN Regiment fight a two-day battle near Tam Ky (Quang Tin Province). Losses: U.S.—5 KIA, 20 WIA; NVA/VC—131 KIA. **10 February 1970**—An NVA force of unknown size attacks a night defensive position (NDP) of A–2/1st Infantry 12 miles northwest of Tam Ky (Quang Tin Province). Losses: U.S.—1 KIA, 8 WIA; NVA/VC—7 KIA. **20 February 1970**—F/17th Cavalry engages an enemy force of unknown size 13 miles northwest of Tam Ky (Quang Tin Province). The American unit loses seven KIA and 12 WIA. Later the same day, A–2/1st Infantry runs across an enemy force in the same location. Five more U.S. soldiers are KIA and 10 WIA. Enemy losses in both firefights are unknown. **19 March 1970**—Nine soldiers are KIA and one WIA from B–1/1st Cavalry when the enemy detonates a mine near Binh Son, 18 miles northwest of Tam Ky (Quang Tin Province). *Casualties:* Casualty totals for **Frederick Hill** are current only to 31 October 1970. U.S.— 426 KIA, 2575 WIA; NVA/VC— 4184 KIA, 50 POWs.

18 March 1969 (begins): *Operation Iron Mountain. Locations:* I Corps; Quang Ngai Province; Song Tra Cau and Song Ve valleys; Nui Hon Vu and Nui Tam Cap mountains; Duc Pho; Mo Duc; Nghia Han; FSB Debbie; LZs Bronco, Pepper and Snoopy. *Type/Objective:* Search and Destroy designed to prevent enemy troop massing and to support local pacification efforts. *Units:* USA—23d Infantry Division (Americal): 3/1st Inf, 4/3d Inf, 1/20th Inf, 4/21st Inf, 1/1st Cav; VNAF—2d ARVN Division (4th and 6th ARVN rgts); NVA/VC—3d NVA Division. *Events:* **9–10 June 1969**—Companies A–1/20th Infan-

try and E–1/1st Cavalry battle a large NVA force in the western Song Tra Cau Valley, 10–15 miles northwest of Duc Pho. Sixty-one enemy bodies are found following the fight. **14 August 1969**—C–1/20th Infantry is rocked by a mine explosion six miles north of Duc Pho (Quang Ngai Province). One soldier is KIA and 30 WIA in the blast. **29 August 1969**—C–1/1st Cavalry kills 51 NVA in a battle six miles south of Duc Pho (Quang Ngai Province). The American unit suffers only five WIA. **12 October 1969**—Company B–1/20th Infantry is inserted into a very hot LZ three miles southeast of Quang Ngai City. Four are KIA and 12 WIA during the combat assault. **3 January 1970**—Elements of the 2d NVA Sapper Battalion attack Company B–4/3d Infantry at its night defensive position (NDP), six miles south of Duc Pho (Quang Ngai Province). Losses in the fight: U.S.—7 KIA, 11 WIA; NVA/VC—29 KIA. **2 April 1970**—Seven U.S. soldiers are KIA and 19 WIA when troopers of D–4/3d Infantry trip a large mine 13 miles northwest of Duc Pho (Quang Ngai Province). **15 April 1970**—Troops attached to C–4/3d Infantry and C–4/21st Infantry accidentally set off a mine which in turn detonates the mortar rounds they are carrying. The tragedy claims 14 KIA and 32 WIA. *Casualties:* Totals for *Iron Mountain* are current only to October 1970. U.S.—363 KIA, 2090 WIA; NVA/VC—3136 KIA, 84 POWs.

23 March–3 April: *Operation Montana Mauler. Locations:* I Corps; Quang Tri Province; Khe Chua Valley; Hill 208; Cam Lo; Con Thien; FSB Fuller. *Type:* Reconnaissance in Force. *Units:* USA—1st Brigade/5th Infantry Division (M): 1/11th Inf, A,B–3/5th Cav; USMC—1–3/9th Marines (3d Marine Division); NVA/VC—27th NVA Regiment. *Events:* **27 March**—B–1/11th Infantry and 3/5th Cavalry battle an NVA force of unknown size near Hill 208. Losses in the day-long fight: U.S.—13 KIA, 30 WIA; NVA/VC—120 KIA. **28 March**—1/11th

Infantry loses one KIA and 46 WIA while conducting a sweep of the previous day's battlefield. The unit reports killing 60 more enemy soldiers. *Casualties:* Totals for *Montana Mauler.* U.S. – 24 KIA, 171 WIA; NVA/VC – 271 KIA.

25 March–15 April: *Operation Darby Crest III. Location:* II Corps; Binh Dinh Province; "The Cresent Plains." *Objective:* The operation is a continuation of the *Darby Crest* series to disrupt enemy food-collection efforts. *Unit:* USA – 173d Airborne Brigade (1/503d Abn). *Casualties:* U.S. – 3 WIA; NVA/VC – 5 KIA.

26–28 March: *Operation Hunter. Location:* III Corps; Long An Province; BoBo Canal. *Type/Objective:* Search and Clear – Reconnaissance in Force operation in support of the ongoing *Toan Thang* series. *Units:* USA – 199th Light Infantry Brigade (C–2/3d Inf, A,C–5/12th Inf). *Casualties:* Not included in source document for the individual operation.

29 March–12 April: *Operation Montana Scout. Location:* III Corps; Tay Ninh Province. *Objective:* Offensive operations in support of the ongoing *Toan Thang* series. *Units:* USA – 1st Cavalry Division: 1st Bde (2/8th Cav, 2/12th Cav), 2d Bde (2/5th Cav). *Casualties:* Not included in source documents for the individual operation.

30 March–29 May: *Operation Oklahoma Hills. Locations:* I Corps; Quang Nam Province; "Charlie Ridge"; "Worth Ridge"; "Happy Valley"; Vu Gia River; Hill 467; Ba Na; Hoi An; FSBs Buckskin, Longhorn, Mustang, Rattlesnake, Rawhide and Stallion; LZs Eagle, Hawk and Robin. *Type/Objective:* Reconnaissance in Force–Search and Clear operation aimed at eliminating a suspected enemy base area. *Units:* USMC – 1/7th Marines, 2/7th Marines, 3/7th Marines, BLT–3/26th Marines; VNAF – 2/51st ARVN Regiment, 3/51st ARVN Regiment; NVA/VC – 31st, 141st and 368th NVA regiments. *Casualties:*

U.S. – 44 KIA, 439 WIA. The Marines report an additional 456 nonbattle injuries during the operation. NVA/VC – 596 KIA, 7 POWs.

7–20 April: *Operation Muskogee Meadow. Locations:* I Corps; Quang Nam Province; "The Arizona"; An Hoa; Duy Xuyen; Phu Nhuan; Thu Don. *Type/Objective: Muskogee Meadow* is a Search and Clear operation in the An Hoa Basin with the mission of denying food to the enemy. *Units:* USMC – 1/5th Marines, 2/5th Marines, 3/5th Marines. *Event:* 13 April – Companies E,G,H– 2/5th Marines report killing 106 of the enemy while engaging an NVA company approximately four miles north of An Hoa (Quang Nam Province). *Casualties:* U.S. – 16 KIA, 121 WIA; NVA/VC – 162 KIA.

8–15 April: *Operation Ellis Ravine. Locations:* I Corps; Quang Tri Province; Ba Long Valley; Ca Lu; Phuoc Mon; LZs Davis, Hill and Sharon. *Type/Objective:* Search and Clear in support of road construction of an alternate supply route from Quang Tri to Vandergrift Combat Base in the event of Route 9 being closed. *Units:* USA – 1st Brigade/5th Infantry Division (M): 1/11th Inf, 3/5th Cav, A–4/12th Cav; VNAF – 1st ARVN Division (1st and 2d ARVN rgts). *Casualties:* NVA/VC – 581 KIA, 30 POWs (U.S. losses not included in source document).

10–15 April: *Operation Atlas Power. Locations:* III Corps; Binh Duong Province; Michelin Rubber Plantation; FSB Gafsa. *Type/Objective:* Search and Destroy follow-up to *Atlas Wedge. Units:* USA – 1st Infantry Division: 1st Bde (1/28th Inf, 1/4th Cav). *Casualties:* U.S. – 1 KIA, 9 WIA; NVA/VC – 30 KIA.

12 April–14 May: *Operations Montana Raider I, III. Locations:* III Corps; Binh Duong, Binh Long and Tay Ninh provinces; War Zone C; "The Crescent"; Dau Tieng; Quan Loi; Thon Le Chon; LZ Jake. *Type/Objective:* Search and Destroy operations targeted at enemy rear service support and transportation area. *Units:* USA — 1st Cavalry Division: 1st Bde (1/8th Cav, 1/9th Cav), 3d Bde (2/7th Cav), 11th Armored Cavalry Regiment (1st and 2d squadrons); NVA/VC — 1st and 7th NVA divisions (elements). *Casualties:* Totals for *Montana Raider I, III.* NVA/VC — 247 KIA, 15 POWs (U.S. losses not included in the source document for the individual operation).

15 April 1969–1 January 1971: *Operations Washington Green I–II.* Locations: II Corps; Binh Dinh Province; An Lao Valley; An Khe; An Loc; An Thinh; Binh Di; Bong Son; Dai Dinh; Hoai An; My Duc; Phu Huu; Phu My; Tam Quan; Xuan Vinh; LZs Crystal, English, Mahoney, Stinger, Tape and Uplift. *Type/Objective:* Combination Search and Clear/Cordon and Search operations in support of the ongoing pacification efforts in Binh Dinh Province. *Units:* USA — 4th Infantry Division: 2d Bde (1/12th Inf), 101st Airborne Division: 3d Bde (2/506th Inf), 173d Airborne Brigade (1/503d Abn, 2/503d Abn, 3/503d Abn, 4/503d Abn, 1/50th Inf [M]); VNAF — 22d ARVN Division (40th and 41st ARVN regiments); NVA/VC — 3d NVA Division (2d, 18th and 22d NVA regiments). *Events:* **2 May 1969** — Enemy forces shoot down a recon chopper of C–7/17th Cavalry, 12 miles north of Bong Son. An aero-rifle platoon (Blue Team) is inserted to retrieve the dead and comes under heavy fire. D–2/503d Airborne is sent as reinforcements. U.S. losses for the day are four KIA and three WIA. Enemy losses are unknown. **9 May 1969** — Company B–1/50th Infantry (M) tangles with an enemy squad seven miles northeast of Bong Son. Losses in the brief firefight: U.S. — 7 WIA; NVA/VC — 2 KIA. **26 May 1969** — An armored personnel carrier (APC) of C–1/50th Infantry (M) is hit by a command-detonated mine approximately five miles west of. Bong Son. Eight Americans are WIA in the

blast. **17 June 1969** — LZ English, four miles north of Bong Son, is hit by an enemy rocket and grenade attack. Sixteen members of 2/503d Airborne and C, N/75th Infantry (Rangers) are WIA. *Casualties:* Totals for *Washington Green I–II.* U.S. — 142+ KIA, 1342+ WIA; NVA/VC — 1957 KIA.

21 April: *Location:* I Corps; Quang Tri Province; "The Rockpile"; Elliott Combat Base. *Action:* An NVA company attacks U.S. Marine positions approximately five miles northeast of "The Rockpile." *Units:* USMC — G–2/9th Marines; NVA/VC — 36th NVA Regiment (elements). *Casualties:* U.S. — 8 KIA, 23 WIA; NVA/VC — 42 KIA, 3 POWs.

22 April–22 September: *Operation Putnam Tiger.* Locations: II Corps; Kontum and Pleiku provinces; LZ Penny. *Type/Objective:* Search and Destroy. *Putnam Tiger* is a continuation of screening efforts along the South Vietnam/Cambodia border. *Units:* USA — 4th Infantry Division. *Event:* **9 May** — "Battle of LZ Penny." Companies A,B–3/8th Infantry repel an attack on the landing zone by an estimated NVA regiment. American losses are at least 25 KIA. *Casualties:* Totals for *Putnam Tiger.* NVA/VC — 563 KIA (U.S. losses not included in source document for the individual operation).

23 April: *Location:* I Corps; Quang Tri Province; Cam Lo, "The Rockpile." *Action:* U.S. Marine and NVA forces clash between Cam Lo and "The Rockpile." *Units:* USMC — E–2/9th Marines; NVA/ VC — 36th NVA Regiment (elements). *Casualties:* U.S. — 8 KIA, 17 WIA; NVA/ VC — 14 KIA.

25 April–15 May: *Operation Bristol Boots.* Locations: I Corps; Thua Thien Province; Ruong Ruong Valley. *Type:* Reconnaissance in Force. *Units:* USA — 101st Airborne Division: 1st Bde (1/327th Abn, 2/327th Abn, 2/502d Abn); attached to the 101st: 3/5th Cav, B–2/17th Cav, C–2/34th Armor, VNAF — 1/54th

ARVN Regiment; NVA/VC—4th and 5th NVA regiments reported in the area of operations. *Casualties:* U.S.—5 KIA, 34 WIA; NVA/VC—22 KIA, 1 POW.

30 April–16 July: *Operation Virginia Ridge. Locations:* I Corps; Quang Tri Province; "Helicopter Valley"; "The Rockpile"; "Mutter's Ridge"; Cam Lo; Gio Linh; FSBs Fuller and Pete; LZs Ironsides, Junior and Sparrow. *Type/ Objective:* Search and Destroy to prevent further enemy infiltration through the DMZ. *Units:* USMC—1/3d Marines, 2/3d Marines, 3/3d Marines, 9th Marines; NVA/VC—308th NVA Division (36th NVA Regiment). *Events:* **10 May**—The night defensive position (NDP) of D–1/3d Marines near LZ Ironsides is attacked by an estimated NVA platoon. Eight Marines are KIA and 10 WIA in the 10-minute battle. **17 June**—Various elements of the 3/3d Marines and an enemy force of unknown size skirmish near Gio Linh, approximately eight miles north of Dong Ha. Losses are heavy in the firefight: U.S.—19 KIA, 28 WIA; NVA/VC—193 KIA, 9 POWs. *Casualties:* Totals for *Virginia Ridge.* U.S.—106 KIA, 475 WIA; NVA/VC—558 KIA, 9 POWs.

May: The monsoon (rainy) season begins in the southern provinces and ends in the north.

2–24 May: *Operation Dirty Devil. Locations:* III Corps; Binh Duong and Hau Nghia provinces; FSB Patton. *Type/Objective:* Search and Destroy. *Dirty Devil* is part of the ongoing *Toan Thang* series of operations in III Corps. *Units:* USA—3d Brigade/82d Airborne Division (1/508th Abn). *Casualties:* Not included in source document for the individual operation.

5–20 May: *Operation Daring Rebel. Location:* I Corps; Quang Tin Province; Barrier Island. *Type/Objective: Daring Rebel* is a Search and Clear "County Fair" type of operation conducted

along the Quang Tin coast. *Units:* USMC—BLT–1/26th Marines; VNAF—51st and 54th ARVN regiments; ROK—2d Korean Marine Brigade; NVA/VC—3d, 36th and 38th NVA regiments. *Casualties:* U.S.—2 KIA, 51 WIA; NVA/VC—303 KIA, 328 POWs.

7 May–18 June: *Operation Massachusetts Bay. Locations:* I Corps; Quang Tri Province; Base Area 101; Dong Ha Combat Base (Camp Red Devil); LZs Nancy and Sharon. *Type:* Search and Clear. *Units:* USA—1st Brigade/5th Infantry Division (M): 1/61st Inf (M), 1/77th Armor, 3/5th Cav, 4/12th Cav. *Casualties:* NVA/VC—61 KIA (U.S. losses not included in source).

9–11 May: *Operation Guess Who. Locations:* III Corps; Binh Duong Province; Phu Cuong; Tan Thanh Dong. *Type/Objective:* Cordon and Search operation of Tan Thanh Dong, approximately five miles southwest of Phu Cuong. *Guess Who* is a suboperation of the ongoing *Toan Thang III. Units:* USA—3d Brigade/82d Airborne Division (A,B–2/505th Abn, A–2/34th Armor); VNAF—168th, 312th and 774th local Regional Force (RF) companies. *Casualties:* Not included in source document for the individual operation.

9–12 May. *Location:* I Corps; Quang Nam Province; "The Arizona Territory"; Hill 67; An Hoa. *Action:* In an effort to defend the area's rice and corn fields, the Marines engage enemy troops near Hill 67 in the "Arizona," about five miles north-northeast of An Hoa. *Units:* USMC—5th Marines. *Casualties:* NVA/VC—233 KIA reported (U.S. losses not included in source).

9 May–16 July: *Operation Herkimer Mountain. Locations:* I Corps; Quang Tri Province; Lang Ho Valley; "The Rockpile"; Khe Sanh; Elliott Combat Base; Vandergrift Combat Base; FSBs Neville and Russell; LZs Dodge and Sierra. *Type/Objective:* Search and Destroy operation to screen the DMZ.

Units: USMC—1/4th Marines, 2/4th Marines, 3/4th Marines, 2/9th Marines. *Casualties:* U.S.—21 KIA, 216 WIA; NVA/VC—137 KIA.

10 May–7 June: *Operation Apache Snow. Locations:* I Corps; Quang Tri and Thua Thien provinces; Ashau Valley; Base Area 611; Hill 937 (Dong Ap Bia Mountain—"Hamburger Hill"; Ka Lou Mountain; FSBs Airborne, Bradley, Currahee and Tiger. *Type/Objective:* Reconnaissance in Force into Base Area 611. *Apache Snow* is a follow-up operation to *Dewey Canyon* and *Massachusetts Striker. Units:* USA—101st Airborne Division: 2d Bde (2/501st Inf, 3/5th Cav), 3d Bde (3/187th Inf, 1/506th Inf, 2/506th Inf); USMC—1/9th Marines, 2/9th Marines; VNAF—1st ARVN Division (2/1st ARVN Regiment, 3/1st ARVN Regiment, 4/1st ARVN Regiment, 1/3d ARVN Regiment); NVA/ VC—6th, 9th, 26th and 29th NVA regiments. *Events:* **10–20 May—"Battle of Hamburger Hill."** 10 May—B–3/ 187th Infantry meets heavy resistance from the 29th NVA Regiment at the base of Dong Ap Bia—"Hamburger Hill." Three Americans are KIA and 33 WIA in the opening round of the battle. 11 May—Friendly fire from two Cobra gunships kills two and wounds 35 at 3/187th Infantry command post. 13 May—"Battle of LZ Airborne." Company A–2/501st Infantry is attacked eight miles northeast of Ta Bat by the 806/6th NVA Regiment. Losses are heavy in the 90-minute firefight: U.S.— 26 KIA, 62 WIA; NVA/VC—39 KIA. 14 May—All three line companies (B,C,D) of 3/187th Infantry assault the hill, but are thrown back. Twelve Americans are KIA and more than 80 WIA. 15 May—Companies A,B–3/187th Infantry lure an NVA rear-guard ambush patrol into battle and then open up on them, wiping out an entire company. Companies A and B then attempt another assault on the hill . . . again they are stopped, taking 36 additional casualties. Both companies are now

down to half-strength. 18 May—Two full battalions (3/187th Infantry and 1/506th Infantry) attack Hill 937, but a tremendous rainfall and lack of reinforcements stop their progress only 50 yards short of the summit. Companies A,B–3/187th Infantry have suffered a 50 percent casualty rate; Companies C,D– 3/187th Infantry, an 80 percent casualty rate. 20 May—A reinforced assault by four battalions (A,C–3/187th Infantry, A–2/501st Infantry, 1/506th Infantry and 2/3d ARVN) finally reaches the summit of Hamburger Hill at 11:45 A.M., only to find that most of the enemy have already left. Total casualties in the 10-day "Battle of Hamburger Hill": U.S.—70 KIA, 373 WIA; NVA/VC—630 KIA. 27 May—American units on Dong Ap Bia (Hill 937) are evacuated. "Hamburger Hill" is abandoned only a couple of weeks (5 June) after it was taken in a bitter and bloody fight. 17 June—Allied intelligence reports that more than 1000 enemy troops have reoccupied Dong Ap Bia. *Casualties:* Totals for *Apache Snow.* U.S.—113 KIA, 627 WIA; NVA/VC— 977 KIA, 5 POWs.

13–14 May: *Operation Guess What. Locations:* III Corps; Binh Duong Province; Saigon River; An Son. *Type/Objective:* Airmobile combat assault northwest of Di An. *Guess What* is a suboperation of *Toan Thang III. Units:* USA—3d Brigade/82d Airborne Division (C,D–2/505th Abn). *Casualties:* Not included in source document for the individual operation.

16 May–13 August: *Operation Lamar Plain. Locations:* I Corps; Quang Tin Province; Base Area 117; Tam Ky; LZs Professional and Rustler. *Type/Objective:* Search and Destroy into enemy Base Area 117, approximately 45 miles south of Da Nang. *Units:* USA—23d Infantry Division (American) (1/46th Inf), 101st Airborne Division: 2d Bde (1/501st Inf, 1/502d Inf); NVA/VC—2d NVA Division. *Events:* **21 May—**1/46th

Infantry (Americal) engages an enemy force of unknown size near Phuoc An, 12 miles southwest of Tam Ky. Losses in the five-hour firefight: U.S.−7 KIA, 19 WIA; NVA/VC−6 KIA. **8 July**−A−1/502d Infantry squares off against an estimated NVA company near Hau Duc, approximately 20 miles southwest of Tam Ky. Losses in the fight: U.S.−9 KIA, 7 WIA; NVA/VC−4 KIA. *Casualties:* Totals for *Lamar Plain.* U.S.−105 KIA, 333 WIA; NVA/VC−524 KIA, 11 POWs.

22 May: *Location:* IV Corps; Dinh Tuong Province; Giao Duc. *Action:* U.S. troops ambush a Viet Cong unit in the Delta. *Units:* USA−9th Infantry Division: 1st Bde (4/39th Inf); NVA/VC−261 (a Viet Cong battalion). *Casualties:* U.S.−none; NVA/VC−167 KIA, 7 POWs.

23–25 May: *Operation Gallant Leader.* *Location:* I Corps; Quang Nam Province; Hill 55; Liberty Bridge. *Objective:* Sweep of the "Dodge City" area. *Units:* USMC−3/5th Marines, BLT−1/26th Marines. *Casualties:* None reported on either side.

26 May–7 November: *Operation Pipestone Canyon.* *Locations:* I Corps; Quang Nam Province; Ky Lam Delta; Que Son Mountains; La Tho River; Go Noi Island; Hill 37; "Dodge City"; Bao An Tay; Dai Loc; Dian Ban. *Type/Objective:* Search and Destroy into the old *Allen Brook/Meade River* area of operations, 6–13 miles south of Da Nang. The purpose of *Pipestone Canyon* is to deny the enemy safe havens in the "Dodge City"–Go Noi Island area. *Units:* USMC−1/1st Marines, 2/1st Marines, 3/5th Marines, SLF Alpha BLT−1/26th Marines; VNAF−1/51st ARVN, 4/51st ARVN, 37th and 39th ARVN Ranger battalions; NVA/VC−36th and 38th NVA regiments. *Casualties:* Totals for *Pipestone Canyon.* U.S.−71 KIA, 606 WIA; NVA/VC−852 KIA, 58 POWs.

29 May–23 June: *Operation Cameron Falls.* *Locations:* I Corps; Quang Tri Province; Da Krong Valley; Hill 824 (Dong Cho); Khe Sanh; Vandergrift Combat Base; FSBs Cates, Henderson, Shepard and Whisman. *Units:* USMC−2/9th Marines, 3/9th Marines; NVA/VC−304th NVA Division (57th NVA Rgt). *Casualties:* U.S.−24 KIA, 137 WIA; NVA/VC−120 KIA, 1 POW.

2–3 June: *Operation Black Swan.* *Locations:* III Corps; Binh Duong Province; Saigon River; An Som Can. *Type/Objective:* Reconnaissance in Force. *Black Swan* is a sweep of the area just northwest of Di An. The mission is a suboperation of *Toan Thang III.* *Units:* USA−3d Brigade/82d Airborne Division (A,B,C−2/505th Abn, 3/17th Cav). *Casualties:* NVA/VC−31 KIA, 4 POWs (U.S. losses not included in source document for the individual operation).

5 June: *Location:* III Corps; Tay Ninh Province; "Renegade Woods." *Type/Objective:* Reconnaissance in Force operation 15 miles from Tay Ninh City to prevent an NVA attack on the town. This RIF is part of the ongoing *Toan Thang III.* *Units:* USA−25th Infantry Division: 1st Bde (C,D−4/9th Inf); NVA/VC−271st NVA Regiment (elements). *Casualties:* U.S.−4 KIA, 14 WIA; NVA/VC−45 KIA.

5–7 June: *Locations:* III Corps; Tay Ninh Province; Xom Vinh; FSB Crook. *Action:* Hundreds of enemy soldiers are killed in a series of senseless, suicidal attacks on FSB Crook, 13 miles northwest of Tay Ninh City. *Units:* USA−25th Infantry Division: 3d Bde (B−3/22d Inf, A−7/11th Artillery); NVA/VC−2/88th NVA Regiment, 3/88th NVA Regiment, 3/272d NVA Regiment. *Casualties:* U.S.−1 KIA, 7 WIA; NVA/VC−402 KIA.

7–8 June: *Operation Sacramento Bee.* *Locations:* III Corps; Gia Dinh Province; Hoc Mon. *Type/Objective:* Cordon and Search conducted on village approximately five miles northwest of Tan Son Nhut Air Base. *Sacramento Bee* is a suboperation of *Toan Thang III*. *Units:* USA—3d Brigade/82d Airborne Division (A–2/505th Abn, 1 plt–B–1/17th Cav). *Casualties:* Not included in source document for the individual operation.

8 June: President Richard Nixon announces plans to begin the withdrawal of American troops from South Vietnam.

8 June–14 August: *Operation Montgomery Rendezvous. Locations:* I Corps; Thua Thien Province; Ashau and Rao Lao valleys; Base Area 611; FSBs Berchtesgaden and Currahee. *Type/ Objective:* Search and Destroy to deny the enemy use of the Ashau Valley. *Units:* USA—101st Airborne Division: 1st Bde (2/327th Abn), 3d Bde (3/187th Inf, 1/506th Inf, 2/506th Inf); VNAF— 3d ARVN Regiment; NVA/VC—6th NVA Regiment, 6/29th NVA Regiment, 9/29th NVA Regiment, 803d NVA Regiment. *Event:* 14 June—Elements of the 6th NVA Regiment (C–2 and C–3 companies; K–3 Battalion) attack the 101st Airborne's FSBs Berchtesgaden and Currahee. The defenders, 2/327th Airborne and B–1/506th Infantry, repel the attacks killing 33 and capturing three. The Screaming Eagles suffer 11 KIA and 47 WIA. *Casualties:* Totals for *Montgomery Rendezvous.* NVA/VC—451 KIA, 8 POWs (U.S. losses not included in source document for the individual operation).

12 June–9 July: *Operation Utah Mesa. Locations:* I Corps; Quang Tri Province; FSB Cates; LZs Bison, Cokawa and Quantico. *Units:* USA—1st Brigade/5th Infantry Division (M)– Task Force Mustang (1/61st Inf); USMC—Task Force Guadalcanal (1/9th Marines); VNAF—2/2d ARVN, 2/3d ARVN; NVA/VC—304th NVA Division (24th NVA Regiment). *Event:*

18 June—An estimated 100 soldiers of the 24th NVA Regiment attack the night defensive position (NDP) of B–1/61st Infantry, just east of Lang Vei. Losses in the attack: U.S.—11 KIA, 15 WIA; NVA/VC—41 KIA. *Comment: Utah Mesa* represents the last operation and combat action for the 1/9th Marines. *Casualties:* Totals for *Utah Mesa.* U.S.—19 KIA, 101 WIA; NVA/ VC—309 KIA, 7 POWs.

19 June: *Location:* III Corps; Tay Ninh Province; Highway 22. *Action:* NVA/ VC units ambush a U.S. convoy 3.5 miles southeast of Tay Ninh City. *Units:* USA—25th Infantry Division (B,C–3/ 4th Cavalry); VNAF—276th Regional Forces (RF) Company; NVA/VC— 271st NVA Regiment (D–1 and D–14 NVA battalions). *Casualties:* U.S.—4 KIA, 9 WIA; NVA/VC—98 KIA.

19 June–25 September: *Operation Iroquois Grove. Location:* I Corps; Quang Tri Province. *Objective:* Followup to *Massachusetts Bay* in eastern Quang Tri. The purpose of *Iroquois Grove* is the protection of the civilian population and rice crop and to assist in pacification efforts. *Units:* USA—1st Brigade/5th Infantry Division (M): Task Force 1/11th Infantry, Task Force 1/61st Inf (M), Task Force 1/77th Armor. *Casualties:* U.S.—13 KIA, 130 WIA; NVA/VC—134 KIA.

24 June–1 November: *Operation Kentucky Cougar. Locations:* III Corps; Binh Duong, Binh Long, Phuoc Long and Tay Ninh provinces; War Zones C and D; Bunard; FSBs Barham, Becky, Caroline, Ike, Jackie and Jamie. *Type/ Objective:* Search and Destroy. *Kentucky Cougar* is an interdiction operation in support of *Toan Thang III*. The two operations are merged on 1 November 1969. *Units:* USA—1st Cavalry Division: 1st Bde (1/5th Cav, 1/8th Cav, 2/8th Cav, 2/12th Cav), 2d Bde (2/5th Cav, 5/7th Cav), 3d Bde (1/7th Cav, 2/7th Cav, 1/12th Cav), 11th Armored

Cavalry Regiment; VNAF—2d ARVN Division. *Events:* **21 June**—An estimated 600 enemy troops attack FSB Ike in Tay Ninh Province. The base is defended by the 3/4th Cavalry. Losses: U.S.—7 KIA, 18 WIA; NVA/VC—98 KIA. **11 August**—FSB Becky is pounded by more than 400 rockets and then assaulted by an estimated two NVA companies. Casualties in the attack: U.S.—8 KIA, 39 WIA, 5 MIA; NVA/VC—54 KIA, 1 POW. **22 August**—3d plt-D-1/7th Cavalry is hit by a small NVA force five miles southeast of Bunard (Phuoc Long Province). Four Americans are killed. Enemy losses are unknown. *Casualties:* Totals for **Kentucky Cougar.** U.S.—131 KIA, 105 WIA; NVA/VC—4171 KIA, 39 POWs.

26 June: *Operation Bayonet. Location:* III Corps; Binh Duong Province; Saigon River; Binh My. *Type/Objective:* Cordon and Search of the village of Binh My. **Bayonet** is a suboperation of the continuing **Toan Thang III.** *Units:* USA—3d Brigade/82d Airborne Division (A,B-2/505th Abn). *Casualties:* Not included in source document.

27 June–6 July: *Operation Bold Pursuit. Location:* I Corps; Quang Tin Province; Tam Ky. *Unit:* USMC—SLF Alpha BLT-1/26th Marines. *Casualties:* U.S.—4 KIA, 37 WIA; NVA/VC—42 KIA, 8 POWs.

28–29 June: *Operation Cold Steel. Location:* III Corps; Gia Dinh Province; An Phu Dong Com. *Type:* Reconnaissance in Force. **Cold Steel** is a suboperation of **Toan Thang III.** *Units:* USA—3d Brigade/82d Airborne Division (A,D-2/505th Abn). *Casualties:* Not included in source document for the individual operation.

1–2 July: *Operation Forsythe Grove. Locations:* I Corps; Quang Nam Province; "The Arizona Territory"; Song Vu Gia River. *Type/Objective:* Cordon and Search. **Forsythe Grove** is a preemptive

strike meant to prevent an NVA attack on Marine positions on Hill 65. *Units:* 1/5th Marines, 2/5th Marines, 1/7th Marines. *Casualties:* U.S.—1 KIA; NVA/VC—4 KIA.

3 July–20 September: *Operation Arlington Canyon. Locations:* I Corps; Quang Tri Province; DMZ; Nui Tia Pong; Vandergrift Combat Base; FSB Cates, LZs Cougar, Pedro, Scotch and Uranus. *Type/Objective:* Search and Destroy five miles northwest of Vandergrift Combat Base. *Units:* USMC—1/4th Marines, 2/4th Marines, 3/4th Marines; NVA/VC—24th Independent Regiment, 3/246th Independent Regiment, 3/9th NVA Regiment. *Casualties:* U.S.—10 KIA, 28 WIA; NVA/VC—23 KIA.

7 July: The first U.S. troops to withdraw from South Vietnam leave Saigon. Eight hundred men of the 3/60th Infantry/9th Infantry Division go home. By 29 August, 25,000 U.S. personnel will have been withdrawn.

7–8 July: *Operation Cold Dawn. Location:* III Corps; Binh Duong Province; Tan Thanh Dong. *Type/Objective:* Reconnaissance in Force—Cordon and Search approximately five miles southwest of Phu Cuong. **Cold Dawn** is a suboperation of **Toan Thang III.** *Units:* USA—3d Brigade/82d Airborne Division (A,B-2/505th Abn). *Casualties:* Not included in source document for the individual operation.

10–20 July: *Operation Mighty Play. Location:* I Corps; Quang Nam Province; Song Vinh Diem River. *Objective:* Marine Special Landing Force operation executed between DaNang and Hoi An. The goal of **Mighty Play** is the prevention of attacks on DaNang. *Units:* USMC—M-3/1st Marines, BLT-1/26th Marines; ROK—2d Korean Marine Brigade; NVA/VC—R-20 Local Force Battalion, V-25 Local Force Battalion. *Casualties:* U.S.—2 KIA, 28 WIA; NVA/VC—31 KIA.

11 July–15 August: *Operation Campbell Streamer.* *Locations:* I Corps; Quang Nam and Thua Thien provinces; Hue; Phu Loc; FSB Tomahawk. *Type: Campbell Streamer* is a joint Search and Destroy/Cordon operation. *Units:* USA—101st Airborne Division: 2d Bde (1/501st Inf, 2/501st Inf, 1/502d Inf); VNAF—54th ARVN Regiment; NVA/VC—4th NVA Regiment, Phu Loc Battalion. *Casualties:* NVA/VC—58 KIA (U.S. losses not included in source for the individual operation).

13 July: The 4/47th Infantry of the 9th Infantry Division departs from South Vietnam.

14 July: The 1/9th Marines of the 3d Marine Division departs from South Vietnam.

16 July–25 September: *Operation Idaho Canyon.* *Locations:* I Corps; Quang Tri Province; Cam Hung Valley; "The Rockpile"; Cam Lo; Con Thien; Elliott Combat Base; LZ Mack. *Type/ Objective: Idaho Canyon* is a series of offensive sweeps of the northern Quang Tri/DMZ area and is a follow-up to *Virginia Ridge.* *Units:* USA—1st Brigade/5th Infantry Division (M) (1/11th Inf, C–1/77th Armor); USMC—1/3d Marines, 2/3d Marines, 3/3d Marines; NVA/VC—304th NVA Division (1st NVA Regiment, 3/9th NVA Regiment). *Events:* **27 July**—K–3/3d Marines is attacked at its night defensive position by 35–50 NVA. Three Marines are KIA and six WIA. **7 August**—Company D–1/11th Infantry clashes with an estimated two NVA companies one-half mile south of the DMZ. Losses in the battle: U.S.—3 KIA, 13 WIA; NVA/VC—56 KIA. **10 August**—Forces of the 9th NVA Regiment attack the night defensive positions of the 2/3d Marines' mortar platoon. U.S.—13 KIA, 58 WIA; NVA/VC—17 KIA. **15 August**—Company K–3/3d Marines tangles with an estimated reinforced NVA platoon while moving from LZ Mack to LZ Sierra. Four Marines are KIA and 36 WIA. **17 August**—Company L–3/3d Marines fights off an estimated reinforced NVA company on Hill 154. Losses in the firefight: U.S.—13 KIA, 23 WIA; NVA/VC—41 KIA. **17 September**—Two Marine outposts near "The Rockpile" are forced to repel two fierce NVA assaults. Losses: U.S.—25 KIA, 47 WIA; NVA/VC—48 KIA. *Casualties:* Totals for *Idaho Canyon.* U.S.—78 KIA, 366 WIA; NVA/VC—565 KIA, 5 POWs.

16 July–25 September: *Operation Georgia Tar.* *Locations:* I Corps; Quang Tri Province; Hill 950; Ca Lu. *Type/Objective:* Search and Destroy operation to eliminate rocket attacks on Elliott and Vandergrift Combat Bases. *Units:* USMC—1/4th Marines, 3/4th Marines, 3/9th Marines. *Casualties:* U.S.—1 KIA, 23 WIA; NVA/VC—40 KIA.

18 July: The 3/47th Infantry of the 9th Infantry Division departs from South Vietnam.

20 July: *Location:* IV Corps; Dinh Tuong Province; Dong Tam. *Action:* A Viet Cong force of unknown size attacks the 9th Infantry Division headquarters at Dong Tam. *Casualties:* U.S.—6 WIA; NVA/VC—losses unknown.

20 July 1969 (begins): *Operation Nantucket Beach.* *Locations:* I Corps; Quang Ngai Province; Batangan Peninsula; LZ Gator. *Type/Objective:* Cordon and Search operations in support of pacification efforts in Quang Ngai. *Units:* USA—23d Infantry Division (Americal): 1/6th Inf, 1/46th Inf, 5/46th Inf, 1/52d Inf; VNAF—4th ARVN Regiment, 1/6th ARVN, 2/6th ARVN; NVA/VC—48th Local Force (VC) Battalion. *Events:* **5 October 1969**—The night defensive position of B–5/46th Infantry is attacked by a VC force of unknown size. Four Americans are KIA and 15 WIA; enemy losses are unknown.

11 August 1970 — Troopers from A–1/6th Infantry hit a mine five miles north of Quang Ngai City. Thirteen U.S. soldiers are hurt in the blast. *Casualties:* Totals for **Nantucket Beach** are current only to 31 October 1970. U.S. — 37 KIA, 278 WIA; NVA/VC — 430 KIA, 25 POWs.

20 July–13 August: *Operation Durham Peak. Locations:* I Corps; Quang Nam Province; Que Son Mountains; Nui Mat Rang; Phu Lac (6). *Type:* Search and Destroy. *Units:* USMC — 1/1st Marines, 2/1st Marines, 2/5th Marines, 3/5th Marines; VNAF — 5th ARVN Regiment, 37th ARVN Ranger Battalion; NVA/VC — 2d NVA Division. *Event:* 25 July — Company H–2/1st Marines is hit by enemy sniper fire near Hill 845 (Nui Mat Rang). Six Marines are KIA and 16 WIA. There are no enemy casualties reported. *Casualties:* Totals for *Durham Peak.* U.S. — 15 KIA, 63 WIA; NVA/VC — 76 KIA.

21 July–21 September: *Operation Strangle. Locations:* III Corps; Binh Duong Province; "Iron Triangle"; "The Trapezoid"; Saigon River. *Objective:* **Strangle** is a suboperation of *Toan Thang III* and is meant to neutralize enemy forces in the "Iron Triangle" and "Trapezoid" areas. *Units:* USA — 1st Infantry Division: 1st Bde (1/28th Inf, B–2/34th Armor, 1/4th Cav), 2d Bde (2/16th Inf), 3d Bde (2/2d Inf [M], 2/28th Inf); VNAF — 8th ARVN Regiment. *Casualties:* NVA/VC — 365 KIA, 35 POWs (U.S. losses not included in source document for the individual operation).

24 July–7 August: *Operation Brave Armada. Location:* I Corps; Quang Ngai Province. *Type/Objective:* Special Landing Force (SLF) operation into area north of Quang Ngai City. *Units:* USMC — SLF Bravo BLT–2/26th Marines. *Casualties:* U.S. — 1 KIA, 51 WIA; NVA/VC — 11 KIA, 5 POWs.

28 July: *Operation Nutcracker. Locations:* III Corps; Hau Nghia Province; "The Citadel"; Trang Bang. *Action:* U.S. and Viet Cong units clash in an area 25 miles northwest of Saigon. *Units:* USA — 25th Infantry Division: 1st Bde (2/14th Inf), 2d Bde (B–1/5th Inf [M]), 3d Bde (A,C–2/12th Inf); NVA/VC — 268th Viet Cong Regiment. *Casualties:* U.S. — 3 KIA, 14 WIA; NVA/VC — 53 KIA, 6 POWs.

29 July: *Location:* III Corps; Hau Nghia Province; "Parrot's Beak." *Action:* U.S. troops reinforce Special Forces/CIDG camp under heavy fire near the "Plain of Reeds." *Units:* USA — 25th Infantry Division: 2d Bde (C,D–2/27th Inf); NVA/VC — 263d NVA/VC Battalion. *Casualties:* U.S. — 8 KIA, 9 WIA; NVA/VC — 65 KIA.

30 July: The 4/39th Infantry of the 9th Infantry Division departs from South Vietnam.

1 August: The U.S. command reports that 5690 planes have been destroyed since the American involvement in South Vietnam began.

1 August: The 2/9th Marines of the 3d Marine Division departs from South Vietnam.

3 August: The 2/39th Infantry of the 9th Infantry Division departs from South Vietnam.

4 August: Secretary of State Henry Kissinger holds his first meeting in Paris with the North Vietnamese representative, Xuan Thuy.

7 August: *Location:* II Corps; Khanh Hoa Province; Cam Ranh Bay. *Action:* A team of Viet Cong commandos penetrates the defenses surrounding the Cam Ranh Bay complex and attacks the base hospital. *Casualties:* U.S. — 2 KIA, 99 WIA.

8 August: The 3/39th Infantry of the 9th Infantry Division departs from South Vietnam.

8–20 August: *The Battle of Northern Binh Long Province. Locations:* III Corps; Binh Long Province; An Loc; Loc Ninh; Quan Loi. *Action:* U.S. and enemy forces clash in the area approximately 60 miles north of Saigon. *Units:* USA — 1st Cavalry Division (1/9th Cav), 1st Infantry Division: 3d Bde (1/16th Inf [M]), 11th Armored Cavalry Regiment (1st and 2d squadrons); VNAF — 9th ARVN Regiment, 1st and 15th ARVN Cavalry, 34th ARVN Ranger Battalion; NVA/VC — 101st NVA Regiment, 7th Viet Cong Division (209th NVA Regiment), 9th Viet Cong Division (271st and 272d VC regiments). *Events:* 12 August — The American installations at Quan Loi are attacked for three hours by the K-3/271st VC Regiment and K-4/272d VC Regiment. Losses: U.S. — 7 KIA, 45 WIA. 13 August — Companies A,D–1/11th ACR and elements of the ARVN Rangers kill 77 of the enemy in a fierce battle near Loc Ninh. *Casualties:* Totals for the Battle of Northern Binh Long Province are not included in the source documents.

11–12 August: *Locations:* I Corps; Quang Tin Province; Hiep Duc. *Action:* "Battle of LZ West." American and NVA/VC forces clash on a hill mass approximately five miles west of Hiep Duc. *Units:* USA — 23d Infantry Division (Americal) (4/31st Inf, C–3/16th Artillery); NVA/VC — 2d NVA Division (elements). *Casualties:* U.S. — none; NVA/VC — 59 KIA, 6 POWs.

12–14 August: *Location:* I Corps; Quang Nam Province; "The Arizona Territory"; Phu An. *Action:* U.S. Marines and NVA regulars are involved in a two-day firefight approximately 20 miles southwest of DaNang. *Units:* USMC — 1/7th Marines; NVA/VC — 8/90th NVA Regiment, 9/90th NVA Regiment, 368–B Rocket Regiment

(elements). *Casualties:* U.S. — 22 KIA, 100 WIA; NVA/VC — 255 KIA.

12 August–22 September: *Operation Thunder Run. Locations:* III Corps; Binh Long Province; *Red Ball* Area of Operations; Route 13; Chon Thanh; Lai Khe; FSB Thunder III. *Objective:* Security of Route 13, the main supply route for 1st Cavalry elements at An Loc, Loc Ninh and Quan Loi. *Thunder Run* is a suboperation of *Toan Thang III. Units:* USA — 1st Infantry Division: 3d Bde (2/2d Inf [M], 1/4th Cav), 11th Armored Cavalry Regiment; NVA/VC — 101st NVA Regiment. *Events:* 12 August — The K-8/101st NVA Regiment ambushes a U.S. convoy led by C–2/2d Infantry (M) and 1/4th Cavalry, eight miles south of An Loc. Losses: U.S. — 2 KIA, 8 WIA; NVA/VC — 54 KIA. 6 September — The K-9/101st NVA Regiment attempts another ambush at the same site as the 12 August attack. B–1/4th Cavalry and companies A,C–2/2d Infantry (M) kill 55 NVA and capture four. American losses are one KIA and seven WIA. *Casualties:* Totals for *Thunder Run* not included in source document for the individual operation.

13 August: The 3/9th Marines of the 3d Marine Division departs from South Vietnam.

15 August–28 September: *Operation Richland Square. Locations:* I Corps; Thua Thien Province; Ashau Valley; Phu Loc Mountains. *Type/Objective:* Search and Destroy operation to interdict enemy lines of communication and to provide security for the local population. *Units:* USA — 101st Airborne Division: 1st Bde (1/327th Abn, 2/327th Abn, 2/502d Abn), 2d Bde (1/501st Inf, 2/501st Inf, 1/502d Inf), 3d Bde (3/187th Inf, 1/506th Inf, 2/506th Inf); VNAF — 1st and 3d ARVN regiments; NVA/VC — 5th and 6th NVA regiments. *Comment: Richland Square* is the "parent" operation to three separate suboperations, each one conducted by an individual brigade: **Cumberland Thunder:** 1st Bde vs 5th NVA Rgt; **Claiborne Chute:** 2d Bde vs 5th/6th NVA rgts; **Louisiana Lee:** 3d Bde. *Casualties:* Totals for **Richland Square** et al. NVA/VC—184 KIA, 5 POWs (U.S. losses not included in the source document for the combined operations).

27 August: The 1st and 2d brigades of the 9th Infantry Division officially depart from South Vietnam. The 3d Brigade/9th Infantry Division remains in-country and is reassigned to the 25th Infantry Division.

3 September: The leader of North Vietnam, Ho Chi Minh, dies in Hanoi at the age of 79.

7–19 September: *Operation Defiant Stand. Locations:* I Corps; Quang Tin Province; Barrier Island; Hoi An; LZ Eagle. *Units:* USMC—BLT-1/26th Marines; ROK—ROK 2d Marine Brigade (two battalions). *Casualties:* U.S.—4 KIA, 49 WIA; NVA/VC—244 KIA, 6 POWs.

10 September–15 November: *Operation Yorktown Victor. Locations:* III Corps; Binh Duong Province; "Iron Triangle"; Saigon and Thi Tinh rivers; Phu Hoa. *Type/Objective:* Search and Destroy operations northwest of Saigon in support of the pacification efforts in Binh Duong Province. *Units:* USA—1st Infantry Division (elements), 3d Brigade/82d Airborne Division (1/505th Abn, 2/505th Abn, 1/508th Abn); NVA/VC—83d Rear Service Force (a VC logistics group). *Comment:* **Yorktown Victor** is the last operation in South Vietnam for the 3d Brigade/82d Airborne Division. *Casualties:* Totals for **Yorktown Victor** not included in source document for the individual operation.

11 September 1969–20 February 1970: *Operation Friendship III. Locations:* III Corps; Bien Hoa, Binh Thuy, Long Khanh and Phuoc Tuy provinces;

Ap Tan Lap; FSB Cristol. *Objective:* **Friendship III** is a multinational offensive operation conducted to try to neutralize the 274th Viet Cong Regiment. *Units:* USA—199th Light Infantry Brigade (2/3d Inf, 4/12th Inf, D/17th Cav); VNAF—18th ARVN Division, 48th ARVN Regiment; Aust—1st Australian Task Force; Thai—Royal Thai Army Volunteer Force; NVA/VC—274th Viet Cong Regiment. *Casualties:* Not included in source documents for the individual operation.

16 September: President Nixon announces that another 35,000 American servicemen will be withdrawn from South Vietnam.

19 September: President Nixon announces that draft calls scheduled for some 50,000 men in November and December 1969 have been cancelled.

21 September 1969 (begins): *Operation Danger Forward I. Location:* III Corps; Binh Duong Province; "Iron Triangle." *Type/Objective:* Search and Destroy operation to neutralize enemy forces northwest of Saigon. **Danger Forward I** is a suboperation of **Toan Thang III.** *Units:* USA—1st Infantry Division: 1st Bde (1/2d Inf, 1/26th Inf, 1/28th Inf), 2d Bde (2/16th Inf, 1/18th Inf, 2/18th Inf), 3d Bde (2/2d Inf [M], 1/16th Inf [M], 2/28th Inf), 3d Brigade/82d Airborne Division (1/505th Abn); VNAF—7th and 8th ARVN regiments; NVA/VC—Dong Nai Regiment (VC), 2d Quyet Thang Battalion (VC). *Casualties:* Totals for **Danger Forward I** are current only to 31 October 1969: NVA/VC—598 KIA, 47 POWs (U.S. losses not included in source document for the individual operation).

29 September–3 November: *Operation Norton Falls. Locations:* I Corps; Quang Tri Province; Mai Loc; Vandergrift Combat Base. *Objective:* To screen the redeployment of the 3d Marine Division's 4th Marines from Quang Tri

Province. *Units:* USA−101st Airborne Division: 3d Bde (1/506th Inf, 2/506th Inf, A−2/17th Cav); VNAF−2/2d ARVN Regiment; NVA/VC−31st and 246th NVA regiments. *Casualties:* U.S.−5 KIA, 19 WIA; NVA/VC−65 KIA.

29 September–6 December: *Operation Republic Square. Location:* I Corps; Quang Tri and Thua Thien provinces; Ashau Valley. *Objective:* Relocation of forces out of the Ashau Valley and into the lowlands to help support population security and pacification operations. *Units:* USA−101st Airborne Division: 1st Bde (1/327th Abn, 2/327th Abn, 2/502d Abn), 2d Bde (1/501st Inf, 2/501st Inf, 1/502d Inf); VNAF−2/2d ARVN Regiment, 3d ARVN Regiment, 2/54th ARVN Regiment; NVA/VC−K−4/5th NVA Regiment, 31st and 246th NVA regiments. *Comment: Republic Square* is the "parent" operation for the 101st's *Norton Falls* and *Saturate. Casualties:* Totals for the combined *Republic Square* operations: U.S.−16 KIA, 86 WIA; NVA/VC−254 KIA, 16 POWs.

October–November: The 3d and 4th Marines of the 3d Marine Division depart from South Vietnam.

5 October–4 December: *Operation Saturate. Locations:* I Corps; Thua Thien Province; Phu Luong; Phu Thu; Vinh Thai. *Type/Objective:* Search and Destroy operation to eliminate the VC infrastructure in the Phu Thai District. *Units:* USA−101st Airborne Division: 1st Bde (1/327th Abn); VNAF−3d and 54th ARVN regiments; NVA/VC−K−4/5th NVA Regiment. *Casualties:* U.S.−1 KIA, 31 WIA; NVA/VC−8 KIA, 9 POWs.

6 October: The 1/3d Marines and 2/3d Marines of the 3d Marine Division depart from South Vietnam.

7 October: The 3/3d Marines of the 3d

Marine Division departs from South Vietnam.

22 October 1969–18 January 1970: *Operation Fulton Square. Locations:* I Corps; Quang Tri Province; Gio Linh; Hai Lang; Mai Linh; Trieu Phong; LZ Sparrow. *Units:* USA−1st Brigade/5th Infantry Division (M) (elements), 101st Airborne Division (elements); NVA/VC−27th NVA Regiment. *Casualties:* NVA/VC−384 KIA (U.S. losses not included in source).

25 October: The 11th Armored Cavalry Regiment turns over its main base camp to the South Vietnamese as part of the ongoing Vietnamization of the war. The Blackhorse Base Camp is located 38 miles northeast of Saigon in Long Khanh Province (III Corps).

25 October 1969 (begins): *Operation Seminoles. Locations:* III Corps; Binh Duong Province; Ben Cat; Chau Thanh; Dau Tieng; Lai Thieu; Tan Uyen. *Type/Objective:* Pacification operation with goal of reducing the strength of specific enemy Local Force (LF) units by one-third as of 1 January 1970. *Units:* USA−1st Infantry Division: 1st Bde (1/2d Inf, 1/26th Inf, 1/28th Inf), 2d Bde (2/16th Inf, 1/18th Inf, 2/18th Inf), 3d Bde (2/2d Inf [M], 1/16th Inf [M], 2/28th Inf); NVA/VC−Local Force (LF) units: C−61, C−62, C−63, C−64, C−65 and C−301. *Casualties:* Not included in source document for the individual operation.

November: The monsoon (rainy) season begins in the northern provinces and ends in the south.

1 November 1969–May 1970: *Operation Toan Thang IV. Locations:* III Corps; Bien Hoa, Binh Duong, Binh Long, Binh Tuy, Gia Dinh, Hau Nghia, Long An, Long Khanh, Phuoc Long, Phuoc Tuy and Tay Ninh provinces; IV Corps; Dinh Tuong and Kien Tuong provinces; War Zones C and D; "Iron

Triangle"; Michelin Plantation; Nui Ba
Den; "Renegade Woods"; "Razorback
Mountain"; Saigon, Song Be and Thi
Tinh rivers; "The Trapezoid"; "Jolly
Road"; "Serge's Jungle Highway"; Bear
Cat; Dau Tieng; Di An; Lai Ke; Minh
Thanh; Phu Hoa; Phu Loi; Song Be;
Tan Linh; FSBs Atkinson, Blackhawk,
Buttons, Carolyn, Elaine, Gettysburg,
Ike, Illingworth, Jay, Jerri, LeLoi,
Ruth, Snuffy and Tina. *Type/Objective:*
Toan Thang IV is a series of combined
offensive operations (Search and De-
stroy/Search and Clear/Cordon and
Search) to prohibit enemy troop infil-
tration and movement in the III and IV
Corps areas. *Units:* USA—1st Cavalry
Division: 1st Bde (1/5th Cav, 1/8th Cav,
2/8th Cav, 2/12th Cav), 2d Bde (2/5th
Cav, 5/7th Cav), 3d Bde (1/7th Cav,
2/7th Cav, 1/12th Cav), 1st Infantry
Division: 1st Bde (1/2d Inf, 2/2d Inf [M],
1/26th Inf, 1/28th Inf, 2/28th Inf), 2d
Bde (2/16th Inf, 1/18th Inf, 2/18th Inf),
3d Bde (1/16th Inf [M]), 9th Infantry
Division: 3d Bde (6/31st Inf, 2/47th Inf
[M], 2/60th Inf, 5/60th Inf [M], D–3/5th
Cav), 25th Infantry Division: 1st Bde
(4/9th Inf, 2/14th Inf, 4/23d Inf [M],
3/4th Cav), 2d Bde (1/5th Inf [M], 2/12th
Inf, 1/27th Inf, 2/27th Inf, B–2/34th Ar-
mor), 3d Bde (2/22d Inf [M], 3/22d Inf),
11th Armored Cavalry Regiment, 199th
Light Infantry Brigade (2/3d Inf, 3/7th
Inf, 4/12th Inf, 5/12th Inf); VNAF—
5th, 18th and 25th ARVN divisions;
NVA/VC—1st, 33d, 88th, 95–C and
101st NVA regiments, 199th, 268th,
271st, 272d, 274th and Dong Nai Viet
Cong regiments, 6th and 265th Main
Force (VC) battalions. *Events:* **4 November**—Elements of the 2/271st NVA
Regiment and the 95th Sapper Recon
Company attack the 2/5th Cavalry (1st
Cav Div) at FSB Ike (Tay Ninh Prov-
ince). Losses: U.S.—1 KIA, 11 WIA;
NVA/VC—54 KIA, 5 POWs. **10 No-
vember**—The recon platoon of 3/7th
Infantry (199th LIB) battles an NVA
company near Signal Mountain in Long
Khanh Province. Fifteen Americans
are WIA in the fray. The enemy body

count is four. **11 November**—An NVA/
VC force of unknown size attacks the
1st Cav's FSB Jerri in Binh Long Prov-
ince. Five cavalrymen are KIA and
seven WIA. **23 November**—The 1st In-
fantry Division's A,C–2/28th Infantry,
D–1/4th Cavalry and elements of
2/2d Infantry (M) clash with a well-
entrenched enemy platoon south of
Dau Tieng (Binh Duong Province).
Losses: U.S.—16 WIA; NVA/VC—30
KIA. **12 December**—Companies D–6/
31st Infantry and B–3/17th Cavalry
tangle with elements from the 1st NVA
Regiment two miles northwest of Binh
Phuoc (III Corps; Long An Province).
Losses: U.S.—2 KIA, 5 WIA; NVA/
VC—28 KIA. **15 December**—Troop
F–2/11th ACR and 2/1st ARVN Regi-
ment engage the enemy in an hour-long
firefight two miles south of Bu Dop (III
Corps; Phuoc Long Province). Losses:
U.S.—4 KIA, 18 WIA; VNAF—2 KIA, 9
WIA; NVA/VC—41 KIA, 2 POWs. **23
December**—Enemy troops launch a
rocket and mortar attack on the 1st
Cavalry's FSB Buttons (III Corps;
Phuoc Long Province). The defenders,
2/12th Cavalry, lose five KIA and eight
WIA. **28 December**—NVA/VC terror-
ists toss explosives into a 25th Infantry
Division camp near Lai Khe (III Corps;
Binh Duong Province). Seven Americans are KIA and five WIA in the blasts.
20 January 1970—"Battle of the Crescent." Troops F,G,H–2/11th ACR defend FSB Ruth and the surrounding
area from elements of the 65th and
141st NVA regiments (III Corps; Phuoc
Long Province). Losses not in source.
21 January—The 1st Cavalry's FSB Buttons (III Corps; Phuoc Long Province)
is again rocketed. Three Americans are
KIA and 10 WIA. **21 January**—"Battle
of the Crossroads." While conducting a
Reconnaissance in Force near FSB
Dennis (III Corps; Binh Long Province), troops B,C–1/11th ACR and
F,G–2/11th ACR encounter a large
enemy force composed of the K–1 and
K–2/141st NVA Regiment. Losses:
U.S.—1 KIA, 6 WIA; NVA/VC—41 KIA.

26 January–13 April — The 2d Brigade/ 1st Cavalry Division and the ARVN Airborne Division conduct an extended Search and Destroy campaign in Phuoc Long Province (III Corps) near Bu Gia Map. The operation pits the 5/7th, 2/8th and 2/12th cavalries against the 174th Viet Cong Regiment (5th VC Division). The most significant action of the operation comes 28 March, as A–1/12th Cavalry is conducting a BDA (Bomb Damage Assessment) sweep near Bu Gia Map. A Company comes into contact with elements of the 174th VC Regiment. Losses in the firefight: U.S. — 5 KIA, 10 WIA; NVA/VC — 44 KIA. Total casualties for this suboperation: U.S. — 34 KIA, 23 WIA; NVA/VC — 495 KIA. 31 January — Company C–4/12th Infantry (199th LIB) is attacked at an ambush position in Binh Tuy Province (III Corps) by elements of the 33d NVA Regiment. U.S. losses are two KIA and 26 WIA. 4 February — Elements from the 95–C NVA Regiment launch a rocket-supported ground attack on the 1st Cavalry's positions at FSB Tina (III Corps; Tay Ninh Province). Losses in the fight: U.S. — 4 KIA, 9 WIA; NVA/ VC — 44 KIA. 14–15 February — C–2/8th Cavalry (1st Cav Div) and C–1/ 11th ACR confront an estimated NVA battalion west of Bau Tam Ung (III Corps; Tay Ninh Province). Losses: U.S. — 10 KIA, 30 WIA; NVA/VC — 46 KIA. 27 February — The Tay Ninh Base Camp of the 25th Infantry Division is mortared. The shelling kills six U.S. soldiers and wounds six more. 27 February — An armored personnel carrier of the 1/5th Infantry (M) (25th Inf Div) hits a mine near the Michelin Plantation (III Corps; Binh Duong Province). The explosion kills seven GIs. 27 February — Elements of the 3/33d NVA Regiment ambush Troop D/17th Cavalry (199th LIB) along Highway 335, five miles northwest of Tanh Linh (III Corps; Binh Tuy Province). Losses: U.S. — 9 WIA; NVA/VC — 9 KIA. 4 March — Heavy fighting erupts

eight miles northwest of Cu Chi (III Corps; Binh Duong Province) between C–2/2d Infantry (M) (25th Inf Div) and an enemy force of unknown size. Losses in the battle: U.S. — 11 KIA, 37 WIA; NVA/VC — 84 KIA. 8 March — An estimated company of NVA soldiers attack C–2/8th Cavalry's (1st Cav Div) positions at FSB Carolyn, approximately 20 miles northeast of Tay Ninh (III Corps; Tay Ninh Province). Losses in the attack: U.S. — 3 KIA, 28 WIA; NVA/VC — 39 KIA. 11 March — While accompanying a convoy, companies A,C–2/22d Infantry (M) (25th Inf Div) are ambushed near the Ben Cui Rubber Plantation, approximately three miles southwest of Dau Tieng (III Corps; Binh Duong Province). Losses in the ambush: U.S. — 2 KIA, 3 WIA; NVA/VC — 77 KIA. 15–16 March — The 4/23d Infantry (M) (25th Inf Div) grinds out a two-day fight with an enemy force of unknown size near Nui Ba Den Mountain (III Corps; Tay Ninh Province). Casualties in the battle: U.S. — 1 KIA, 11 WIA; NVA/VC — 56 KIA. 26 March — A U.S. reconnaissance patrol stumbles onto a well-entrenched platoon of NVA regulars from the 1/272d NVA Regiment in Tay Ninh Province (III Corps). The patrol is quickly reinforced by A,C–2/8th Cavalry (1st Cav Div) and A–1/11th ACR. Casualties: U.S. — 3 KIA, 22 WIA; NVA/VC — 88 KIA. 29 March — "Battle of FSB Jay." The 3/95th NVA Regiment attacks the 1st Cav's FSB Jay, 20 miles northwest of Tay Ninh City (III Corps; Tay Ninh Province). The battle is carried for the U.S. by companies A,B,C–2/7th Cavalry, B–2/12th Artillery and B–2/14th Artillery. Losses in the fight: U.S. — 13 KIA, 53 WIA; NVA/VC — 74 KIA, 3 POWs. 1 April — D/17th Cavalry (199th LIB) is ambushed again by the 33d NVA Regiment at the site of the 27 February attack — four miles northwest of Tanh Linh (III Corps; Binh Tuy Province). Losses: U.S. — 5 KIA, 16 WIA; NVA/VC — 9 KIA. 1 April — "Battle of FSB Illingworth." An estimated two reinforced companies of NVA regulars attack the 1st Cavalry's FSB Ill-ingworth, situated near the Cambodian border approximately 25 miles north-west of Tay Ninh City (III Corps; Tay Ninh Province). Defending the base are the 2/8th Cavalry and Troop A–1/11th ACR. Losses in the bloody attack: U.S.—24 KIA, 54 WIA; NVA/VC—74+ KIA. **5 April**—A–4/23d Infantry (M) (25th Inf Div) engages an enemy force of unknown size near Tay Ninh's Nui Ba Den Mountain (III Corps). Losses in the battle: U.S.—2 KIA, 11 WIA; NVA/VC—6 KIA. **15–16 April**—NVA/VC forces launch a rocket and mortar-supported ground attack on the 1st Cav's FSB Atkinson, 23 miles north-west of Tay Ninh City (III Corps; Tay Ninh Province). Seven Americans are KIA and 12 WIA in the assault. The enemy body count is reported at 79 KIA. *Casualties:* Totals for **Toan Thang IV** are incomplete. Partial figures are as follows: 1st Infantry Division—65 KIA, 460 WIA; 9th/25th Infantry divi-sions—113 KIA, 1112 WIA, totals—178 KIA, 1572 WIA. Casualty information for the 1st Cavalry Division, 11th Ar-mored Cavalry Regiment and 199th Light Infantry Brigade not included in source documents. NVA/VC casualty figures reflect only those inflicted by the 1st, 9th and 25th Infantry divisions: NVA/VC—2431 KIA, 175 POWs.

7–9 November: *Operation Long Reach I. Locations:* III Corps; Binh Long and Phuoc Long provinces; Bo Duc; Bu Dop; Loc Ninh; FSBs Deb, Jerri, Joel and Marge. *Objective:* The goal of **Long Reach I** is to open High-way 14 and relieve pressure on the Bo Duc/Bu Dop area, approximately 22 miles northeast of Loc Ninh. *Units:* USA—1st Cavalry Division (elements), 11th Armored Cavalry Regiment (2d Squadron); VNAF—36th ARVN Ranger Battalion. *Casualties:* Totals for **Long Reach I** not included in source document for the individual opera-tion.

9 November: The 2/4th Marines of the 3d Division departs from South Vietnam.

12–13 November: *Location:* I Corps; Quang Tri Province; Con Thien. *Ac-tion:* NVA forces launch two days of fierce attacks on American units in the Con Thien area. *Units:* USA—1st Bri-gade/5th Infantry Division (M). *Casu-alties:* U.S.—22 KIA, 53 WIA.

20 November: The Cleveland *Plain Dealer* newspaper publishes photog-rapher Ron Haeberle's pictures of the massacre at My Lai.

20 November: The 3/4th Marines of the 3d Marine Division departs from South Vietnam.

24 November: The 3d Recon Battal-ion of the 3d Marine Division departs from South Vietnam. The planned withdrawal of 35,000 more U.S. troops from South Vietnam is completed.

24–28 November: *Operation Texas Traveler. Locations:* III Corps; Binh Long and Tay Ninh provinces; War Zone C; Route 246; FSBs Jackie, Jake, Jamie and Vickie. *Type/Objective:* **Texas Traveler** is a Long Range Recon-naissance (LRRP) mission to help with the screening and interdicting of enemy infiltration from Cambodia into eastern War Zone C. *Units:* USA—11th Armored Cavalry Regiment (3d Squad-ron). *Casualties:* Not included in source document for the individual operation.

30 November: The 3d Marine Divi-sion officially departs from South Viet-nam. The division was the commanding unit of the 3d, 4th and 9th Marines.

3 December 1969–January 1970: *Operation Long Reach II. Locations:* III Corps; Phuoc Long Province; "Serge's Jungle Highway"; Bu Dop. *Type/Ob-jective:* **Long Reach II** is a "Rome Plow" land-clearing operation along QL 14.

Units: USA—11th Armored Cavalry Regiment (2d Squadron). *Casualties:* Not included in source document for the individual operation.

7 December 1969–31 March 1970: *Operation Randolph Glen. Locations:* I Corps; Thua Thien Province; Ashau, Ba Long, Da Krong and Ruong Ruong valleys; La Chu; Nam Hoa; Phong Diem; Phu Vang. *Type/Objective:* Search and Clear operation in support of the pacification efforts in the Thua Thien lowlands. *Units:* USA—101st Airborne Division: 1st Bde (1/327th Abn, 2/327th Abn, 2/502d Abn), 2d Bde (1/501st Inf, 2/501st Inf, 1/502d Inf), 3d Bde (3/187th Inf, 1/506th Inf, 2/506th Inf); VNAF— 1st ARVN Division; NVA/VC—324-B Division (4th NVA Regiment, 2/246th NVA Regiment, 804th NVA Battalion), 800/6th VC Regiment, Phu Loc (VC) Battalion. *Casualties:* U.S.—123 KIA, 257 WIA, 4 MIA; NVA/VC—721 KIA, 19 POWs.

11 December: The 3d Brigade/82d Airborne Division officially departs from South Vietnam. Leaving with the brigade are its three organic infantry battalions: 1/505th Airborne, 2/505th Airborne and the 1/508th Airborne.

15 December: President Nixon announces the beginning of the third phase of troop reductions in Southeast Asia. Nixon promises the removal of 50,000 more U.S. personnel from Vietnam by 15 April 1970.

15 December 1969 (begins): *Operation Danger Forward II. Locations:* III Corps; Binh Duong Province; "The Trapezoid"; Michelin Rubber Plantation; Lai Khe. *Objective: Danger Forward II* is an offensive operation with the mission of neutralizing enemy forces in the area northwest of Saigon. *Units:* USA—1st Infantry Division: 2d Bde (1/18th Inf, 2/18th Inf); VNAF—5th ARVN Division, 2d Quyet Thang Regiment; NVA/VC—Dong Nai (VC) Regiment. *Casualties:* Not included in source document for the individual operation.

30 December 1969 (begins): *Operation Chameleon. Location:* III Corps; Bien Hoa and Phuoc Tuy provinces; Bear Cat. *Objective: Chameleon* is supposed to increase Allied troop density in the area of operations. *Units:* USA— 1st Infantry Division: 2d Bde (1/18th Inf, 2/18th Inf), Aust—1st Australian Task Force; Thai—Royal Thai Army Volunteer Force; NVA/VC—274th Viet Cong Regiment; 5th Main Force Heavy Weapons Battalion (VC). *Casualties:* (current only to 31 January 1970) NVA/VC—41 KIA (U.S. losses not included in source document for the individual operation).

31 December: There are still approximately 475,000 U.S. personnel in Southeast Asia. U.S. ground forces total 385,000 and end the year in the following strengths: Army—330,650, Marines—55,040. So far, some 60,000 troops have returned home. American losses for the year: 9414 KIA, 62,946 WIA. Total American losses in Vietnam since 1960: 40,024 KIA, 270,441 WIA. VNAF strength at the end of 1969: 897,000–1,000,000. VNAF losses for the year: 21,833 KIA. Total VNAF losses since 1965: 110,176 KIA. Estimated NVA/VC strength at the end of 1969: 240,000+. NVA/VC losses for the year: 45,000+. Estimated NVA/VC losses since 1965: 400,000+.

1970

As of 1 January 1970, more than 475,000 U.S. personnel still remain in South Vietnam and Thailand. U.S. ground force strength is down to 385,000. VNAF strength is estimated at 900,000. A large contingent of Australian, Korean and Thai soldiers supplements the American/South Vietnamese forces. The opposition still is formidable . . . numbers of enemy troops are estimated at more than 240,000.

4 January: *Location:* I Corps; Quang Nam Province; DaNang. *Action:* An enemy unit attacks 1st Marine Division positions at Outpost Piranha, 1.5 miles southwest of the divisional Command Post near DaNang. *Units:* USMC—1st Tank Battalion/26th Marines. *Casualties:* U.S.—4 WIA; NVA/VC—1 KIA.

4–11 January: *Operation Cliff Dweller IV. Locations:* III Corps; Tay Ninh Province; Nui Ba Den; Nui Cau; Phu Kuong. *Type/Objective:* Search and Clear on the eastern slope of Nui Ba Den, near Phu Kuong—eight miles northeast of Tay Ninh City. *Cliff Dweller IV* is a suboperation of *Toan Thang IV. Units:* USA—25th Infantry Division: 1st Bde (A–4/9th Inf, 3/22d Inf, A–2/34th Armor); NVA/VC—271st NVA Regiment (F–31, F–51 Sappers). *Casualties:* U.S.—3 KIA, 55 WIA; NVA/VC—156 KIA.

6 January: *Location:* I Corps; Quang Nam Province; Que Son Valley; FSB Ross. *Action:* VC units attack Marine positions at FSB Ross approximately 30 miles south of DaNang. *Units:* USMC— HHC,A,B–1/7th Marines, G–3/11th Marines, K–4/13th Marines (560 Marines); NVA/VC—409th Local Force (VC) Battalion. *Casualties:* U.S.—13 KIA, 63 WIA; NVA/VC—38 KIA, 3 POWs.

6 January: *Location:* I Corps; Quang Nam Province; DaNang/Marble Mountain. *Type/Objective:* "Kingfisher" patrol five miles south of DaNang. *Unit:* USMC—A–2/1st Marines. *Casualties:* U.S.—0; NVA/VC—15 KIA, 1 POW.

13 January: *Location:* I Corps; Quang Nam Province; "Arizona Territory"; Vu Gia River. *Type/Objective:* "Kingfisher" patrol into area approximately 22 miles southwest of DaNang. *Units:* USMC— I–3/5th Marines. *Casualties:* U.S.—2 WIA; NVA/VC—10 KIA, 1 POW.

14 January: *Location:* I Corps; Quang Nam Province; LZ Baldy. *Action:* Marines clash with enemy in a firefight near LZ Baldy. The fight takes place 19 miles south of DaNang. *Unit:* USMC—F-2/7th Marines. *Casualties:* U.S.—2 KIA, 3 WIA; NVA/VC—10 KIA.

19 January–22 July: *Operation Greene River.* *Locations:* I Corps; Quang Tri Province; Ba Long Valley; Cua Viet; Dong Ha; Hai Lang; Trieu Phong; Vandergrift Combat Base; FSBs Fuller, Holcomb and Pedro. *Type/Objective:* Reconnaissance in Force and Search and Clear operations in support of provincial pacification programs. *Units:* USA—1st Brigade/5th Infantry Division (M) (1/11th Inf, 1/61st Inf [M], 3/5th Cav, 1/77th Armor); VNAF—1st ARVN Division (2d ARVN Regiment, 7th ARVN Regiment [M]). *Events:* **28 May**—A-1/77th Armor and 1/61st (M) battle an NVA squad north of Dong Ha. Losses: U.S.—5 WIA; NVA/VC—5 KIA. **15 July**—Company B-1/77th Armor is ambushed by an enemy force of unknown size between Quang Tri and Vandergrift Combat Base. One American is KIA and three WIA in the ambush. Only one enemy body is found following the fight. *Casualties:* Totals for *Greene River.* Allied—68 KIA, 967 WIA; NVA/VC—400+ KIA.

30 January–16 April: *Operation York Market.* *Locations:* I Corps; Quang Tri Province; O Giang and Thac Ma rivers; Hai Lang; Hai Truong. *Type/Objective:* Reconnaissance in Force–Search and Clear into the area approximately 8–10 miles southeast of Quang Tri City. *Units:* USA—1st Brigade/5th Infantry Division (1/77th Armor); VNAF—Regional Forces/Popular Forces (elements). *Casualties:* Totals for **York Market.** U.S.—9 WIA; NVA/VC—20 KIA, 1 POW.

10 February: *Location:* I Corps; Quang Nam Province; DaNang. *Action:* A Marine unit skirmishes with an enemy force three miles south of Marble Mountain. *Unit:* USMC—E-2/1st Marines. *Casualties:* U.S.—none; NVA/VC—4 KIA.

10 February–29 March: *Operation Dakota Clint.* *Locations:* I Corps; Quang Tri Province; Cam Lo; Mai Loc. *Type/Objective:* Combined Reconnaissance in Force and Search and Clear operation into area west of Quang Tri City to deny the enemy food and support pacification of the province. *Units:* USA—1st Brigade/5th Infantry Division (M) (1/11th Inf); VNAF—Regional Forces/Popular Forces (elements). *Casualties:* U.S.—15 WIA; NVA/VC—19 KIA, 1 POW.

12 February: *Locations:* I Corps; Quang Nam Province; Que Son Valley; Ly Ly River; FSB Ross. *Action:* North Vietnamese units ambush a U.S. Marines force near FSB Ross. Site of the ambush is 8.5 miles west of Hiep Duc. *Units:* USA—23d Infantry Division (American) (3/21st Infantry—as reinforcement); USMC—B-1/7th Marines, C-1/7th Marines (as reinforcements); NVA/VC—31st NVA Regiment reported in area of operations. *Casualties:* U.S.—13 KIA, 13 WIA; NVA/VC—6 KIA.

16 February–9 March: *Operation Wayne Stab II.* *Locations:* II Corps; Binh Dinh Province; Kim Son Valley ("Crows Foot"); FSBs Abby, Augusta, Challenge and Hooper; LZ English. *Objective:* **Wayne Stab II** is a search mission for a suspected POW camp and is a suboperation of the ongoing *Dan Quyen/Hines.* *Units:* USA—4th Infantry Division: 1st Bde (3/8th Inf, 1/14th Inf, 1/22d Inf), 173d Airborne Brigade (elements); VNAF—22d ARVN Division; NVA/VC—3d NVA Division (elements). *Casualties:* Not included in source document for the individual operation.

19 February: *Locations:* I Corps; Quang Nam Province; Que Son Valley; Son Thang (Thang Tay [1]). *Action:* "Massacre at Son Thang." A five-man patrol ("killer team") enters the small village of Son Thang (Thang Tay [1]),

8.5 miles northeast of Hiep Duc. Seeking NVA/VC, the patrol finds only civilians. A woman attempts to run away, apparently spooking the Marines who unleash a hail of bullets that kill five women and 11 children. Efforts by the unit's commanding officer to cover the tragedy fail and the five members of the patrol are charged with premeditated murder . . . two are convicted. *Unit:* USMC — B–1/7th Marines (five-man patrol).

March: The 26th Marines departs from South Vietnam. The 26th conducts its last combat patrol in March and then stands down.

1 March–? 1970: *Operation Park Silver.* *Location:* II Corps; Pleiku Province. *Objective:* Security of Highway 19–E. *Park Silver* is a suboperation of *Dan Quyen/Hines.* *Units:* USA — 4th Infantry Division (1/10th Cav). *Casualties:* Not included in source document for the individual operation.

11–18 March: *Operation Earhart White.* *Locations:* II Corps; Binh Dinh Province; Dak Som River; LZs Hardtimes and Susie. *Type/Objective:* Search and Destroy. *Earhart White* is a suboperation of *Dan Quyen/Hines.* *Units:* USA — 4th Infantry Division: 1st Bde (1/8th Inf, 3/8th Inf, 1/22d Inf), 2d Bde (1/12th Inf, 1/35th Inf, 2/35th Inf); NVA/VC — 3d NVA Division (elements). *Casualties:* Not included in source document for the individual operation.

24 March–24 April: *Operation Eichelberger Black.* *Locations:* II Corps; Binh Dinh Province; Base Area 226; Dak Som and Soui Lon River valleys; LZ Hardtimes. *Type/Objective:* Search and Destroy into valleys 15–30 miles west of Bong Son. *Eichelberger Black* is a suboperation of *Dan Quyen/Hines.* *Units:* USA — 4th Infantry Division: 1st Bde (1/22d Inf), 2d Bde (1/12th Inf, 2/35th Inf); NVA/VC — 3d NVA Division (elements reported in area of

operation). *Casualties:* Not included in source document for the individual operation.

1 April–5 September: *Operation Texas Star.* *Locations:* I Corps; Quang Tri and Thua Thien provinces; Ashau Valley; Phong Dien; Phu Loc; FSBs Arsenal, Bastogne, Gladiator, Henderson, Kathryn, Los Banos, Maureen, Mink, O'Reilly, Ripcord, Sarge and Tomahawk. *Type/Objective:* Search and Destroy. *Texas Star* is the follow-up to *Randolph Glen* and is a series of offensive operations in support of provincial pacification. *Units:* USA — 101st Airborne Division: 1st Bde (1/327th Abn, 2/327th Abn, 2/502d Abn), 2d Bde (1/501st Inf, 2/501st Inf, 1/502d Inf), 3d Bde (3/187th Inf, 1/506th Inf, 2/506th Inf); VNAF — 1st ARVN Division (1st, 3d and 54th ARVN regiments); NVA/VC — 304th and 320th NVA divisions (4th, 6th, 66th, 803d and 812th NVA rgts). *Events:* 1 April — B–2/506th Infantry air assaults onto hill near FSB Ripcord, 30 miles west of Hue. The American attack is turned back. 11 April — C–2/506th Infantry is finally able to take the crest of the hill near Ripcord. 30 April — FSB Granite, approximately 20 miles southwest of Hue is mortared five times during the course of the day wounding 34 Americans. 6 May — "Battle of FSB Henderson." A combined force of A,C–2/501st Infantry and 2/2d ARVN Regiment is attacked at FSB Henderson, approximately 25 miles west of Hue, by the 8/66th NVA Regiment. NVA flamethrower assaults cause more than 1000 rounds of 155 mm Howitzer ammunition to "cook off" (explode) within the American perimeter. Losses in the fight: U.S. — 32 KIA, 33 WIA, 2 MIA; VNAF — 19 KIA, 45 WIA; NVA/VC — 29 KIA. 7 May — Six Americans from D–1/506th Infantry are KIA and 12 WIA when FSB Maureen, 20 miles east of Hue, is mortared and a brief firefight erupts just beyond the base perimeter. The enemy body count is only four. 16 May — A–2/506th

Infantry is attacked at a night defensive position, 15 miles east of Hue, by an enemy force of unknown size. Losses: U.S.—4 KIA, 22 WIA; NVA/VC—5 KIA. **20 May**—A recon platoon and A–2/502d Airborne are ambushed 15 miles southwest of Hue. Three Americans are KIA and nine WIA. **23 May**—Positions manned by A–1/506th Infantry at FSB Kathryn are mortared. Losses: U.S.—3 KIA, 25 WIA. **23 July**—Extractions begin as the U.S. command decides to abandon FSB Ripcord, 35 miles west of Hue. Ripcord and its defenders had been under almost constant attack during the period 13 March–23 July by elements of the 6th NVA Regiment. Losses inflicted on the 101st Airborne during that time frame: 112 KIA, 698 WIA. *Casualties:* Totals for *Texas Star.* U.S.—386 KIA, 1978 WIA, 7 MIA; NVA/VC—4138 KIA, 49 POWs.

4–5 April: *Location:* I Corps; Quang Tri Province; Con Thien. *Action:* Heavy fighting erupts near DMZ, southwest of Con Thien. *Units:* USA—1st Brigade/ 5th Infantry Division (M) (elements). *Casualties:* U.S.—6 KIA, 40 WIA; NVA/ VC—unknown.

7–8 April: Nine infantry battalions from the 1st Infantry Division depart South Vietnam. Leaving for home are the following: 1/2d Infantry; 2/2d Infantry (M); 1/16th Infantry (M); 2/16th Infantry; 1/18th Infantry; 2/18th Infantry; 1/26th Infantry; 1/28th Infantry and 2/28th Infantry.

10 April: The 1/8th Infantry and 1/35th Infantry of the 4th Infantry Division depart from South Vietnam.

15 April: The 1st Infantry Division officially leaves South Vietnam, bound for duty in Germany and Fort Riley, Kansas.

15 April: 12,900 U.S. Marines are withdrawn from South Vietnam. Among the troops returning are the 26th Marines.

15 April: *Location:* I Corps; Quang Nam Province; Le Bac (2). *Action:* Firefight and its resulting tactical air support accidentally kill 30 civilians in the village of Le Bac (2), approximately nine miles northeast of An Hoa. *Unit:* USMC—B–1/5th Marines.

15–27 April: *Locations:* I Corps; Quang Nam Province; "Charlie Ridge"; FSB Crawford. *Type/Objective:* Reconnaissance in Force into area 12–15 miles southwest of DaNang. *Units:* USMC— 1/1st Marines, A,B–1/5th Marines, L–3/5th Marines; NVA/VC—102d/31st NVA Regiment, Q–84 Main Force (VC) Battalion. *Casualties:* U.S.—2 KIA, 5 WIA; NVA/VC—13 KIA.

20 April: President Nixon announces his pledge to withdraw 150,000 more troops from South Vietnam over the next 12 months.

22 April: *Operation Wayne Wind. Location:* II Corps; Binh Dinh Province; Base Area 226; "VC Valley." *Type:* Search and Clear. *Units:* USA—4th Infantry Division: 1st Bde (3/8th Inf, 1/14th Inf), 3d Bde (3/12th Inf), 173d Airborne Brigade–Task Force Pursuit (3/506th Inf, C/75th Inf, C–7/17th Cav); NVA/VC—3d NVA Division (elements). *Casualties:* Not included in source document for the individual operation.

24 April: *Location:* I Corps; Quang Nam Province; Que Son Valley; FSB Ross. *Action:* U.S. Marines and a company of NVA regulars clash in a five-hour firefight approximately 10 miles east of Hiep Duc. *Unit:* USMC— H–2/7th Marines. *Casualties:* U.S.—6 WIA; NVA/VC—6 KIA.

May: The monsoon (rainy) season begins in the southern provinces and ends in the north.

May : 1970

1 May–30 June: *The Cambodian Incursion.* *Locations:* III Corps; Binh Long, Hau Nghia, Kien Tuong, Phuoc Long and Tay Ninh provinces; Cambodia. *Type/Objective:* The Cambodian Incursion is a series of 13 offensive Search and Destroy operations to find and eliminate NVA/VC sanctuaries in Cambodia and the troops defending them. *Units:* USA—1st Cavalry Division, 4th Infantry Division, 9th Infantry Division, 25th Infantry Division, 11th Armored Cavalry Regiment, 199th Light Infantry Brigade. *Note:* See individual entries for U.S. assets used in the Cambodian Incursion. VNAF—1st ARVN Airborne Division (2d, 3d, 4th ARVN Airborne brigades); 5th, 9th, 21st, 22d and 23d ARVN divisions; 2d ARVN Armored Brigade; NVA/VC—5th and 7th NVA divisions (101st NVA Regiment), 5th Viet Cong Division. *Casualties:* Totals for the Cambodian Incursion. U.S.—338 KIA, 1525 WIA; VNAF—538 KIA, 3009 WIA; NVA/VC—11,336 KIA, 2328 POWs.

1 May–30 June: *Operation Toan Thang–43.* *Locations:* III Corps; Phuoc Long and Tay Ninh provinces; Bu Dop; FSBs Corral, Mini, Ranch, Ready, Smith and Thor; Cambodia; Snoul; Mimot; Base Areas 353 and 707; "The Fishhook"; "The City." *Type/Objective:* Search and Destroy to locate and eliminate COSVN, the command headquarters for communist activities in South Vietnam. Part of the Cambodian Incursion. *Units:* USA—Task Force Shoemaker–1st Cavalry Division: 1st Bde (2/5th Cav, 2/7th Cav, 1/9th Cav), 9th Infantry Division: 3d Bde (2/47th Inf [M]), 25th Infantry Division: 1st Bde (4/9th Inf, 2/34th Armor, 3/4th Cav), 2d Bde (1/27th Inf), 11th Armored Cavalry Regiment; VNAF—1st ARVN Airborne Division (4th ARVN Airborne Brigade), 1st ARVN ACR; NVA/VC—5th and 7th NVA divisions (101st NVA Rgt), 5th Viet Cong Division. *Events:* 5 May—2/11th ACR captures a huge NVA supply area that comes to be known simply

as "The City." 20 May—The night defensive position (NDP) of B–1/11th ACR near Choam Kravien, Cambodia, is mortared. Three Americans are KIA and 25 WIA. *Casualties:* Totals for *Toan Thang–43* not included in sources for the individual operation.

4 May: Ohio National Guardsmen shoot and kill four student protesters at Kent State University.

6 May: There are now more than 50,000 Allied troops in Cambodia, 31,000 of them American.

6–14 May: *Operation Toan Thang–44.* *Locations:* III Corps; Tay Ninh Province; Cambodia; Rach Ben Go River; Base Area 354; Tasuos. *Type/Objective:* Search and Destroy into enemy Base Area 354. *Units:* USA—9th Infantry Division: 1st Bde (6/31st Inf attached to 25th Infantry Division), 25th Infantry Division: 1st Bde (3/22d Inf, D–3/4th Cav), 2d Bde (1/5th Inf [M], 3/17th Cav), 3d Bde (2/14th Inf, 2/22d Inf [M]). *Casualties:* NVA/VC—557 KIA, 28 POWs (U.S. losses not included in sources for the individual operation).

6–16 May: *Operation Binh Tay I.* *Locations:* II Corps; Pleiku Province; Cambodia; Base Area 702; LZs Jackson Hole and Meredith. *Type/Objective:* Search and Destroy into enemy Base Area 702. *Units:* USA—4th Infantry Division: 1st Bde (3/8th Inf, 1/14th Inf, 3/506th Inf), 2d Bde (1/12th Inf, 1/22d Inf, 2/35th Inf, 2/1st Cav), 3d Bde (2/8th Inf [M], 3/12th Inf, 1/10th Cav); VNAF—40th ARVN Regiment. *Comment:* U.S. involvement in *Binh Tay I* ended after 10 days (16 May). *Casualties:* U.S.—43 KIA, 118 WIA; NVA/VC—212 KIA, 7 POWs.

6 May–20 June: *Operation Toan Thang–45.* *Locations:* III Corps; Phuoc Long Province; Cambodia; "The Fishhook"; Base Area 351; "Rock Island East"; FSBs Brown, Mo, Myron, Neil,

Speer and Nguyen Trai. *Type/Objective:* Search and Destroy into Base Area 351. *Units:* USA—1st Cavalry Division: 1st Bde (2/8th Cav), 2d Bde (5/7th Cav, 2/12th Cav), 199th Light Infantry Brigade (5/12th Inf); VNAF—2d ARVN Airborne Brigade, 7th ARVN Regiment; NVA/VC—275th NVA Regiment. *Event:* 13 May—Companies B,C–5/12th Infantry repel an assault on FSB Brown by an estimated two NVA companies. Losses: U.S.—1 KIA; NVA/VC—55 KIA. *Casualties:* Totals for *Toan Thang–45* not included in sources for the individual operation.

7–12 May: *Operation Toan Thang–500.* *Locations:* Cambodia; "Parrot's Beak"; Ba Thu; Chantrea; FSB Seminole. *Type:* Search and Destroy. *Units:* USA—9th Infantry Division: 1st Bde (6/31st Inf). *Event:* 8 May—6/31st Infantry battles an estimated 200 enemy soldiers near Chantrea, Cambodia, approximately 40 miles west of Saigon. U.S. losses are five KIA and 11 WIA. *Casualties:* Totals for *Toan Thang–500.* U.S.—7 KIA, 29 WIA; NVA/VC—159 KIA, 18 POWs.

15–28 May: *Operation Cheadle Blue.* *Location:* II Corps; Pleiku Province; "Rocket Box." *Type/Objective:* Search and Clear in area northeast and west of Pleiku City. *Unit:* USA—4th Infantry Division (2/8th Inf [M]). *Casualties:* None reported.

15 May–30 June: *Operation Barber Glade.* *Locations:* I Corps; Quang Tri Province; Khe Sanh Plain; Da Krong River Valley; Mai Loc. *Objective:* Reconnaissance and tactical exploitation of intelligence. *Units:* USA—5th Special Forces Group (B-52 Detachment). *Casualties:* NVA/VC—15 KIA (U.S. losses not included in source document for the individual operation).

16–26 May: *Operation Wayne Jump.* *Locations:* II Corps; Pleiku Province; Plei Trap Valley; New Plei Djereng;

Cambodia; Base Area 702. *Objective:* **Wayne Jump** is an offensive action in support of an ARVN Search and Destroy mission in to Base Area 702. *Units:* USA—4th Infantry Division: 1st Bde (3/8th Inf, 1/14th Inf, 3/506th Inf). *Casualties:* None reported.

18–30 May: *Operation Fredenall Gold.* *Locations:* II Corps; Pleiku Province; Plei Djereng; Pleiku City. *Objective:* Road Security operation charged with the protection of Highway 19 from Pleiku to New Plei Djereng. *Units:* USA—4th Infantry Division (2/1st Cav); NVA/VC—95-B NVA Regiment elements reported in the area of operations. *Casualties:* None reported.

18 May–12 October: *Operation Putnam Paragon.* *Locations:* II Corps; Binh Dinh Province; Base Area 226; Suoi Kon Valley; An Khe; Camp Radcliff; LZ Uplift. *Type/Objective:* Combined Search and Clear/Search and Destroy operation into area north of An Khe. **Putnam Paragon** is a suboperation of *Dan Quyen/Hines.* *Units:* USA—4th Infantry Division: 1st Bde (3/8th Inf, 1/14th Inf), 2d Bde (1/12th Inf, 1/22d Inf, 2/35th Inf); VNAF—22d ARVN Division; NVA/VC—3d NVA Division (C-2/407th Sapper Bn). *Casualties:* Not included in source document for the individual operation.

26 May–13 June: *Locations:* I Corps; Quang Nam Province; Que Son Mountains; Hill 800; FSBs Baldy, Buzzard, Crow, Ross and Ryder. *Type/Objective:* Search and Destroy into area northeast of Hiep Duc. *Units:* USMC—3/7th Marines, 3/11th Marines, 1st Recon Battalion. *Casualties:* U.S.—1+ KIA, 1+ WIA; NVA/VC—9 KIA, 4 POWs.

28 May: *Location:* III Corps; Binh Tuy Province; Tanh Linh; FSB Sun. *Action:* Enemy attack on FSB Sun. *Unit:* USA—199th Light Infantry Brigade (elements). *Casualties:* U.S.—9 WIA; NVA/VC—45 KIA.

1-9 June: *Operation Robertson White. Location:* II Corps; Pleiku Province; Hill 666. *Objective:* Security of engineers working along Highway 508. *Robertson White* is a suboperation of *Dan Quyen/Hines. Units:* USA—4th Infantry Division (2/8th Inf [M]); NVA/VC—K-361 Composite Battalion reported in the area of operations. *Casualties:* None reported.

1-26 June: *Operation Wayne Hurdle. Locations:* II Corps; Pleiku Province; Dak Payou Valley ("VC Valley"); Base Area 202; LZs Buckeye and Doris. *Type/Objective:* Search and Clear of Dak Payou—"VC Valley." *Wayne Hurdle* is a suboperation of *Dan Quyen/Hines. Units:* USA—4th Infantry Division: 1st Bde (3/8th Inf, 3/12th Inf, 1/4th Inf); NVA/VC—95-B NVA Regiment reported in area of operations. *Casualties:* Not included in source documents for the individual operation.

11 June: *Location:* I Corps; Quang Nam Province; Thanh My. *Action:* Two companies of VC sappers attack the village of Thanh My. U.S. Marines assist local forces in driving the enemy from the area. Losses in the day's action: U.S.—1 KIA, 10 WIA; NVA/VC—3 KIA; Civilians—74 KIA, 63 WIA (300 homes destroyed).

23-28 June: *Operation Wright Blue. Location:* II Corps; Pleiku Province; Thanh Binh. *Objective: Wright Blue* is to provide road security from the intersection of Highway 19–W and Highway 14 west to the Cambodian border. *Wright Blue* is a suboperation of *Dan Quyen/Hines. Units:* USA—4th Infantry Division (2/8th Inf [M]); NVA/VC—95-B NVA Regiment elements reported in area of operation. *Casualties:* None reported.

25 June: *Location:* III Corps; Long Khanh Province; Vo Dat; FSB Rita. *Action:* Firefight five miles south of Vo Dat. *Units:* USA—199th Light Infantry

Brigade (C–4/12th Inf). *Casualties:* U.S.—5 KIA, 10 WIA; NVA/VC—3 KIA.

26 June: *Location:* I Corps; Quang Nam Province; LZ Baldy. *Action:* Booby traps and ambushes plague Marines south of DaNang. *Units:* USMC—1/7th Marines. *Casualties:* U.S.—5 KIA.

28 June-14 July: *Operation Wayne Fast. Locations:* II Corps; Binh Dinh Province; An Lao Valley; LZs Armageddon and Welch. *Type/Objective:* Search and Clear into area 40 miles north of An Khe. *Wayne Fast* is a suboperation of *Dan Quyen/Hines. Units:* USA—4th Infantry Division: 1st Bde (3/8th Inf, 1/14th Inf), 2d Bde (2/35th Inf); NVA/VC—3d NVA Division (elements). *Casualties:* Totals for *Wayne Fast* not included in source document for the individual operation.

29-30 June: The final troop withdrawals from Cambodia are completed. Casualties in the two-month incursion: U.S.—338 KIA, 1525 WIA; NVA/VC—11,000+ (estimated).

1-23 July: *Location:* I Corps; Thua Thien Province; FSB Ripcord. *Action:* "Battle of FSB Ripcord." A part of *Texas Star* (1 April–5 September), the "Battle of FSB Ripcord" proves to be the costliest fight of 1970. For 23 days, elements of the 101st Airborne Division withstand heavy rocket, mortar and ground attacks by an NVA regiment 25 miles west of Hue. *Units:* USA—101st Airborne Division: 3d Bde (2/506th Inf); NVA/VC—803d NVA Regiment. *Casualties:* 1-23 July: U.S.—61 KIA, 345 WIA.

2 July-25 August: *Operation Brandies Blue. Location:* II Corps; Binh Dinh Province; An Khe. *Type/Objective:* Search and Clear southwest of Camp Radcliff/An Khe. *Units:* USA—4th Infantry Division (2/8th Inf [M]); NVA/VC—95-B NVA Regiment.

Casualties: Not included in source document for the individual operation.

8 July: *Location:* I Corps; Quang Tri Province; Khe Sanh. *Action:* Gunships from the 101st Airborne decimate an estimated 150–200 NVA soldiers trying to cross into South Vietnam from Laos. *Units:* USA—101st Airborne Division (2/17th Cav). *Casualties:* U.S.—4 KIA, 7 WIA; NVA/VC—139 KIA, 3 POWs.

9–15 July: *Operation Clinch Valley.* *Location:* I Corps; Quang Tri Province; Khe Sanh. *Type/Objective:* Search and Destroy. *Clinch Valley* is an airmobile assault into the South Vietnam/Laos border area to exploit the enemy sightings from 8 July. *Units:* USA—1st Brigade/5th Infantry Division (M): 101st Airborne Division (3d Brigade elements, 2/17th Cav); VNAF—1st ARVN Division (3d ARVN Regiment); NVA/VC—304th NVA Division (9th NVA Regiment). *Casualties:* U.S.—none reported; NVA/VC—226 KIA.

12 July–25 August: *Operations Elk Canyon I–II.* *Locations:* I Corps; Quang Tin Province; Song Tranh River; Kham Duc; FSBs Judy and Mary Ann; LZ Boxer. *Objective:* Disruption of enemy supply lines and rear areas west of Tam Ky. *Units:* USA—23d Infantry Division (Americal) (2/1st Inf, 1/46th Inf); VNAF—4th and 5th ARVN regiments; NVA/VC—36th NVA Regiment (K–80 NVA Battalion). *Events:* **13 August**—D-2/1st Infantry tangles with an enemy force of unknown size two miles north of Kham Duc. Losses: U.S.—1 KIA, 9 WIA; NVA/VC—2 KIA. **26 August**—Thirty-one Americans are KIA and nine injured when enemy forces shoot down a CH–47 "Chinook" while on a flight from Kham Duc to FSB Judy. *Casualties:* Totals for *Elk Canyon I–II.* U.S.—36 KIA, 90 WIA; NVA/VC—78 KIA, 1 POW.

13 July–31 August: *Operation Ripley Center.* *Location:* I Corps; Quang Nam

Province; Que Son Mountains. *Type/Objective:* Search and Destroy into mountains south of DaNang to find and eliminate the enemy's Front–4 Headquarters. *Units:* USMC—A–1/5th Marines, 1/7th Marines, 2/7th Marines, D,I,L–3/7th Marines. *Casualties:* U.S.—27 WIA; NVA/VC—25 KIA, 8 POWs.

16 July–24 August: *Operation Picken's Forest.* *Locations:* I Corps; Quang Nam Province; Song Thu Bon Valley; "Charlie Ridge"; Nong Son; Thuong Duc; FSBs Dart, Defiant, Hatchet and Mace; LZs Bluejay and Starling. *Type/Objective:* Search and Destroy into southern Quang Nam aimed at enemy Base Areas 112 and 127. *Units:* USMC—1/5th Marines, 1/7th Marines, 2/7th Marines; NVA/VC—1st and 38th NVA regiments, 1st VC Battalion; 490th Sapper Battalion, 577th Rocket Battalion (1500 enemy troops estimated in area of operations). *Casualties:* U.S.—4 KIA, 51 WIA; NVA/VC—99 KIA.

17–27 July: *Operation Wayne Span I.* *Location:* II Corps; Binh Dinh Province; Nui Mieu Mountains; Base Area 226. *Type/Objective:* Search and Clear of enemy Base Area 226. *Wayne Span I* is a suboperation of *Dan Quyen/ Hines.* *Units:* USA—4th Infantry Division: 1st Bde (3/8th Inf, 3/12th Inf), 2d Bde (2/35th Inf), 173d Airborne Brigade (elements); VNAF—40th and 41st ARVN regiments; NVA/VC—3d NVA Division (elements). *Casualties:* Totals for *Wayne Span I* not included in source document for the individual operation.

24–27 July: *Operation Barren Green.* *Locations:* I Corps; Quang Nam Province; "Arizona Territory"; Vu Gia River; My Hiep. *Objective: Barren Green's* mission is to prevent the enemy from harvesting the local corn crop and to destroy unharvested portion. *Units:* USMC—2/5th Marines, 3/5th Marines, C–1st Tank Battalion; NVA/VC—38th

NVA Regiment. *Casualties:* U.S.—none listed; NVA/VC—18 KIA.

25 July–12 August: *Operation Chicago Peak/Lam Son–363. Locations:* I Corps; Thua Thien Province; Ashau Valley; FSBs Goodman and Maureen. *Type/Objective:* Search and Destroy to locate enemy cache sites and logistics facilities. *Units:* USA—101st Airborne Division (1st Brigade elements); VNAF—1st ARVN Division (3d ARVN Regiment); NVA/VC—29th and 803d NVA regiments. *Casualties:* U.S.—none; VNAF—3 KIA; NVA/VC—97 KIA.

28 July–6 August: *Operation Wayne Span II. Locations:* II Corps; Binh Dinh Province; An Lao Valley; Nui Mieu Mountains; "Fishhook." *Type:* Search and Destroy. **Wayne Span II** is a suboperation of *Dan Quyen/Hines. Units:* USA—4th Infantry Division: 1st Bde (3/8th Inf, 3/12th Inf), 173d Airborne Brigade (elements); VNAF—22d ARVN Division (elements). *Casualties:* Not included in source document for the individual operation.

4 August: *Location:* I Corps; Quang Nam Province; Quang Ha (1); Camp Lauer. *Action:* Combat assault on the village of Quang Ha (1), 10 miles southwest of DaNang. *Unit:* USMC—3d plt-G-2/1st Marines. *Casualties:* U.S.—none; NVA/VC—12 KIA.

6–27 August: *Operation Wayne Pierce. Locations:* II Corps; Binh Dinh Province; An Lao Valley; "Fishhook." *Type/Objective:* Search and Destroy into area north of An Khe. **Wayne Pierce** is a suboperation of *Dan Quyen/Hines. Units:* USA—4th Infantry Division: 1st Bde (3/8th Inf, 3/12th Inf, 1/14th Inf), 2d Bde (2/35th Inf); NVA/VC—3d NVA Division (elements). *Casualties:* NVA/VC—10 KIA (U.S. losses not included in source document for the individual operation).

12 August: The 1st Brigade/1st Cavalry Division is the only remaining U.S. combat unit left along the South Vietnam/Cambodia border area.

16–24 August: *Operation Lyon Valley. Location:* I Corps; Quang Nam Province; "Arizona Territory." *Objective:* Preventing the movement of food and supplies from the northern "Arizona Territory" to the base areas of the 38th NVA Regiment. *Units:* USMC—F,H-2/5th Marines, L-3/5th Marines; NVA/VC—38th NVA Regiment. *Casualties:* U.S.—11 WIA (the Marines' casualties are the result of accidents or heat stroke); NVA/VC—5 KIA, 1 POW.

28 August–14 October: *Operation Wayne Forge. Locations:* II Corps; Binh Dinh, Phu Bon and Phu Yen provinces; An Khe. *Type/Objectives:* Search and Destroy. **Wayne Forge** is a suboperation of *Dan Quyen/Hines. Units:* USA—4th Infantry Division: 1st Bde (3/8th Inf, 3/12th Inf, 1/14th Inf), 2d Bde (1/22d Inf, 2/35th Inf); NVA/VC—3d NVA Division, 6/12th NVA Regiment. *Casualties:* NVA/VC—16 KIA, 1 POW (U.S. losses not included in the source document for the individual operation).

31 August 1970–7 May 1971: *Operation Imperial Lake. Locations:* I Corps; Quang Nam Province; Que Son Mountains; Que Son Valley; FSBs Ross and Ryder; LZs Baldy and Vulture. *Type/ Objective:* Search and Destroy. **Imperial Lake** is the last Marine effort to clear the enemy from the Que Son Mountains south of DaNang. *Units:* USA—23d Infantry Division (Americal) (elements); USMC—2/5th Marines, 3/5th Marines, 1/7th Marines, 2/7th Marines, 3/7th Marines, 1st Recon Battalion; NVA/VC—D-3, R-20 and V-25 NVA/VC battalions reported in the area of operations. *Events:* **31 August**—Ten Marine artillery batteries pound the Que Son Mountains in one of the largest preparatory artillery strikes of the war. Shells rain down on 53 different target areas for six hours. Ordnance expended: 13,400 shells with a total weight of 370 tons. The barrage was followed by two hours of fixed wing air strikes in which 63 tons more of explosives are used. **5–9 September—** The 2/7th Marines trap and battle 30–50 North Vietnamese in a ravine near LZ Vulture. Three Marines are KIA and 12 WIA in the minisiege. Marine aircraft are called in to pound the ravine with 40 tons of bombs. *Casualties:* Totals for *Imperial Lake.* U.S.—24 KIA, 205 WIA; NVA/VC—305 KIA.

September–October: The 7th Marines (1st Marine Division) departs from South Vietnam.

5–8 September: *Operation Nebraska Rapids. Locations:* I Corps; Quang Nam Province; Thu Bon River Route 534; Hiep Duc; LZ Baldy. *Type/Objective:* Search and Destroy with mission of clearing and securing Route 534 from LZ Baldy west to Hiep Duc. *Units:* USA—23d Infantry Division (Americal) (2/1st Inf, 3/21st Inf, 4/31st Inf); USMC—B-1/7th Marines; I,K,M-3/7th Marines. *Casualties:* U.S.—1 KIA, 13 WIA; NVA/VC—2 KIA, 1 POW.

5 September 1970–8 October 1971: *Operation Jefferson Glen. Locations:* I Corps; Thua Thien Province; "Elephant Valley"; FSBs Arsenal, Bastogne, Birmingham, Blitz, Normandy, Tomahawk and Veghel. *Type/Objective:* Combined Search and Destroy–Search and Clear offensive operations to prevent an NVA buildup and to support pacification programs in Thua Thien. *Units:* USA—101st Airborne Division: 1st Bde (1/327th Abn, 2/327th Abn, 2/502d Abn), 2d Bde (1/501st Inf, 2/501st Inf, 1/502d Inf), 3d Bde (3/187th Inf, 1/506th Inf, 2/506th Inf); VNAF— 1st ARVN Division (1st and 3d ARVN regiments); NVA/VC—304th NVA Division (9th, 24th and 66th NVA regiments), 320th NVA Division (52d and 64th NVA regiments), 325th NVA Division (36th, 88th and 102d NVA regiments). *Event:* **15 September**—FSB Blitz is mortared, killing six U.S. soldiers of the 1/502d Infantry. *Comment: Jefferson Glen* is the last major combat operation for U.S. ground forces in South Vietnam. *Casualties:* Totals for *Jefferson Glen.* NVA/VC—2026 KIA (U.S. losses not included in the source document for the individual operation).

9–19 September: *Operation Dubois Square. Locations:* I Corps; Quang Nam Province; Cu De River; DaNang; FSB Sam. *Type/Objective:* Reconnaissance in Force 15 miles northwest of DaNang. *Units:* USMC—B-1/1st Marines, F-2/1st Marines, K-3/1st Marines. *Casualties:* None reported—no enemy contact.

18–21 September: *Operation Catawba Falls. Locations:* I Corps; Quang Nam Province; Base Area 112; FSB Dagger. *Type/Objective:* Artillery bombardment of enemy Base Area 112. *Units:* USMC—11th Marines (artillery). *Comment:* The *Catawba Falls* target area is hit with more than 11,500 rounds of artillery fire, and air strikes account for an additional 141 tons of ordnance. *Casualties:* U.S.—none; NVA/VC—Uncertain.

25 September–11 October: *Operation Murray Blue. Location:* II Corps; Binh Dinh Province; An Khe. *Type/Objective:* Search and Destroy seven miles north of An Khe. *Unit:* USA—4th Infantry Division (2/8th Inf [M]). *Casualties:* Not included in source document for the individual operation.

2–15 October: *Operation Tulare Falls I. Location:* I Corps; Quang Nam Province; Que Son Mountains; Hill 55; LZ Baldy. *Objective: Tulare Falls I* is meant to prevent communist attacks on Hill 55 in the Que Son Mountains, south of DaNang. *Units:* USA—23d Infantry Division (American)–Task Force Saint (2/1st Inf, 1/1st Cav); USMC—5th

Marines. *Casualties:* U.S.—19 WIA; NVA/VC—30 KIA, 21 POWs.

10 October–?: *Operation Wayne Sabre. Locations:* II Corps; Binh Dinh Province; An Khe; Camp Radcliff. *Type/Objective:* Search and Destroy to provide security for the populated areas around An Khe. *Units:* USA—4th Infantry Division: 1st Bde (3/8th Inf, 3/12th Inf, 1/14th Inf); NVA/VC—95-B NVA Regiment reported in the area of operation. *Casualties:* Not included in source document for the individual operation.

11 October: The 3d Brigade/9th Infantry Division officially leaves South Vietnam.

11–12 October: The 199th Light Infantry Brigade officially leaves South Vietnam for Fort Benning, Georgia, and deactivation. The Brigade takes with it its four organic infantry battalions: 2/3d Infantry; 3/7th Infantry; 4/12th Infantry and 5/12th Infantry.

12 October: Four of the 9th Infantry Division's organic infantry battalions depart from South Vietnam. Going home are 6/31st Infantry, 2/47th Infantry (M), 2/60th Infantry and 5/60th Infantry (M).

13–24 October: *Operation Putnam Valley. Location:* II Corps; Binh Dinh Province; Vinh Thanh Valley ("Happy Valley"). *Type/Objective:* Search and Destroy into area northeast of An Khe to strengthen the security of the local population and territorial forces. *Putnam Valley* is a suboperation of *Dan Quyen/Hines. Units:* USA—4th Infantry Division (1/12th Inf). *Casualties:* Not included in source document.

22 October–30 November: *Operation Hoang Dieu. Location:* I Corps; Quang Nam Province. *Objective: Hoang Dieu* is a systematic search of the majority of the villages and hamlets in

Quang Nam Province in an effort to root out the Viet Cong infrastructure. *Units:* USA—23d Infantry Division (American)–Task Force Burnett (2/1st Inf, 1/1st Cav); USMC—1st Marine Division (elements); VNAF—2d ARVN Division (51st ARVN Regiment, ARVN Ranger Group). *Casualties:* U.S.—3 KIA, 62 WIA; NVA/VC—590 KIA (reported).

23 October–3 November: *Operation Noble Canyon. Locations:* I Corps; Quang Nam Province; Que Son Mountains; Hill 441; FSB Ross. *Type/Objective:* Search and Clear near Hill 441, 10 miles east of Hiep Duc. *Unit:* USMC—3/5th Marines. *Casualties:* U.S.—8 WIA; NVA/VC—4 KIA, 1 POW.

27 October–30 November: *Operation Tulare Falls II. Location:* I Corps; Quang Nam Province; Que Son Mountains; LZ Baldy. *Type:* Search and Destroy. *Units:* USA—23d Infantry Division (American)–Task Force Burnett (2/1st Inf, 1/1st Cav). *Casualties:* U.S.—4 KIA, 26 WIA; NVA/VC—22 KIA, 2 POWs.

November: The monsoon (rainy) season begins in the northern provinces and ends in the south.

8 November: The 2d Brigade/25th Infantry becomes a separate command, allowing the bulk of the division to prepare to return to the United States.

21 November: *Location:* North Vietnam. *Action:* "The Sontay Raid." Col. Bull Simon leads a team of 50 commandos on a raid west of Hanoi to locate and free U.S. prisoners of war. However, the team find no POWs and have to fight their way out. Luckily, they sustain no casualties.

7 December: The 4th Infantry Division officially departs South Vietnam for Fort Carson, Colorado. Leaving with the division are three of its organic infantry battalions: 2/8th Infantry (M); 3/8th Infantry; 3/12th Infantry.

7 December: The 2/22d Infantry (M) of the 25th Infantry Division departs from South Vietnam.

8 December: The 4th Infantry Division's 1/14th Infantry and 2/35th Infantry battalions depart South Vietnam.

8 December: The 25th Infantry Division officially departs from South Vietnam. Joining the division are four of its organic infantry battalions. Going back to the world are 4/9th Infantry, 2/14th Infantry, 4/23d Infantry (M) and 2/27th Infantry.

18 December 1970–19 January 1971: *Operation Hoang Dieu 101.* *Location:* I Corps; Quang Nam Province.

Objective: Hoang Dieu 101 is a continuation of the search and clear efforts begun in *Hoang Dieu.* *Units:* USMC— 1st Marines; VNAF—51st ARVN Regiment. *Casualties:* U.S.—5 KIA, 87 WIA; NVA/VC—690 KIA (estimated), 87 POWs.

31 December: About 350,000 total U.S. personnel remain in the Southeast Asian theater. U.S. ground forces are in the following strengths: Army— 255,000, Marines—25,400. Nearly 200,000 troops have returned home so far. American losses for the year: 4204 KIA. Number of Americans killed in the Vietnam War since 1959: 44,228. VNAF strength at the end of 1970: 968,000+. VNAF losses for 1970: 20,914 KIA. Total VNAF killed in Vietnam War since 1965: 133,522.

1971

As of 1 January 1970 more than 135,000 U.S. troops have returned home, but 350,000 remain in South Vietnam. American ground forces in Vietnam are composed of some 330,650 Army soldiers and 25,400 Marines. ARVN strength is estimated at 968,000.

7 January: The *New York Times* reports on MACV's estimate that some 65,000 U.S. soldiers and Marines were involved with drug abuse in 1970.

11 January–29 March: *Operation Upshur Stream. Location:* I Corps; Quang Nam Province; "Charlie Ridge." *Type/Objective:* Search and Clear of the "rocket belt" area around DaNang. *Units:* USMC – 1/1st Marines, 2/1st Marines; NVA/VC – 575th Artillery Battalion. *Events:* **20 January** – A member of B-1/1st Marines accidentally trips a booby trap that wounds four and sets off a tragic series of events. While securing an LZ for a medevac chopper to land and pick up the four wounded Marines, another booby trap explodes, wounding four more men. When the "dustoff" finally does arrive, its rotor wash sets off more mines that wound three more. Total wounded: 11. **21 January** – Misfortune again plagues B Company of the 1/1st Marines: a CH-46 helicopter crashes and burns while attempting to land. Five Marines are KIA and 16 injured. *Casualties:* Totals for *Upshur Stream.* U.S. – 1 KIA, 19 WIA; NVA/VC – 13 KIA.

30 January–7 February: *Operation Dewey Canyon II. Locations:* I Corps; Quang Tri Province; "Red Devil Road." *Objective:* Preliminary support operation in preparation for *Lam Son–719.* American troops are charged with the clearing of Route 9 toward Khe Sanh to pave the way for the ARVN incursion into Laos. *Units:* USA – 1st Brigade/5th Infantry Division (M) (1/11th Inf, 1/77th Armor), 23d Infantry Division (Americal) (2/1st Inf, 4/3d Inf), 101st Airborne Division (Aviation and Infantry elements). *Note:* Some 9000 U.S. troops participate in *Dewey Canyon II. Casualties:* U.S. – 55 KIA, 431 WIA; NVA/VC losses not included in the source document for the individual operation.

3 February–29 March: *Operation Hoang Dieu–103. Location:* I Corps; Quang Nam Province. *Type/Objective:* Search and Clear. *Hoang Dieu–103* is a continuation of the *Hoang Dieu* series to secure the majority of the villages

124

and hamlets in Quang Nam. *Unit:*
USMC—1st Marines. *Casualties:* U.S.—
2 KIA, 99 WIA; NVA/VC—329 KIA, 10
POWs (totals for enemy casualties are
combined VNAF/USMC figures).

8 February–6 April: *Operation Lam
Son–719. Locations:* I Corps; Quang Tri
Province; Khe Sanh; Route 9; Vandergrift Combat Base; Laos; Base Areas
604 and 611; Tchepone. *Type/Objective:*
Search and Destroy into NVA staging
areas and strongholds in Laos. The
United States' role in this VNAF operation is to clear the Khe Sanh area and
provide aviation and artillery support.
Units: USA—1st Bde/5th Infantry Division (M) (1/11th Inf, 1/77th Armor), 23d
Infantry Division (American) (2/1st Inf,
4/3d Inf), 101st Airborne Division
(2/17th Cav), 101st Aviation Group
(more than 650 U.S. aircraft and 10,000
troops participated in *Lam Son–719*);
VNAF—1st ARVN Division (1st, 2d and
3d ARVN regiments), 1st ARVN Airborne Division, 1st ARVN Armored Brigade (7th, 11th and 17th ACR squadrons); VNMC—1st ARVN Ranger
Group (21st, 37th and 39th ARVN
Ranger battalions). (17,000 VNAF
troops participate in *Lam Son–719*.)
NVA/VC—2d NVA Division, 304th
NVA Division (304th NVA Regiment),
308th NVA Regiment (36th, 88th and
102d NVA regiments), 324–B NVA
Division (29th, 803d and 812th NVA
regiments), 4th, 5th and 6th NVA regiments. (22,000 enemy troops reported
in area of operations.) *Casualties:*
U.S.—215 KIA, 1149 WIA, 42 MIA (108
U.S. helicopters destroyed and 600
others damaged in the operation);
VNAF—1483 KIA, 5420 WIA, 691
MIA; NVA/VC—13,636 KIA, 69
POWs.

March–April: The 5th Marines of the
1st Marine Division departs from South
Vietnam.

1 March: *Operation Phoenix* is expanded to include the jailing and selec-

tive assassination of Viet Cong agents,
suspects and sympathizers.

5 March: The 1st and 3d squadrons of
the 11th Armored Cavalry Regiment
depart from South Vietnam.

22 March: *Location:* I Corps; Quang
Tin Province; Tam Ky; FSB Mary Ann.
Action: An estimated 50 NVA attack the
250 defenders of FSB Mary Ann, 32
miles west of Chu Lai. *Units:* USA—
23d Infantry Division (American)
(1/46th Inf). *Comment:* Fifty NVA soldiers penetrate the base defenses and
run amok shooting and tossing satchel
charges. Almost half of the base's personnel are KIA or WIA. The Army in-
vestigates the incident and finds that
lax perimeter security allowed the attack to happen. The Army files formal
charges against several high ranking
officers of the 23d Infantry Division.
Casualties: Totals for attack on Mary
Ann. U.S.—33 KIA, 76 WIA; NVA/
VC—10 KIA.

27–28 March: The 5/7th Cavalry,
1/8th Cavalry and 2/12th Cavalry of the
1st Cavalry Division depart from South
Vietnam.

7 April: Three of the 1st Infantry Division's organic infantry battalions depart
South Vietnam. Going home are the
1/2d Infantry, 1/16th Infantry (M) and
1/26th Infantry.

7–12 April: *Operation Scott Orchard.
Locations:* I Corps; Quang Nam Province; Base Area 112; FSB Dagger. *Objective:* Marines search for an alleged
VC POW camp—none was found.
Units: USMC—1/1st Marines (elements), 2/1st Marines, 3/1st Marines
(elements), A/1st Recon Battalion.
Casualties: NVA/VC—4 KIA.

8 April: Six of the 1st Infantry Division's organic infantry battalions depart
from South Vietnam. Going home are
2/2d Infantry (M), 2/16th Infantry,

1/18th Infantry, 2/18th Infantry, 1/28th Infantry and 2/28th Infantry.

9 April: The 1/5th Cavalry of the 1st Cavalry Division departs from South Vietnam.

11 April–11 July: *Operation Montana Mustang. Locations:* I Corps; Quang Tri Province; DMZ; Base Area 101; Ba Long and Son Thach Han rivers; Cam Lo; Hai Lang; Mai Linh; FSBs Anne and Pedro. *Type/Objective:* Search and Destroy. *Montana Mustang* is a follow-up mission to *Lam Son–719. Units:* USA – 1st Brigade/5th Infantry Division (M) (1/11th Inf, 1/77th Armor, 3/5th Cav). *Casualties:* Totals for *Montana Mustang* not included in the source document for the individual operation.

13 April: The 1st Marines cease all offensive operations.

14 April: The 1st Marine Division officially departs from South Vietnam.

16 April: The 2/12th Infantry of the 4th Infantry Division departs from South Vietnam.

20 April: The 3/22d Infantry of the 4th Infantry Division departs from South Vietnam.

20 April: MACV acknowledges that fragging incidents, or the killing or injuring of unpopular noncoms and officers, are on the rise. The U.S. command admits to 34 deaths in 209 fragging incidents in 1970.

27 April: The 1/503d Airborne of the 173d Airborne Brigade departs from South Vietnam.

29 April: The majority of the 1st Cavalry Division officially departs South Vietnam for Fort Hood, Texas. The remaining 3d Brigade becomes a separate command with the following assets: 2/5th Cavalry, 1/7th Cavalry, 2/8th

Cavalry and 1/12th Cavalry. The brigade remains active in South Vietnam until 26 June 1972.

30 April: The 2d Brigade/25th Infantry Division (separate) departs South Vietnam for its headquarters at Scho-field Barracks, Hawaii. Leaving with the brigade are two of its organic infantry battalions: the 1/5th Infantry (M) and 1/27th Infantry.

May: The monsoon (rainy) season begins in the southern provinces and ends in the north.

May: The 1st Marines of the 1st Marine Division departs South Vietnam.

May–?: *Operation Caroline Hill. Location:* I Corps; Quang Nam Province; DaNang. *Type/Objective:* Search and Destroy into the mountains and low-lands west and south of DaNang. *Units:* USA – 23d Infantry Division (Americal) (elements). *Casualties:* Casualty figures current only for 29 April–1 July. U.S. – 15 KIA, 125 WIA; NVA/VC – 162 KIA, 11 POWs.

5 May: 2/7th Cavalry of the 1st Cavalry Division departs from South Vietnam.

7 May: All Marine forces of III MAF cease combat operations and stand down awaiting transfer back to the world.

15 May: The 3/506th Infantry of the 101st Airborne Division departs South Vietnam.

16 May: MACV acknowledges that heroin addiction among the troops in South Vietnam has reached epidemic proportions. The official estimate is 10–15 percent of all lower-ranked enlisted men are addicts, amounting to some 37,000 soldiers.

19–22 May: *Location:* I Corps; Quang Tri Province; DMZ; FSB Charlie II.

Action: NVA rocket attack on FSB Charlie II. One incoming round scores a direct hit on a bunker. *Units:* USA—1st Brigade/5th Infantry Division. *Casualties:* U.S.—30 KIA, 50 WIA.

21 May: The 5/46th Infantry (198th Light Infantry Brigade), 23d Infantry Division (American) departs South Vietnam.

13 June: The *New York Times* begins publishing the "Pentagon Papers."

28 June: The 1/9th Cavalry of 1st Cavalry Division and the 4/21st Infantry (11th Light Infantry Brigade) of the 23d Infantry Division (American) depart from South Vietnam.

9 July: The United States turns over complete responsibility for the DMZ area to South Vietnamese units. It is understood that U.S. bombers will continue their missions in a supporting role.

30 July: The 2/503d Airborne of the 173d Airborne Brigade departs from South Vietnam.

1 August: The 1/61st Infantry (M) of the 1st Brigade/5th Infantry Division (M) departs from South Vietnam.

5 August: Three more units depart South Vietnam. Going home are 1/12th Infantry of the 4th Infantry Division, 1/11th Infantry of the 1st Brigade/5th Infantry Division and 3/503d Airborne of the 173d Airborne Brigade.

20 August: The 4/503d Airborne of the 173d Airborne Brigade departs from South Vietnam.

25 August: The 173d Airborne Brigade officially departs from South Vietnam.

27 August: *Location:* I Corps; Quang Nam Province; DaNang. *Action:* NVA units attack elements of the 23d Infantry Division (American) at a night defensive position (NDP) 16 miles southwest of DaNang. *Casualties:* U.S.—5 KIA, 7 WIA.

27 August: The 1st Brigade/5th Infantry Division officially departs South Vietnam for Fort Carson, Colorado.

8 October: The 101st Airborne's Operation *Jefferson Glen* ends in I Corps. This is the final major ground operation for U.S. ground forces.

25 October: The 4/31st Infantry (196th Light Infantry Brigade) of the 23d Infantry Division (American) departs from South Vietnam.

29 October: The 3/1st Infantry (11th Light Infantry Brigade) of the 23d Infantry Division (American) departs from South Vietnam.

30 October: There are still more than 197,000 U.S. troops in South Vietnam.

1 November: The 1/52d Infantry (198th Light Infantry Brigade) of the 23d Infantry Division (American) departs from South Vietnam.

5 November: The 4/3d Infantry (11th Light Infantry Brigade) of the 23d Infantry Division (American) departs from South Vietnam.

13 November: Two of the 23d Infantry Division's organic infantry brigades, 11th Light Infantry and 198th Light Infantry, officially leave South Vietnam.

21 November: The 1/6th Infantry (196th Light Infantry Brigade) of the 23d Infantry Division (American) departs South Vietnam.

29 November: The 23d Infantry Division (American) is deactivated in South Vietnam.

30 November: The 1/20th Infantry (11th Light Infantry Brigade) of the 23d Infantry Division (Americal) departs South Vietnam.

December: The last troops of the Royal Australian Regiment depart from South Vietnam.

9 December: The Paris peace talks stall and for the first time, both sides schedule no new meetings.

10 December: The 3/187th Infantry of the 101st Airborne Division departs from South Vietnam.

14 December: The 2/506th Infantry of the 101st Airborne Division departs from South Vietnam.

21 December: The 1/506th Infantry of the 101st Airborne Division departs from South Vietnam.

26 December 1971–1 January 1972: The U.S. launches the heaviest bombings of North Vietnam since the November 1968 hiatus began. Secretary of State Melvin Laird justifies the attacks by saying the communists have failed to live up to the agreements made prior to the 1968 halt. The raids are part of the effort to disrupt communist preparations for an anticipated offensive during the TET holidays of 1972.

31 December: U.S. troop strength in South Vietnam is down to 158,000. More than 177,000 Americans have returned home. American losses for the year: 1386 KIA. Total of Americans KIA in Vietnam War since 1959: 45,626. VNAF troop strength at the end of 1971: 1,050,000. VNAF losses for the year: 21,500 KIA. Total VNAF losses in Vietnam War to date: 156,260 KIA. NVA/VC troop strength estimate for end of 1971: 250,000+. NVA/VC losses estimated for 1971: 97,000 KIA. Total losses estimated for NVA/VC since 1965: 347,000+ KIA. The year ends on an ominous note for the U.S. command. The Army reports that between 1969 and 1971 more than 700 fragging incidents have occurred resulting in 82 deaths and 651 injured.

1972

As of 1 January 1972 more than 155,000 U.S. troops still remain in South Vietnam. VNAF strength is up to more than 1,000,000. NVA/VC strength is still estimated at more than 250,000.

6 January: The peace talks resume in Paris.

7 January: *Location:* III Corps; Binh Duong Province; FSB Fiddler's Green. *Action:* Enemy forces pound FSB Fiddler's Green, some 20 miles northwest of Saigon. *Casualties:* U.S.—18 WIA.

13 January: President Nixon announces that 70,000 more U.S. troops will be withdrawn from South Vietnam over the next three months.

19 January: The 2/502d Airborne of the 101st Airborne Division departs from South Vietnam.

20 January: The 1/327th Airborne of the 101st Airborne Division departs from South Vietnam.

25 January: President Nixon announces that Henry Kissinger has held secret meetings with key North Vietnamese representatives since August of 1969.

30 January: The 1/22d Infantry of the 4th Infantry Division departs from South Vietnam.

February: The Republic of Korea's 2d Marine Corps Brigade departs from South Vietnam.

4 February: The 1/501st Infantry of the 101st Airborne Division departs from South Vietnam.

8 February: The 1/502d Infantry of the 101st Airborne Division departs from South Vietnam.

10 February: The Paris peace talks break down again.

21 February: President Nixon arrives in Peking to begin his historic visit to China.

24 February: The peace talks resume in Paris. However, the communist delegates leave after only 17 minutes to protest the United States' renewed bombing missions over North Vietnam.

29 February: The first ROK troop withdrawal is completed. 11,000 of the United States' allies have returned home. 37,000 Korean fighting men remain in South Vietnam.

129

10 March: The 101st Airborne Division officially departs South Vietnam for Fort Campbell, Kentucky.

23 March: U.S. negotiators in Paris announce that President Nixon has ordered the peace talks suspended indefinitely.

30 March: *Locations:* I Corps; Quang Tri Province; II Corps; Kontum Province. *Action:* The North Vietnamese launch a huge attack into South Vietnam using six divisions (more than 150,000 men) supported by 500+ tanks.

April: The 2d Squadron of the 11th Armored Cavalry Regiment departs from South Vietnam.

1 April: The 2/5th Cavalry of the 1st Cavalry Division departs from South Vietnam.

10 April: U.S. aircraft begin to pound North Vietnam above the 19th Parallel for the first time since the November 1968 bombing halt. The U.S. command acknowledges that B–52s are hitting the north for the first time since November 1967.

16 April: American B–52s fly missions over Hanoi and Haiphong in the first bombings of those cities since 1 November 1968.

21 April: The 2/327th Airborne of the 101st Airborne Division departs from South Vietnam.

26 April: President Nixon announces that another 20,000 U.S. troops will be withdrawn from Vietnam in May and June.

27 April: Official peace talks resume in Paris, but are described as "fruitless."

29–30 April: U.S. B–52s fly 700 raids over North Vietnam.

May: The monsoon (rainy) season begins in the southern provinces and ends in the north.

May: Quang Tri Province falls to the communists. 66,000 U.S. troops remain in South Vietnam.

2 May: Secret meetings between Secretary of State Henry Kissinger and the North Vietnamese representative, Le Duc Tho, resume in Paris.

4 May: American and South Vietnamese officials agree to another indefinite suspension of the formal (public) peace talks.

8 May: President Nixon announces the mining of all ports in North Vietnam. This action is to prevent the flow of arms and supplies to the communists. Nixon adds that the mining, search and seizure of ships and bombing of the north will stop if all American POWs are returned and an internationally supervised cease-fire begins.

9 May: The U.S. bombing of North Vietnam reaches the all-time high levels of the years 1967–1968.

10 May–23 October: *Operation Linebacker I. Locations:* North Vietnam; Gia Lam; Haiphong; Hanoi; Phuc Yen. *Type/Objective:* Aerial bombardment of North Vietnam in an effort to reduce their ability to wage war by destroying all their vital logistic, communications and port facilities. *Units:* United States Air Force, United States Navy.

23 May: The bombing campaign over North Vietnam is widened to now include more industrial and nonmilitary targets.

14 June: U.S. aircraft fly a record 340 missions over North Vietnam.

20 June: The 1/46th Infantry (196th Light Infantry Brigade) of the 23d

Infantry Division (Americal) departs from South Vietnam.

26 June: The 3d Brigade (separate) of the 1st Cavalry Division departs from South Vietnam. Also leaving is one of its organic battalions, the 1/12th Cavalry.

28 June: The 2/8th Cavalry of the 1st Cavalry Division departs from South Vietnam.

28 June: President Nixon announces that no more draftees will be sent involuntarily to South Vietnam.

29 June: The 196th Light Infantry Brigade of the 23d Infantry Division (Americal) officially departs from South Vietnam.

29 June: The 2/1st Infantry (196th Light Infantry Brigade) of the 23d Infantry Division (Americal) departs from South Vietnam.

1 July: The 2/501st Infantry of the 101st Airborne Division departs from South Vietnam.

13 July: The formal peace talks begin again in Paris after a 10-week layoff.

11 August: The last U.S. ground combat unit in South Vietnam, the 3/21st Infantry (196th Light Infantry Brigade) of the 23d Infantry Division (Americal), is deactivated.

22 August: The 1/7th Cavalry of the 1st Cavalry Division departs from South Vietnam.

23 August: The 3/21st Infantry (196th Light Infantry Brigade) of the 23d Infantry Division (Americal) departs from South Vietnam.

43,500 U.S. airmen and support personnel remain in South Vietnam.

29 August: President Nixon announces

the withdrawal of 12,000 more U.S. troops from South Vietnam is to be completed by 1 December 1972.

3 October: The United States Department of Defense reports that American planes have dropped more than 7,555,800 tons of bombs on Indo-China between February 1965 and August 1972. *Note:* To put this into perspective, the *combined* Allied tonnage dropped in World War II was 2,056,244 tons.

21 October: North Vietnamese Premier Pham Van Dong announces his country will accept a cease-fire. The Premier says the cessation of hostilities will be followed by a complete withdrawal of all U.S. forces and that all American POWs will be released after a settlement has been agreed on. It is also stipulated that Saigon and the Viet Cong will join in a coalition with general elections to follow in six months.

24 October: As a sign of good faith, President Nixon orders all bombing of North Vietnam stopped above the 20th Parallel.

7 November: The 1st Signal Brigade officially departs from South Vietnam.

8 November: The Republic of Korea's (ROK) troops cease all combat operation and schedule a December departure.

22 November: The first American B–52 of the war to be shot down by a surface-to-air (SAM) missile crashes near Vinh, North Vietnam.

14 December: President Nixon issues a statement demanding that the North Vietnamese begin to negotiate seriously or suffer the consequences.

18–31 December: *Operation Linebacker II. Locations:* North Vietnam; Haiphong and Hanoi. *Action:* The aerial bombardment of North Vietnam with the intention of pounding them into submission and forcing them to negotiate seriously. *Units:* United States Air Force, United States Navy. *Comments:* U.S. officials confirm the resumption of bombing and mining over North Vietnam. Between 18 and 24 December, U.S. planes drop an amount of bombs over North Vietnam that is equal to half the total tonnage dropped on England during all of World War II . . . or the destructive equivalent of 20 Hiroshima-sized atomic bombs. *Casualties:* 15 B–52s shot down, 11 other aircraft shot down, 93 pilots/crew members KIA or POW.

31 December: U.S. troop levels are down to 24,000 remaining in South Vietnam. U.S. losses in 1972: 4300 KIA. Total U.S. losses in Vietnam War since 1959: 45,926 KIA. VNAF troop strength at the end of 1972: 1,000,000+. VNAF losses in 1972: 39,587 KIA. VNAF losses in Vietnam War to date: 195,847 KIA. Enemy troop strength in South Vietnam is estimated at more than 150,000.

1973 –1975

As of 1 January 1973 only 24,000 U.S. personnel remain in South Vietnam. VNAF strength is more than a million men. Enemy forces are estimated at 150,000.

23 January: President Nixon announces that a peace agreement ending the Vietnam War has been reached and signed in Paris.

27 January: The last U.S. soldier to die in the Vietnam War, Lt. Col. William Nolde, is KIA by an enemy artillery burst near An Loc (III Corps; Binh Long Province).

28 January: Hostilities in South Vietnam end. The formal cease-fire begins at 7 p.m. EST.

March: The Royal Thai Volunteer Force departs from South Vietnam.

10 March: The Republic of Korea's (ROK) Capital Division departs from South Vietnam.

16 March: The Republic of Korea's (ROK) 9th Infantry Division departs from South Vietnam.

28 March: The United States' 1st Aviation Brigade officially departs from South Vietnam.

29 March: The last U.S. troops leave South Vietnam. North Vietnam releases the last 67 American POWs. For the United States, the war is finally over. The war's statistics are staggering: More than 3,000,000 Americans served in Vietnam. 47,253 Americans were KIA or as the result of combat. 10,449 Americans died of nonbattle injuries. 313,919 Americans were WIA. 153,300 classified as "seriously" wounded. 1340 Americans are listed as MIA. 4865 helicopters and 3720 fixed-wing aircraft were shot down or destroyed. Eight million tons of bombs were expended in the Vietnam War . . . four times that of the total tonnage dropped in all of World War II. 223,748 Vietnamese Armed Forces (VNAF) personnel were KIA in the war. 499,026 VNAF personnel WIA. 924,048 NVA/VC deaths estimated in the Vietnam War. 415,000 civilians KIA and an estimated 935,000 more WIA.

4 January 1974: South Vietnam's president, Nguyen Van Thieu claims that the war has resumed.

6 January 1974: The communist Khmer Rouge attack Phnom Penh, Cambodia's capital.

27 January 1974: The South Vietnamese government states some 13,700 government troops, 2200 civilians and 45,000 communists have died in fighting since the truce.

6 May 1974: The United States Senate turns down an Administration request for $266,000,000 in military aid for South Vietnam.

22 May 1974: The House of Representatives rejects a proposed 100,000-man reduction in U.S. forces abroad. The House does approve a $474,000,000 cutback in aid to South Vietnam.

9 August 1974: Facing certain impeachment, Richard Nixon resigns as President of the United States. Vice President Gerald Ford succeeds Nixon.

8 January 1975: North Vietnamese forces take Phuoc Long Province, north of Saigon (III Corps). The United States does nothing to prevent the province's fall.

10 March 1975: North Vietnamese

forces begin the siege of the provincial capital of Ban Me Thout (II Corps; Darlac Province).

30 March 1975: DaNang (I Corps; Quang Nam Province) is captured by communist forces.

10 April 1975: Congress rejects President Ford's call for $722,000,000 in military aid to South Vietnam.

15 April 1975: Xuan Loc (III Corps; Long Khanh Province), 38 miles east of Saigon, falls to the communists after days of heavy fighting.

17 April 1975: Forces of the Khmer Rouge take Phnom Penh, Cambodia.

21 April 1975: South Vietnamese President Nguyen Van Thieu resigns his post.

28 April 1975: Duong Van Minh assumes the presidency of South Vietnam in Thieu's absence.

29 April 1975: *Operation Frequent Wind. Location:* III Corps; Gia Dinh Province; Capital Military District; Saigon. *Objective:* The final evacuation of American staff and their dependents from Saigon. Four thousand, eight hundred and seventy people are evacuated in less than 24 hours.

30 April 1975: Communist troops enter Saigon as the last Americans and their dependents rush to evacuate. The final chopper lifts off from the roof of the American embassy at 7:53 a.m. carrying the last 11 Marines. President Duong Van Minh announces the unconditional surrender of the Saigon government to the communist forces. For the South Vietnamese, the war is finally over too.

Appendix I

*An alphabetical listing of Army and Marine combat operations
of the Vietnam War contained in* Vietnam Battle Chronology.

Abilene: 30 March–15 April 1966 (1st Infantry Division)

Adair: 15–25 June 1967 (USMC)

Adairsville: 1 February–23 March 1968 (11th ACR)

Adams: 26 October 1966–5 April 1967 (4th Infantry Division)

Adelaide I: 30 May–9 June 1966 (1st Infantry Division)

Aiea: 8 August–1 September 1966 (25th Infantry Division)

Akron II: 22–27 August 1967 (9th Infantry Division)

Akron V: 11–21 January 1968 (9th Infantry Division)

Alcorn Cove: 21 March–7 April 1968 (11th ACR)

Alexandria: 4–5 December 1966 (11th ACR)

Alice: 2–8 September 1966 (196th LIB)

All the Way: 23 October–9 November 1965 (1st Cavalry Division)

Allen Brook: 4 May–24 August 1968 (USMC)

Amarillo: 23 August–1 September 1966 (1st Infantry Division)

An Truyen: 8–9 August 1968 (101st Airborne Division)

A–0 Strike: 1–18 August 1967 (1st Infantry Division)

Apache Snow: 10 May–7 June 1969 (101st Airborne Division; USMC)

Ardmore: 17 July–31 October 1967 (USMC)

Arizona: 14–22 June 1967 (USMC)

Arkansas City: 18–23 September 1967 (11th ACR; 9th Infantry Division)

Arlington Canyon: 3 July–20 September 1969 (USMC)

Athens: 15 May–25 June 1966 (USMC)

Athol: 8–13 September 1966 (196th LIB)

Atlanta: 20 October–8 December 1966 (11th ACR)

Atlanta: 18 November–23 December 1967 (25th Infantry Division)

Atlas Wedge: 17–24 March 1969 (1st Cavalry Division; 1st Infantry Division; 11th ACR; 25th Infantry Division)

Attala/Casey: 21–30 January 1968 (1st Infantry Division; 11th ACR; 101st Airborne Division)

Attleboro: 14 September–24 November 1966 (1st Infantry Division; 4th Infantry Division; 11th ACR; 25th Infantry Division; 173d Airborne Brigade; 196th LIB)

Aurora I: 9–17 July 1966 (173d Airborne Brigade)

Aurora II: 17 July–3 August 1966 (173d Airborne Brigade)

Austin II/VI: 12 April–18 May 1966 (101st Airborne Division)

Badger Catch: 23–26 January 1968 (USMC)

Badger Tooth: 26 December 1967–2 January 1968 (USMC)

Baker: 19 April–20 September 1967 (4th Infantry Division; 25th Infantry Division)

Ballistic Arch: 24–27 November 1967 (USMC)

Ballistic Armor: 22–26 January 1968 (USMC)

Ballistic Charge: 16–22 September 1967 (USMC)

Barber Glade: 15 May–30 June 1970 (101st Airborne Division)

Barking Sands: 18 May–7 December 1967 (25th Infantry Division)

Barren Green: 24–27 July 1970 (USMC)

Baton Rouge: 4 September–8 October 1966 (1st Infantry Division)

Beacon Gate: 7–11 August 1967 (USMC)

Beacon Guide: 21–30 July 1967 (USMC)

Beacon Hill: 20 March–1 April 1967 (USMC)

Beacon Point: 1–6 September 1967 (USMC)

Beacon Star: 22 April–12 May 1967 (USMC)

Beacon Torch/Calhoun: 18 June–2 July 1967 (USMC)

Bear Bite: 2–12 June 1967 (USMC)

Bear Chain: 20–21 July 1967 (USMC)

Beau Charger: 18–26 May 1967 (USMC)

Beauregard: 24 June–15 July 1966 (101st Airborne Division)

Beaver: 1–7 June 1966 (USMC)

Beaver Cage: 28 April–12 May 1967 (USMC)

Beaver Track: 5–13 July 1967 (USMC)

Belt Drive: 27 August–5 September 1967 (USMC)

Belt Tight: 20–23 May 1967 (USMC)

Benton: 14 August–1 September 1967 (101st Airborne Division)

Bethlehem/Allentown: 20–27 October 1966 (1st Infantry Division)

Big Spring: 1–16 February 1967 (9th Infantry Division; 173d Airborne Brigade)

Billings: 12–26 June 1967 (1st Infantry Division)

Binh Tay I: 6–16 May 1970 (4th Infantry Division)

Birmingham: 24 April–17 May 1966 (1st Infantry Division)

Black Ferret: 3–5 November 1965 (USMC)

Black Swan: 2–3 June 1969 (3d Brigade/82d Airborne Division)

Blastout I: 2–3 August 1965 (USMC)

Bloodhound/Bushmaster: December 1965 (1st Infantry Division)

Blue Marlin I: 10–12 November 1965 (USMC)

Blue Marlin II: 16–18 November 1965 (USMC)

Bluefield I: 5–9 June 1967 (1st Infantry Division)

Bluefield II: 23–28 September 1967 (1st Infantry Division)

Bold Mariner: 13 January–9 February 1969 (USMC)

Bold Pursuit: 27 June–6 July 1969 (USMC)

Bolling II: 19 September 1967–31 January 1969 (1st Cavalry Division; 173d Airborne Brigade)

Box Springs: 16–22 March 1968 (101st Airborne Division)

Boyd: 25–29 September 1966 (1st Infantry Division)

Brandies Blue: 2 July–25 August 1970 (4th Infantry Division)

Brave Armada: 24 July–7 August 1969 (USMC)

Bremerton: 25 October–28 November 1966 (4th Infantry Division)

Bristol Boots: 25 April–15 May 1969 (101st Airborne Division)

Buffalo: 2–14 July 1967 (USMC)

Burlington Trail: 8 April–11 November 1968 (23d Infantry Division [Americal])

Byrd: 26 August 1966–20 January 1968 (1st Cavalry Division)

Camden: 17–31 December 1968 (25th Infantry Division)

Cameron Falls: 29 May–23 June 1969 (USMC)

Campbell Streamer: 11 July–15 August 1969 (101st Airborne Division)

Canary/Duck: 7 December 1966–5 January 1967 (173d Airborne Brigade)

Carentan I–II: 8 March–17 May 1968 (3d Brigade/82d Airborne Division; 101st Airborne Division)

Catawba Falls: 18–21 September 1970 (USMC)

Cedar Falls: 8–26 January 1967 (1st Infantry Division; 11th ACR, 25th Infantry Division; 173d Airborne Brigade; 196th LIB)

Cedar Rapids: 17–21 July 1966 (1st Infantry Division)

Champaign Grove: 4–24 September 1968 (23d Infantry Division [Americal])

Chattachoochee Swamp: 19–29 June

1968 (23d Infantry Division [Americal])

Cheadle Blue: 15–28 May 1970 (4th Infantry Division)

Checkerboard: December 1965 (1st Infantry Division; 101st Airborne Division; 173d Airborne Brigade)

Cherokee: 5–7 May 1966 (USMC)

Cheyenne: 2–5 August 1966 (1st Infantry Division)

Chicago Peak/Lam Son 363: 25 July–12 August 1970 (101st Airborne Division)

Chinook I: 19 December 1966–6 February 1967 (USMC)

Cimmaron: 1 June–2 July 1967 (USMC)

Cincinnati: 18–25 May 1967 (173d Airborne Brigade)

Clean House I–II–III: 17–31 December 1965 (1st Cavalry Division)

Cliff Dweller IV: 4–11 January 1970 (25th Infantry Division)

Clinch Valley: 9–15 July 1970 (101st Airborne Division)

Cochise: 11–28 August 1967 (USMC)

Cochise Green/Dan Sinh: 30 March 1968–31 January 1969 (23d Infantry Division [Americal], 173d Airborne Brigade)

Cocoa Beach: 3–6 March 1966 (1st Infantry Division)

Colby: 20–28 January 1967 (9th Infantry Division)

Cold Dawn: 7–8 July 1969 (3d Brigade/82d Airborne Division)

Cold Steel: 28–29 June 1969 (3d Brigade/82d Airborne Division)

Colorado/Lien Ket 52: 6–22 August 1966 (USMC)

Comanche Falls: 11 September–7 November 1968 (1st Cavalry Division)

Comanche Falls III: 2–7 November 1968 (1st Cavalry Division)

Concordia I: 19–21 June 1967 (9th Infantry Division)

Concordia II: 10–14 July 1967 (9th Infantry Division)

Concordia Square: 9–17 May 1968 (1st Cavalry Division)

Cook: 2–9 October 1967 (101st Airborne Division)

Coronado I: 1 June–26 July 1967 (9th Infantry Division)

Coronado II: 28 July–1 August 1967 (9th Infantry Division)

Coronado III: 5–17 August 1967 (9th Infantry Division)

Coronado IV: 19 August–9 September 1967 (9th Infantry Division)

Coronado V: 12 September–8 October 1967 (9th Infantry Division)

Coronado VI: 11–18 October 1967 (9th Infantry Division)

Coronado IX: 1 November 1967–21 January 1968 (9th Infantry Division)

Coronado X: 18 January–13 February 1968 (9th Infantry Division)

Coronado XI: 13 February–6 March 1968 (9th Infantry Division)

County Fair I: 24–25 February 1966 (USMC)

County Fair II: 26 April 1966 (USMC)

Crazy Horse: 16 May–5 June 1966 (1st Cavalry Division)

Crimp/Buckskin: 8–14 January 1966 (1st Infantry Division; 173d Airborne Brigade)

Crockett: 13 May–16 July 1967 (USMC)

Cumberland: 7–11 March 1967 (1st Infantry Division)

Cumberland: 3 June–15 September 1967 (USMC)

Cussetta: 4–7 April 1967 (199th LIB)

Dagger Thrust: 25 September 1965 (USMC)

Dagger Thrust V: 5–6 December 1965 (USMC)

Dakota Clint: 10 February–29 March 1970 (1st Infantry Brigade/5th Infantry Division)

Dale Common: 18–19 October 1968 (23d Infantry Division [Americal])

Dallas: 17–25 May 1967 (1st Infantry Division; 11th ACR)

Dan Tam 81: 16 November 1966–12 January 1967 (11th ACR)

Danbury: 15–21 September 1966 (1st Infantry Division)

Daniel Boone: May 1967 (MACV-SOG)

Darby Crest I: 1 February–3 March 1969 (173d Airborne Brigade)

Darby Crest III: 25 March–15 April 1969 (173d Airborne Brigade)

Darby March I: 1–3 February 1969 (173d Airborne Brigade)

Darby March II: 8 February–6 March 1969 (173d Airborne Brigade)

Darby Trail: 1–7 February 1969 (173d Airborne Brigade)

Daring Endeavor: 10–17 November 1968 (USMC)

Daring Rebel: 5–20 May 1969 (USMC)

Davy Crockett: 3–16 May 1966 (1st Cavalry Division)

Dawson River: 28 November 1968–27 January 1969 (USMC)

Dawson River South: 22–25 January 1969 (USMC)

Dayton: 5–17 May 1967 (173d Airborne Brigade)

Decatur: 3 September–8 October 1966 (1st Infantry Division)

Deckhouse I: 18–30 June 1966 (USMC)

Deckhouse II: 16–18 July 1966 (USMC)

Deckhouse III: 16–29 August 1966 (USMC)

Deckhouse IV: 15–24 September 1966 (USMC)

Deckhouse V: 6–15 January 1967 (USMC)

Deckhouse VI: 16 February–3 March 1967 (USMC)

Defiant Measure: 10–16 February 1969 (USMC)

Defiant Stand: 7–19 September 1969 (USMC)

Delaware/Lam Son 216: 19 April–17 May 1968 (1st Cavalry Division; 23d Infantry Division [Americal]; 101st Airborne Division)

Desoto: 26 January–7 April 1967 (USMC)

Dewey Canyon I: 22 January–19 March 1969 (USMC)

Dewey Canyon II: 30 January–7 February 1971 (23d Infantry Division [Americal]; 101st Airborne Division)

Dexter: 4–6 May 1966 (173d Airborne Brigade)

Diamond Head: 18 May–7 December 1967 (25th Infantry Division)

Dirty Devil: 2–24 May 1969 (3d Brigade/82d Airborne Division)

Dodge: 17–23 June 1966 (USMC)

Double Eagle I: 28 January–19 February 1966 (USMC)

Double Eagle II: 20 February–1 March 1966 (USMC)

Drum Head: 26–27 October 1965 (USMC)

Dubois Square: 9–19 September 1970 (USMC)

Dukes Glade: 2–9 October 1968 (23d Infantry Division [Americal])

Duong Cua Dan: 17 March–30 July 1968 (9th Infantry Division)

Durham Peak: 20 July–13 August 1969 (USMC)

Eager Hunter/Garrard Bay: 25 October–6 December 1966 (USMC)

Eager Pursuit: 1–10 March 1969 (USMC)

Eager Pursuit II: 10–27 March 1969 (USMC)

Eager Yankee: 9–16 June 1968 (USMC)

Earhart White: 1–18 March 1970 (4th Infantry Division)

Eichelberger Black: 24 March–24 April 1970 (4th Infantry Division)

El Dorado: 13–14 August 1966 (1st Infantry Division)

El Paso II: 2 June–13 July 1966 (1st Infantry Division)

El Paso III: 13 July–3 September 1966 (1st Infantry Division)

Elk Canyon I–II: 12 July–25 August 1970 (23d Infantry Division [Americal])

Ellis Ravine: 8–15 April 1969 (1st Brigade/5th Infantry Division)

Emporia: 21 July–14 September 1967 (11th ACR)

Enterprise: 13 February 1967–11 March 1968 (9th Infantry Division; 25th Infantry Division; 199th LIB)

Essex: 6–17 November 1967 (USMC)

Evansville: 5–15 August 1966 (1st Infantry Division)

Fairfax/Rang Dong: 30 November 1966–14 December 1967 (1st Infantry Division; 4th Infantry Division; 25th Infantry Division; 199th LIB)

Fargo: 21 December 1967–21 January 1968 (11th ACR)

Farragut: 26 January–23 March 1967 (101st Airborne Division)

Fayette Canyon: 15 December 1968–

28 February 1969 (23d Infantry Division [Americal])

Fitchburg: 25 November 1966–8 April 1967 (196th LIB)

Florida/Doan Ket: 9–12 June 1966 (USMC)

Formation Leader: 17–18 October 1967 (USMC)

Forsythe Grove: 1–2 July 1969 (USMC)

Fort Wayne: 1–4 May 1967 (173d Airborne Brigade)

Fortress Attack: 27 January 1968 (USMC)

Fortress Ridge: 21–24 December 1967 (USMC)

Fortress Sentry: 17–25 September 1967 (USMC)

Foster/Badger Hunt: 13–30 November 1967 (USMC)

Francis Marion: 5 April–12 October 1967 (4th Infantry Division; 173d Airborne Brigade)

Fredenall Gold: 18–30 May 1970 (4th Infantry Division)

Frederick Hill: Began 18 March 1969 (23d Infantry Division [Americal])

Fremont: 10 July–31 October 1967 (USMC)

Frequent Wind: 29 April 1975 (USMC)

Fresno: 8–16 September 1966 (USMC)

Friendship III: 11 September 1969–20 February 1970 (199th LIB)

Fulton Square: 22 October 1969–18 January 1970 (1st Brigade/5th Infantry Division [M])

Gadsden: 2–21 February 1967 (4th Infantry Division)

Gallant Leader: 23–25 May 1969 (USMC)

Gatling I–II: 1–15 February 1967 (101st Airborne Division)

Geneva Park: Began 18 March 1969 (23d Infantry Division [Americal])

Georgia: 21 April–10 May 1966 (USMC)

Georgia Tar: 16 July–25 September 1969 (USMC)

Geronimo: 31 October–4 December 1966 (101st Airborne Division)

Gibraltar: 18–21 September 1965 (101st Airborne Division)

Golden Fleece: 8 September–27 October 1965 (USMC)

Golden Fleece II: 14–30 March 1966 (USMC)

Golden Fleece 7–1: 16–27 September 1966 (USMC)

Golden Valley: 10–12 May 1968 (23d Infantry Division [Americal])

Good Friend: 20 October–15 November 1965 (1st Cavalry Division)

Granite: 26 October–4 November 1967 (USMC)

Great Bend: 13 June–26 July 1967 (9th Infantry Division)

Greeley: 17 June–11 October 1967 (1st Cavalry Division; 173d Airborne Brigade)

Green House: 20–26 November 1965 (1st Cavalry Division)

Greene River: 19 January–22 July 1970 (1st Infantry Brigade/5th Infantry Division [M])

Greenleaf: 6–24 February 1967 (9th Infantry Division)

Guess What: 13–14 May 1969 (3d Bde/82d Airborne Division)

Guess Who: 9–11 May 1969 (3d Bde/82d Airborne Division)

Hancock: 26 April–22 May 1967 (4th Infantry Division)

Happy Valley I–II: 6 October–19 November 1965 (1st Cavalry Division)

Hardihood: 16 May–8 June 1966 (173d Airborne Brigade)

Hardin Falls: 2 December 1968–28 February 1969 (23d Infantry Division [Americal])

Harvest Moon: 8–20 December 1965 (USMC)

Harvest Moon: 5 April–9 May 1967 (1st Infantry Division)

Hastings: 7 July–3 August 1966 (USMC)

Hattiesburg: 1–5 March 1966 (1st Infantry Division)

Hawthorne I–II: 2–21 June 1966 (1st Cavalry Division; 101st Airborne Division)

Henderson Hill: 24 October–6 December 1968 (USMC)

Henry Clay: 2–30 July 1966 (1st Cavalry Division; 101st Airborne Division)

Herkimer Mountain: 9 May–16 July 1969 (USMC)

Hickory: 7–15 October 1966 (11th ACR)

Hickory: 18–28 May 1967 (USMC)

Hickory II: 14–16 July 1967 (USMC)

Highland: 22 August–2 October 1965 (101st Airborne Division)

Hoang Dieu: 22 October–31 November 1970 (USMC)

Hoang Dieu 101: 18 December 1970–19 January 1971 (USMC)

Hoang Dieu 103: 3 February–29 March 1971 (USMC)

Hollandia: 9–18 June 1966 (173d Airborne)

Holt: 2–6 July 1966 (USMC)

Honolulu: March 1966 (25th Infantry Division)

Hood River: 2–13 August 1967 (101st Airborne Division)

Hooker I: 10–21 June 1966 (1st Cavalry Division)

Hot Springs: April 1966 (USMC)

Houston: 26 February–12 September 1968 (USMC)

Hue City: 2 February–2 March 1968 (1st Cavalry Division; USMC)

Hump: 5 November 1965 (173d Airborne Brigade)

Hunter: 26–28 March 1969 (199th LIB)

Idaho Canyon: 16 July–25 September 1969 (USMC)

Imperial Lake: 31 August 1970–7 May 1971 (USMC)

Independence: 1–9 February 1967 (USMC)

Indiana: 28–30 March 1966 (USMC)

Iron Mountain: Began 18 March 1969 (23d Infantry Division [Americal])

Iroquois Grove: 19 June–25 September 1969 (1st Brigade/5th Infantry Division [M])

Irving: 1–24 October 1966 (1st Cavalry Division)

Jackstay: 26 March–6 April 1966 (USMC)

Jay: 25 June–4 July 1966 (USMC)

Jeb Stuart: 19 January–31 March 1968 (1st Cavalry Division; 101st Airborne Division)

Jeb Stuart III: 17 May–3 November 1968 (1st Cavalry Division)

Jefferson Glen: 5 September 1970–8

October 1971 (101st Airborne Division)

Jim Bowie: 7–28 March 1966 (1st Cavalry Division)

John Paul Jones: 21 July–5 September 1966 (4th Infantry Division; 101st Airborne Division)

Join Hands: 6–15 September 1967 (1st Cavalry Division)

Junction City: 22 February–17 March 1967 (1st Infantry Division; 4th Infantry; 9th Infantry Division; 11th ACR; 173d Airborne Brigade; 196th LIB)

Junction City II: 21 March–14 April 1967 (1st Infantry Division; 11th ACR)

Kamuela: 20 September–4 October 1966 (25th Infantry Division; 196th LIB)

Kangaroo Kick: 1–3 August 1967 (USMC)

Kansas: 17–22 June 1966 (USMC)

Kentucky: 1 November 1967–28 February 1969 (USMC)

Kentucky Jumper: 1 March–14 August 1969 (101st Airborne Division)

Kien Giang 9–1: 16–24 November 1967 (9th Infantry Division)

Kingfisher: 16 July–31 October 1967 (USMC)

Kings: 19–28 March 1966 (USMC)

Kipapa: 31 August–12 September 1966 (25th Infantry Division)

Kittyhawk: 14 February 1967–21 March 1968 (11th ACR)

Klamath Falls: 1 December 1967–8 January 1968 (1st Cavalry Division; 101st Airborne Division)

Knox: 24 October–4 November 1967 (USMC)

Koko Head: 22 July–6 August 1966 (25th Infantry Division)

Kole Kole: 14 May–7 December 1967 (25th Infantry Division)

Ky Lam Campaign: May 1966 (USMC)

Lahaina: 7 August–1 September 1966 (25th Infantry Division)

Lake: 6–12 July 1967 (101st Airborne Division)

Lam Son 68: 1 February–10 March 1968 (1st Infantry Division)

Lam Son 719: 8 February–6 April 1971 (101st Airborne Division)

Lamar Plain: 16 May–13 August 1969 (23d Infantry Division [Americal]; 101st Airborne Division)

Lancaster I: 1 November 1967–20 January 1968 (USMC)

Lancaster II: 21 January–23 November 1968 (USMC)

Lanikai: 15 September 1966–13 February 1967 (25th Infantry Division)

Laurel: 16–17 February 1967 (1st Infantry Division)

Lejeune: 7–22 April 1967 (1st Cavalry Division)

Lewis and Clark: 3–16 May 1966 (1st Cavalry Division)

Lexington I: 17 April 1966 (1st Infantry Division)

Lexington III: 21 May–9 June 1966 (1st Infantry Division)

Liberty I: 7–30 June 1966 (USMC)

Liberty II: 19–24 October 1967 (USMC)

Lien Ket-10: 29–30 October 1965 (USMC)

Lincoln: 25 March–8 April 1966 (1st Cavalry Division)

Linn River: 27 January–7 February 1969 (USMC)

Little Rock: 2–4 October 1966 (1st Infantry Division)

Lonesome End: 14–19 October 1965 (1st Cavalry Division)

Long Reach: 23 October–26 November 1965 (1st Cavalry Division)

Long Reach I: 7–9 November 1969 (1st Cavalry Division; 11th ACR)

Long Reach II: 3 December 1969–1 January 1970 (11th ACR)

Lulu: 12–14 March 1969 (9th Infantry Division; 199th LIB)

Lyon Valley: 16–24 August 1970 (USMC)

MacArthur/Binh Tay: 12 October 1967–31 January 1969 (4th Infantry Division; 173d Airborne Brigade)

McLain: 20 January 1968–31 January 1969 (173d Airborne Brigade)

Macon: 4 July–27 October 1966 (USMC)

Maine Crag: 15 March–2 May 1969 (1st Infantry Brigade/5th Infantry Division [M]; USMC)

Makalapa: 18 March–21 April 1967 (25th Infantry Division)

Makii: 3 June 1966 (25th Infantry Division)

Malheur I–II: 11 May–2 August 1967 (25th Infantry Division; 101st Airborne Division; 196th LIB)

Mallard: 10–17 January 1966 (USMC)

Mallet: February 1966 (1st Infantry Division)

Mameluke Thrust: 18 May–23 October 1968 (USMC)

Manchester: 18 December 1967–12 January 1968 (199th LIB)

Manhattan: 22 April–12 May 1967 (1st Infantry Division)

Marauder: 1–8 January 1966 (173d Airborne Brigade)

Marshaltown: 2–8 November 1966 (4th Infantry Division)

Maryland: 25–27 June 1967 (USMC)

Masher/Whitewing: 25 January–6 March 1966 (1st Cavalry Division)

Massachusetts Bay: 7 May–18 June 1969 (USMC)

Massachusetts Striker: 1 March–8 May 1969 (101st Airborne Division)

Mastiff: 21–27 February 1966 (1st Infantry Division)

Matador I–II: 1–19 January 1966 (1st Cavalry Division)

Maui Peak: 6–19 October 1968 (USMC)

Meade River: 20 November–9 December 1968 (USMC)

Medina/Bastion Hill: 11–20 October 1967 (USMC)

Meridian: 7–11 November 1966 (173d Airborne Brigade)

Midnight: 12 August 1965 (USMC)

Mighty Play: 10–20 July 1969 (USMC)

Miracle: 6–9 February 1968 (23d Infantry Division [Americal])

Montana Mauler: 23 March–3 April 1969 (1st Infantry Brigade/5th Infantry Division [M])

Montana Mustang: 11 April–11 July 1971 (1st Infantry Brigade/5th Infantry Division [M])

Montana Raider I–II: 12 April–14 May 1969 (1st Cavalry Division; 11th ACR)

Montana Scout: 29 March–12 April 1969 (1st Cavalry Division)

Montgomery Rendezvous: 8 June–14 August 1969 (101st Airborne Division)

Mosby I: 11–17 April 1966 (1st Cavalry Division)

Mosby II: 21 April–3 May 1966 (1st Cavalry Division)

Muncie: 4–14 February 1967 (11th ACR)

Murray Blue: 25 September–11 October 1970 (4th Infantry Division)

Muscatine: 19 December 1967–10 June 1968 (23d Infantry Division [Americal])

Muskogee Meadow: 7–20 April 1969 (USMC)

Nam Hoa I: 18 November–7 December 1968 (101st Airborne Division)

Nantucket Beach: Began 29 July 1969 (23d Infantry Division [Americal])

Napoleon/Saline: 5 November 1967–9 December 1968 (USMC)

Nathan Hale: 19 June–1 July 1966 (1st Cavalry Division; 101st Airborne Division, USMC)

Navajo Warhorse I: 15 December 1968–17 January 1969 (1st Cavalry Division)

Navajo Warhorse II: 17 January–29 March 1969 (1st Cavalry Division)

Nebraska Rapids: 5–8 September 1970 (USMC)

Neosho I: 1 November 1967–20 January 1968 (USMC)

Neosho II: 21–24 January 1968 (USMC)

Nevada Eagle: 17 May 1968–28 February 1969 (101st Airborne Division)

New Life: 21 November–31 December 1965 (1st Infantry Division; 173d Airborne Brigade)

New York: 27 February–3 March 1966 (USMC)

Newark: 18–30 April 1967 (173d Airborne Brigade)

Newcastle: 22–25 March 1967 (USMC)

Niagara Falls: 5–7 January 1967 (173d Airborne Brigade)

Noble Canyon: 23 October–3 November 1970 (USMC)

Norfolk Victory: 9–19 April 1968 (23d Infantry Division [Americal])

Norton Falls: 29 September–3 November 1969 (101st Airborne Division)

Nutcracker: 28 July 1969 (25th Infantry Division)

Oahu: 1–31 August 1966 (25th Infantry Division)

Ohio Rapids: 24 January–28 February 1969 (101st Airborne Division)

Oklahoma Hills: 30 March–29 May 1969 (USMC)

Oregon: 19–23 March 1966 (USMC)

Osage: 27 April–1 May 1966 (USMC)

Osceola I: 20 October 1967–20 January 1968 (USMC)

Osceola II: 21 January–16 February 1968 (USMC)

Paddington: 8–15 July 1967 (9th Infantry Division; 11th ACR)

Palm Beach: 28 January–31 May 1967 (9th Infantry Division)

Paul Revere I/Than Phong–14: 10 May–30 July 1966 (9th Infantry Division)

Paul Revere II: 1–25 August 1966 (1st Cavalry Division; 25th Infantry Division)

Paul Revere III: 26 August–18 October 1966 (1st Cavalry Division; 4th Infantry Division; 25th Infantry Division)

Paul Revere IV: 18 October–30 December 1966 (1st Cavalry Division; 25th Infantry Division)

Pegasus/Lam Son–207: 1–15 April 1968 (1st Cavalry Division; USMC)

Pershing I: 11 February 1967–21 January 1968 (1st Cavalry Division; 25th Infantry Division)

Pershing II: 22 January–29 February 1968 (1st Cavalry Division)

Phu Vang I: 27 September–10 October 1968 (101st Airborne Division)

Phu Vang II–III: 25 October–6 November 1968 (101st Airborne Division)

Phu Vang IV: 11 December 1968–4 January 1969 (101st Airborne Division)

Pickens Forest: 16 July–24 August 1970 (USMC)

Pickett: 6 December 1966–19 January 1967 (101st Airborne Division)

Pipestone Canyon: 26 May–7 November 1969 (USMC)

Piranha: 7–10 September 1965 (USMC)

Pitt: December 1967 (USMC)

Pittsburg: 25 February–3 March 1967 (9th Infantry Division)

Platte Canyon: 6 January–5 February 1969 (101st Airborne Division)

Pocahontas Forest: 6 July–4 August 1968 (23d Infantry Division [Americal])

Portland: 12–21 August 1967 (1st Infantry Division)

Portsea: 3–15 April 1967 (9th Infantry Division)

Prairie I: 3 August 1966–31 January 1967 (USMC)

Prairie II: 31 January–18 March 1967 (USMC)

Prairie III: 18 March–19 April 1967 (USMC)

Prairie IV: 20 April–30 May 1967 (USMC)

Proud Hunter: 18–21 August 1968 (USMC)

Purple Martin: 27 February–8 May 1969 (USMC)

Putnam Paragon: 18 May–12 October 1970 (4th Infantry Division)

Putnam Tiger: 22 April–22 September 1969 (4th Infantry Division)

Putnam Valley: 13–24 October 1970 (4th Infantry Division)

Quick Kick I–II–III: 3–14 January 1966 (1st Infantry Division)

Quick Kick IV: 3–9 February 1966 (1st Infantry Division)

Quicksilver: 27 June–2 July 1967 (9th Infantry Division; 11th ACR)

Quyet Thang: 11 March–7 April 1968 (1st Infantry Division; 9th Infantry Division; 25th Infantry Division)

Randolph Glen: 7 December 1969–31 March 1970 (101st Airborne Division)

Rawlins Valley: 16–24 December 1968 (101st Airborne Division)

Red Snapper: 22–25 October 1965 (USMC)

Reno: 30 May–8 June 1966 (USMC)

Republic Square: 26 September–6 December 1969 (101st Airborne Division)

Rich: 23–25 October 1968 (1st Infantry Brigade/5th Infantry Division [M])

Richland Square: 15 August–28 September 1969 (101st Airborne Division)

Richmond: 22–28 September 1967 (11th ACR)

Ripley Center: 13 July–31 August 1970 (USMC)

River Raider I: 16 February–20 March 1967 (9th Infantry Division)

Roadrunner: November 1965 (1st Infantry Division)

Robertson White: 1–9 June 1970 (4th Infantry Division)

Robin: 10 October 1966 (4th Infantry Division)

Robin North/Robin South: 28 May–19 June 1968 (USMC)

Rolling Stone: 10 February–2 March 1966 (1st Infantry Division)

Rolling Thunder: 2 March 1965–31 October 1968 (USAF/USN)

Rose: 11–30 November 1967 (101st Airborne Division)

Russell Beach: 13 January–21 July 1969 (23d Infantry Division [Americal]; USMC)

Sacramento Bee: 7–8 June 1969 (3d Bde/82d Airborne Division)

Sam Houston: 1 January–5 April 1967 (4th Infantry Division; 25th Infantry Division)

San Angelo: 16 January–9 February 1968 (101st Airborne Division)

Santa Fe: 3 November–3 December 1967 (11th ACR)

Saratoga: 8 December 1967–11 March 1968 (25th Infantry Division)

Saturate: 5 October–4 December 1969 (101st Airborne Division)

Scotland I: 1 November 1967–31 March 1968 (USMC)

Scotland II: 15 April 1968–28 February 1969 (1st Cavalry Division; USMC)

Scott Orchard: 7–12 April 1971 (USMC)

Seward: 5 September–25 October 1966 (4th Infantry Division; 101st Airborne Division)

Shawnee/Choctaw: 22 April–10 July 1967 (USMC)

Shenandoah II: 27 September–19 November 1967 (1st Infantry Division)

Sheridan Sabre: 7 November 1968–2 April 1969 (1st Cavalry Division)

Sherman Peak: 24 January–9 February 1969 (101st Airborne Division)

Shining Brass: Begins October 1965 (MACV-SOG)

Shiny Bayonet: 3–14 October 1965 (1st Cavalry Division)

Sierra: 12 December 1966–21 January 1967 (USMC)

Silver Bayonet I: 10–20 November 1965 (1st Cavalry Division)

Silver Bayonet II: 21–26 November 1965 (1st Cavalry Division)

Silver City: 7–23 March 1966 (173d Airborne Brigade)

Silver Lake: 9–19 January 1967 (9th Infantry Division)

Somerset Plain/Lam Son–246: 4–20 August 1968 (1st Cavalry Division; 101st Airborne Division)

Spanway: 27–29 October 1966 (4th Infantry Division)

Speedy Express: 1 December 1968–31 May 1969 (9th Infantry Division)

Spokane Rapids: 26 February–3 March 1969 (101st Airborne Division)

Springfield I: 27 July–1 August 1966 (1st Infantry Division)

Starlite: 18–24 August 1965 (USMC)

Stomp: 5–7 September 1965 (USMC)

Stone: 10–12 February 1967 (USMC)

Strangle: 21 July–21 September 1969 (1st Infantry Division)

Strangler I: 4–12 February 1969 (199th LIB)

Strangler II: 12–16 February 1969 (199th LIB)

Strike: 1 September–17 November 1967 (9th Infantry Division)

Strike Force: 31 August–1 September 1967 (101st Airborne Division)

Suitland: 19–20 February 1967 (1st Infantry Division)

Summerall: 30 March–29 April 1967 (101st Airborne Division)

Sunset Beach: 2 September–8 October 1966 (25th Infantry Division)

Swift: 4–15 September 1967 (USMC)

Swift Move: 20 November–9 December 1968 (USMC)

Swift Play: 23–24 July 1968 (USMC)

Swift Pursuit: 23 August–19 September 1968 (USMC)

Swift Sabre: 7–14 June 1968 (USMC)

Taylor Common: 7 December 1968–8 March 1969 (USMC)

Texas/Lien Ket–26: 19–24 March 1966 (USMC)

Texas Star: 1 April–5 September 1970 (101st Airborne Division)

Texas Traveler: 24–28 November 1969 (11th ACR)

Thayer I: 13 September–1 October 1966 (1st Cavalry Division)

Thayer II: 25 October 1966–12 February 1967 (1st Cavalry Division)

Thunder Run: 12 August–22 September 1969 (1st Infantry Division; 11th ACR)

Thunderbolt: 6–7 August 1965 (USMC)

Toan Thang I: 8 April–31 May 1968 (1st Infantry Division; 9th Infantry Division; 25th Infantry Division; 101st Airborne Division; 199th LIB)

Toan Thang II: 1 June 1968–16 February 1969 (1st Cavalry Division; 1st Infantry Division; 9th Infantry Division; 11th ACR; 25th Infantry Division; 3d Bde/82d Airborne Division; 101st Airborne Division; 199th LIB)

Toan Thang III: 17 February–31 October 1969 (1st Cavalry Division; 1st Infantry Division; 9th Infantry Division; 11th ACR; 3d Bde/82d Airborne Division; 199th LIB)

Toan Thang IV: 1 November 1969–1 May 1970 (1st Infantry Division; 9th Infantry Division; 25th Infantry Division)

Toan Thang–43: 1 May–30 June 1970 (1st Cavalry Division; 9th Infantry Division; 11th ACR; 25th Infantry Division)

Toan Thang–44: 6–14 May 1970 (25th Infantry Division)

Toan Thang–45: 6 May–20 June 1970 (1st Cavalry Division)

Toan Thang–500: 7–12 May 1970 (9th Infantry Division)

Todd Forest: 31 December 1968–13 January 1969 (101st Airborne Division)

Trailblazer: 18–24 October 1965 (USMC)

Triple Play: 18–20 October 1965 (USMC)

Troui Bridge Cordon: 10–18 November 1968 (101st Airborne Division)

Troy: 2–3 March 1966 (USMC)

Truong Cong Dinh: 7 March–30 July 1968 (9th Infantry Division)

Tucson Delta: 14–21 February 1967 (1st Infantry Division)

Tulare Falls I: 2–15 October 1970 (23d Infantry Division [Americal]; USMC)

Tulare Falls II: 27 October–30 November 1970 (23d Infantry Division [Americal]; USMC)

Turner: 23 June 1966 (USMC)

Twinkletoes: 14–16 March 1969 (11th ACR)

Union I: 21 April–17 May 1967 (USMC)

Union II: 25 May–5 June 1967 (USMC)

Uniontown: 28 January–18 April 1967 (1st Infantry Division; 9th Infantry Division)

Uniontown/Strike: 1–17 December 1967 (199th LIB)

Upshur Stream: 11 January–29 March 1971 (USMC)

Utah/Lien Ket–26: 4–8 March 1966 (USMC)

Utah Mesa: 12 June–9 July 1969 (USMC)

Valdosta I–II: 1 September–23 October 1967 (9th Infantry Division; 11th ACR)

Valiant Hunt I–II: 15 December 1968–5 January 1969 (USMC)

Van Buren: 19 January–21 February 1966 (101st Airborne Division)

Vance Canyon: 20 June–3 July 1968 (23d Infantry Division [Americal])

Vernon Lake I: 15 October–2 November 1968 (23d Infantry Division [Americal])

Vernon Lake II: 2 November 1968–28 February 1969 (23d Infantry Division [Americal])

Vinh Loc: 10–20 September 1968 (101st Airborne Division)

Virginia: 17 April–1 May 1966 (USMC)

Virginia Ridge: 30 April–16 July 1969 (USMC)

Waco: 25 November–2 December 1966 (173d Airborne Brigade)

Waialua: 8 March–8 April 1967 (25th Infantry Division)

Waimea: 22–26 August 1967 (25th Infantry Division)

Wallowa: 4 October–11 November 1967 (1st Cavalry Division; 23d Infantry Division [Americal])

Washington: 6–14 July 1966 (USMC)

Washington Green I–II: 15 April 1969–1 January 1971 (4th Infantry Division; 101st Airborne Division; 173d Airborne Brigade)

Wayne: 10–12 May 1966 (USMC)

Wayne Fast: 28 June–14 July 1970 (4th Infantry Division)

Wayne Forge: 28 August–14 October 1970 (4th Infantry Division)

Wayne Grey: 1 March–14 April 1969 (4th Infantry Division)

Wayne Hurdle: 1–26 June 1970 (4th Infantry Division)

Wayne Jump: 16–26 May 1970 (4th Infantry Division)

Wayne Pierce: 6–27 August 1970 (4th Infantry Division)

Wayne Span I: 17–27 July 1970 (4th Infantry Division)

Wayne Span II: 28 July–6 August 1970 (4th Infantry Division; 173d Airborne Brigade)

Wayne Stab II: 16 February–9 March 1970 (4th Infantry Division; 173d Airborne Brigade)

Wayne Wind: 22 April 1970 (4th Infantry Division; 173d Airborne Brigade)

Weatherford: 6–9 April 1968 (1st Infantry Division)

Wheeler: 11 September–11 November 1967 (23rd Infantry Division [Americal]; 101st Airborne Division)

Wheeler/Wallowa: 11 November 1967–11 November 1968 (23d Infantry Division [Americal])

Williston: 2–12 February 1967 (1st Infantry Division; 11th ACR)

Worth: 13–26 March 1968 (USMC)

Wright Blue: 23–28 June 1970 (4th Infantry Division)

Yazoo: 27 August–5 September 1967 (USMC)

Yellowstone: 8 December 1967–24 February 1968 (25th Infantry Division)

York Market: 30 January–16 April 1970 (1st Infantry Brigade/5th Infantry Division [M])

Yorktown: 24 June–9 July 1966 (173dAirborne Brigade)

Yorktown Victor: 10 September–15 November 1969 (1st Infantry Division; 1st Infantry Brigade/5th Infantry Division [M])

Appendix II

A *chronological listing of the Army and Marine combat operations of the Vietnam War contained in* Vietnam Battle Chronology *listed by major command unit.*

1st Cavalry Division

Shiny Bayonet (3–14 October 1965)
Happy Valley I-II (6 October–19 November 1965)
Lonesome End (14–19 October 1965)
Good Friend (20 October–15 November 1965)
All the Way (23 October–9 November 1965)
Long Reach (23 October–26 November 1965)
Silver Bayonet I (10–20 November 1965)
Green House (20–26 November 1965)
Silver Bayonet II (21–26 November 1965)
Clean House I-II-III (17–31 December 1965)
Matador I-II (1–19 January 1966)
Masher/Whitewing (25 January–6 March 1966)
Jim Bowie (7–28 March 1966)
Lincoln (25 March–8 April 1966)
Mosby I (11–17 April 1966)
Mosby II (21 April–3 May 1966)
Davy Crockett (3–16 May 1966)
Lewis and Clark (3–16 May 1966)
Crazy Horse (16 May–5 June 1966)
Hawthorne I-II (2–21 June 1966)
Hooker I (10–21 June 1966)
Nathan Hale (19 June–1 July 1966)
Henry Clay (2–30 July 1966)
Paul Revere I (1–25 August 1966)
Paul Revere III (26 August–18 October 1966)
Byrd (26 August 1966–20 January 1968)

Thayer I (13 September–1 October 1966)
Irving (1–24 October 1966)
Paul Revere IV (18 October–30 December 1966)
Thayer II (25 October 1966–12 February 1967)
Pershing I (11 February 1967–21 January 1968)
Lejeune (7–22 April 1967)
Greeley (17 June–11 October 1967)
Join Hands (6–15 September 1967)
Bolling II (19 September 1967–31 January 1969)
Wallowa (4 October–11 November 1967)
Klamath Falls (1 December 1967–8 January 1968)
Jeb Stuart (19 January–31 March 1968)
Pershing II (22 January–29 February 1968)
Hue City (2 February–2 March 1968)
Pegasus/Lam Son–207 (1–15 April 1968)
Scotland II (15 April 1968–28 February 1969)
Delaware/Lam Son–216 (19 April–17 May 1968)
Concordia Square (9–17 May 1968)
Jeb Stuart III (17 May–3 November 1968)
Toan Thang II (1 June 1968–16 February 1969)
Somerset Plain/Lam Son–246 (4–20 August 1968)
Comanche Falls (11 September–7 November 1968)
Comanche Falls III (2–7 November 1968)

(1st Cavalry Division cont.)
Sheridan Sabre (7 November 1968–2 April 1969)
Navajo Warhorse I (15 December 1968–17 January 1969)
Navajo Warhorse II (17 January–29 March 1969)
Toan Thang III (17 February–31 October 1969)
Atlas Wedge (17–24 March 1969)
Montana Scout (29 March–12 April 1969)
Montana Raider I–II (12 April–14 May 1969)
Long Reach I (7–9 November 1969)
Toan Thang–43 (1 May–30 June 1970)
Toan Thang–45 (6 May–20 June 1970)

1st Infantry Division

Roadrunner (November 1965)
New Life (21 November–31 December 1965)
Checkerboard (December 1965)
Bloodhound/Bushmaster (December 1965)
Quick Kick I–II–III (3–14 January 1966)
Crimp/Buckskin (8–14 January 1966)
Mallet (February 1966)
Quick Kick IV (3–9 February 1966)
Rolling Stone (10 February–2 March 1966)
Mastiff (21–27 February 1966)
Hattiesburg (1–5 March 1966)
Cocoa Beach (3–6 March 1966)
Abilene (30 March–15 April 1966)
Lexington I (17 April 1966)
Birmingham (24 April–17 May 1966)
Lexington III (21 May–9 June 1966)
Adelaide I (30 May–9 June 1966)
El Paso II (2 June–13 July 1966)
El Paso III (13 July–3 September 1966)
Cedar Rapids (17–21 July 1966)
Springfield I (27 July–1 August 1966)
Cheyenne (2–5 August 1966)
Evansville (5–15 August 1966)
El Dorado (13–14 August 1966)
Amarillo (23 August–1 September 1966)

Decatur (3 September–8 October 1966)
Baton Rouge (4 September–8 October 1966)
Attleboro (14 September–24 November 1966)
Danbury (15–21 September 1966)
Boyd (25–29 September 1966)
Little Rock (2–4 October 1966)
Bethlehem/Allentown (20–27 October 1966)
Fairfax/Rang Dong (30 November 1966–14 December 1967)
Cedar Falls (8–26 January 1967)
Uniontown (28 January–18 April 1967)
Williston (2–12 February 1967)
Tucson Delta (14–21 February 1967)
Laurel (16–17 February 1967)
Suitland (19–20 February 1967)
Junction City (22 February–17 March 1967)
Cumberland (7–11 March 1967)
Junction City II (21 March–14 April 1967)
Harvest Moon (5 April–9 May 1967)
Manhattan (22 April–12 May 1967)
Dallas (17–25 May 1967)
Bluefield I (5–9 June 1967)
Billings (12–26 June 1967)
A–O Strike (1–18 August 1967)
Portland (12–21 August 1967)
Bluefield II (23–28 September 1967)
Shenandoah II (27 September–19 November 1967)
Attala/Casey (21–30 January 1968)
Lam Son–68 (1 February–10 March 1968)
Quyet Thang (11 March–7 April 1968)
Weatherford (6–9 April 1968)
Toan Thang I (8 April–31 May 1968)
Toan Thang II (1 June 1968–16 February 1969)
Toan Thang III (17 February–31 October 1969)
Atlas Wedge (17–24 March 1969)
Strangle (21 July–21 September 1969)
Thunder Run (12 August–22 September 1969)
Yorktown Victor (10 September–15 November 1969)
Toan Thang IV (1 November 1969–1 May 1970)

4th Infantry Division

John Paul Jones (21 July–5 September 1966)

Paul Revere III (26 August–18 October 1966)

Seward (5 September–25 October 1966)

Attleboro (14 September–24 November 1966)

Robin (10 October 1966)

Bremerton (25 October–28 November 1966)

Adams (26 October 1966–5 April 1967)

Spanway (27–29 October 1966)

Marshaltown (2–8 November 1966)

Fairfax/Rang Dong (30 November 1966–14 December 1967)

Sam Houston (1 January–5 April 1967)

Gadsden (2–21 February 1967)

Junction City (22 February–17 March 1967)

Francis Marion (5 April–12 October 1967)

Baker (19 April–20 September 1967)

Hancock (26 April–22 May 1967)

MacArthur/Binh Tay (12 October 1967–31 January 1969)

Wayne Grey (1 March–14 April 1969)

Washington Green I–II (15 April 1969–1 January 1971)

Putnam Tiger (22 April–22 September 1969)

Wayne Stab II (16 February–9 March 1970)

Earhart White (11–18 March 1970)

Eichelberger Black (24 March–24 April 1970)

Binh Tay I (6–16 May 1970)

Cheadle Blue (15–28 May 1970)

Wayne Jump (16–26 May 1970)

Fredenall Gold (18–30 May 1970)

Putnam Paragon (18 May–12 October 1970)

Wayne Wind (22 April 1970)

Robertson White (1–9 June 1970)

Wayne Hurdle (1–26 June 1970)

Wright Blue (23–28 June 1970)

Wayne Fast (28 June–14 July 1970)

Brandies Blue (2 July–25 August 1970)

Wayne Span I (17–27 July 1970)

Wayne Span II (28 July–6 August 1970)

Wayne Pierce (6–27 August 1970)

Wayne Forge (28 August–14 October 1970)

Putnam Valley (13–24 October 1970)

Murray Blue (25 September–11 October 1970)

1st Infantry Brigade/5th Infantry Division (Mech.)

Rich (23–25 October 1968)

Maine Crag (15 March–2 May 1969)

Montana Mauler (23 March–3 April 1969)

Ellis Ravine (8–15 April 1969)

Massachusetts Bay (7 May–18 June 1969)

Iroquois Grove (19 June–25 September 1969)

Fulton Square (22 October 1969–18 January 1970)

Greene River (19 January–22 July 1970)

York Market (30 January–16 April 1970)

Dakota Clint (10 February–29 March 1970)

Montana Mustang (11 April–11 July 1971)

9th Infantry Division

Silver Lake (9–19 January 1967)

Colby (20–28 January 1967)

Uniontown (28 January–18 April 1967)

Palm Beach (28 January–31 May 1967)

Big Spring (1–16 February 1967)

Greenleaf (6–24 February 1967)

Enterprise (13 February 1967–11 March 1968)

River Raider I (16 February–20 March 1967)

Junction City (22 February–17 March 1967)

Pittsburg (25 February–3 March 1967)

Portsea (3–15 April 1967)

Coronado I (1 June–26 July 1967)

Great Bend (13 June–26 July 1967)

Concordia I (19–21 June 1967)

Quicksilver (27 June–2 July 1967)

Paddington (8–15 July 1967)

Concordia II (10–14 July 1967)

(9th Infantry Division cont.)
Coronado II (28 July–1 August 1967)
Coronado III (5–17 August 1967)
Coronado IV (19 August–9 September 1967)
Akron II (22–27 August 1967)
Valdosta I–II (1 September–23 October 1967)
Strike (1 September–17 November 1967)
Coronado V (12 September–8 October 1967)
Arkansas City (18–23 September 1967)
Coronado VI (11–18 October 1967)
Coronado IX (1 November 1967–21 January 1968)
Kien Giang 9–1 (16–24 November 1967)
Akron V (11–21 January 1968)
Coronado X (18 January–13 February 1968)
Coronado XI (13 February–6 March 1968)
Truong Cong Dinh (7 March–30 July 1968)
Quyet Thang (11 March–7 April 1968)
Duong Cua Dan (17 March–30 July 1968)
Toan Thang I (8 April–31 May 1968)
Toan Thang II (1 June 1968–16 February 1969)
Speedy Express (1 December 1968–31 May 1969)
Toan Thang III (17 February–31 October 1969)
Lulu (12–14 March 1969)
Toan Thang IV (1 November 1969–1 May 1970)
Toan Thang–43 (1 May–30 June 1970)
Toan Thang–500 (7–12 May 1970)

Cedar Falls (8–26 January 1967)
Williston (2–12 February 1967)
Muncie (4–14 February 1967)
Kittyhawk (14 February 1967–21 March 1968)
Junction City (22 February–17 March 1967)
Junction City II (21 March–14 April 1967)
Dallas (17–25 May 1967)
Quicksilver (27 June–2 July 1967)
Paddington (8–15 July 1967)
Emporia (21 July–14 September 1967)
Valdosta I–II (1 September–23 October 1967)
Arkansas City (18–23 September 1967)
Richmond (22–28 September 1967)
Santa Fe (3 November–3 December 1967)
Fargo (21 December 1967–21 January 1968)
Attala/Casey (21–30 January 1968)
Adairsville (1 February–23 March 1968)
Alcorn Cove (21 March–7 April 1968)
Toan Thang II (1 June 1968–16 February 1969)
Toan Thang III (17 February–31 October 1969)
Twinkletoes (14–16 March 1969)
Atlas Wedge (17–24 March 1969)
Montana Mauler I–II (12 April–14 May 1969)
Thunder Run (12 August–22 September 1969)
Long Reach I (7–9 November 1969)
Texas Traveler (24–28 November 1969)
Long Reach II (3 December 1969–1 January 1970)
Toan Thang–43 (1 May–30 June 1970)

11th Armored Cavalry Regiment

Attleboro (14 September–24 November 1966)
Hickory (7–15 October 1966)
Atlanta (20 October–8 December 1966)
Dan Tam–81 (16 November 1966–12 January 1967)
Alexandria (4–5 December 1966)

23d Infantry Division (Americal)

Wheeler (11 September–11 November 1967)
Wallowa (4 October–11 November 1967)
Wheeler/Wallowa (11 November 1967–11 November 1968)
Muscatine (19 December 1967–10 June 1968)

Miracle (6–9 February 1968)
Cochise Green/Dan Sinh (30 March 1968–31 January 1969)
Burlington Trail (8 April–11 November 1968)
Norfolk Victory (9–19 April 1968)
Delaware/Lam Son-216 (19 April–17 May 1968)
Golden Valley (10–12 May 1968)
Chattachoochee Swamp (19–29 June 1968)
Vance Canyon (20 June–3 July 1968)
Pocahontas Forest (6 July–4 August 1968)
Champaign Grove (4–24 September 1968)
Dukes Glade (2–9 October 1968)
Vernon Lake I (15 October–2 November 1968)
Dale Common (18–19 October 1968)
Vernon Lake II (2 November 1968–28 February 1969)
Hardin Falls (2 December 1968–28 February 1969)
Fayette Canyon (15 December 1968–28 February 1969)
Russell Beach (13 January–21 July 1969)
Frederick Hill (Began 18 March 1969)
Geneva Park (Began 18 March 1969)
Iron Mountain (Began 18 March 1969)
Lamar Plain (16 May–13 August 1969)
Nantucket Beach (Began 20 July 1969)
Elk Canyon I-II (12 July–25 August 1970)
Tulare Falls I (2–15 October 1970)
Tulare Falls II (27 October–30 November 1970)
Dewey Canyon II (30 January–7 February 1971)

25th Infantry Division

Honolulu (March 1966)
Paul Revere I/Than Phong-14 (10 May–30 July 1966)
Makii (3 June 1966)
Koko Head (22 July–6 August 1966)
Paul Revere II (1–25 August 1966)
Oahu (1–31 August 1966)
Lahaina (7 August–1 September 1966)

Aiea (8 August–1 September 1966)
Paul Revere III (26 August–18 October 1966)
Kipapa (31 August–12 September 1966)
Sunset Beach (2 September–8 October 1966)
Attleboro (14 September–24 November 1966)
Lanikai (15 September 1966–13 February 1967)
Kamuela (20 September–4 October 1966)
Paul Revere IV (18 October–30 December 1966)
Fairfax/Rang Dong (30 November 1966–14 December 1967)
Sam Houston (1 January–5 April 1967)
Cedar Falls (8–26 January 1967)
Pershing I (11 February 1967–21 January 1968)
Enterprise (13 February 1967–11 March 1968)
Waialua (8 March–8 April 1967)
Makalapa (18 March–21 April 1967)
Baker (19 April–20 September 1967)
Malheur I-II (11 May–2 August 1967)
Kole Kole (14 May–7 December 1967)
Barking Sands (18 May–7 December 1967)
Diamond Head (18 May–7 December 1967)
Waimea (22–26 August 1967)
Atlanta (18 November–23 December 1967)
Yellowstone (8 December 1967–24 February 1968)
Saratoga (8 December 1967–11 March 1968)
Quyet Thang (11 March–7 April 1968)
Toan Thang I (8 April–31 May 1968)
Toan Thang II (1 June 1968–16 February 1969)
Camden (17–31 December 1968)
Atlas Wedge (17–24 March 1969)
Nutcracker (28 July 1969)
Toan Thang IV (1 November 1969–1 May 1970)
Cliff Dweller IV (4–11 January 1970)
Toan Thang-43 (1 May–30 June 1970)
Toan Thang-44 (6–14 May 1970)

3d Brigade/82d Airborne Division

Carentan II (8 March–17 May 1968)
Toan Thang II (1 June 1968–16 February 1969)
Toan Thang III (17 February–31 October 1969)
Dirty Devil (2–24 May 1969)
Guess Who (9–11 May 1969)
Guess What (13–14 May 1969)
Black Swan (2–3 June 1969)
Sacramento Bee (7–8 June 1969)
Cold Steel (28–29 June 1969)
Cold Dawn (7–8 July 1969)
Yorktown Victor (10 September–15 November 1969)

101st Airborne Division

Highland (22 August–2 October 1965)
Gibraltar (18–21 September 1965)
Checkerboard (December 1965)
Van Buren (19 January–21 February 1966)
Austin II, VI (12 April–18 May 1966)
Hawthorne I–II (2–21 June 1966)
Nathan Hale (19 June–1 July 1966)
Beauregard (24 June–15 July 1966)
Henry Clay (2–30 July 1966)
John Paul Jones (21 July–5 September 1966)
Seward (5 September–25 October 1966)
Geronimo (31 October–4 December 1966)
Pickett (6 December 1966–19 January 1967)
Farragut (26 January–23 March 1967)
Gatling I–II (1–15 February 1967)
Summerall (30 March–29 April 1967)
Malheur I–II (11 May–2 August 1967)
Lake (6–12 July 1967)
Hood River (2–13 August 1967)
Benton (14 August–1 September 1967)
Strike Force (31 August–1 September 1967)
Wheeler (11 September–11 November 1967)
Cook (2–9 October 1967)
Rose (11–30 November 1967)

Klamath Falls (1 December 1967–8 January 1968)
San Angelo (16 January–9 February 1968)
Jeb Stuart (19 January–31 March 1968)
Attala/Casey (21–30 January 1968)
Carentan II (8 March–17 May 1968)
Box Springs (16–22 March 1968)
Toan Thang I (8 April–31 April 1968)
Delaware/Lam Son–216 (19 April–17 May 1968)
Nevada Eagle (17 May 1968–28 February 1969)
Toan Thang II (1 June 1968–16 February 1969)
Somerset Plain/Lam Son–246 (4–20 August 1968)
An Truyen (8–9 August 1968)
Vinh Loc (10–20 September 1968)
Phu Vang I (27 September–10 October 1968)
Phu Vang II–III (25 October–6 November 1968)
Troui Bridge Cordon (10–18 November 1968)
Nam Hoa I (18 November–7 December 1968)
Phu Vang IV (11 December 1968–4 January 1969)
Rawlins Valley (16–24 December 1968)
Todd Forest (31 December 1968–13 January 1969)
Platte Canyon (6 January–5 February 1969)
Sherman Peak (24 January–9 February 1969)
Ohio Rapids (24 January–28 February 1969)
Spokane Rapids (26 February–3 March 1969)
Massachusetts Striker (1 March–8 May 1969)
Kentucky Jumper (1 March–14 August 1969)
Washington Green I–II (15 April 1969–1 January 1971)
Bristol Boots (25 April–15 May 1969)
Apache Snow (10 May–7 June 1969)
Lamar Plain (16 May–13 August 1969)
Montgomery Rendezvous (8 June–14 August 1969)

Campbell Streamer (11 July–15 August 1969)

Richland Square (15 August–28 September 1969)

Republic Square (26 September–6 December 1969)

Norton Falls (29 September–3 November 1969)

Saturate (5 October–4 December 1969)

Randolph Glen (7 December 1969–31 March 1970)

Texas Star (1 April–5 September 1970)

Barber Glade (15 May–30 June 1970)

Clinch Valley (9–15 July 1970)

Chicago Peak/Lam Son–363 (25 July–12 August 1970)

Jefferson Glen (5 September 1970–8 October 1971)

Dewey Canyon II (30 January–7 February 1971)

Lam Son–719 (8 February–6 April 1971)

173d Airborne Brigade

Hump (5 November 1965)

New Life (21 November–31 December 1965)

Checkerboard (December 1965)

Marauder (1–8 January 1966)

Crimp/Buckskin (8–14 January 1966)

Silver City (7–23 March 1966)

Dexter (4–6 May 1966)

Hardihood (16 May–8 June 1966)

Hollandia (9–18 June 1966)

Yorktown (24 June–9 July 1966)

Aurora I (9–17 July 1966)

Aurora II (17 July–3 August 1966)

Deckhouse III (16–29 August 1966)

Attleboro (14 September–24 November 1966)

Meridian (7–11 November 1966)

Waco (25 November–2 December 1966)

Canary/Duck (7 December 1966–5 January 1967)

Niagara Falls (5–7 January 1967)

Cedar Falls (8–26 January 1967)

Big Spring (1–16 February 1967)

Junction City (22 February–17 March 1967)

Francis Marion (5 April–12 October 1967)

Newark (18–30 April 1967)

Fort Wayne (1–4 May 1967)

Dayton (5–17 May 1967)

Cincinnati (18–25 May 1967)

Greeley (17 June–11 October 1967)

Bolling II (19 September 1967–31 January 1969)

MacArthur/Binh Tay (12 October 1967–31 January 1969)

McLain (20 January 1968–31 January 1969)

Cochise Green/Dan Sinh (30 March 1968–31 January 1969)

Darby March I (1–3 February 1969)

Darby Trail I (1–7 February 1969)

Darby Crest I (1 February–3 March 1969)

Darby March II (8 February–6 March 1969)

Darby Crest III (25 March–15 April 1969)

Washington Green I–II (15 April 1969–1 January 1971)

Wayne Stab II (16 February–9 March 1970)

Wayne Wind (22 April 1970)

Wayne Span II (28 July–6 August 1970)

196th Light Infantry Brigade

Alice (2–8 September 1966)

Athol (8–13 September 1966)

Attleboro (14 September–24 November 1966)

Kamuela (20 September–4 October 1966)

Fitchburg (25 November 1966–8 April 1967)

Cedar Falls (8–26 January 1967)

Junction City (22 February–17 March 1967)

Malheur I–II (11 May–2 August 1967)

198th Light Infantry Brigade

Wallowa (4 October–11 November 1967)

Appendix II

(198th Light Infantry Brigade cont.)
Wheeler/Wallowa (11 November 1967–11 November 1968)
Muscatine (19 December 1967–10 June 1968)
Miracle (6–9 February 1968)
Burlington Trail (8 April–11 November 1968)
Golden Valley (10–12 May 1968)
Vance Canyon (20 June–3 July 1968)
Champaign Grove (4–24 September 1968)

199th Light Infantry Brigade

Fairfax/Rang Dong (30 November 1966–14 December 1967)
Enterprise (13 February 1967–11 March 1968)
Cussetta (4–7 April 1967)
Uniontown/Strike (1–17 December 1967)
Manchester (18 December 1967–12 January 1968)
Toan Thang I (8 April–31 May 1968)
Toan Thang II (1 June 1968–16 February 1969)
Strangler I (4–12 February 1969)
Strangler II (12–16 February 1969)
Toan Thang III (17 February–31 October 1969)
Lulu (12–14 March 1969)
Hunter (26–28 March 1969)
Friendship III (11 September 1969–20 February 1970)

United States Marine Corps

Blastout I (2–3 August 1965)
Thunderbolt (6–7 August 1965)
Midnight (12 August 1965)
Starlite (18–24 August 1965)
Stomp (5–7 September 1965)
Piranha (7–10 September 1965)
Golden Fleece (8 September–27 October 1965)
Dagger Thrust I (25 September 1965)
Triple Play (18–20 October 1965)
Trailblazer (18–24 October 1965)
Red Snapper (22–25 October 1965)

Drum Head (26–27 October 1965)
Lien Ket–10 (29–30 October 1965)
Black Ferret (3–5 November 1965)
Blue Marlin I (10–12 November 1965)
Blue Marlin II (16–18 November 1965)
Dagger Thrust V (5–6 December 1965)
Harvest Moon (8–20 December 1965)
Mallard (10–17 January 1966)
Double Eagle I (28 January–19 February 1966)
Double Eagle II (20 February–1 March 1966)
County Fair (24–25 February 1966)
New York (27 February–3 March 1966)
Troy (2–3 March 1966)
Utah/Lien Ket–26 (4–8 March 1966)
Golden Fleece II (14–30 March 1966)
Oregon (19–23 March 1966)
Texas/Lien Ket–26 (19–24 March 1966)
Kings (19–28 March 1966)
Jackstay (26 March–6 April 1966)
Indiana (28–30 March 1966)
Hot Springs (April 1966)
Virginia (17 April–1 May 1966)
Georgia (21 April–10 May 1966)
County Fair II (26 April 1966)
Osage (27 April–1 May 1966)
Ky Lam Campaign (May 1966)
Cherokee (5–7 May 1966)
Wayne (10–12 May 1966)
Athens (15 May–25 June 1966)
Reno (30 May–8 June 1966)
Beaver (1–7 June 1966)
Liberty (7–30 June 1966)
Florida/Doan Ket (9–12 June 1966)
Kansas (17–22 June 1966)
Dodge (17–23 June 1966)
Deckhouse I (18–30 June 1966)
Nathan Hale (19 June–1 July 1966)
Turner (23 June 1966)
Jay (25 June–4 July 1966)
Holt (2–6 July 1966)
Macon (4 July–27 October 1966)
Washington (6–14 July 1966)
Hastings (7 July–3 August 1966)
Deckhouse II (16–18 July 1966)
Prairie I (3 August 1966–31 January 1967)
Colorado/Lien Ket–52 (6–22 August 1966)
Deckhouse III (16–29 August 1966)
Fresno (8–16 September 1966)

Deckhouse IV (15–24 September 1966)
Golden Fleece 7–1 (16–27 September 1966)
Sierra (12 December 1966–21 January 1967)
Chinook I (19 December 1966–6 February 1967)
Deckhouse V (6–15 January 1967)
Desoto (26 January–7 April 1967)
Prairie II (31 January–18 March 1967)
Independence (1–9 February 1967)
Stone (10–12 February 1967)
Deckhouse VI (16 February–3 March 1967)
Prairie III (18 March–19 April 1967)
Beacon Hill (20 March–1 April 1967)
Newcastle (22–25 March 1967)
Prairie IV (20 April–30 May 1967)
Union (21 April–17 May 1967)
Beacon Star (22 April–12 May 1967)
Shawnee/Choctaw (22 April–10 July 1967)
Beaver Cage (28 April–12 May 1967)
Crockett (13 May–16 July 1967)
Beau Charger (18–26 May 1967)
Hickory (18–28 May 1967)
Belt Tight (20–23 May 1967)
Union II (25 May–5 June 1967)
Cimmaron (1 June–2 July 1967)
Bear Bite (2–12 June 1967)
Cumberland (3 June–15 September 1967)
Arizona (14–22 June 1967)
Adair (15–25 June 1967)
Beacon Torch/Calhoun (18 June–2 July 1967)
Maryland (25–27 June 1967)
Buffalo (2–14 July 1967)
Beaver Track (5–13 July 1967)
Fremont (10 July–31 October 1967)
Hickory II (14–16 July 1967)
Kingfisher (16 July–31 October 1967)
Ardmore (17 July–31 October 1967)
Bear Chain (20–21 July 1967)
Beacon Guide (21–30 July 1967)
Kangaroo Kick (1–3 August 1967)
Beacon Gate (7–11 August 1967)
Cochise (11–28 August 1967)
Belt Drive (27 August–5 September 1967)
Yazoo (27 August–5 September 1967)
Beacon Point (1–6 September 1967)

Swift (4–15 September 1967)
Ballistic Charge (16–22 September 1967)
Fortress Sentry (17–25 September 1967)
Medina/Bastion Hill (11–20 October 1967)
Formation Leader (17–18 October 1967)
Liberty II (19–24 October 1967)
Osceola I (20 October 1967–20 January 1968)
Knox (24 October–4 November 1967)
Granite (26 October–4 November 1967)
Lancaster (1 November 1967–20 January 1968)
Neosho I (1 November 1967–20 January 1968)
Scotland I (1 November 1967–31 March 1968)
Kentucky (1 November 1967–28 February 1969)
Napoleon/Saline (5 November 1967–9 December 1968)
Essex (6–17 November 1967)
Foster/Badger Hunt (13–30 November 1967)
Pitt (December 1967)
Ballistic (24–27 November 1967)
Fortress Ridge (21–24 December 1967)
Badger Tooth (26 December 1967–2 January 1968)
Neosho II (21–24 January 1968)
Osceola II (21 January–16 February 1968)
Lancaster II (21 January–23 November 1968)
Ballistic Armor (22–26 January 1968)
Badger Catch (23–26 January 1968)
Fortress Attack (27 January 1968)
Hue City (2 February–2 March 1968)
Houston (26 February–12 September 1968)
Worth (13–26 March 1968)
Pegasus/Lam Son–207 (1–15 April 1968)
Scotland II (15 April 1968–28 February 1969)
Allen Brook (4 May–24 August 1968)
Mameluke Thrust (18 May–23 October 1968)
Robin North/Robin South (28 May–19 June 1968)

(United States Marine Corps cont.)
Swift Sabre (7–14 June 1968)
Eager Yankee (9–16 June 1968)
Swift Play (23–24 July 1968)
Proud Hunter (18–21 August 1968)
Swift Pursuit (23 August–19 September 1968)
Maui Peak (6–19 October 1968)
Henderson Hill (24 October–6 December 1968)
Eager Hunter/Garrard Bay (25 October–6 December 1968)
Daring Endeavor (10–17 November 1968)
Swift Move (20 November–9 December 1968)
Meade River (20 November–9 December 1968)
Dawson River (28 November 1968–27 January 1969)
Taylor Common (7 December 1968–8 March 1969)
Valiant Hunt I–II (15 December 1968–5 January 1969)
Bold Mariner (13 January–9 February 1969)
Russell Beach (13 January–21 July 1969)
Dawson River South (22–25 January 1969)
Dewey Canyon I (22 January–19 March 1969)
Linn River (27 January–7 February 1969)
Defiant Measure (10–16 February 1969)
Purple Martin (27 February–8 May 1969)
Eager Pursuit (1–10 March 1969)
Eager Pursuit II (10–27 March 1969)
Maine Crag (15 March–2 May 1969)
Oklahoma Hills (30 March–29 May 1969)
Muskogee Meadow (7–20 April 1969)
Virginia Ridge (30 April–16 July 1969)
Daring Rebel (5–20 May 1969)
Herkimer Mountain (9 May–16 July 1969)
Apache Snow (10 May–7 June 1969)
Gallant Leader (23–25 May 1969)
Pipestone Canyon (26 May–7 November 1969)
Cameron Falls (29 May–23 June 1969)
Utah Mesa (12 June–9 July 1969)

Bold Pursuit (27 June–6 July 1969)
Forsythe Grove (1–2 July 1969)
Arlington Canyon (3 July–20 September 1969)
Mighty Play (10–20 July 1969)
Georgia Tar (16 July–25 September 1969)
Idaho Canyon (16 July–25 September 1969)
Durham Peak (20 July–13 August 1969)
Brave Armada (24 July–7 August 1969)
Defiant Stand (7–19 September 1969)
Ripley Center (13 July–31 August 1970)
Pickens Forest (16 July–24 August 1970)
Barren Green (24–27 July 1970)
Lyon Valley (16–24 August 1970)
Imperial Lake (31 August 1970–7 May 1971)
Nebraska Rapids (5–8 September 1970)
Dubois Square (9–19 September 1970)
Catawba Falls (18–21 September 1970)
Tulare Falls I (2–15 October 1970)
Hoang Dieu (22 October–30 November 1970)
Noble Canyon (23 October–3 November 1970)
Tulare Falls II (27 October–30 November 1970)
Hoang Dieu–101 (18 December 1970–19 January 1971)
Upshur Stream (11 January–29 March 1971)
Hoang Dieu–103 (3 February–29 March 1971)
Scott Orchard (7–12 April 1971)
Frequent Wind (29 April 1975)

Other Significant Operations

Flaming Dart I (7–8 February 1965) USN
Flaming Dart II (11 February 1965) USN
Rolling Thunder (2 March 1965–31 October 1968) USAF, USN
Shining Brass (Begins October 1965) MACV-SOG
Daniel Boone (Begins May 1967) MACV-SOG

Bibliography

Books

Anderson, Charles. *The Grunts*. Berkley Books, 1985.

Baker, Mark. *NAM*. Quill, 1982.

Berry, F. Clifton. *Air Cav — The Illustrated History of the Vietnam War*. Bantam Books, 1989.

_____. *Sky Soldiers — The Illustrated History of the Vietnam War*. Bantam Books, 1987.

Bonds, Ray, ed. *The Vietnam War*. Crown Publishers, 1979.

Bowman, John S. *The Vietnam War: An Almanac*. World Almanac Publications, 1985.

Brennan, Matthew. *Brennan's War*. Presidio Press, 1987.

_____, ed. *Headhunters*. Presidio Press, 1985.

Browne, Malcolm. *The New Face of War (Revised Edition)*. Bantam Books, 1985.

Caputo, Philip. *A Rumor of War*. Ballantine Books, 1983.

Carhart, Tom. *Battles and Campaigns in Vietnam: 1954–1984*. The Military Press, 1984.

_____. *The Offering*. William Morrow, 1987.

Clark, Johnnie M. *Guns Up*. Ballantine Books, 1984.

Clodfelter, Micheal. *Mad Minutes and Vietnam Months*. McFarland, 1988.

Coleman, J. D. *Pleiku: The Dawn of Helicopter Warfare in Vietnam*. St. Martin's Press, 1988.

Croizat, Lt. Col. Victor. *Vietnam River Warfare: 1945–1975*. Blandford Press, 1986.

Cutler, Lt. Cmdr. Thomas J. *Brown Water, Black Berets*. The Naval Institute Press, 1988.

Davidson, Lt. Col. Phillip B. *Vietnam at War: The History: 1946–1975*. Presidio Press, 1988.

Donovan, David. *Once a Warrior King*. Ballantine Books, 1985.

Drake, Hal, ed. *Vietnam Front Pages*. Bonanza Books, 1987.

Edelman, Bernard, ed. *Dear America: Letters Home from Vietnam*. Pocket Books, 1985.

Ehrhart, W. D. *Vietnam–Perkasie: A Combat Marine Memoir*. McFarland, 1983.

Flesch, Ron. *Redwood Delta*. Berkley Books, 1988.

Gadd, Charles. *Line Doggie*. Presidio Press, 1987.

Garland, Lt. Col. Albert N. *Infantry in Vietnam*. Jove Publishing, 1985.

Goff, Stanley and Robert Sanders. *Brothers: Black Soldiers in the Nam*. Berkley Books, 1982.

Goldman, Peter and Tony Fuller. *Charlie Company: What Vietnam Did to Us*. William Morrow, 1983.

Hackworth, David and Julie Sherman. *About Face: The Odyssey of an American Warrior*. Simon and Schuster, 1989.

Herr, Michael. *Dispatches*. Discus (Avon Books), 1980.

Infantry Magazine. *A Distant Challenge*. Jove Books, 1985.

Karnow, Stanley. *Vietnam: A History*. The Viking Press, 1983.

Kimball, William R. *Vietnam: The Other Side of Glory*. Ballantine Books, 1987.

Klein, Joe. *Payback*. Ballantine Books, 1985.

Kovic, Ron. *Born on the Fourth of July*. Pocket Books, 1987.

Krepinevich, Andrew F. *The Army and Vietnam*. Johns Hopkins University Press, 1986.

Lanning, Michael Lee. *The Only War We Had*. Ivy Books, 1987.

―――. *Vietnam 1969–1970: A Company Commander's Journal*. Ivy Books, 1988.

Lowry, Timothy S. *And Brave Men, Too*. Crown Publishers, 1985.

McDonough, James R. *Platoon Leader*. Bantam Books, 1986.

MacLear, Michael. *The Ten-Thousand Day War: Vietnam 1945–1975*. St. Martin's Press, 1981.

Marigold, Tom and John Penycate. *The Tunnels of Cu Chi—The Untold Story of Vietnam*. Random House, 1985.

Marshall, S. L. A. *Ambush*. The Battery Press, 1969.

―――. *Battles in the Monsoon*. The Battery Press, 1984.

―――. *Bird*. The Battery Press, 1968.

―――. *The Fields of Bamboo*. The Battery Press, 1971.

―――. *West to Cambodia*. Jove Books, 1986.

Mason, Robert. *Chickenhawk*. Penguin Books, 1983.

Newcomb, Richard F. *What You Should Know About Vietnam*. The Associated Press, 1968.

Nolan, Keith William. *Death Valley*. Presidio Press, 1987.

―――. *Into Laos*. Dell Publishing Company, 1988.

―――. *The Battle for Hue: TET 1968*. Dell, 1985.

101st Airborne Division. *Vietnam Odyssey*. Ferguson Communications, 1986.

145th Combat Aviation Battalion. *First in Vietnam: A Pictorial History of the 145th*. Dai Nippon, 1967.

O'Brien, Tim. *If I Die in a Combat Zone*. Dell, 1984.

Ogden, Richard. *Green Knight, Red Mourning*. Zebra Books, 1986.

Palmer, Dave Richard. *Summons of the Trumpet*. Ballantine Books, 1984.

Pimlott, John, ed. *Vietnam: The History and the Tactics*. Crescent Books, 1982.

Pisor, Robert. *The End of the Line: The Siege of Khe Sanh*. W. W. Norton, 1982.

Santoli, Al. *Everything We Had*. Ballantine Books, 1982.

―――. *To Bear Any Burden*. Ballantine Books, 1986.

Sharp, Adm. U. S. G. *Strategy for Defeat*. Presidio Press, 1978.

―――and Gen. William C. Westmoreland. *Report on the War*. U.S. Government Printing Office, 1969.

Sheehan, Neil. *A Bright and Shining Lie*. Random House, 1988.

Simmons, Edwin H. *Marines. The Illustrated History of the Vietnam War*. Bantam Books, 1987.

Spencer, Ernest. *Welcome to Vietnam, Macho Man*. Corps Press, 1987.

Stanton, Shelby. *Anatomy of a Division: The First Cav in Vietnam*. Presidio Press, 1987.

―――. *The Rise and Fall of an American Army*. Presidio Press, 1985.

―――. *Vietnam Order of Battle*. Galahad Books, 1986.

Starry, Gen. Donn A. *Armored Combat in Vietnam*. The Bobbs-Merrill Company, 1980.

Summers, Col. Harry G. *On Strategy: A Critical Analysis of the Vietnam War*. Dell, 1984.

25th Infantry Division. *Tropic Lightning Yearbook (10 October 1967–10 October 1968).* 1968.
Uhlig, Frank, Jr. *Vietnam: The Naval Story.* Naval Institute Press, 1986.
Westmoreland, Gen. William C. *A Soldier Reports.* Doubleday, 1976.
Zaffiri, Samuel. *Hamburger Hill.* Presidio Press, 1988.
Zumbro, Ralph. *Tank Sergeant.* Pocket Books, 1988.

Government Publications

Berger, Carl. *The United States Air Force in Southeast Asia: 1961–1973 (Revised Edition).* Office of Air Force History, 1984.
Cash, John A., et al. *Seven Firefights in Vietnam* (part of the Vietnam Studies Series). U.S. Government Printing Office, 1970.
Cosmas, Graham A. and Lt. Col. T. P. Murray (USMC). *U.S. Marines in Vietnam: Vietnamization and Redeployment (1970–1971).* History and Museums Division, U.S. Marine Corps, 1986.
Fulton, Maj. Gen. William B. *Riverine Operations: 1966–1969* (part of the Vietnam Studies Series). U.S. Government Printing Office, 1985.
Matloff, Maurice, ed. *American Military History.* Office of the Chief of Military History—U.S. Army, 1969.
Pearson, Lt. Gen. Willard. *The War in the Northern Provinces* (part of the Vietnam Studies Series). U.S. Government Printing Office, 1975.
Shore, Capt. Moyers S., Jr. *The Battle for Khe Sanh.* History and Museums Division, U.S. Marine Corps, 1977.
Shumlinson, Jack. *U.S. Marines in Vietnam: An Expanding War: (1966).* History and Museums Division, U.S. Marine Corps, 1982.
———— and Maj. Charles N. Johnson (USMC). *U.S. Marines in Vietnam: The Landing and the Build-Up (1965).* History and Museums Division, U.S. Marine Corps, 1978.
Smith, Charles R. *U.S. Marines in Vietnam: High Mobility and Standdown (1969).* History and Museums Division, U.S. Marine Corps, 1988.
Telfer, Maj. Gary L., Lt. Col. Lane Rogers and V. Keith Fleming, Jr. *U.S. Marines in Vietnam: Fighting the North Vietnamese (1967).* History and Museums Division, U.S. Marine Corps, 1984.
Tolson, Lt. Gen. John J. *Airmobility: 1961–1971* (part of the Vietnam Studies Series). U.S. Government Printing Office, 1973.
United States Air Force. *Air War—Vietnam.* Arno Press, 1978.
United States Marine Corps. *The Marines in Vietnam: 1954–1973: An Anthology and Annotated Bibliography.* History and Museums Division, U.S. Marine Corps, 1983.
West, Capt. Francis J., Jr. *Small Unit Action: Summer 1966.* History and Museums Division, U.S. Marine Corps, 1977.

Other Sources

Military (a monthly magazine published by MR Publishing Company, Sacramento, California).
New York Times (1965–1975).
Vietnam (a quarterly magazine published by Empire Press, Leesburg, Virginia).
Vietnam Veteran (a monthly newspaper published by Michael Kukler, Gastonia, North Carolina).

Vietnam War Newsletter (a monthly newsletter published by Tom Hebert, Collins-ville, Connecticut).

Unpublished Government Documents

Author's note: For those readers wishing to read the actual documents themselves, please note the code numbers in each entry. The first code number, usually beginning with **OACSFOR** is for the filing system used by the National Archives.

The second series of codes begin with the letters **AD** and are used to order documents through the National Technical Information Service.

1st Cavalry Division

Quarterly Command Report (period ending September 1965). Dated: 1 December 1965. OACSFOR-OT-RD-650110, AD 390 502.

Operational Report—Lessons Learned (1 October–30 November 1965). Dated: 10 January 1966. OACSFOR-OT-RD-650109, AD 390 501.

Operational Report—Lessons Learned: The Pleiku Campaign (March 1966). Dated: 4 March 1966. OACSFOR number not listed on document. AD 855 112.

Operational Report—Lessons Learned (1 January–30 April 1966). Dated: 5 May 1966. OACSFOR-OT-RD-660119, AD 390 504.

Operational Report—Lessons Learned (1 May–31 July 1966). Dated: 28 November 1966. OACSFOR-OT-RD-660292, AD 390 505.

Operational Report—Lessons Learned (1 August–31 October 1966). Dated: 22 November 1966. OACSFOR-OT-RD-660505, AD 390 507.

Operational Report—Lessons Learned (1 November 1966–31 January 1967). Dated: 15 February 1967. OACSFOR-OT-RD-670226, AD 388 156.

Operational Report—Lessons Learned (1 May–31 July 1967). Dated: 15 August 1967. OACSFOR-OT-RD-670798, AD 386 215.

Operational Report—Lessons Learned (1 August–31 October 1967). Dated: 15 November 1967. OACSFOR-OT-RD-T674236, AD 387 543.

Operational Report—Lessons Learned (1 November 1967–31 January 1968). Dated: 17 March 1968. OACSFOR-OT-RD-681288, AD 390 249.

Operational Report—Lessons Learned (1 February–30 April 1968). Dated: 13 June 1968. OACSFOR-OT-RD-682337, AD 392 381.

Operational Report—Lessons Learned (1 May–31 July 1968). Dated: 20 August 1968. OACSFOR-OT-UT-683305, AD 394 701.

Operational Report—Lessons Learned (1 November 1968–31 January 1969). Dated: 15 February 1969. OACSFOR-OT-UT-691115, AD 502 597.

Operational Report—Lessons Learned (1 February–30 April 1969). Dated: 15 April 1969. OACSFOR-OT-UT-692094, AD 504 499.

Operational Report—Lessons Learned (1 August–31 October 1969). Dated: 15 November 1969. OACSFOR-OT-UT-694007, AD 508 303.

Operational Report—Lessons Learned (1 November 1969–31 January 1970). Dated: 15 February 1970. OACSFOR-OT-UT-701072, AD 509 704.

Operational Report—Lessons Learned (1 February–30 April 1970). Dated: 12 November 1970. OACSFOR-OT-UT-702040, AD 512 505.

Operational Report—Lessons Learned (1 May–31 July 1970). Dated: 14 August 1970. OACSFOR-OT-UT-703016, AD 514 580.

Operational Report—Lessons Learned (1 August–31 October 1970). Dated: 14 November 1970. OACSFOR-OT-UT-704030, AD 516 259.

Operational Report—Lessons Learned (1 August–31 October 1971). Dated: 13 November 1971. RCSCSFOR-65 (R-3), AD 630 055.

Combat After Action Report: *Jim Bowie* (7–28 March 1966). Dated: 8 May 1966. OACSFOR-OT-RD-66X114, AD 829 472.

Combat After Action Report: *Lincoln* (25 March–8 April 1966). Dated: 21 April 1966. OACSFOR-OT-RD-66X263, AD 833 869.

Combat After Action Report: *Davy Crockett* (3–16 May 1966). Dated: 25 May 1966. OACSFOR-RD-File-66X031, AD 823 475.

Senior Officer Debriefing Report (23 April 1969–5 May 1970). Dated: 18 April 1970. OACSFOR-OT-UT-70B017, AD 509 767.

Senior Officer Debriefing Report (13 December 1971–20 June 1972). Dated: 4 December 1972. DAFD-OTT-72B012, AD 523 510.

1st Infantry Division

Operational Report—Lessons Learned (1 January–30 April 1966). Dated: 30 May 1966. OACSFOR-OT-UT-660122, AD 513 858.

Operational Report—Lessons Learned (1 May–31 July 1966). Dated: 15 August 1966. OACSFOR-OT-RD-660291, AD 391 481.

Operational Report—Lessons Learned (1 August–31 October 1966). Dated: 23 May 1967. OACSFOR-OT-RD-660504, AD 385 847.

Operational Report—Lessons Learned (1 February–30 April 1967). Dated: 9 November 1967. OACSFOR-OT-RD-670468, AD 388 163.

Operational Report—Lessons Learned (1 May–31 July 1967). Dated: 25 May 1967. OACSFOR-OT-RD-670742, AD 387 145.

Operational Report—Lessons Learned (1 August–31 October 1967). Dated: 3 December 1967. OACSFOR-OT-RD-674246, AD 389 325.

Operational Report—Lessons Learned (1 February 1968). Dated: 1 February 1968. OACSFOR-OT-RD-682001, AD 830 338.

Operational Report—Lessons Learned (1 February–30 April 1968). Dated: 27 May 1968. OACSFOR-OT-RD-682342, AD 392 802.

Operational Report—Lessons Learned (1 May–31 July 1968). Dated: 25 November 1968. OACSFOR-OT-RD-683262, AD 394 109.

Operational Report—Lessons Learned (1 August–31 October 1968). Dated: 16 November 1968. OACSFOR-OT-UT-684282, AD 500 799.

Operational Report—Lessons Learned (1 November 1968–31 January 1969). Dated: 19 February 1969. OACSFOR-OT-UT-691257, AD 502 283.

Operational Report—Lessons Learned (1 February–30 April 1969). Dated: 15 May 1969. OACSFOR-OT-UT-692281, AD 504 754.

Operational Report—Lessons Learned (1 May–31 July 1969). Dated: 29 August 1969. OACSFOR-OT-UT-693296, AD 506 277.

Operational Report—Lessons Learned (1 August–31 October 1969). Dated: 1 December 1969. OACSFOR-OT-UT-694230, AD 508 672.

Operational Report—Lessons Learned (1 November 1969–31 January 1970). Dated: 10 March 1970. OACSFOR-OT-UT-701235, AD 509 060.

Combat After Action Report: *Cocoa Beach* (3–6 March 1966). Dated: 3 April 1966. OACSFOR-OT-RD-66X269, AD 833 870.

Combat After Action Report: *Lexington 3* (21 May–9 June 1966). Dated: 20 June 1966. OACSFOR-OT-RD-66X151, AD 386 121.

Senior Officer Debriefing Report (10 August 1969–21 March 1970). Dated: 11 June 1970. OACSFOR-OT-UT-70B013, AD 509 880.

4th Infantry Division

Operational Report—Lessons Learned (1 August–31 October 1966). Dated: 22 December 1966. OACSFOR-OT-RD-660546, AD 510 787.

Operational Report—Lessons Learned (1 November 1966–31 January 1967). Dated: 1 February 1967. OACSFOR-OT-RD-670230, AD 388 158.

Operational Report—Lessons Learned (1 November 1966–31 January 1967). Dated: 20 March 1967. OACSFOR-OT-RD-670232, AD 388 159.

Operational Report—Lessons Learned (1 November 1966–31 January 1967). Dated: 23 February 1967. OACSFOR-OT-RD-670223, AD 388 890.

Operational Report—Lessons Learned (1 February–30 April 1967). Dated: 15 June 1967. OACSFOR-OT-RD-670469, AD 385 851.

Operational Report—Lessons Learned (1 May–31 July 1967). Dated: 20 August 1967. OACSFOR-OT-RD-670698, AD 386 284.

Operational Report—Lessons Learned (1 August–31 October 1967). Dated: 26 December 1967. OACSFOR-OT-RD-674280, AD 388 843.

Operational Report—Lessons Learned: 3d Brigade Task Force (1 August–31 October 1967). Dated: 10 November 1967. OACSFOR-OT-RD-T674264, AD 388 976.

Operational Report—Lessons Learned (1 November 1967–31 January 1968). Dated: 7 March 1968. OACSFOR-OT-RD-681187, AD 390 612.

Operational Report—Lessons Learned (1 February–30 April 1968). Dated: 21 May 1968. OACSFOR-OT-RD-682163, AD 392 678.

Operational Report—Lessons Learned (1 May–31 July 1968). Dated: 18 August 1968. OACSFOR-OT-UT-683153, AD 394 812.

Operational Report—Lessons Learned (1 August–31 October 1968). Dated: 15 November 1968. OACSFOR-OT-UT-684152, AD 500 751.

Operational Report—Lessons Learned (1 February–30 April 1969). Dated: 21 May 1969. OACSFOR-OT-UT-692256, AD 504 855.

Operational Report—Lessons Learned (1 February–30 April 1970). Dated: 31 May 1970. OACSFOR-OT-UT-702179, AD 511 160.

Operational Report—Lessons Learned (1 May–31 July 1970). Dated: 20 August 1970. OACSFOR-OT-UT-703083, AD 513 854.

Operational Report—Lessons Learned (1 August–31 October 1970). Dated: 20 November 1970. OACSFOR-OT-UT-704063, AD 516 045.

Combat After Action Report: *Gadsden* (2–12 February 1967). Dated: 10 March 1967. OACSFOR-OT-RD-67X013, AD 390 546.

Senior Officer Debriefing Report (1967–1968). Dated: 7 June 1969. OACSFOR-OT-UT-69B017, AD 502 432.

Senior Officer Debriefing Report (30 November 1968–14 November 1969). Dated: 10 November 1969. OACSFOR-OT-UT-69B050, AD 506 705.

1st Infantry Brigade/5th Infantry Division (Mech)

Operational Report—Lessons Learned (1 August–31 October 1968). Dated: 13 December 1968. OACSFOR-OT-UT-684335, AD 849 495.

Operational Report—Lessons Learned (1 February–30 April 1969). Dated: 30 May 1969. OACSFOR-OT-UT-692327, AD 504 857.

Operational Report—Lessons Learned (1 February–30 April 1970). Dated: 21 May 1970. OACSFOR-OT-UT-702211, AD 510 576.

Operational Report—Lessons Learned (1 May–31 July 1970). Dated: 12 August 1970. OACSFOR-OT-UT-703139, AD 513 710.

Operational Report—Lessons Learned (19 June–19 August 1971). Dated: 19 August 1971. DAFD-DOU-712182, AD 530 751.
Senior Officer Debriefing Report (30 June 1970–18 May 1971). Dated: 9 June 1971. OACSFOR-OT-UT-71B025, AD 516 498.

9th Infantry Division

Operational Report—Lessons Learned (1 February 1966–31 January 1967). Dated: 8 June 1967. OACSFOR-OT-RD-670236, AD 829 461.
Operational Report—Lessons Learned (1 February–30 April 1967). Dated: July 1967. OACSFOR-OT-RD-670474, AD 386 676.
Operational Report—Lessons Learned (1 August–31 October 1967). Dated: 23 December 1967. OACSFOR-OT-RD-T674255, AD 388 749.
Operational Report—Lessons Learned (1 November 1967–31 January 1968). Dated: 15 February 1968. OACSFOR-OT-RD-681181, AD 389 810.
Operational Report—Lessons Learned (1 May–31 July 1968). Dated: 20 August 1968. OACSFOR-OT-UT-683300, AD 394 511.
Operational Report—Lessons Learned (1 August–31 October 1968). Dated: 15 November 1968. OACSFOR-OT-UT-684329, AD 500 939.
Operational Report—Lessons Learned (1 November 1968–31 January 1969). Dated: 15 February 1969. OACSFOR-OT-UT-691216, AD 503 258.
Operational Report—Lessons Learned (1 February–30 April 1969). Dated: 15 May 1969. OACSFOR-OT-UT-692280, AD 504 835.
Operational Report—Lessons Learned (1 May–30 June 1969). Dated: 15 July 1969. OACSFOR-OT-UT-693234, AD 506 525.
Operational Report—Lessons Learned: 3d Brigade (1 August–31 October 1969). Dated: 15 November 1969. OACSFOR-OT-UT-694175, AD 508 091.
Operational Report—Lessons Learned: 3d Brigade (1 November 1969–31 January 1970). Dated: 1 February 1970. OACSFOR-OT-UT-701298, AD 509 173.
Operational Report—Lessons Learned: 3d Brigade (1 February–30 April 1970). Dated: 14 May 1970. OACSFOR-OT-UT-702276, AD 511 070.
Operational Report—Lessons Learned: 3d Brigade (1 May–31 July 1970). Dated: 15 August 1970. OACSFOR-OT-UT-703101, AD 514 461.
Senior Officer Debriefing Report (1 June 1967–25 February 1968). Dated: 25 February 1968. OACSFOR-OT-UT-68B032, AD 511 311.

11th Armored Cavalry Regiment

Operational Report—Lessons Learned (11 March–31 October 1966). Dated: 31 October 1966. OACSFOR-OT-RD-660507, AD 386 101.
Operational Report—Lessons Learned (1 November 1966–31 January 1967). Dated: 17 June 1967. OACSFOR-OT-RD-670233, AD 386 099.
Operational Report—Lessons Learned (1 February–30 April 1967). Dated: 30 April 1967. OACSFOR-OT-RD-670472, AD 388 893.
Operational Report—Lessons Learned (1 May–31 July 1967). Dated: 31 July 1967. OACSFOR-OT-RD-670883, AD 387 684.
Operational Report—Lessons Learned (1 August–31 October 1967). Dated: 20 November 1967. OACSFOR-OT-RD-T674248, AD 388 840.
Operational Report—Lessons Learned (1 November 1967–31 January 1968). Dated: 15 February 1968. OACSFOR-OT-RD-681188, AD 390 149.
Operational Report—Lessons Learned (1 February–30 April 1968). Dated: 10 May 1968. OACSFOR-OT-RD-682336, AD 392 230.

Operational Report—Lessons Learned (1 May–31 July 1968). Dated: 10 August 1968. OACSFOR-OT-UT-683090, AD 395 033.
Operational Report—Lessons Learned (1 August–31 October 1968). Dated: 10 November 1968. OACSFOR-OT-UT-684271, AD 500 745.
Operational Report—Lessons Learned (1 November 1968–31 January 1969). Dated: 10 February 1969. OACSFOR-OT-UT-691274, AD 502 458.
Operational Report—Lessons Learned (1 February–30 April 1969). Dated: 15 May 1969. OACSFOR-OT-UT-692322, AD 504 794.
Operational Report—Lessons Learned (1 May–31 July 1969). Dated: 18 August 1969. OACSFOR-OT-UT-693340, AD 506 335.
Operational Report—Lessons Learned (1 August–31 October 1969). Dated: 22 November 1969. OACSFOR-OT-UT-694306, AD 507 384.
Operational Report—Lessons Learned (1 November 1969–31 January 1970). Dated: 18 February 1970. OACSFOR-OT-UT-701254, AD 506 538.
Operational Report—Lessons Learned (1 February–30 April 1970). Dated: 21 May 1970. OACSFOR-OT-UT-702199, AD 510 766.

23d Infantry Division (Americal)

Operational Report—Lessons Learned (1 August–31 October 1967). Dated: 26 November 1967. OACSFOR-OT-RD-674289, AD 388 576.
Operational Report—Lessons Learned (1 November 1967–31 January 1968). Dated: 8 February 1968. OACSFOR-OT-RD-681060, AD 389 940.
Operational Report—Lessons Learned (1 February–30 April 1968). Dated: 7 May 1968. OACSFOR-OT-RD-682332, AD 392 637.
Operational Report—Lessons Learned (1 May–31 July 1968). Dated: 7 August 1968. OACSFOR-OT-UT-683371, AD 394 911.
Operational Report—Lessons Learned (1 August–31 October 1968). Dated: 7 November 1968. OACSFOR-OT-UT-684321, AD 500 558.
Operational Report—Lessons Learned (1 November 1968–31 January 1969). Dated: 10 February 1969. OACSFOR-OT-UT-691316, AD 502 518.
Operational Report—Lessons Learned (1 February–30 April 1969). Dated: 10 May 1968. OACSFOR-OT-UT-692339, AD 504 330.
Operational Report—Lessons Learned (1 May–31 July 1969). Dated: 10 August 1969. OACSFOR-OT-UT-693290, AD 505 536.
Operational Report—Lessons Learned (1 August–31 October 1969). Dated: 10 November 1969. OACSFOR-OT-UT-694285, AD 508 093.
Operational Report—Lessons Learned (1 November 1969–31 January 1970). Dated: 10 February 1970. OACSFOR-OT-UT-701205, AD 508 671.
Operational Report—Lessons Learned (1 February–30 April 1970). Dated: 10 May 1970. OACSFOR-OT-UT-702210, AD 512 565.
Operational Report—Lessons Learned (1 August–31 October 1970). Dated: 15 November 1970. OACSFOR-OT-UT-704121, AD 515 335.
Operational Report—Lessons Learned (1 May–15 October 1971). Dated: 1 November 1971. DAFD-OTT-712166, AD 520 351.
Senior Officer Debriefing Report (1 March 1967–18 October 1968). Dated: 7 October 1968. OACSFOR-OT-UT-68B023, AD 513 370.
Senior Officer Debriefing Report (September 1967–June 1968). Dated: 2 June 1968. OACSFOR-OT-UT-68B020, AD 513 369.
Senior Officer Debriefing Report (June 1968–May 1969). Dated: 13 June 1969. OACSFOR-OT-UT-69B023, AD 502 065.

25th Infantry Division

Operational Report—Lessons Learned (1–31 August 1966). Dated: September 1966. OACSFOR-OT-RD-660580, AD 385 846.
Operational Report—Lessons Learned (1 August–31 October 1966). Dated: 4 November 1966. OACSFOR-OT-RD-660514, AD 391 485.
Operational Report—Lessons Learned (1 August–31 October 1966). Dated: 18 November 1966. OACSFOR-OT-RD-660510, AD 385 848.
Operational Report—Lessons Learned (1 February–30 April 1967). Dated: 19 May 1967. OACSFOR-OT-RD-670470, AD 390 303.
Operational Report—Lessons Learned (1 February–30 April 1967). Dated: 10 May 1967. OACSFOR-OT-RD-670750, AD 365 641.
Operational Report—Lessons Learned (1 May–31 July 1967). Dated: 10 August 1967. OACSFOR-OT-RD-670701, AD 387 363.
Operational Report—Lessons Learned (1 August–31 October 1967). Dated: 31 October 1967. OACSFOR-OT-RD-674216, AD 388 381.
Operational Report—Lessons Learned (1 November 1967–31 January 1968). Dated: 14 February 1968. OACSFOR-OT-RD-681191, AD 390 530.
Operational Report—Lessons Learned (1 February–30 April 1968). Dated: 30 April 1968. OACSFOR-OT-RD-682244, AD 392 127.
Operational Report—Lessons Learned (1 May–31 July 1968). Dated: 1 August 1968. OACSFOR-OT-UT-683310, AD 395 425.
Operational Report—Lessons Learned (1 August–31 October 1968). Dated: 5 November 1968. OACSFOR-OT-UT-684286, AD 500 768.
Operational Report—Lessons Learned (1 November 1968–31 January 1969). Dated: 1 February 1969. OACSFOR-OT-UT-691258, AD 502 976.
Operational Report—Lessons Learned (1 February–30 April 1969). Dated: 1 May 1969. OACSFOR-OT-UT-692282, AD 504 766.
Operational Report—Lessons Learned (1 May–31 July 1969). Dated: 18 December 1969. OACSFOR-OT-UT-?, AD 506 604.
Operational Report—Lessons Learned (1 August–31 October 1969). Dated: 1 November 1969. OACSFOR-OT-UT-694221, AD 508 335.
Operational Report—Lessons Learned (1 November 1969–31 January 1970). Dated: 1 February 1970. OACSFOR-OT-UT-701223, AD 509 705.
Operational Report—Lessons Learned (1 February–30 April 1970). Dated: 30 April 1970. OACSFOR-OT-UT-702160, AD 512 358.
Operational Report—Lessons Learned (1 May–31 July 1970). Dated: 31 July 1970. OACSFOR-OT-UT-703026, AD 514 626.
Combat After Action Report: *Saratoga* (8 December 1967–11 March 1968). Dated: 13 April 1968. OACSFOR-OT-RD-68X015, AD 390 664.
Senior Officer Debriefing Report (30 July 1967–20 March 1969). Dated: 27 April 1969. OACSFOR-OT-UT-69B013, AD 513 164.
Senior Officer Debriefing Report (3 August 1968–15 September 1969). Dated: 26 September 1969. OACSFOR-OT-UT-69B039, AD 505 393.
Senior Officer Debriefing Report (15 September 1969–2 April 1970). Dated: 20 May 1970. OACSFOR-OT-UT-70B015, AD 509 875.
Senior Officer Debriefing Report (March 1969–December 1970). Dated: 20 January 1971. OACSFOR-OT-UT-71B011, AD 514 361.

3d Brigade/82d Airborne Division

Operational Report—Lessons Learned (1 February–30 April 1968). Dated: 12 May 1968. OACSFOR-OT-RD-682329, AD 392 622.

Operational Report—Lessons Learned (1 August–31 October 1968). Dated: 30 November 1968. OACSFOR-OT-UT-684283, AD 500 366.

Operational Report—Lessons Learned (1 February–30 April 1969). Dated: 15 May 1969. OACSFOR-OT-UT-692078, AD 504 592.

Operational Report—Lessons Learned (1 May–31 July 1969). Dated: 18 August 1969. OACSFOR-OT-UT-693231, AD 506 020.

Operational Report—Lessons Learned (1 August–31 October 1969). Dated: 20 November 1969. OACSFOR-OT-UT-694208, AD 508 165.

101st Airborne Division

Operational Report—Lessons Learned: 1st Brigade (1 May–31 July 1966). Dated: 13 August 1966. OACSFOR-OT-RD-660296, AD 388 883.

Operational Report—Lessons Learned: 1st Brigade (1 August–31 October 1966). Dated: 12 November 1966. OACSFOR-OT-UT-660508, AD 512 778.

Operational Report—Lessons Learned: 1st Brigade (1 November 1966–31 January 1967). Dated: 21 April 1967. OACSFOR-OT-RD-670225, AD 394 055.

Operational Report—Lessons Learned: 1st Brigade (1 February–30 April 1967). Dated: 2 October 1967. OACSFOR-OT-RD-670466, AD 388 162.

Operational Report—Lessons Learned: 1st Brigade (1 May–31 July 1967). Dated: 2 February 1968. OACSFOR-OT-RD-670577, AD 387 285.

Operational Report—Lessons Learned: 1st Brigade (1 August–31 October 1967). Dated: 13 March 1968. OACSFOR-OT-RD-T674249, AD 388 845.

Operational Report—Lessons Learned: 1st Brigade (1 November 1967–31 January 1968). Dated: 12 February 1968. OACSFOR-OT-RD-681261, AD 390 024.

Operational Report—Lessons Learned (1 February–30 April 1968). Dated: 16 May 1968. OACSFOR-OT-RD-682251, AD 390 901.

Operational Report—Lessons Learned (1 February–30 April 1968). Dated: 24 May 1968. OACSFOR-OT-RD-682315, AD 392 520.

Operational Report—Lessons Learned (1 May–31 July 1968). Dated: 15 August 1968. OACSFOR-OT-UT-683306, AD 394 951.

Operational Report—Lessons Learned (1 August–31 October 1968). Dated: 22 November 1968. OACSFOR-OT-UT-684306, AD 501 007.

Operational Report—Lessons Learned (1 November 1968–31 January 1969). Dated: 24 February 1969. OACSFOR-OT-UT-691328, AD 502 771.

Operational Report—Lessons Learned (1 May–31 July 1969). Dated: 20 August 1969. OACSFOR-OT-UT-693240, AD 506 515.

Operational Report—Lessons Learned (1 November 1969–31 January 1970). Dated: 13 February 1970. OACSFOR-OT-UT-701245, AD 509 174.

Operational Report—Lessons Learned (1 February–30 April 1970). Dated: 17 May 1970. OACSFOR-OT-UT-702186, AD 510 686.

Operational Report—Lessons Learned (1 May–31 July 1970). Dated: 15 August 1970. OACSFOR-OT-UT-703152, AD 515 469.

Operational Report—Lessons Learned (1 August–31 October 1970). Dated: 31 October 1970. OACSFOR-OT-UT-704119, AD 515 195.

Operational Report—Lessons Learned (1 February–30 April 1971). Dated: 24 May 1971. DAFD-OTT-711143, AD 518 927.

Operational Report—Lessons Learned (1 August–31 October 1971). Dated: 31 October 1971. DAMO-ODU-712196, AD 531 137.

Combat After Action Report: *Lam Son 719* (8 February–6 April 1971). Dated: 1 May 1971. OACSFOR-OT-UT-71X010, AD 516 603.

Senior Officer Debriefing Report (19 July 1968–25 May 1969). Dated: 23 June 1969. OACSFOR-OT-UT-69B018, AD 502 564.
Senior Officer Debriefing Report (25 May 1969–25 May 1970). Dated: 11 May 1970. OACSFOR-OT-UT-70B024, AD 510 128.
Senior Officer Debriefing Report (May 1970–January 1971). Dated: 15 January 1971. OACSFOR-OT-UT-71B017, AD 514 578.
Senior Officer Debriefing Report (February 1971–February 1972). Dated: 13 July 1972. DAFD-OTT-72B005, AD 521 407.

173d Airborne Brigade

Operational Report—Lessons Learned (1 May–31 July 1966). Dated: 12 January 1967. OACSFOR-OT-RD-660297, AD 388 152.
Operational Report—Lessons Learned (1 November 1966–31 January 1967). Dated: 15 February 1967. OACSFOR-OT-RD-670235, AD 391 484.
Operational Report—Lessons Learned (1 February–30 April 1967). Dated: 1 July 1967. OACSFOR-OT-RD-670471, AD 386 888.
Operational Report—Lessons Learned (1 May–31 July 1967). Dated: 15 August 1967. OACSFOR-OT-RD-670819, AD 386 216.
Operational Report—Lessons Learned (1 August–31 October 1967). Dated: 15 November 1967. OACSFOR-OT-RD-T674257, AD 388 578.
Operational Report—Lessons Learned (1 May–31 July 1968). Dated: 15 August 1968. OACSFOR-OT-UT-683298, AD 394 510.
Operational Report—Lessons Learned (1 August–31 October 1968). Dated: 15 November 1968. OACSFOR-OT-UT-684235, AD 500 664.
Operational Report—Lessons Learned (1 February–30 April 1969). Dated: 15 May 1969. OACSFOR-OT-UT-692284, AD 504 329.
Operational Report—Lessons Learned (1 May–31 July 1969). Dated: 15 August 1969. OACSFOR-OT-UT-693233, AD 506 708.
Operational Report—Lessons Learned (1 August–31 October 1969). Dated: 1 December 1969. OACSFOR-OT-UT-694283, AD 507 245.
Operational Report—Lessons Learned (1 November 1969–31 January 1970). Dated: 14 February 1970. OACSFOR-OT-UT-701244, AD 509 676.
Operational Report—Lessons Learned (1 August–31 October 1970). Dated: 15 November 1970. OACSFOR-OT-UT-714245, AD 515 473.
Operational Report—Lessons Learned: *Crimp* (8–14 January 1966). Dated: 22 March 1966. OACSFOR-OT-RD-Report 1-66, AD 855 104.

196th Light Infantry Brigade

Operational Report—Lessons Learned (1 August–31 October 1966). Dated: 29 November 1966. OACSFOR-OT-RD-660511, AD 388 885.
Operational Report—Lessons Learned (1 November 1966–31 January 1967). Dated: 7 March 1967. OACSFOR-OT-RD-670221, AD 388 888.
Operational Report—Lessons Learned (1 May–31 July 1967). Dated: 22 September 1967. OACSFOR-OT-RD-670772, AD 387 362.
Operational Report—Lessons Learned (1 August–31 October 1967). Dated: 10 November 1967. OACSFOR-OT-RD-674210, AD 387 537.

199th Light Infantry Brigade

Operational Report—Lessons Learned (1 February–30 April 1967). Dated: 15 May 1967. OACSFOR-OT-RD-670467, AD 388 892.

Operational Report—Lessons Learned (1 May–31 July 1967). Dated: 15 August 1967. OACSFOR-OT-RD-670657, AD 388 894.

Operational Report—Lessons Learned (1 August–31 October 1967). Dated: 15 November 1967. OACSFOR-OT-RD-T674237, AD 386 675.

Operational Report—Lessons Learned (1 November 1967–31 January 1968). Dated: 18 February 1968. OACSFOR-OT-RD-681260, AD 390 150.

Operational Report—Lessons Learned (1 May–31 July 1968). Dated: 22 August 1968. OACSFOR-OT-RD-683335, AD 393 814.

Operational Report—Lessons Learned (1 August–31 October 1968). Dated: 25 February 1969. OACSFOR-OT-UT-684269, AD 500 213.

Operational Report—Lessons Learned (1 February–30 April 1969). Dated: 30 April 1969. OACSFOR-OT-UT-692289, AD 504 765.

Operational Report—Lessons Learned (1 May–31 July 1969). Dated: 31 July 1969. OACSFOR-OT-UT-693235, AD 506 276.

Operational Report—Lessons Learned (1 August–31 October 1969). Dated: 31 October 1969. OACSFOR-OT-UT-694231, AD 507 858.

Operational Report—Lessons Learned (1 November 1969–31 January 1970). Dated: 31 January 1970. OACSFOR-OT-UT-701239, AD 509 286.

Operational Report—Lessons Learned (1 February–30 April 1970). Dated: 4 September 1970. OACSFOR-OT-UT-702147, AD 511 159.

Operational Report—Lessons Learned (1 May–31 July 1970). Dated: 31 July 1970. OACSFOR-OT-UT-703148, AD 513 911.

Name and Subject Index

See also following index of military units. Operations are listed below in bold italic.

169

Military Unit Index